ORGANS FOR SALE

Bioethics, Neoliberalism, and Public Moral Deliberation

Organs for Sale is a study of the bioethical question of how to increase human organ supply. But it is also an inquiry into public moral deliberation and the relationship between economic worth and the value systems of a society. Looking closely at human organ procurement debates, the author offers a critique of neoliberalism in bioethics and asks what kind of society we truly want.

While society has shown concern over debates surrounding organ procurement, a better understanding of the rhetoric of advocates and philosophical underpinnings of the debate might indeed improve our public moral deliberation in general and organ policy more specifically. Examining public arguments, this book uses a range of source material, from medical journals to congressional hearings to newspaper op-eds, to provide the most up-to-date and thorough analysis of the topic. *Organs for Sale* posits that deciding together on the limits of markets, and on what is and ought to be for sale, sheds light on the moral fibre of our society and what it needs to thrive.

RYAN GILLESPIE is a lecturer in the Study of Religion program at University of California, Los Angeles.

Organs for Sale

Bioethics, Neoliberalism, and Public Moral Deliberation

RYAN GILLESPIE

UNIVERSITY OF TORONTO PRESS
Toronto Buffalo London

© University of Toronto Press 2021
Toronto Buffalo London
utorontopress.com
Printed and bound by CPI Group (UK) Ltd, Croydon, CR0 4YY

ISBN 978-1-4875-0603-2 (cloth)   ISBN 978-1-4875-3316-8 (EPUB)
ISBN 978-1-4875-2405-0 (paper)   ISBN 978-1-4875-3315-1 (PDF)

_____

Library and Archives Canada Cataloguing in Publication

Title: Organs for sale : bioethics, neoliberalism, and public moral deliberation /
    Ryan Gillespie.
Names: Gillespie, Ryan, 1982– author.
Description: Includes bibliographical references and index.
Identifiers: Canadiana (print) 20200278940 | Canadiana (ebook) 20200278967 |
    ISBN 9781487506032 (hardcover) | ISBN 9781487524050 (softcover) |
    ISBN 9781487533168 (EPUB) | ISBN 9781487533151 (PDF)
Subjects: LCSH: Donation of organs, tissues, etc – Moral and ethical aspects. |
    LCSH: Bioethics. | LCSH: Medical ethics.
Classification: LCC RD129.5 .G55 2020 | DDC 174.2/97954—dc23

_____

University of Toronto Press acknowledges the financial assistance to its
publishing program of the Canada Council for the Arts and the Ontario Arts
Council, an agency of the Government of Ontario.

**Canada Council   Conseil des Arts
for the Arts   du Canada**

Funded by the   Financé par le
Government   gouvernement
of Canada   du Canada

Contents

Acknowledgments

Making one's debts explicit is tricky business, and not just because someone who helped shaped this project will inevitably be accidently unacknowledged. Rather, it is that the relationality of debt, gift, and repayment, and of clap and echo, is impossibly entangled: *who can these Gordian knots undo?*

There are the debts that you can point to, and the debts that you cannot, and then there are the ones you can kinda point to. Part of me wants use this space to buck the trend of only highlighting academic influence, but of course that list would be a book in itself and no one really wants to read my thank yous to Flannery O'Connor, The Cure, K Records, and Krzysztof Kieslowski, and Brian Eno, Bob Dylan, and The Beatles don't care or will never read my gratitude anyway.

The kind of debt that one cannot, at least usually, point to is just as influential as the kind one can. Tolstoy captures this kind in *A Confession* when he tells of a friend who lost his faith when an older brother saw him praying and said, "Do you still do that?" And that was it; the utterance – let alone the intellectual assents – carrying so little water compared to the surrounding complex of assertion, disapproval, attitude, positionality in altering aim, path, and worldview. And then there are all the encounters, glances, intonations that we don't even recall! Marilynne Robinson's Reverend Ames is convincing when he says "you never do know the actual nature even of your own experiences." But now I'll cease with highlighting these less obvious kinds of debts and formations, even if they are equal to the more obvious kinds.

The two clearest kinds of debts for a book like this are the intellectual and the direct. In terms of the former, citations and references run through nearly every page to document those debts. It is a pretty cool practice, when you think about it, to document one's debts in these ways. You don't see folksongs or novels so annotated. Now to the direct debts.

Thank you to Meg Patterson, who took a chance on this project and carefully oversaw it from start to finish, and Lisa Jemison and the entire editorial board and team at the University of Toronto Press. Two anonymous reviewers gave extensive and helpful critiques, clearly improving the book, Catherine Plear carefully copyedited the manuscript, and Naomi Pauls constructed the index. Of course all the errors and oversights were and remain mine.

Carol Bakhos has been a wonderful colleague here at UCLA, and I am also grateful to her and the Center for the Study of Religion for institutional support. My gratitude to Dean David Schaberg and the Humanities Division for providing financial support for producing this book. The first major dive into this research came thanks to an Annenberg Fellowship during my time in the Annenberg School at the University of Southern California. Tom Goodnight, Randy Lake, and Stephen Finlay provided serious and substantive engagement at an earlier stage of the arguments in this book; they were incisive in their comments and collegial and generous with their time.

I've benefited enormously from dialogue on many of the themes in this book and beyond, both encouraging and critical and most especially when they combine the two, with Christopher H. Smith, Sarah Banet-Weiser, Larry Gross, Manuel Castells, Jon Taplin, Eleanor Kaufman, Scott Bartchy, Jeffrey Guhin, Mary Katherine Sheena, Megan Remington, Nicholas Burnett, Jacqueline Irwin, Nicholas Crowe, James Murphy, Carol Poster, Robin Reames, Paul Strait, Beth Boser, Martin Hilbert, Garrett Broad, Ritesh Mehta, Don Waisanen, Nikki Usher, Zoltan Majdik, Carrie Platt, Angela Gorrell, Matt Croasmun, Ryan McAnnally-Linz, Sarah Farmer, Drew Collins, Nichole Flores, Michael Balboni, Ben Warf, and Derek Johnson. My students over the past decade or so have been of great assistance in critical sharpening, especially in better presentation of arguments that become mere abstractions quite quickly.

Perhaps no conversation has benefited my academic life more practically than one I had with Gary Ferngren in 2018. There's a more-than-possible world in which this book doesn't happen without that lunch; thank you for the advice – and the spirit – of that conversation.

Mark Williams taught me how to think clearer and be better, and I'm grateful that he still motivates me on both fronts. Your friendship, good sir, is a godsend.

The personal support and encouragement from loving friends and family is the largest debt and the deepest well. My love and gratitude to Ryan Lindow, Tyler Gee, and Gabe Garcia; and to Marvi, Jim, Billie Anne, Steve, James, Daniella, and Paul for being the kind of family that most people don't even think it is possible to have.

Part of this book is motivated by the desire to preserve and promote these sorts of conversations and themes for a subsequent generation, at least in my own little world of nieces and nephews. So, Graham, Heidi, Cora, Henry, Caleb, Addie, Samantha, Kyle, and Kierstin, someday may you read this book and argue with me about the is and oughts and hopes. Robinson/Ames again captures it: writing has always felt like praying ...

My parents Tim and Patti model unending love as parents and now as grandparents, and my wonderful sister Kelli is always the great encourager, especially for projects like this. Thank you.

Aideyn, Liam, Emmeline: you are the joy of my life, and inspired me every day during this project – even though only two of you were alive for half this book, and one of you arrived just a few months ago. Backward causation, surely, must be a thing. Your beauty, verve, and creativity are a salubrious contagion: infect the world!

And finally, Amber: to you and for you, all ways and always ...

ORGANS FOR SALE

SECTION ONE

Morals, Markets, and Medicine

1 Organs for Sale? Normative Entanglements in the Public Sphere

Imagine two scenarios. Let's call the first one *Child on the Range:*

> *Suppose I am shooting a gun at a firing range. You approach me and say, "You know, to hit the furthest target, you ought to aim a bit higher." I respond by informing you that I'm aiming at a different target – the one just inside that furthest one. Given my intention, given my goal, it would be natural for you to respond, "Oh, well never mind, then. Carry on." Now suppose a child wanders out onto the range. "Wait, stop firing!" you scream. But I say, "Why? Because of the stupid brat wandering around out there? I don't care if I hit him." You then start screaming at me, calling for help, and moving to physically restrain me.*

Notice the contrast between the two conversations in regard to aims and ends. In the first one, when you learn that I am aiming at a different target than you thought, you withdraw the *ought* claim. You are happy to say you are mistaken about what you perceived my aim to be, or just to let it go, thinking that while you might want to aim at the furthest target, it is no big deal that I don't share that aim. You don't go on insisting, "Well, you really ought to aim at that furthest target." But in the second conversation, that's exactly what you do. Despite my intention and disinterest in your goal, you nevertheless press me into pursuit of a different aim – even calling for assistance and perhaps physically wrestling the gun from my hand.

Now consider a different scenario. Let's call it *Family Heirloom:*

> *Your wealthiest friend is over at your apartment. She notices an exquisite goblet on your counter, and asks if she might buy it from you. You are going to be short on rent this month, and anyway, you never found much use for it, so you agree to sell it to her. "How much is it worth?" she asks you. It is from your grandmother, and so you call her to ask. Grandma is aghast that you'd want to sell the goblet, for it is an*

heirloom that has been in the family for generations. "You cannot sell it," Grandma says. "It is priceless." But you don't feel connected to it. Your friend then offers you $10 million for it. Overhearing, Grandma laughs and says, "Well in that case, of course you can sell it!" So you do. A few weeks later, you get a knock on your door, and it is the police. "You are under arrest," they say. "Don't you know it is illegal to sell family heirlooms?"

Notice here that what Grandma seems to mean at first is that you cannot morally sell the goblet, even if physically you can, and that it is an informing understanding of value, purpose, meaning, kinship, or the like that pulls significant weight. But once an outlandish money offer is made, all those sorts of informing things disappear. It is just too much money to turn down, as you and your grandmother agree, and so you then can sell the goblet. That is, the object can be sold, and from your and your grandmother's perspective, you've done nothing morally wrong; and so it comes as a surprise learn that, in this fictitious scenario, such transactions are illegal.

There are likely several intuitions firing here to indicate differences in the two scenarios. In the *Child* scenario, the weight of the end (or potential outcome) seems to do much of the intuitional work here, for there is not much at stake regarding which target someone aims at on a firing range – even if you are perfectly correct and rational that *if* I want to hit that furthest target, I ought to aim a bit higher. But when a life is in danger, particularly a child's life, the agent's stated goals and aims and interests – or lack thereof – seem to count for much less, if anything at all. Most of us would consider your response rationally justified, contextually appropriate, or both; there are some ends (or at least one) that trump other (the agent's) ends, some that might be absolute or categorical. That the contrast between the relative (aiming at a certain target) and the absolute (not shooting at innocent children) is readily grasped suggests an intuitive distinction between categorical and hypothetical (or instrumental) value. At least since Kant, there has been a persistent belief that it is the categorical that makes up morality, with the hypothetical/instrumental kind of rationality given over to desires or inclinations. Given the distinction of the problem and the intuitive grip that such a scenario presents, I will dub this issue *The Categorical Grip*, and refer to it often throughout the book.

But is nothing of the moral happening in the *Heirloom* scenario? Claims of identity, memory, kinship, and honouring ancestors are clearly present, as are notions of responsibility (to kinship and rent contracts), prudence, and, of course, a citizen's duty to uphold legal structures and the law. Still, most of us would want to say that even if some *one* held family heirlooms to be in the categorical, surely enacting a *law* that demanded that *all* citizens subscribe to as much would be a step too far. After all, by making it legal to sell family heirlooms, we are hardly requiring that you *have* to sell them. That legality maximizes freedom: you are free to sell them or not sell them. If we push that line of reasoning to its logical conclusion, what would be illegal? Don't all instances of law rest on some underlying moral position that is contestable by some citizen somewhere?

The major themes of this book are now coming into focus. We have, it seems, a strong desire (rationally justified or not at this point) to press pursuit of an end on a fellow citizen *despite* her not sharing that end *and at the same time* an aversion to such formulations. It is precisely this pressing of an end on a fellow citizen that becomes the grist for the mill of public moral deliberation.

The Big Questions I'm interested in, as present in the two scenarios and discussion above, are these: whether or not there are right answers to moral questions, what a society values and how it engages in valuing, and what ought to be for sale and who gets to decide.

While I won't shy away from Big Questions here, I want to try to get at them in a narrower way, and through a single case study in bioethics and public moral deliberation, that of human organ procurement rhetoric. While the essential question of human organ procurement in the United States and most nations is clear – how do we get more organs, given that supply is not meeting demand – I am much less concerned with that practical question than I am with the rhetoric of advocates.

I'll set three tasks for this book: (1) to analyse how advocates rhetorically construct the relationship between morals and markets in human organ procurement debates; (2) to offer a critique of neoliberalism in bioethics in specific and public moral deliberation more generally; (3a) to ask, deliberatively and not (just) rhetorically, what kind of society we want and to highlight (3b) that deciding relationships between morals and markets, in deciding what kind of laws and bioethical policies we want, *is coextensive with and performative of* deciding what kind of society we want. The bulk of the book is dedicated to the first task, with the secondary goal being a critique of neoliberalism and, finally, consideration of the broader question of what kind of policy we want for what kind of society.

To be clear, while I am not directly concerned with the practical question of how to get more organs and immediate policy, it is my hope that better understanding of the rhetoric of advocates and philosophical underpinnings and implications of the procurement debate will indeed improve our public moral deliberation in general and organ policy in specific. Seeing what public thinking is and how public arguments go on the topic and providing philosophical interrogation, critical-historical analysis, and rhetorical analysis and extensions might be a way to begin to engage more effectively and answer practical questions together.

A key task for our moral life together in the twenty-first century, pace organ sales and *Child* and *Heirloom* scenarios, seems to me to be how to conceptually and practically keep alive public moral deliberation, to keep alive a rhetoric between privatization and totalization, where morality is not reducible to (subjective, private) autonomy nor is it synonymous with whatever the public decides it is or an absolute decree.

At the very least, I hope to show how and why the question of organ procurement – and any moral question in the contemporary era – is *so hard* to answer in public moral deliberation. I also hope to give some theoretical resources for easing this problem and make it clear that, while there is a full and significant amount of choice and autonomy involved in this particular and all moral decisions, there are still right answers, even if we do not know or see them, and that we need each other to help make better moral judgments in individual, social, and public life.

Organs for Sale?

This book is a study of a lively public moral debate in the United States: the bioethical question of how to increase human organ supply. It is about the human organ shortage – a major practical biomedical problem facing the United States and many advanced nations – but it is also, perhaps even more, an extended analysis of what a society values and how it engages in the process of valuing. In short, it is a book about how we deliberate on what we value. One prominent solution to the shortage is to pay people for organs, placing, say, kidneys for sale. An overarching idea in this book is that deciding the legality of questions that concern markets and their limits in the buying and selling of human organs *is the same as* deciding what kind of society we are or what kind of society we want to be – in short, deciding what we value, how we value it, and why we value it. In other words, the moral and the legal are intertwined in a way that is not always obvious, especially in liberal-democratic societies. Furthermore, the changing support for the idea of buying and selling organs – once anathema to all but the most economically liberal – indicates the prevalence of economic value not as *one* way of valuing among several, but as the *dominant* system by which value is established. That the market has become *the* organ that filters value in the body politic is of unprecedented historical implication. The (at)traction of buying and selling human organs is a symptom of the body politic being sick.[1]

The compatibility of liberal democracy and liberal markets, in which individual liberty trumps all other concerns of morality, politics, and so forth, represents a crucial, nearly inescapable privatization of almost everything, including and especially morality and potentially political disagreement altogether. The idea of human organs being for sale might be read as but one instantiation of a broader debate in liberal capitalistic democracies: what does letting the market determine value – and defending the market as arbiter of value on liberal moral terms – mean? *Organs for Sale* is thus about organs for sale, literally and figuratively: literally in the sense of buying and selling human body parts, and figuratively in the sense of making organs of public moral deliberation reducible to the single organ of markets and market mechanisms.

That is, one of the most pervasive features of contemporary life in the West is that questions of value are reduced, simply, to questions of markets and market mechanisms. Markets determine value. What is your home worth? Put it up for sale and find out. What are your skills worth? Put out your resume and find out. What is your life worth? Call a life insurance company and find out. Moral value, when it is distinguished (if at all) from economic value, is often conceived as a privatized affair and distinct from legality. In this view, morality is largely – if not completely – reducible to autonomy. In the language of bioethics, autonomy trumps all other principles and concerns (such as beneficence or justice). That these answers *make sense* and are part of (much) common understanding in the twenty-first century is part of what will be interrogated in these pages, with the fusion of autonomy, markets, and efficiency forming the crux of a neoliberal ethos.

But of course this view of value is not the only one. That there is a market value does not mean that there is *solely* market value, one might argue; more strongly, one might accuse me of equivocating on value and worth in the preceding paragraphs. What, then, is the defence of something like public morality or democratic principles, irreducible to privatization and autonomy, or the pushback to the subjectivity of all value against increasing encroachment of markets, cost-benefit analysis, and monetization – in short, against the pressures and practices of neoliberalism? Or, in the language of much bioethical discussion, of beneficence or justice against the triumph of autonomy? One place to start is the promotion and maintenance of the ideals of altruism and the forging of a public morality – and currently in the United States, the law is on the side of this approach.

There is a reassertion, an attempted reclaiming of the common good, or public spiritedness, against the individualizing ethos of biomedical practice, forging in towards more robust deliberative democratic practices.[2] In the language of prominent bioethicist Donna Dickenson, the struggle is for "we medicine" in the face of "me medicine."[3] The challenge of neoliberalism in health care is articulated clearly by Salmaan Keshavjee: "Neoliberalism's success as an ideology, as a significant social force, is demonstrated by the way the components of this ideology have been absorbed by individuals, transplanted by NGOs, and – through its infiltration of practice – embodied in the local world in the form of poor health outcomes."[4] *Organs for Sale* adds to this growing literature by showing how and why neoliberalism has achieved success and resonance in the public moral argumentation process for democratic societies, particularly in the area of biomedical practices and, to some degree, bioethical theory. Strongly overlapping with Ezekiel Emanuel's political conception of medical ethics and his critiques of liberal theory, the aim here is particular attention to the contours, implications, and practices of neoliberal rhetoric for what otherwise might be a pursuit of the common good and public morality for democratic regimes.[5]

But isn't *public morality* really *someone's* morality? Isn't the common good *someone's take* on the common good? And in a liberal democracy, aren't we entitled, by legal right, to pursue our vision of the good life and make our evaluations of moral worth with limited (if any) interference from the state and the law? These are the kind of situations and questions to be explored and unpacked – questions of what ought to be for sale – and why – in a market economy, the broader context of increasing neoliberalism and the privatization of morality, tensions of categorical morality and individual rights, and the relationship between morality, legality, and democracy writ large. Here we will utilize and expand on common bioethical terms such as autonomy, beneficence, and justice in an instantiated debate of organ procurement in the pursuit of robust bioethical debate in the public sphere.[6] For now, let's lay the issues out clearly.

As of this writing, we are approaching 120,000 Americans on the waiting list for an organ transplant, and, despite efforts of public campaigns and social media, the gap between organ supply and demand continues to widen.[7] Estimates claim that one in three on the waiting list, or nearly 40,000 people, will die due to the current organ shortage.[8] The practical question, then, is quite simple – and urgent: how does the United States get more organs? The same question stands for many nations and their health care systems, countries like Japan, Belgium, Mexico, and Taiwan, as the global need for donors continues to increase at a rate of 5 per cent to 8 per cent per year.[9]

Many strategies exist for increasing organ supply to meet the growing demand. While there are solutions such as vouchers and tax incentives, strategies tend to focus on alleviating one side of the equation.[10] For example, demand-side fixes aspire to extinguish the need for new organs in the first place with such strategies as health campaigns aimed at preventing disease and promoting healthy lifestyle and well-being choices. If we can head off significant causes of organ failure further upstream – obesity, diabetes, and alcohol immoderation, to name a few – then the demand for organs should decrease. More generally, the idea that there is a significant misallocation of resources (particularly time and money) in health care systems towards one-off, heroic, and often late-stage interventions and that we ought to rethink this asymmetry is, rightly, gaining traction. From both a health-outcomes and a financial-cost perspective, the thinking goes, we'd be better off redeploying and reallocating resources through a systematic restructuring of medical education, training, and financial incentives for patient, insurer, and physician alike to frequent, consistent, and relational health care. Atul Gawande gives a forceful articulation of the idea of *incrementalism* as a solution to any number of problems that plague current health systems – distrust, rising costs, inefficiency, and health outcomes.[11] So, incrementalism, public health, and preventive medicine represent tools which may assist in fixing the organ shortage problem, but these are partial solutions at best.

There are also two prevalent solutions aimed at the supply side: presumed consent (opt-out structuring) and artificial organs. The opt-out model shifts the status quo of organ donation from a system in which each citizen must make a decision to opt in and somehow record that and make it known to one in which citizens are assumed to be donors unless they speak out and/or register otherwise. Some of the countries with the highest donor rates – Austria, Spain – have the opt-out policy. A recent study suggests that a switch to an opt-out policy in the United States, for example, would modestly reduce the shortage.[12] While the default position fundamentally changes, the core principle of choice – to opt in/out – remains intact. Artificial organs represent probably *the* significant potential solution to the supply-side problem. The potential to bypass human or animal organs altogether is rapidly increasing, with researchers able to harvest, grow, or even outright manufacture organs in the lab, using biomedical engineering (including bioprinting, the ability to print organs on demand), scaffold-tissue engineering, and so forth, and eventually print them out on 3D printers.[13] Though ethically underdetermined, the manufacturing of organs in this way seems promising, and potentially a more permanent and robust solution to the shortage in a way that opt-out, incrementalism, and preventive medicine likely never can be.[14]

But this is not a book about the practical question of how to increase organ supply – at least not directly. Rather, the focus here is on the rhetoric of advocates of two distinct strategies to increase human organ supply: one based on the maintenance and expansion of the current volunteer-donation system rooted in public altruism, and the other based on incentivizing organ giving through financial compensation and/or through an outright market for human organs, both currently prohibited under federal law. The focus here is on procurement strategies only and not distribution.[15] And the concerns are at core philosophical: what ought to be for sale and why and who gets to decide; tensions of morality and legality; challenges of the categorical under conditions of ethical and political pluralism; and the background conditions in which this debate arises and the contingencies therein. I am not as concerned with how to explicitly motivate donors or the alignment of stated values with registration practices.[16] (One excellent book already exists on that subject.[17])

The reason for my focus is simple: how we talk about what has worth, how we engage in the valuing process – be it in discursive public argument, codified law, or protest – matters. One of the most striking features of contemporary discourse – formal and informal – is the degree to which questions of value are often reduced to questions of market value, that debates about what has worth, or what worth something has, tend to mean almost exclusively *economic* worth, even if as a proxy.[18] This book is a philosophically informed analysis of why that is the case and critical-historical account of how we got here, using an extended case study of organ procurement. The content and strategies of our communication and especially our public argumentation inform – and reveal – our ideas of who we are personally, communally, and globally, and what we think has value and why. Talk matters, and here I will explore our talk about three things that many of us think matter – morality, markets, and medicine – as rendered in public arguments about organ sales.

At its most basic level, this book offers a (bio)ethical and philosophical-rhetorical analysis of two dominant strategies for increasing human organ supply, engaging in a reconstruction of public moral argumentation in terms of more nuanced concepts and categories in order to better understand this deliberative moment – and how to best choose among alternatives. The book is situated at the intersection of bioethics and public moral deliberation, and is intended to be appealing and challenging to an interdisciplinary host of scholars and practitioners and policymakers alike. How we talk about our policies and our vision for who, as a society, we want to be is vital to becoming, morally and legally, who it is that we ought to be.

The Key Problems: Moral, Legal, Economic, and Political

To reiterate, the primary concern of this book is not directly with the practical question of how the United States or any nation struggling with a gap can increase its organ supply but rather with the rhetoric of advocates, most specifically with the arguments that advocates make to justify their strategies. The contesting strategies are traced through congressional hearings, presidential advisory committee hearings, interest groups' and non-profit organizations' websites and documents, and popular media coverage. Relevant bioethical, legal, and philosophical literature is also drawn upon to establish and parse out key arguments in the respective arenas. The analysis focuses on the normative dimensions of the strategies. Specific attention is paid to the interplay of, and the rhetorically constructed limits between, morality and markets in terms of justification for the two strategies.

This study also outlines the context within which the procurement strategies appear in the public sphere. It considers the broader political-economic relations currently at work in many Western societies – namely, increasing neoliberalism – and draws implications for public moral deliberation. The two intersecting strands – the collapse of the shared backdrop of moral discourse and the ensuing fragmentation of morality, and the increasing economization of everyday life under liberal democracy and global capitalism – make the normative justification of a market mechanism for moral matters persuasive and resonant neoliberal rhetoric. Under present conditions, one can see why a market mechanism is also desirable for adjudication, given the difficulty of moral coherence under pluralistic constitutional democracies with strong rights-based interpretative paradigms.

There are elements of common ground among advocates. That is, while an altruistic system is significantly different from a free market, advocates share a commitment to two overarching arguments. These will be called the General Moral Argument (GMA) and the General Economic Argument (GEA):

> GMA: All things being equal, it is wrong to let people die who ought to otherwise live.
> GEA: All things being equal, the strategy that costs less financially is a better strategy.

The GMA is largely enthymematic in the United States: it is a value that is shared and generally does not need to be argued for. Applied specifically to the case of human organs, it means that the fact that supply is not meeting demand is unacceptable to all advocates and fellow citizens. As James Greenwood, the chair of a 2003 congressional hearing, put it in his opening statement, "What is particularly frustrating about these numbers, these missed chances to save a life, is that we know more organs could be made available."[19] The point is that supply is out there, and citizens know that they want and need it; the supply just needs to be harnessed.

The economics of transplantation are staggering. For example, the current amount spent in the United States on people with end-stage renal disease is $33 billion – and that is just through Medicare, not private insurance.[20] To put that in perspective, that is almost *double* the amount spent since just 2005.[21] When the $64 billion spent for patients suffering from chronic kidney disease is added, there is nearly $100 billion spent through Medicare on kidney medical interventions. No one wants to waste money, and no one wants to waste lives.[22]

There is thus significant agreement among citizens, politicians, and the medical community that transplantation is morally acceptable, that it is safe, and that it is cheaper for individuals, companies, and the government than treatment through processes like dialysis. In some sense, then, these could be thought of as shared aims among otherwise competing advocates. At an abstract level, that is indeed true, but as analysis in future chapters will indicate, there are often significantly different assumptions and justifications for these shared aims, and it is those that constitute much of the argumentative conflict.

The problems, then, are at the level of both ends and means, despite some level of shared aims and means discussed above. In short, organ transplantation *is* the moral and economic answer to the question of organ failure. While there are many potential concerns about transplantation, from the politics of the waiting list and distribution to the procedure itself, my focus here is on organ procurement strategies.

While there are "six main possible modes of transfer or acquisition of human body parts (HBPs),"[23] James Childress informs that the "primary debate" focuses on express donation and sale/purchase.[24] But there is an in-between position here as well: that of financial incentives *towards* express donation. So, there are two main positions being evaluated, which I will call "altruistic donation" and "compensated offering," with the latter being divisible into financial incentives for express donation and financial compensation under a market mechanism for procurement. Therefore, while there are essentially two "sides," there are three positions being considered.

So far I have been describing what might be considered the practical problems associated with organ procurement, particularly the question of how best to achieve the goal of increasing organ supply. The theoretical problems are partly evident in this discussion, but let me make them explicit.

Chapters 3 and 4 outline the key arguments and rhetorical elements of altruistic donation and compensated offerings respectively. Given that there are differing conclusions based on differing assumptions and justifications for action, the key theoretical problem of this book is how societies can and should manage conflicting justifications in contemporary liberal democracies. This focus follows the driving question of much political philosophical work, articulated perhaps most succinctly by John Rawls: "How is it possible that there may exist over time a stable and just society of free and equal citizens profoundly divided by reasonable though incompatible religious, philosophical, and moral doctrines?"[25]

In the same way that this study is not as concerned with directly answering the practical question of how best to increase human organ supply, its primary theoretical concern is not how to directly answer the liberal-democratic justificatory question but is instead to provide an analysis of how arguers answer (either implicitly or explicitly) that question, particularly in the context of neoliberal rhetoric and organ sales. I am interested in the way that categorical moral claims are argued as part of or antithetical to capitalistic liberal democracy. The rhetorical construction of the limits and boundaries between morals and markets in general, and bioethics and biomedical practices like organ donation in particular, represents the primary motivating question for this book.

The challenge in the contemporary era as I see it is precisely how to negotiate the tension between limits, ethical injunctions, and moral purpose against the powerful and pervasive sweep of morality as reducible to autonomy and social life as reducible to market and market mechanisms. The concept of neoliberalism represents a shorthand for the confluence of privatization, autonomy, and efficiency as the three criteria for sociopolitical life in liberal democracies like the United States.

While this study analyses a very practical, concrete problem, there is a critical-historical background and much philosophy and rhetorical theory involved. This is because I want to explain how and why the questions of organ procurement – and any moral question in the contemporary era – are *so hard* to answer.

My goal is to analyse responses to, and eventually weigh in on, these two driving questions:

Q1: Is financial compensation for human organs morally permissible?
Q2: Should a society allow it?

The fundamental problems, then, are how arguers do and ought to construct the relationship between moral categoricity and community in moral debates – in this case, human organ procurement – in the liberal-democratic political public sphere, and what role market rationality does and ought to play in managing, deflecting, and deciding the outcome of those debates. The relationship between Q1 and Q2 is *the* important wedge issue in this debate – not just in how each is answered *per se* but in how arguers and advocates construct the *relationship* between the two questions. The simple versions, on each end of the spectrum, are that to an idealized neoliberal, Q1 has *nothing* to do with Q2, and to an idealized civic republican, the answer to Q1 is tantamount to answering Q2.

Moral Disagreement and Controversy in Liberal Democracies

The general backdrop for this book is rational disagreement in democracies, and particularly the way in which controversies are argued and (potentially) settled in the public sphere,[26] occasioning moral reflection on a specific problem and moving to more general conclusions for ethics and human life together. As Michael Sandel observes, "Moral reflection is not a solitary pursuit but a public endeavor."[27] Moral judgment, individually and collectively, is, and ought to be, rhetorical deliberation.

Moral disagreement is a significant feature of contemporary life in the United States. Moral disagreement occurs within already established norms and over the very attempt to establish a reasonable "basic structure of society."[28] The process of argumentation itself affects (if not fully licences and legitimates) the outcome of the public debates. Thus what is felt is the *intersubjective nature* of the enterprise of public deliberation, something articulated in the work of Jürgen Habermas. As Tom Goodnight writes, "Habermas' own work is self-consciously to transform the 'telos of reaching understanding' developed in religious traditions to the secular, argumentative realm of making informed, meaningful, collaborative life choices."[29]

Publics sort out conflicts in desires and beliefs resting in comprehensive doctrines, principles, practices, institutional systems, and political parties. Everyone is entitled to her own opinion, of course, and those opinions can be amalgamated pragmatically (e.g., voting for results). But public processes continue in aspiration for reasoned deliberation.[30]

There are normative constraints for reasoned public deliberation in constitutional democracies oriented towards maintaining a just society.[31] The most important is for citizens to engage in intersubjective reason giving as a reciprocal and reflexive enterprise. *Reciprocity* "holds that citizens owe one another justifications for the mutually binding laws and public policies they collectively enact."[32] *Reflexivity*, as the ability to turn criticism back on oneself, invokes the "conversational skills and virtues involved in the ongoing practice of moral dialogue and discourse."[33] Reflexivity also promotes and breeds what Habermas calls the "appropriate epistemic attitudes," which is a reflexive stance in which interlocutors are able to self-reflect on their own limitations and potential blind spots in argumentative engagement.[34]

The aim of a just society is both to distribute goods (and in particular relation to our discussion, scarce resources) the right way and to value things the right way.[35] The "right way" is of course a normative claim and therefore subject to debate and disagreement. But rather than ethical controversy over the right way to value being evidence of a lack of consensus, it is precisely debate and disagreement that offer the possibility to *affirm* a civic community and shared social relations. This is in line with a contractualist view of human social relations in which people are "moved by the aim of finding principles that others, similarly motivated, could not reasonably reject"; this is what we owe to each other as members of the same society.[36] The cooperative search is for the reasons that matter and the principles that will guide a just society.

A challenge to inquiries of ethical disagreements is to not settle for simply describing differing moral positions. It is indeed true that two arguers can disagree over ethical claims and yet still both be rational. "But," as moral philosopher Ralph Wedgwood succinctly puts it, "it is perfectly possible for false beliefs to be rational."[37]

That is, in order to discuss substantive judgment in matters of moral disagreement in constitutional democracies beyond sociological description – the fact of moral pluralism and how people account for and justify claims – this study must engage with conceptual metaethics and normativity.[38] The conceptual level, which is neither principle nor application, is where a significant amount of argument and debate takes place, at least implicitly and presuppositionally. So normative concepts must be addressed.

Normative concepts – the constituents of thoughts about normative terms such as *right, good,* and *just* – are a significant part of moral disagreement in contemporary US society. Christine Korsgaard notes,

> Normative concepts exist because human beings have normative problems. And we have normative problems because we are self-conscious rational animals, capable of reflection about what we ought to believe and do. That is why the normative question can be raised in the first place: because even when we are inclined to believe that something is right and to some extent feel ourselves moved to do it we can still *always* ask: but is this really true? and must I really do this?[39]

To that end, conceptual analysis, a fundamental component of metaethics and moral philosophy in the analytic tradition, is part of the enquiry for the organ debate. Concepts can be removed and rationally analysed outside particular cases, and thus furnish content for theoretical work. Thinking about the Big Ideas and the Tough Moral Questions needs to be addressed, and not only by practitioners in the clinic and on the field.[40]

The challenge of rhetorical reflection on ethical controversies is negotiating the relationship between analysis (describing, categorizing, and aiding in understanding the debate) and judgment (who is right, or what ought to be done). This study's goal is not primarily to make a first-order judgment about the ethics of human organ procurement. Such a judgment and the corresponding work are unavoidable, of course, as the work of moral psychology is making it clearer by the day that most moral arguments are simply rationalizations of one's immediate and intuitively made first-order judgments.[41] But significantly, intuitive judgments and corresponding rationalizations do not *necessarily* exhaust the possibilities for moral discourse. Spaces for rational deliberation, such as this book itself, aid in thinking through the poststructural era of hybridity in ethical systems, in which little thought is given to the ethical implications of such societally shaped and charged choice mechanisms, or in which it is assumed that *harm* is somehow self-evidently understandable in a way that *good* is not. Put differently, following in the Aristotelian tradition, the immediate character of judgment is due to cultivating intuitions through processes of education and socialization. But these processes of education and community are meant to reinforce what is *rationally* given as the Good Life, not as a substitute for reflective thought or reason. As Aristotle writes in Book II of the *Nicomachean Ethics*, "We ought to have been brought up in a particular way from our very youth, as Plato says, so as both to delight in and to be pained by the things that we ought; for this is the right education."[42] What one *ought* to be pained by or delight in, however, is precisely part of the contestation in liberal democracies. Aristotle gets to assume a collective backdrop of shared values that is either not currently enjoyed, is precisely what is an open question, or, most profoundly, is what we claim we *don't* enforce or need to share with one another in contemporary liberal democracies.

Categorical morality would fix ends and guide means for an otherwise ethically pluralistic age. *Categorical morality* is a public morality that does not rest upon subjective beliefs and desires. The concept of categorical morality in general is largely what neoliberalism and many market advocates attack, as will be seen in the coming chapters. *Neoliberalism* is a theory of political economy that asserts the centrality and priority of individual rights, privatization, and free markets in human well-being and also the necessity that society be structured accordingly. Ideas like "private property rights, free markets, and free trade" and "deregulation, privatization, and withdrawal of the state from many areas of social provision" characterize the view, as do the policy trends in Western countries such as the United States from the 1970s forward.[43] The political economic element of neoliberalism is vital to our discussion, of course, but the most salient element is the related ethical dimension of neoliberalism – namely, moral individualism. That is, neoliberal ethics are a type of moral individualism, in which morality is a private and subjective affair. The combination of autonomy and efficiency as the watchwords for all sociopolitical decision-making and collective life are what I mean to capture in my usage of the term "neoliberalism."

A civic republican pushback – what might also be seen as egalitarian, or communitarian, and so forth – makes do not just with emphasis on collective deliberation en route to judgment but also – and this is something important to my discussion – with the notion that there are such things as right ends and wrong ends in morality. In short, the notion of categorical morality is *central* to my supplement to the logic of good reasons as well as a full understanding of the pressures of neoliberalism on disarticulating morality from public life. As Tom Koch notes in the conclusion to his *Thieves of Virtue*, "without a strong and generally accepted core value as an a priori, perhaps all that is left is the brutal accountancies of the neoliberal."[44]

To better understand what is meant by the categorical, consider Ludwig Wittgenstein's image of the difference between *relative* judgments of value (i.e., values relative to a certain goal) and *absolute* judgments of value (i.e., unrelativized, categorical, universal-type values).[45] As ethical pluralism and moral disagreement are such common features of contemporary US life, the notion of absolute judgments of value might seem questionable, and an inherited tradition of scepticism towards logically establishing moral practice bolsters as much.

In the *Child* scenario at the start of this chapter, few would disagree that I ought to stop firing into a field with a child running through it.[46] But not all matters are so clear-cut. That is to say, the Categorical Grip gets tighter and more complicated when competing ends or goal are not shared *and yet* people must still live together in the same community.[47] Neoliberalism pushes against such categorical pressures and articulations from the state or fellow citizens.

Suffice it to say, the problem of *categoricity and community*, as managed by rhetorical engagement, on the specific questions of bioethics and biopractice has extensive literature and history. But few have put the conversation between moral disagreement, bioethics, neoliberalism, and democracy together. The problems of moral disagreement in general and in liberal democracies in particular are not new but they are persistent, and becoming intensified and wrought with vast implications for individual and collective life in the contemporary moment. And the problems of bioethics and biopolitics are relatively new problems, becoming more prevalent and pressing in contemporary society. How, then, ought we understand – and construct – the relationship between morality, markets, and medicine?

Previewing the Structure and Arguments of the Book

This introductory chapter has set up the key problems of this study and situated them in the broader discussion of bioethics and public moral deliberation. To reiterate, the two primary positions under analysis for organ procurement are altruistic donation and compensated donation, with the latter including subcamps of a market in human organs and financial incentives for the act of donation.

Organ donation is an important case study as a public controversy that generally advocates public morality and civic republican norms against market logic and monetization norms. To isolate the normative stakes of the controversy, the rhetorical logic of good reasons has to be tested, redefined, and extended in ways that account for alternative views of the relations between norms, ethics, justifications, and communities. This book engages in this discussion to explicate the tensions of a specific bioethical question, that of human organ procurement strategies, as well as to illuminate the broader socio-political-ethical context in the current era. It intends to expose the explicit and implied moral thinking on each side within theoretical, philosophical, and historical analyses.

This book has ten chapters (including the conclusion) and is divided into four sections. The first section sets the stage for the debate, offering this introduction to the theoretical and practical issues in this bioethical debate and in moral disagreements in constitutional democracies more broadly (chapter 1), and providing an account of altruism and public policy (chapter 2), explicating legal, philosophical, and historical antecedent arguments and motivations. The second section details the specifics of each side in the debate, the rhetoric, key arguments and narrative, and structure of justification for the altruism-based supply side (chapter 3) and the market-based supply side (chapter 4).

A certain kind of study might proceed from chapters 1 through 4 to an intervention and declaration of a winner, so to speak. But to go from the establishment *that* there is disagreement on what to do about it misses *why* it is that these positions can come to such different conclusions and yet still be respectively rationally justified. To put it in the form of a question: Why is it that a market solution arises and is so rhetorically resonant in the twenty-first century whereas such a solution would have been nearly unthinkable in, say, the seventeenth century?

The third section of the book is thus a theoretically rich investigation of the ascendancy of neoliberalism in the public sphere, shaping reasoning, law, policy, and civic participation, with specific reference to medicine (chapter 5); the ways in which the implications of a kind of neoliberal rationality map onto moral discourse more generally and why such a mapping is philosophically mistaken (chapter 6), and how moral disagreement in the public sphere can be better understood and potentially reformulated via a rhetorical theory of good reasons and moral disagreement (chapter 7).

With such an understanding in place, we then return to the bioethical debate of organ procurement. Section 4 of the book puts the arguments, motivations, and narratives in full conflict with each other in chapters 8 and 9. The essential moral issues and questions, then, of what has rhetorical and normative force in this debate will thus be made clear, and the conclusion will tie the conversation back together and expand the scope and stakes of the debate. Undoubtedly, certain audiences will be more interested in certain sections. For example, clinical bioethicists, policymakers, and health care practitioners might be most interested in sections 2 and 5, while philosophical bioethicists and humanities academics more generally might be most interested in sections 3 and 4. Or perhaps scholars interested in altruism and dignity will be interested in chapters 2, 9, and 10, while those studying narrative medicine might be most interested in chapters 3 and 4. Scholars, and not just critics, of neoliberalism and the relationships between morals and markets and the public sphere might be interested in chapters 5, 8, 9, and 10. It is my hope, however, that all ten chapters hang together as one cohesive argument, and that, while certain parts can be read out of context, all are necessary to understanding – and engaging in – current public (bioethical) (moral) disagreement.

Previewing the overarching argument, the organ donation system in the United States is built on and maintained by the values of altruism and dignity. Neoliberalism tends to be successfully transgressive in the current era, dominating forms of life in both market and non-market arenas. The rhetorical appeal of neoliberalism as a solution – either a positive, best-case scenario or even as a lowest common denominator of appeal under conditions of ethical pluralism – is articulated and analysed. Market challenges and neoliberal ethos – the economization of everyday life – might be resisted through a logic of good reasons and the process of public moral deliberation.

The key theoretical move is this: moral deliberation is not philosophically reducible to privatization, and the pragmatic outcome of such a theoretical error is a reification of the privatization and efficiency logics of neoliberalism. The logic of neoliberalism both assumes and affirms moral fragmentation. It replaces substantive moral disagreements with nonmoral ones by prizing efficiency and consistency. The key turn is claiming autonomy, which is a moral consideration, as the *only* relevant moral consideration. Thus the neoliberal logic becomes clear: moral disagreement writ large is both understood as and resolved by appeals to autonomy, efficiency, and consistency. If autonomy, efficiency, and consistency are not the only or not the proper concepts with which to think through and perform moral deliberation, then a different conception of what morality – and by extension moral deliberation – *is* must be articulated.

Thus, a metaethical and morally normative supplement to the logic of good reasons provides a robust defence of moral realism in the face of the fact of ethical pluralism, thereby articulating a kind of public morality for policy and practice against the privatization of morality and the neoliberal ethos of markets determining all value and values.

What has the most normative force in this debate is the question of human dignity. Market advocates' case turns on the fact that markets do not violate human dignity, but altruistic advocates respond that a good society would be one that actually *promotes* attitudes that *enhance* human dignity and altruism, not simply avoiding violations and harm.

The society that buys and sells human body parts is unlikely to have much concern for human dignity, just as the relationship built on the buying and selling of sex is unlikely to have much concern for love. It is not the *acts* that *remove* such things as human dignity or love but *the acts and communicative patterns around them that promote and reinforce* attitudes towards ourselves and others. Payment does not inherently diminish the virtues of one's behaviour, but in practice it promotes an attitude that absolves oneself and society of gratitude and deeper conceptions of justice. While the ultimate attitude of this book is deliberative, aiming to explicate key tensions and better understand the debate, normative arguments proceed as well, in what we might see as the beginnings of an attempt to *degraft* neoliberalism from bioethics in specific and public deliberation in democratic society in general, based on the idea that a healthy, functioning democratic society is one that avoids the twin poles of individualization and totalization. On offer is an attempt to highlight the drift to individualization – triumph of autonomy in the privatization of morality and markets alike – while maintaining consciousness of the danger that certain kinds of categoricity lead to totalization.

Organs for Sale means to be a reappraisal of the increasing drift towards the self-interested, market logics side of medicine and medical practice. While there is much ethical argument and critical analysis of practice, bioethics, and overarching biopolitics, the central task here is to further public deliberation on substantive moral commitments and encouragement to maintain reflective and reflexive moral engagement in the public sphere. Albert Jonsen, in his excellent *The New Medicine and the Old Ethics*, writes, "In medicine's moral history and present, [the central] axis forms at the point where altruism and self-interest meet. At that intersection a profound moral paradox pervades medicine."[48] *Organs for Sale* documents and cautions about the latter practically and rhetorically overtaking the former, either through active ideological commitment or by secular pluralistic default, and argues for increased deliberation on the cross-pressures of morality and markets in medicine, keeping the dialectical tensions between the opposing logics of altruism and self-interest alive and healthy. To that end, it is argued that US society should speak of morality and – not or – markets, collective democratic deliberation and – not or – moral categoricity, normative force and – not or – rhetorical force.

Though sometimes uncomfortable, public moral disagreements like those over human organ procurement strategies are expected in an ethically pluralistic society such as the United States. Human organ procurement is a problem symbolically at the heart of contemporary moral and sociopolitical disagreements in liberal democracies, with "organs for sale" marking a metaphor for the economization of everyday life under the continued expansion and rhetorical resonance of neoliberalism for public moral deliberation. Deciding together about the limits of markets, of what is and ought to be for sale and why, is about organ policy in particular but, more significantly, it is also about the very kind of society in which citizens and markets exist, deliberate, and thrive.

2 Public Morality: Altruism, Rhetoric, and Bioethics

In the fourth century CE, twin-brother physicians named Cosmas and Damien travelled from Arabia through Syria performing medical works and good deeds.[1] The men were called *Anagyroi*, which means money-less ("without silver"), because they refused to accept payment for their work. The strength of their charity and the witness of their acts converted many to Christianity, which upset Lycias, the Roman proconsul, who condemned them to death if they would not recant their faith. They refused and were beheaded.

After their death and upon the religious conversion of Rome, Emperor Justinian credited prayers to Cosmas and Damien for curing him from a severe illness. Later, the most enduring Cosmas and Damien story is told: that of a Roman custodian with a gangrenous leg. Cosmas and Damien reappear in human form and, using the leg of a recently dead Ethiopian gladiator, successfully transplant the healthy leg onto the custodian's body.[2]

So goes the earliest story of human body-part transplantation. Easier-to-explain transplantation doesn't become a reality until the twentieth century, with an Austrian ophthalmologist performing a cornea transplant in 1906 and experiments with animal body parts (e.g., monkey and lamb kidneys) being inserted into humans. But none of these early experiments worked. The first successful – that is, non-rejected – vital-organ transplant occurred in Boston in 1954, in which Joseph Murray performed a living-donor kidney transplant between (in echo of Cosmas and Damien) twin brothers. In response to this new medical ability, in 1968 the United States adopted the Uniform Anatomical Gift Act (UAGA), which, following the spirit of *Anagyroi*, permitted the gifting of human organs.[3]

For nearly fifteen years, the UAGA stood as the primary statement on organ transplantation until a few incidents led to the establishment of a more comprehensive policy and law.[4] One of those incidents occurred in 1983, as Ashley Bailey, an eleven-month-old baby, was in need of a new liver. With the lack of medical or social infrastructure for the procurement of organs – and with death imminent – her grandfather contacted Charles Stenholm, his local congressman. Stenholm was so moved by the story that he brought it to the attention of President Reagan, who then brought up Ashley Bailey on his weekly radio address. He said,

> I'm taking to the airwaves today in hopes we can save one little eleven-month-old girl from Texas and many others like her ... she is now in critical condition ... and has but two or three weeks to live unless she receives a liver transplant ... Time is running out. I'm issuing a plea to the nation to find Ashley a donor.
>
> Once one is found, an Air Force jet is standing ready ... [5]

Though a number of more complicated and rapidly growing problems led to the moment, Ashley Bailey largely catalysed the 1983 congressional hearings on forming and reforming organ-transplantation policy, procedure, and law in the United States. As Thomas Luken, a Congressman from Ohio, said at the opening of one hearing, "To sum it up, Air Force One isn't a national policy."[6]

After the hearings, the United States passed its most significant piece of human organ legislation to date, the National Organ Transplant Act (NOTA) in 1984. In addition to creating the Organ Procurement and Transplant Network (OPTN), the act also explicitly created a prohibition under Section 301(a): "It shall be unlawful for any person to knowingly acquire, receive, or otherwise transfer any human organ for valuable consideration for use in human transplantation if the transfer affects interstate commerce."[7] The key wording here is *valuable consideration*, and what it means, inter alia, is that it is illegal to sell or buy human organs.

After the 1983 hearings that led to the enactment of NOTA in 1984, the altruism-based model remained largely uncontested for approximately a decade.[8] Then ideas about repealing parts of this act or reinterpreting the *valuable consideration* clause began to surface.[9] Relatively steady academic debates, particularly in bioethics and the medical-transplant community, appear in the late 1990s and early 2000s,[10] and the 2003 congressional hearing, *Assessing Initiatives to Increase Organ Donation*, put the issue squarely before a US Congress subcommittee. Since that hearing in the early 2000s, the controversy surrounding paid organ supply[11] and a (free or regulated) market in human organs has become increasingly a part of public concern.[12] Furthermore, while in general the public attitude towards organ donation is extremely positive (over

90 per cent), there is also increased positivity towards financial incentives or compensation.

In fact, what had been overwhelming resistance to incentives or buying organs in both the transplant community and the public has significantly lessened. For example, a 2004 study of attitudes towards organ donation within the transplant community found that among a mass of transplant surgeons, transplant coordinators, and critical care nurses, nearly *half* of the respondents deemed some sort of financial incentive to be morally permissible.[13] Perhaps more interesting is a 2012 NPR-Thomson Reuters Poll:

> If compensation took the form of credits for health care needs, about 60 percent of Americans would support it. Tax credits and tuition reimbursement were viewed favorably by 46 percent and 42 percent, respectively. Cash for organs was seen as OK by 41 percent of respondents.[14]

A 2015 study found that 51 per cent of US residents believed payment for organs acceptable, and when a process of explanation about the organ shortage and potential for market mechanisms to alleviate this shortage occurred, more than 70 per cent found such a payment process acceptable.[15] So while attitudes towards organ donation are still extremely positive, public and professional attitudes towards incentives and compensation, once anathema to all but the most economically liberal, are also becoming more positive.

The push against the status quo – of altruism and the volunteer-based model and the legal prohibition against commodification – cannot be fully understood until there is an account of the current system. This chapter provides an overview of the altruism-based organ procurement system as it is currently practised, how and why it came into effect, and how the argument of and for the status quo theoretically hangs together. But before diving into that system, it is worth briefly revisiting the deep historical entwinement between altruism and medical practice.

Altruism and Medicine: Religious and Secular Orientations

The practice of healing as an altruistic act has precedence in antiquity, with the linkage most notably forged by the Hippocratic Oath and early Christianity. With the Hippocratic Oath, one gets the establishment of more than a code of conduct or prescriptive on-the-job rules; one gets something closer to a way of life. The Oath's emphasis on character and ethical uprightness both in the clinical setting and outside it and the (even-then) countercultural prohibition on abortion and euthanasia due to what was seen as an overarching emphasis on benevolence and the cultivation of healing and restoration of life indicate a seriousness of medicine, of medical practice being more than transactional and technical.

While a significant part of the Hippocratic Corpus is the rejection, or at least diminishment, of supernatural etiologies and cures, the Oath itself is sworn before the gods, and the guarding of the art of medicine is itself considered a holy act: "in purity and in holiness I will guard my life and my art." This "demand for holiness," as Ludwig Edelstein highlights, "can hardly be understood as resulting from practical thinking or technical responsibility ... [as] [h]oliness belong to another realm of values, and is indicative of standards of a different, more elevated character."[16] Vivian Nutton goes so far as to say that it is precisely this *religious* tone of the Oath that accounts for both its difference from other medical ethical writings of the time and its enduring appeal.[17]

With Hippocratic medicine we get the push, then, for both a rational, empirical care and a values-oriented care. In short, body and soul care. The idea is that medical care is to be given in accordance with if not religious then at least an elevated realm of values, and namely those values that include emphasizing something *more* than the transactional being necessarily a part of practising the art of medicine.

The impetus of care beyond the transactional sees perhaps its fullest articulation in early Christianity and its enduring legacies, particularly with its emphasis on treating anyone in need, regardless of ability to pay. The authoritative *Western Medical Tradition* puts it this way: "The Jewish tradition of hospitality was extended by the Christians [following Christ's orders to make] a commitment to all in need, Christians and non-Christians alike."[18]

Furthermore a special emphasis existed in early Christianity on care for the poor and the sick, a special philanthropic calling. In the West, the contemporary notion of philanthropy likely resonates more readily with the Christian notion of *agape* than the Greco-Roman notion of *philanthropia*. The redistribution by the wealthy more equally throughout society and the discounting of pity as a valid motivation for medical philanthropy characterized *philanthropia*, whereas the Christian *agape* concerned both God's love for humanity that humans were meant to endorse and enact, as well as a special emphasis on the marginalized.[19]

That is, the impetus to care in the early Christian medical care was one that *emphasized* the sick and the poor. As historian Gary Ferngren writes, "No pre-Christian institutions in the ancient world served the purpose for which Christian hospitals were created, which was to offer charitable aid to those in need."[20] It is from these Christian principles, and their enacted practices in the Roman republic, that we get the founding, essentially, of hospitals – and most notably, hospitals that were not steeped in an economic or military purpose.

The transition from these kind of institutions and altruistic motives to the technical-bureaucratized medicine of the contemporary is well-charted.[21] The rise of science in medicine, for better or worse, changes the emphasis in medicine from care to cure, and the primary core of medicine from the clinical patient-physician encounter to the laboratory. The most significant moment in recounting this history is this: the transformation of the hospital as a site of care run by doctors and nurses and lay clergy on the principle of compassion to a site of heroic medical intervention run by business administrators on the principle of efficiency.[22]

But altruism, and motives of care and concern beyond the transactional, are hardly absent in the contemporary, even if they are muted. There are remainders of the Hippocratic-Christian system within the transactional, rational-technical-bureaucratized medicine of the contemporary, and the organ donation system is exactly one such instance. Let me offer that account now.

An Overview of the Organ Procurement System

As organ transplantation became a medical reality in the 1950s and 1960s, the news of a patient needing a new vital organ – heart, kidney, liver – soon ceased to be a death sentence. The use of technology, such as pacemakers and dialysis machines, to assist in repair and life improvement remains a possibility but is hardly ideal. Dialysis, for example, is so miserable a process – requiring patients to be hooked up to a machine to filtrate their system for four to five hours, often three days a week – that as many as 12 per cent of patients choose death over the process.[23] Transplantation, then, is the preferred option.

So how does one legally obtain an organ for transplant? The establishment of the UAGA in 1968 and NOTA in 1984 are the two most significant pieces of legislation governing the organ procurement and distribution process. The UAGA made federal law of the altruistic process of organ and tissue giving, which had previously been handled state by state. NOTA established not just the federal ban on organ selling but also the system of organ procurement and allocation. NOTA created a national body, the OPTN, that governs, grants, and otherwise ties together the local organ procurement organizations (OPOs). The OPTN federal contract was granted exclusively to the private, non-profit United Network for Organ Sharing (UNOS) in 1986. The localized OPOs serve counties and regions across the United States. The fifty-eight

OPOs do not compete against one another for organs, and have a single national representative, called the Association of Organ Procurement Organizations (AOPO), headquartered in Washington, DC.

Organs come directly from humans through a process known as referral, typically via doubly bad news. That is, in addition to the bad news of a patient being in organ failure, organ procurement is also often replete with the tragic news of premature death. As prominent medical researcher Jeffrey Prottas puts it, "The archetypical organ donor is a young man who is in an auto accident and untimely dies of his injuries."[24] In such an occurrence, the situation is referred to the local OPO.[25] While the hospital and the organ donor are extremely necessary, it is ultimately the responsibility of the OPO to procure (and then allocate) the organ.[26]

Whether or not physicians can procure the deceased's organ is an individual decision, frequently indicated by driver's licence permission in the United States. But in practice, the family's approval often trumps the donor's wishes. This is one of several complicated questions surrounding cadaveric donation, as the decision to donate thus comes, ultimately, in a "single, reactive decision in the midst of personal tragedy."[27] Trying to influence and shape against this problem, public campaigns stemming from OPOs – such as "share your decision, share your life" – are designed to make one's organ decision clear to family members as well as to protect the family from feelings of being harsh and insensitive about their loved one's body in that vulnerable moment.

While not everyone is an organ donor, there is significant public support and a prevailing attitude of altruism that undergirds status quo policy. How altruism came to be a familial and community-supported concept in the context of organ donation is discussed next.

Establishing Altruism as a Communal Concept in Context of Modern Medicine

In the context of organ donation, altruism is both public and familial. In a legal sense, the decision to donate one's organs is strictly a private, individual decision. Straightforwardly, one can check the *yes* box to being an organ donor or check the *no* box. But, as alluded to above, it is, in actuality, a family decision.[28] In practice, then, the act of organ donation is not fully individualistic voluntary but what bioethicists Arthur Caplan and Paul Welvang describe as "assisted voluntary."[29]

Assisted voluntary donation suggests that family is pivotal to the act of donation. Research by health communication scholars Susan Morgan and Jenny Miller demonstrates as much, as they find that individuals with knowledge of organ transplantation (i.e., being free from misconceptions and myths) and high levels of altruism were the most likely to speak about organ donation with their family.[30] Potential organ donors must have factual knowledge about donation to make a decision and reasonably defend it should they encounter disagreement from family members. Potential donors also need to understand that "next of kin must grant consent under the current medical system."[31]

The notion of assisted voluntarism and the related issue of individual altruism needing to be supported by next of kin result in the establishment of altruism, in the context of organ donation, as a communal concept. The importance of family and next of kin knowing one's wishes is not always sufficient in this picture, given that wishes, even a signed donor card, might be overruled. The next of kin, therefore, must not only know but *understand* and *support* one's individual decision and wishes for her organs.

The resources for an individual's decision and the ensuing or supporting material and evidence for her family to understand and support that decision are provided by a matrix of medical, legal, social, moral, religious, and media messages. This makes, to some degree, significantly public affairs of both the process of organ donation as resting on factual and correct knowledge and the virtue of altruism.

The systemization and public institutionalization of altruism as the cornerstone of organ donor policy in the United States began with the UAGA passing in 1968. In 1970, Richard Titmuss published a famous and influential study of the gift relationship in medical contexts, arguing empirically and philosophically that the non-profit, altruistic-based blood donor system in Britain yielded better results in terms of quality and quantity than the then-for-profit market mechanism system in the United States.[32] His book and arguments in the medical sphere and the resulting public policy and law decisions have been influential in persuading a number of bioethicists and lawmakers that "commercialization ... has serious destructive effects, ethical and nonethical, on the whole of a society."[33]

Part of Titmuss's argument is that the ways "in which society organizes and structures its social institutions ... can encourage or discourage the altruistic in [people]."[34] The establishment of altruism, then, as a communal concept backed by public institutions is what allows Prottas to say, in 1994, that organ transplantation in the United States is characterizable as a continuum: on one end, "the development of highly advanced biotechnology," and, on the other end, "widespread public altruism," with "public policies designed to allow technology and kindness to support one another" in the middle.[35] The establishment of the organ procurement process – the technology, the medical practices, the organizations, institutions, and laws – was built around and in turn continues to self-justify a public notion of altruism.[36]

There is further evidence to suggest that monetary incentives dampen altruism, public spiritedness, and practical norms. Consider two oft-cited studies in which a sense of altruism and/or the common good (fellow-feeling, public spirit, social solidarity, civic duty, etc.) is said to be crowded out by money and market mechanisms. A study conducted in Switzerland presented residents with a scenario.[37] The government had identified two potential sites for radioactive waste, and respondents were asked about their willingness for the site to be located nearby their homes. About 50 per cent of residents said they would support it, while about 45 per cent said they would not, with the remaining percentage claiming they had no preference.[38] Roughly speaking, then, approximately 55 per cent of residents found the prospect acceptable. The same study was conducted again, but this time by offering residents financial compensation for the waste facility in their backyard. Curiously, the level of acceptance then dropped to less than 25 per cent. The authors interpret this result to suggest that when intrinsic motivation to civic duty is high, money can have deleterious effects.[39]

Another study, this one involving parents and a day care, concerned money and attempts at behavioural deterrence/modification.[40] The day care imposed a fine on parents who were more than ten minutes late picking up their children. The interesting outcome was that the introduction of the fine *increased* the number of parents coming late to pick up their children. An explanation here is that perhaps the pay element absolved a certain sense of obligation to a fellow person, with a parent no longer treading on a worker's goodwill, but instead compensating them for their time. While the language of the study is in behaviour modification and deterrence, the connection to civic republicanism (the common good, fellow feeling, public spirit, social solidarity, civic duty, etc.) is rather striking. In a preview of the discussion in chapter 9, the introduction of pay might absolve guilt or gratitude.

The degree to which we interpret these empirical results as evidence for the replacing of a sense of community (public morality, common good, etc.) and mutual support with a sense of entitlement or individuality is less important to me than the way in which we *talk* about altruism and the common good, including in reference to studies like these. That is, I do not mean to draw too heavily on the more empirical literature in this chapter, for the argument on offer is not about the nature of altruism, nor whether altruism *really* crowds out civic republican virtues and practices, nor what really *motivates* altruistic acts. Rather, the aim of this chapter has been to suggest how altruism becomes, and is maintained as, a *public moral* concept, central to *debates* about normativity, what we owe to each other, what bioethical policies and laws are worthwhile, and the like.

Public Morality and Altruism

The primary justification for the organ donation system is altruism. This section suggests how the links between altruism and community in organ transplantation systems form a public morality. Altruism, as a moral concept, engenders stronger communal associations and builds from *civic republicanism* – a notion of citizen community engagement on social, moral, and political matters.[41] Civic republicanism is then supported, maintained, and enlarged through institutions in a wholly rhetorical, reflexive process.

This process – of using reason, affect, and argument to build a public morality – is well explained by rhetorician Celeste Condit.[42] She holds that a collective and shared public morality is built through the argumentative establishment of social norms, which become reinforced throughout society at the institutional level (law, policy, organizations, etc.). Normative processes allow for a movement beyond individual moral codes and thereby engender possibilities for, and maintenance of, moral communities.

Medical practitioners and sociologists alike specify this process. Jeffrey Prottas posits the entire system of institutional medicine as dependent on fostering a willingness to donate organs through rhetorical appeals and institutions. Writing in the early establishment of the organ donation system, Prottas says that the cornerstone principle is "altruism and its exploitation for the common good."[43]

Altruism needs strengthening and fostering. Sociologist Kieran Healy, tying in to the notion of *fostering altruism*, observes the significant difference between altruistic acts and their sustainability. Conceived as a sort of four-square matrix, she claims that there are so-called one-shot altruistic acts (helping an innocent bystander), conventional acts of kindness (letting someone in a hurry go in front of you in line at the grocery store), institutionally supported or socially organized one-shot events (Race for the Cure), and routine institutionalized giving, community participation, and regular volunteering. Drawing on established literature, Healy claims,

> Studies of rates of charitable giving find that having effective "communities of participation" is the best way to channel social norms, prior dispositions, or available resources into actual donations. Similarly, ethnographic evidence shows that charitable acts and volunteering are common when they are embedded in the social structure of a community.[44]

The twofold mechanism of *harnessing* altruism and *creating* it should be apparent. There is the idea of forming institutions to support and harness those already donating, but through this process there is both the possibility to expand and encourage more acts of altruism, as well as the continued solidification of the practice as a public moral virtue with local inflections. In her words, "As organizations create contexts for giving they generate altruistic action differently across populations. Rather than simply drawing from sui generis donor populations, they help create them."[45] In turn, then, following Andrew Michael Flescher, we can create and foster organ donation as a "civic duty."[46]

Establishing, circulating, and encouraging public morals (and something like a civic duty) is not new to sociology and sociologically informed thinking. Titmuss argues that the way "in which society organizes and structures its social institutions ... can encourage or discourage the altruistic." Roberta Simmons documents the centrality of altruism in the classical structural-functionalist view of sociology that seeks to understand the ways society is glued together or rent asunder. Herbert Spencer and Emile Durkheim, for example, discuss altruism and community at length, and, most relevantly, Auguste Comte "is not only the Father of Sociology, but coined the word 'altruism'" as well.[47] The generating ethical connection here is that "society has developed norms to better insure help for the helpless,"[48] and that these norms are maintained best via institutional and consistent communal support.

It becomes clear, then, that public morality in the context of medicine is a mix of Christian virtues and practices, social structures and message circulation, and continued and renewed discussions and practices of what makes a society hold together. Altruism forms a core public moral concept in the West, particularly and potentially most saliently in medicine.

In *The Altruistic Species*, Andrew Michael Flescher and Daniel Worthen canvass and critique altruism as it is understood and employed in scientific, philosophical, and religious theories. They summarize their book by suggesting that cultivating altruism is worthwhile and necessary for human community, making an important point that humans are neither fundamentally altruistic nor are they fundamentally selfish. That is, one of their seven conclusions states that "altruism is neither a given nor an impossibility for human beings, but rather an ongoing opportunity ... [b]eing more a matter of skill than talent."[49] This means, inter alia, that altruism's *contingency* thus requires cultivation, participation, and shaping. In short, it requires "hard work."[50]

Flescher and Worthen support this view not (or not only) by discussing classical virtues from antiquity (as I'll do, too), but by highlighting the results of the psychological research published in the almost thousand-page *Cambridge Handbook of Expertise and Expert Performance*.[51] The gloss of that work is that what makes someone excel – at soccer, chess, or surgery alike – is much more the result of *desire to excel* than it is attributable to given talent, because it is only with the former that you will get the drive to practise and the persistence of pursuit of the end that excellence requires. The argument Flescher and Worthen make throughout their book is that morality (and in particular altruism) is precisely the same: the desire to be morally excellent must be present, must be cultivated, and must be practised.

Socrates's description of the pursuit of wisdom as akin to physical training bears recall here.[52] The degree to which we *desire* to be moral matters in the same way that we desire to be physically in good shape (and especially for a professional athlete). The claim that "I'm a pretty good person" is familiar to us (and probably is sort of a psychological requirement for self-preservation/existence). But like the Socratics, let's use the analogy of health. Most of us also probably claim, "I'm a pretty healthy person." We often think of morality and health in a similar way: Well, I could probably stand to exercise a little more, and eat a little less ice cream, and I could probably stand to be a bit more generous with my time and resources with others. The Socratic point is that this type of person is not going to be serious about physical excellence or moral excellence. "I want to be an Olympian but I am going to change nothing about my life" strikes us, rightly, as laughable. But why wouldn't moral development be similarly conceived, Socrates wondered.[53]

That altruism is a significant and motivating public moral concept is a point underscored by the empirical literature on organ donation as well. For example, a series of studies has shown that altruism and humanitarian attitudes have been some of the most significant predictors of willingness to donate.[54] A study by Margareta Sanner employed traditional survey analysis to measure attitudes and willingness to donate organs but also included follow-up interviews with selected participants. Of fourteen undecided potential donors, half of them moved towards donation based on a sort of rational reflection, a combination of altruism appeals and rationality (getting certain facts about transplantation straight).[55]

The foregoing is not to suggest that there are uncomplicated and simplistic relationships between donors and recipients in the transplant community and that there is a dichotomy between altruistic motives and self-interested motives. Indeed, significant work done in bioethics and (medical) anthropology has show the contrary.[56] But recall that my primary emphasis and analysis is on the *language* and overarching rhetoric of the advocates, and in particular the ways in which the rhetoric is deployed in public moral deliberation.

In short, the establishment and maintenance of altruism as a public moral norm turns on a discourse of civic republicanism. Public morality embraces *communitas*, a social solidarity of helping one another individually and in turn embedding that notion in public institutions and organizations. Rhetorical scholars, sociologists, and empirical communication research lend credence to this perspective. Philosopher Peter Singer describes this circulatory public-moral-norms process succinctly: "I find it hardest to act with consideration for others when the norm in the circle of people I move in is to act egoistically. When altruism is expected of me, however, I find it much easier to be genuinely altruistic."[57]

Individual altruism, community, and citizenship can be mixed into a blend we might call *civic altruism*.[58] The results of such a blend would be strong cohesiveness. In Prottas's words: "Altruism is valuable not merely for itself but also for the coherence it encourages."[59] The organ donation system based on altruism is more than individuals helping individuals: it also taps into the deeper communal structures of altruism as a public moral concept, engendering reciprocally good acts and social coherence.

Or so the argument goes. What I've offered in this chapter is, at a minimum, an account of the rationale for altruism and public morality in medicine in general and organ procurement in specific. In the next two chapters, we will see more specifically and in greater detail the defence of organ procurement as a civic altruistic program and the market-informed critique of it.

SECTION TWO

The Rhetorical Positions, Arguments, and Justifications in Human Organ Procurement

3 The Case for an Altruistic Supply System

This chapter describes and categorizes the multifaceted rhetoric of advocates championing an altruistic supply system of human organs. The rhetoric comes from academics and medical professionals advocating the principles and policies for the federal government, as evidenced in the work of United Network for Organ Sharing, the localized organ procurement organizations, and current law. Given that currently no organ can be given "valuable consideration" under the National Organ Transplant Act, the attempt is to defend the current system as rational, efficient, and promoting (as well as consistent with) public morality.

Rhetoric here is meant in the full Aristotelian sense of *ethos, pathos,* and *logos,* and is not, then, simply shorthand for discursive claims. Substantial space will be given to the analysis of narratives, as narratives are both a fundamental way in which humans make sense of the world and play a significant and overt role in altruistic rhetoric. Narrative is meant in both the rational-critical sense of storytelling that subsumes all rational engagement – as a kind of story (that there was a transition from mythos to logos, say) – as well as in the colloquial sense of telling a story. In this way I am following Alasdair MacIntyre's notion of narrative, in which the human is the "storytelling animal," with the narratives we "live out hav[ing] both an unpredictable and partially teleological character."[1] Narratives can also constitute a way of improving beliefs and determining veracity.[2] Following Wayne Booth, "To talk of improving beliefs implies that we are seeking truth, since some beliefs are 'truer' than others" – so, then, the differences between warranted belief in shared discourse or between argumentative (logos) and narrative (pathos) reasons, are not so "sharply definable."[3]

Following rhetoric in the Ciceronian tradition, the rhetorician has three functions: *docere, delectare,* and *movere,* that is, as Cicero tells us (*De Oratore* II.128), to inform, to delight, and to move.[4] The interplay of ethos, pathos, and logos that is not so sharply definable, as discussed above, can be seen to have its fullest effect in the concept of *movere*. The key theoretical link, for present purposes, is that *movere* in the classical rhetorical tradition is both an epideictic and a deliberative event. As Aristotle (*Rhet.*1367.b35) tells us, "To praise a man is in one respect akin to urging a course of action."[5]

Overall, this chapter will describe and categorize the rhetoric of altruistic donation, leading to an analysis of the overarching structure of justification for the rhetoric. There are four sections: (a) the narratives of and about organ donation that fortify the position; (b) discussion of specific word clusters and the defining of semantic space; (c) the primary arguments for the altruistic system; and (d) an examination of the role and invitations of trust and contingencies. The culminating section of this chapter will offer analysis of the overall position, clustering the persuasive appeals based on justifications and then turning them explicitly into guiding principles.

Stories: Representing and Circulating Altruism

The stories of organ donors and organ recipients play a significant role in the structure of the altruistic system. The emphasis on narratives and pathos plays out in terms of both volume of appeals and rhetorical resonance. Several representative stories carry out the ways in which narratives function to install altruism as a norm. This section will examine the way in which *stories* illustrate and perform the interrelationship between interpersonal conversation, cognition, and mass media.[6]

Three styles of stories are associated with altruistic rhetoric. Let's call the first kind *official stories*. These are told and circulated within official transplant institutional networks, namely those affiliated with the Organ Procurement and Transplant Network (OPTN) and the subsequent organ procurement organizations (OPOs), and those repeated in congressional hearings. The second we'll call *mainstream stories*, which are true stories of donation and transplantation that are reported and circulated by media unaffiliated with the OPTN. The final style, *fictional stories*, involves fictional narratives of donation and transplantation. Each has a different way of employing altruism and establishing donation as a civic practice.

Official Stories

Official stories are (re)told by state-backed institutions in relation to organ donation and transplantation. The government's official organ donation awareness website, OrganDonor.gov, maintains a homepage full of images and videos. At the top of the screen one can click on "Stats and Stories" and be taken to a page where the viewer can read true stories of organ donation, reception, and advocacy. The stories are short (typically less than two paragraphs) and are not usually written in the first person. A representative description here tells the story of Carlee Baladez, who was born with a "life threatening heart condition and was just shy of 2 years old when she received a new heart."[7] On the right-hand column are several videos that are short public service announcements (PSAs) giving information and requesting that individuals become donors. At the time I accessed the site, the default video featured NBA All-Star Alonzo Mourning speaking into the camera and telling of his own kidney transplant and encouraging others, especially ethnic minorities, to register.

More stories are found on the websites of localized OPOs or by statewide systems. For example, Donate Life California's website also features snapshot images at the top of the page which, when clicked, take viewers to stories. But here, one is taken to an eleven-minute-plus video (an embedded YouTube video) that features a host giving information on registration but also three donor or recipient stories, narrated by and featuring the main persons and brief interviews with their family and friends. In the first story told, we meet Sarah Donnett, a working model who has received two liver transplants due to being born with a rare disease. After a first-person narrative with B-roll featuring her as a child and a brief interview with Sarah's mother, the host then comes back onto the screen and says, "Knowing that after you pass away you could help someone like Sarah live a long and full life with a bright future, perhaps organ donation is right for you."[8]

Personal struggles of transplantation are present in the testimony of, for example, Cheryl Koller, mother of heart-transplant recipient Caitlyn. The testimony, as part of the 2003 congressional hearings on organ supply, gives factual elements such as being at the top of the recipient list because "we had the sickest child in the southeastern United States" and the requisite pleas to become donors (sharing this story "in the hopes that it will encourage more people to give").[9] But there are more revealing elements in Koller's testimony that serve to increase audience identification. "We were very afraid of the possibility of facing the future without our daughter ... and eight days into our wait [for a transplant], the doctors told us to prepare ourselves to say goodbye, because they didn't believe Caitlyn could make it through another night," she reports.[10]

In those days of waiting, unsure which night would be her daughter's last, Koller then tells a miraculous story:

> On the evening of March 14, my husband and I had gone to the hospital chapel to pray. We spent a lot of time praying and asking God to inspire a family faced with the death of their child, to give the gift of life to our child.

It was a very difficult prayer to offer up, but we prayed with a great deal of faith and hope ...

When we returned to Caitlyn's room a few minutes later, we were told that a heart had been found for Caitlyn. We spent a lot of time that evening praying for a very brave family that we didn't know but owed our future happiness to.[11]

That Koller admits that praying was "difficult" speaks to something seemingly universal in the human condition: crying out to the divine in moments of significant personal tragedy and turmoil, further pulling people into her narrative. Furthermore, the story is moving even if one may not believe in God or any causal connection between the prayers and the material result, for it reveals an intimate struggle and discloses the psyche of a mother at the end of her list of options. That we see the heart as a reward for her faith despite struggle or as a coincidence of timing is secondary to the point here of the power of a revealing and honest personal story.

A final story to share from the official government record comes from All-Pro football player Everson Walls, who donated a kidney to his friend and fellow player Ron Springs.[12] This story is representative of a growing trend in altruistic stories from deceased to living donors (more prevalent in the next two sections) and also emphasizes *character*. Walls says that he was shaped by his former college football coach who, in the first instance was less concerned about football, "because he always wanted you first to emulate an American citizen in life ... [and if you could do that, then he could] make you into a good football player."[13] In this connection of character and citizenship, Walls makes a further leap to that of hero, in which it is not because of his football exploits but his donation that he should be singled out and elevated. This is not an "unattainable feat," for, "as long as you have got two good kidneys," it can "done by anyone, whether he is a football player, whether he is a Congressman. It doesn't matter."[14] This story is meant to both model character and inspire other people to become living kidney donors.

Mainstream Stories

In addition to these official stories, there is a plethora of mainstream cultural stories bolstering the rhetorical positioning of organ donation. Like the story of Caitlyn, the story of Ashley Bailey, as recounted in the previous chapter, was included in the congressional record. But it was President Reagan who first told Ashley's story during his national radio address. Nearly everyone who knew the story knew it from that or the subsequent media circulation and amplification of the story, and not from the congressional record. This is indicative of the role that mainstream stories – true stories circulated through (potentially) mass media – play in the rhetoric of altruistic organ supply.

Celebrity organ stories follow this pattern on the surface. Some high-profile organ recipients include the baseball superstar Mickey Mantle (liver), singer Natalie Cole (kidney), inventor and cultural icon Steve Jobs (liver), the aforementioned basketball player Alonzo Mourning (liver), film director Robert Altman (heart), and comedian/actor Tracy Morgan (kidney). Most celebrities exhibit a reluctance to talk about the process, with the exception of Mourning[15] and Morgan.[16] Rather, most of these stories are simply broadcasted as news items. But it is the celebrity element that makes, say, liver disease "newsworthy" to a private citizen and thereby gives a broad reach to the phenomenon and at least some degree of incorporation into everyday cultural life.

Non-celebrity mainstream transplant stories, while following the same pattern of broadcast, are more encompassing than their celebrity counterparts. There are two versions to the deeper, non-bullet-point-news-item version of mainstream stories: the true story version with non-celebrities, in cases of extreme or unlikely circumstances or results, then picked up by mass media; and fictional stories, which are discussed in the next subsection.

There are several standouts of true stories of non-celebrities in a mass media environment. The first and perhaps most melodramatic is the story of Baby Jesse, made public through Phil Donahue's daytime talk show, *Donahue*. In 1986, an unwed couple's dying infant, who was in need of a heart, was denied transplantation at Loma Linda University Medical Center, supposedly because they were not married, with the hospital later agreeing to do the transplantation should they relinquish custody. The couple then took to the airwaves with their sad story of Baby Jesse. While onstage, a phone call with a hospital in Michigan took place, in which a spokeswoman for the hospital declared that they would be donating a heart for Jesse – all on live television. The parents and the "audience bursts into tears and applause" in what was "the stuff of soap operas."[17] Fairness and questions of circumvention aside, the power of an individual true story with a mass broadcast is evident here, as it was with Reagan's Ashley Bailey. The desperation of the acts themselves serves as a reminder of the direness of the situation, as then-Congressman Al Gore put it in 1983: "There is no more compelling plight than that of ... parents who must mount nationwide media campaigns to plead for an organ donation."[18]

The New Yorker provides two less overtly emotional but no less dramatic narratives of organ donation via in-depth profiles: one of a man, Zell

Kravinsky; and the other of the types of people who, while still alive, give kidneys to strangers. Kravinsky's story, told and framed by Ian Parker in 2004, is of a multimillionaire who gave his kidney to a stranger.[19] As a young man who had "an active social conscience," participating in protests and fighting for social justice and public interest, "by the standards of the late sixties, Kravinsky was [still] unfashionably curious about money."[20] Though he possessed two PhDs and had worked in education in varying capacities, including at an inner-city high school, he was left unfulfilled by the experiences, and turned to investing and real estate. At the peak of his very successful business career, Kravinsky, still feeling unfulfilled, gave away almost all of his $45 million to charities and organizations focused on public health.

Kravinsky's motivation, as crafted by *The New Yorker*, was a sense of morality, of distributive justice in particular, and in the most abstract senses of the terms.[21] He did not place any special emphasis on the individuals whom he desired to help, and failed to distinguish strongly between people – including strangers and his own family. When asked to calculate the relationship of his love of strangers and of his own kids, he says, "I don't know where I'd set it [exactly, but] ... I don't think that two kids should die so that one of my kids has comfort."[22] Moral controversy regarding this line of thought aside,[23] the implication, combined with his philanthropic attitude, of not just giving a kidney to a stranger but to "fantasize ... about" giving away his other kidney and just live on dialysis, or give his "whole body" – is made explicit as the logical conclusion to his thought that "other lives are equal to my own, and I could save at least three or four."[24]

Kravinsky is not unique in his desires and actions, as documented and explored in another *New Yorker* article. In her story "The Kindest Cut: What Sort of Person Gives a Kidney to a Stranger?" Larissa MacFarquhar discusses a variety of people who have engaged in the same type of nondirected living donation as Kravinsky.[25] Whether "you find the idea of donating a kidney to a stranger noble ... or freakish," one of the main sticking points is that living people are willing to donate their kidneys to strangers. Through websites like MatchingDonors.com, which has donors register and potential recipients post profiles and pleas in an effort at match making, and through traditional hospitals, "about six hundred [living people have given kidneys to strangers] ... each for his own reasons."[26]

Among these people is Melissa Stephens, a twenty-four-year-old who was strongly inspired by the character of her recently deceased grandmother. She wanted to do something as a "fitting tribute" to a woman who took in and fed strangers, and not "just going on a sponsored walk – something big, something that people would remember" and "something that would set an example, that would inspire other good deeds."[27] She logged onto MatchingDonors.com, found a man in need of a kidney in her area, and gave him one.[28]

In conclusion, mainstream stories have two primary styles: the celebrity version, which is typically not very detailed but nonetheless circulates widely, and the non-celebrity version, which is typically quite detailed and often severe in terms of need or action, bolstering altruism as a public moral trope.

Fictional Stories

Fictional stories have the media features of the mainstream stories but are instead imagined and often commercial. The altruism trope circulates in culture and highlights the shortage problem through films, television shows, and novels. In spite of being fictional portrayals, the narratives can still exhibit tangible, real-world effects.

Bestselling author Jodi Picoult's *My Sister's Keeper* from 2003 (which was also made into a film starring Abigail Breslin and Cameron Diaz in 2009) details the story of Anna, a young girl who donates several body elements to her sick and dying teen sister, Kate.[29] Her parents are not candidates for any bodily donations, and so the task falls to Anna, who has gone along willingly – until Kate needs a kidney. Her parents try to persuade and "force" her to go through with it, but Anna draws the line, and in turn sues her parents, aiming for legal emancipation. The twist is that this is not Anna acting un-altruistically or stubbornly; rather, the idea is Kate's. Kate believes the emancipation of Anna to be the only way to stop her parents from delaying the inevitable. Anna wins the case but then, in melodramatic fashion, gets hit by a car and goes brain dead, allowing her kidney to be donated to her sister anyway.

The book sold widely and the film grossed nearly $50 million at the US domestic box office alone.[30] Though it is not a story of much reflective depth, it does go beyond informational awareness of the organ shortage to portray the struggle and pressure of family members by pushing into questions of bodily autonomy and the at-least-eventual futility of the life-prolonging act. Other stories followed.

Seven Pounds starred Will Smith and was released in 2008. The story is of a man who has a secret in his past: while not paying attention to the road, he accidentally killed seven people in a car crash. Haunted, and needing to atone, he decides to kill himself and leave his organs to seven people. The twist here is that he selects all the recipients, through some covert research and pretended just-bumping-into-you-on-the-street, wanting to be sure that each is worthy of his gift. He then kills himself (inexplicably in a bathtub with a poisonous jellyfish), and the donations are made per his will. Though mostly panned by critics – A.O. Scott called it "among the most transcendently, eye-poppingly, call-your-friend-in-the-middle-of-the-night-just-to-go-over-it-one-more-time crazily awful motion picture ever made" – it was widely viewed, and grossed more than $160 million.[31] Minus the crushing guilt part (so far as I can tell), one can see the Will Smith character as a similar breed as Zell Kravinsky.

Less extreme stories of donation have featured in the subplots of television shows. I'll highlight two comedy shows from the 2000s, NBC's *30 Rock* and HBO's *Curb Your Enthusiasm*. In *30 Rock*, Jack (played by Alec Baldwin), an executive at NBC, finally meets his biological father after forty-some years. The father (played by Alan Alda), thinks the event is fortuitous, as he needs a new kidney. The irony of this being a family dynamic is played to comedic effect. Jack, himself not a match, decides that he will help his father by mobilizing his resources (i.e., a television network) to help find the organ. A benefit show is assembled, complete with a "We Are the World"-type song entitled "He Needs Kidney," performed by both characters on the show and musical celebrities ranging from Clay Aiken to Elvis Costello to Talib Kweli.[32] The show then is a send-up of both the family drama of desperately needing a vital organ (like *My Sister's Keeper*) and the media spectacle of benefits and melodrama (like the *Donahue* episode). Even in the comedic register, the show still functions to communicate the message of organ shortage.

Similarly, 2005's season of *Curb Your Enthusiasm* has the misanthropic lead character, Larry David, in an organ-donation situation with one of his dearest friends, fellow comedian Richard Lewis. Lewis needs a kidney, and this causes Larry and his other close friend/manager Jeff to debate whether or not they will help. They both decide that *somebody* should volunteer, but of course each thinks the other should be the one to do it. The decision is then arrived at through a game of "Eennie Meanie Miny Moe" in which the concluding line to pick goes, "and out goes y-o-u." The "u/you" lands on Larry. Both Jeff and Larry start cheering, each thinking that this means the *other* has to give the kidney. The moment devolves into a high-pitched debate over what *out goes you* means in the game, whether you have or haven't been selected.[33] The nobility of live organ donation as a sort of supreme altruistic act, as demonstrated in so many of the stories so far, is here turned on its head, as falling, instead, to the loser of casting lots. The audience can at some level identify with the reluctance and laugh at the lengths gone to avoid the call of "duty." The interplay of (social) duty and (individual) conscience (or with Larry, a lack thereof) played to comedic effect allows a cathartic moment not otherwise offered in this serious-as-life-and-death debate.

Though the previous two plots are comedic examples, and we are meant to laugh at the characters' responses, again they still remind us of the tragedy of organ shortage and keep that message circulating throughout culture. But aside from awareness, is there a possibility of any real-world effects of such fictional media storytelling? Cultivation theory suggests that the answer is yes. Though the concept of cultivation is a thoroughly rhetorical one, with roots in Aristotle, the documentation of it in media storytelling is seen in the empirical-based communication scholarship of George Gerbner and Larry Gross. Rather than look for *effects* of media in a cause-effect relationship, "continued exposure to [television] messages is likely to reiterate, confirm, nourish – that is cultivate – its own values and perspectives."[34] The idea is that exposure and circulation reiterate and inform/confirm values. Stories powerfully cultivate altruism as part of public morality.

And anecdotally, there exists at least one example of a direct media effect with regard to organs. Susan Kantrowitz recounts in congressional testimony her husband dying tragically and his organs being used for thirteen people.[35] Aside from being an inspiring story in its own right, the connection to media circulation and cultivation is that Kantrowitz reported that her husband's wishes to be an organ donor were informed by an episode of the hugely popular television show *ER*. The couple were apparently watching the show together, and the plot line was of a female teenager who needed a lung transplant just as a man is dying in the room next to her. The episode had "incredible discussion" about "whether they could hasten death" or not.[36] The episode so moved the two people that they talked about it the next day. "We agreed that if it ever came to pass, we would gladly give each other's organs," Kantrowitz reported.[37] *ER* prompted reflection and dialogue within a family, and that dialogue resulted in thirteen saved lives.

Though the above example is likely unrepresentative, there is the possibility for such a one-to-one connection. Furthermore, there is a continual circulation of stories of donation that have resonant effects, from celebrity endorsers (Michael Jordan, Alonzo Mourning) as official PSA-style announcements to media-amplified true stories of donors and recipients, to the fictional construction of compelling situations and characters. This prevalent circulation of ideas represents the power to shape public awareness, action, and norms to highlight – sometimes plainly, sometimes comedically, sometimes dramatically – the need for organs and the altruistic model for combating the shortage.

Social Media Stories and Chains of Awareness

In May 2012, Facebook debuted the most aggressive and perhaps talked-about organ donation campaign in recent memory. The website, which boasts over one billion users worldwide at the time and over two billion currently,[38] launched a feature that allows users to indicate organ donor status on their timeline. The origin story of this feature indicates precisely the power of personal connections and networked problem solving. Prior to his twenty-year reunion at Harvard, Dr. Andrew Cameron, a transplant surgeon at Johns Hopkins, posted on the crisis of the organ shortage in a class note. He reconnected with old friend Sheryl Sandberg (Facebook's COO) at the reunion, and she said to Cameron, "I remember what you wrote. We can fix this problem."[39] According to data collected between May and September 2012, 275,000 US users indicated their donor status, and Facebook launched the program in Canada and Mexico.[40]

The Facebook campaign creates conversation through the public announcement of the program, circulation of the news story about Facebook's feature, and provides a direct link from Facebook to organ donation registries. Beyond the immediate announcement effect, the site provides an opportunity for people to think about organ donation – and have the choice in front of them – while online and throughout the year. This is quite different than the yearly driver's licence renewal checkpoint.

The most explicit connection of the moral and the mimetic dimension of storytelling for altruistic advocates is made via kidney donor chains. In living donation, it is sometimes the case that none of the patient's loved ones is a compatible donor. But rather than wait for a match, one can exchange donors with another pair of donor-patients. Given the complications of matches, though, sometimes a single swap is not enough to generate a connection, and this can kick off a donor chain. Through interpersonal and public media channels, the chain can grow longer and longer. For example, a 2015 chain included sixty-eight people and twenty-six hospitals.[41] Coverage of these chains amplifies both the moral public spiritedness of citizens as well as the organ shortage. A 2018 *CBS News* headline puts it succinctly: "Stranger's Kidney Donation Sets Off a Chain Reaction of Good Deeds."[42] Some hospitals and programs, such as the UCLA Kidney Exchange Program, have built dynamic online and offline networks to aid, support, and enact transplantation, highlighting the degree to which this "paying it forward" mentality and action "creates opportunities for endless recipient-donor pairings."[43]

News stories circulating about a social media campaign to highlight the organ-shortage crisis have a mimetic outcome. This mimetic effect has been attempted on a smaller scale in the case of a tweeted organ transplantation. In what is called a Twittercast (given that it uses the so-cial networking website and application Twitter), University of Indiana hospital live tweeted during a kidney transplant. The tweets sought to harness social media to get the word out about organ shortage, encour-aging people to follow the surgery, receive updates and graphic pho-tos, and to tweet and retweet using "#calebskidney" – after the recipient, Caleb Johnson.[44]

These campaigns are designed precisely to create conversation about the shortage of organ donors. The idea is, simply, to create a news story that will circulate through traditional and social media channels and thereby raise awareness of the problem and inspire or motivate people to register.[45]

In conclusion, it must be admitted that there are not many statistics available on the impact that any of these stories – from official to com-mercial to social media campaigns – have on increasing donor registra-tion in the United States. However, there are frequent booms correlated with such narrative strategies. For example, Donate Life California, the official organ registry for California, reported an increase of four thousand donors in the first twenty-four hours of the Facebook cam-paign.[46] Hélène Campbell, a young double-lung-transplant recipient who received highly visible support from Ellen DeGeneres and Justin Bieber, is credited with seven thousand registered consent donors – an increase of 23 per cent – over a three-month period in what was called the "Hélène Campbell effect."[47]

Language and Word Choices

While plots create powerful dramas, certain words and phrases create and evoke powerful effects as well. The language of an advocacy cam-paign or argument sheds light on the underlying position and character of the movement. Thus, clusters of key terms can be analysed to shed light on motivations and fuller discursive positions of the advocates.

The touchstone and most familiar phrase of the altruistic formation is "the gift of life."[48] It operates as the sort of master trope or ultimate rhetorical phrase for the altruistic side.[49] The key word, *gift*, connotes something that is not just given to someone else, but given *freely* and *optimistically*. While the word choice of *gift* is problematized in the next chapter, at face value, it is a straightforward motivation and relation: gifts are worth giving, no gift is greater than that of life itself, and therefore the gift of life is the greatest and most worthy gift. That which is the greatest and most worthy of course should be pursued by the virtuous individual, and so, packed into the phrase is both a judgment (life is a gift, and one worth giving) and, when spoken as "donate the gift of life," an imperative. Taken together, the judgment-imperative construction is a promotion for a particular view of the virtuous citizen.

Further support for this view is seen in surrounding clusters of terms and statements. For example, one advocate says that "you cannot put a price tag in human terms on such a gift," indicating the supreme value (in a nonmonetary sense) of human life.[50] Repeated reference to the act of donation and subsequent transplant as a *miracle* also underscores this view. For example, "We want this miracle to be available," and for that we need "to get more people to sign up to be organ donors because we know the miracle that results when we do."[51] What is interesting here is that the transplantation, of course, is not a miracle in any traditional religious sense of the term; in fact, it is an example of progressive science par excellence. The miracle seems to focus more on the donation, the gift itself, the selfless act. The combination of these two things results in, to borrow the name of an officially endorsed documentary on organ transplantation, the "science of miracles."[52]

Related to (or perhaps given) this language, there is commonly a reverence for donors. We hear of donors described as "heroes" and that it is an "honor" to meet them.[53] In the words of one recipient, "There is no way that I can express my appreciation and gratitude for the donor heart which gave me a second chance, the 'Gift of Life.'"[54] The families, too, and not just the donors themselves are considered heroes:[55] "The real heroes are the donor families," says another recipient, and "I am forever grateful."[56]

So that families know the wishes of individuals prior to death, and to avoid having to guess or make what can sound like gruesome choices in a time of grieving, an official campaign slogan from the late 1990s ran, "Share your life, share your decision."[57] In this phrase, one reads the double meaning in *share your life*, with one being to share your life with another person by *donating* your organs, by donating your life, and another being to share your life with another person by *speaking* with them. The latter meaning is highlighted in the second clause of *share your decision*, thereby making the former meaning more resonant in the first clause. This phrase, given the historical emphasis on the Gift of Life trope, serves not just to promote the sharing of one's decision but also indicates belief that supply will increase by encouraging conversation around donation.

Given these word choices and language, specific narratives take shape: donors are *heroes* who perform *miracles* by giving the *gift of life*, and recipients are eternally *grateful* and *honoured*. The language is noble and elevated; it signals something *important* and *virtuous* happening in the act of donation and transplantation.

Primary Positive Arguments

There are just two main discursive arguments for the altruistic side, which is a small number. But this small number makes sense given that the altruistic system is status quo and enshrined in US law, and therefore the burden of proof (to change) lies on the other side. There are, however, a significant number of rebuttals (negative arguments) produced by the altruistic camp, and these are discussed more fully in chapters 8 and 9, thereby giving a fuller account of the position.

The first, and most popular, argument for the altruistic system is

A1: Public awareness will sufficiently increase organ supply.

This claim is both about what to do (action) and what will happen (result). The action proposed is to spend resources of time, energy, and money on increasing public awareness through media campaigns, educational curricula, and interpersonal conversation. Doing this, the argument suggests, will result in an increase in the supply of organs and will thereby eliminate the need for even a debate about compensated organ supply systems.

The two main congressional hearings on increasing supply after the enactment of NOTA advanced this argument. For example, in 1999's *Putting Patients First: Increasing Organ Supply for Transplantation*, Howard Nathan, president of the Coalition on Donation, says, "Increasing consent rates requires significant public education and information."[58] Robert Higgins, speaking on behalf of the Patient Access Transplantation Coalition, lists the first "main" strategy as "public awareness and education to encourage families to consider donating healthy organs in the event of imminent death."[59] In 2003's *Assessing Initiatives to Increase Organ Donations*, three testimonies in a row (from relatives of organ transplant recipients or donors) assert that, in the words of one speaker, "education, first and foremost, is probably the most important thing that we need to do."[60]

To increase public consciousness for advocates in these hearings is to "put the message in every level of society."[61] Such effort requires (a) spending significant money on advertising campaigns, (b) developing and implementing instructional curricula in schools, (c) more storytelling, and (d) continued localized but nationally coordinated public awareness efforts. In terms of (a), the idea is to reach audiences via media, using in particular public service announcements on television and taking out billboard space, using popular figures like Michael Jordan and working with the Ad Council and agencies to craft memorable messages.[62]

In terms of (b), age-appropriate curriculum can teach the effects, harm, and need of human organs and transplantation. One example is that in

North Carolina, such curriculum is a part of ninth- and tenth-grade health classes.[63] In September 2012, Governor Jerry Brown signed legislation to include organ and tissue donation as part of public school curriculum in California for the next course adoption/submission cycle.[64]

Sometimes billboards and other mass media approaches do not appropriately flag audiences, and more effective methods are sought, particularly in face-to-face and more personal storytelling.[65] Thus, (c) is geared around narrative strategies featuring actual donors and recipients in local communities, as well as the circulation of stories in both local face-to-face environments and national media-amplified stories of the same ilk. The sparking of individual conversations through broader storytelling is evidenced in the example of *ER* resulting in a donor decision, as discussed earlier in this chapter.

Finally, in terms of (d), localized and nationally coordinated public awareness campaigns, one can see all of the previous strategies (a–c) coming together with awareness campaigns like National Donor Day (14 February), National Donate Life Month (April), National Minority Donor Awareness Day (1 August), and National Donor Sabbath (the Friday–Sunday two weeks prior to Thanksgiving).[66] The purpose of these efforts is to increase awareness in both the announcement of the day itself and by having figures, organizations, and local and national media use the federally declared days to run stories and news items pertaining to organ donation, thereby signalling the shortage and inspiring more donors. Similarly, the Workplace Partnership for Life initiative gets businesses to sign on to a program of organ donation awareness and education for their company.[67] Inaugurated in July 2012, the Transplant Games of America, meant to follow the Olympics and Paralympics, complements both the World Transplant Games and other holidays as another eventful way of raising awareness and cultivation of positive and uplifting stories – stories worthy of mimesis – to circulate through society.[68]

The efforts to increase public education and public awareness combine under a heading of public consciousness. The idea of getting the message out to every level society is deemed to be effective not just out of saturation but as evidenced in the effective practice of anti-tobacco consciousness-raising along similar lines.[69] Furthermore, such a multilayered approach is seemingly necessary: "Given the diversity of our country, one message is not enough."[70]

Overall, A1 is seen as the first and foremost strategy in filling the organ shortage gap. Given that both the 1999 and 2003 hearings were debating alternatives to the current system, including the repeal of the NOTA prohibition on "valuable consideration" (the phrase that effectively means the ban of monetary compensation for human organs), it is clear that A1 was deemed, via congressional (in)action, to be the most beneficial (policy) action – and to be the most persuasive argument in human organ procurement rhetoric.

The second substantial positive argument supporting the altruistic system is

A2: Altruistic donation promotes community.

There are two levels to the argument of altruism promoting community: the first is the *literal-physical* community connection of family members and strangers via the act of donation (A gives to B), and the second is that of a *sense-feeling* of community engendered in society given the altruistic structure (the positive feeling one gets from being involved with such a gift). These two levels of community, the literal-physical and the sense-feeling, will be discussed in turn.

Assuming the donor does not remain anonymous, the literal connection forged by donation is transparent: in the rhetoric of the supporters, one person has given the gift of life to another person. The physical intensity and emotional drama of near-death experiences have unification power, as evidenced most clearly in the bonds formed by military platoons.[71] In the case of post-mortem donation, the families of the donor are able to provide someone else with what could not be provided by their own kin. As in the story of Caitlyn and her family in the opening subsection of this chapter, the parents of the donor found "comfort in getting to know Caitlyn and [her parents]," even feeling like their own "son lives on through her."[72]

The sense of community that comes from directly helping others is evidenced in the case of Susan Kantrowitz (the woman who testified in regard to her husband's tragic death and the donation of his organs to save thirteen people). She felt that the act of donating her husband's organs and tissues helped to "take a tragedy and put a positive spin on it," despite not knowing to whom the donations were going.[73] Liver recipient Amelia Brown-Wilson says, "I look at it this way: there could have been two tragedies, but my donor family turned their tragedy into a blessing."[74]

There is significant evidence of the *sense-feeling* of community as well. As in the military example, the idea that there is a common enemy at work in organ donation (death) that everyone is fighting against has a similar galvanizing effect throughout a society, and that individuals work together to "fight" it provides a sense of community. The sense of community engendered via organ donation has both concrete and abstract potential. In the abstract sense, the idea of an individual *doing good* plays into the equation, as does the notion of *helping people*, thereby harnessing and performing that Smithean virtue of public spiritedness. The overall sense of doing good and helping someone form an abstract sense of community that can motivate donation.

The abstract sense of community, the feeling of community as motivating ethical action is evidenced in the so-called moral point of view of acting beyond the self, or what T.M. Scanlon might say is acting in accordance with what is right, in which rightness is what we owe each other.[75] The basic moral point: human life is to be valued, and we ought to work together to value it.[76] Humans are able to distinguish, as rational creatures, rather quickly and perhaps even intuitively, between needs and wants, and it is in this ability to separate out and weigh needs and wants[77] – that I do not need my organs once I am dead, and someone else does – that the decision is made swiftly, and the ease and prevalence of this calculus is some indication of human community, of an ability to focus on others and not ourselves.

More drastically, the story of Zell Kravinsky above illustrates the power of the abstract *good* motive and a focus on *others*: "What I aspire to is ethical ecstasy ... *ex stasis*: standing outside of myself, where I'd lose my punishing ego ... and once there, the significant locus would be in the sphere of others."[78] And furthermore, the types of people discussed in MacFarquhar's article seem to have some sense of others and *community*: "[Stephens] believed that most people were selfish and materialistic, but that if they were reminded that others had needs and wants, as important as their own, they would be a little less so."[79] In less ambitious moral-philosophical language, the football player Everson Walls' story connects character and citizenship in a way as to promote living donation, as he did for his friend: this is what people of good character do, this is how virtuous citizens act.

A *sense* of community is not always abstract. For example, the fact that Walls's gift was for a friend and not as an abstract citizen do-gooder indicates another possibility: the less abstract element of a feeling of community can come from localized interaction. The concreteness here is the most important element; that is, it is the non-abstraction of the process that is both motivating and promoting community and its feeling. Congresswoman Barbara Cubin asserts that people would be "more likely to want to give it to someone if they thought it would be in their community, in their area."[80] While there is no evidence offered for this view, she more clearly expresses later that she does not mean to be making an empirical claim but rather is speaking of an *attitude* to be cultivated and harnessed:

> I am absolutely convinced that the old barn raising mentality that we still have in the West, where neighbors help neighbors, people in communities

build communities instead of having government do it ... you start with your family, your city, your county, your State, and you go out as far as you can and be as generous as you can with the resources you have.[81]

This localized community sentiment stemming to practice is endorsed by the National Kidney Foundation, represented by John R. Campbell, who, in a written supplement to the 1999 hearing, says that the "sense of identification with local patients, and with the patients across an OPO's home state, is integral to the success of an organ donor program," and he continues by saying that certainly, "OPO staff want to help any patient in need, but the drive that is needed to perform this kind of heart-wrenching work day after day is further fueled by the knowing the names and identities of those local patients who wait."[82] In this version, then, we see that it is not *doing good for people* that is the key; it is *doing good for Jane Smith* that both motivates and promotes attitudes of community commitment. And while the abstract moral motivation may have been there for those involved with sites like MatchingDonors.com, it seems it is the (virtual) face-to-face element, of connecting faces and stories with the act of donation, that effectuates.

These two versions of community, the literal face-to-face connection version and the feeling of community in both the abstract and concrete sense, while differing on motivational and effectiveness details, all share a commitment to the argument that it is *human community* that can and will solve the shortage problem. Francis Delmonico, representing the National Kidney Foundation, puts the matter succinctly: everyone needs to "embrace a social responsibility about organ donation, rather than say we'll throw money to it."[83]

The community element, then, is twofold: it is because of feelings of community, or an attitude of community – we are all in this together – that one would become an organ donor, and it is the act of organ donation that reinforces and recommits oneself to that ideal. Put into more conspicuous language of political community, Congressman Gerry Sikorski paraphrases Hubert Humphrey in one of the NOTA hearings from 1983, saying, "The true test of a society's greatness is how it treats those in the dawn of life, the children, and those in the shadows of life, the ill."[84]

Trust and Contingencies

For altruistic rhetoric, *trust* is invited in two key places: in people and in institutions. That is, there is implicit trust that people, once they know the facts of the shortage and the good that can come, will do the right thing and become donors. There is also implicit trust, then, in the state and NGO institutions to collect and distribute this information and these scarce organs quickly and fairly. Contingencies to this strategy are almost always some variation of the current strategy, just increased: more PSAs, more school curriculum, more stories, more word-of-mouth. That is, the strategy does not really change: *public awareness* will be enough once messages are relayed at every level of society, because people know that organ donation is the correct thing to do.

The OrganDonor.gov homepage once visually summed up the main sort of rhetorical strategy.[85] In the centre-left of the screen, there were bold-face statistics of the shortcomings (the waiting list numbers) and how to help (one person can save up to eight lives), and in the centre top, and on the right-hand side of the screen, are narratives and pathos appeals, personifying and giving voice to those statistics. In short, stats and stories. The overarching rhetoric of information-giving and pathos appeals, with some ethos of celebrities thrown in, indicate that *trust* resides in the official government *institutions* and their disbursement of organs, and in *fellow citizens* to *do the right thing*. That is, the rhetorical strategy is premised on the *logos* of the information and the *pathos* of the stories; the trust is in the audience to put the two together and donate their organs.

Justifications and Principles

The four key justifications for altruistic rhetoric are *virtue, inspiration, justice,* and *civic community*. These compact terms serve as grounds for the claim of altruism being the best system for increasing human organ supply. I have moved from the concrete up to the more abstract, starting with the stories and arguments and word choices, showing how these can be condensed and succinctly captured in key justificatory terms. The justifications will be explained more clearly, and then they can, in turn, serve as guiding principles for altruistic organ rhetoric.

Virtue is seen as a justification for the altruistic model in a most basic sense.[86] That which is morally good is virtuous, and that altruistic donation is morally good is a case most plainly made in the language and word choices. Discussion of *heroes*, of being *honoured* to meet these people or their families, of giving the ultimate, priceless *gift of life* indicates the highest normative distinctions of people, and hence it seems fair to call these people virtuous. So as virtue is plainly *present* in these people or at least in their supreme act, and that, at some level, basically everyone wants to be (at least considered) virtuous, the formation of virtue as an underlying justification, as a warranted appeal, is clear.

Taking virtue or the virtuous as an implicit justification at work in the altruistic side, I can then turn it into an explicit principle:

Virtue Principle: morally upstanding individuals donate their organs.

The next key justificatory term is inspiration. That *inspiration* can serve as a justification for an action is documented by Boltanski and Thévenot.[87] For organ rhetoric, here the virtuous element is mobilized, serving as an inspiring model for human relations. This is most evident in the circulation of stories about organ donors and recipients, in which ordinary people have extraordinary impact, as was the case with Kantrowitz, Koller, and Baby Jesse, and ordinary people do extraordinary things, as was the case with Kravinsky and the Will Smith character. These stories serve as models for mimicry and circulate in the larger media landscape and thereby, via cultivation theory, work to reiterate and entrench values at a minimum, and serve to outright inspire individuals to change their mind or action at best. The inspiring element is to pull individuals out of their everyday life, work, and details and to point to something bigger than themselves.

As an implicit justification at work in the altruistic side, inspiration can be turned into an explicit principle:

Inspiration Principle: donating one's organs inspires self and others to think and act beyond the mundane, everyday details in life.

The penultimate justification is the abstract concept of *justice.* Like virtue, I do not mean to invoke too substantive a concept of justice (that is, a theory of justice here) but simply an Aristotelian definition of justice as treating like things alike and in proportion to the differences.[88] In this, the idea of treating humans, of treating each other as alike and therefore as worthy of respect and imbued with the same sense of dignity is prevalent in altruistic organ donation rhetoric.[89]

Specifically, this justification is evidenced in the overall rhetorical strategies of stories and information present in the first primary argument A1 and in the official government and NGO literature. Here justice – treating people alike and with alike dignity – is seen in that, from the altruistic advocates' perspective, all that needs to be done to rectify the loss of lives and imbalance of donors and potential recipients is appeal to this basic justice formula. By giving the information of deaths and shortages, combined with pathos appeals to induce sympathy and compassion, the altruistic side implicitly rests its case on this sort of version of what justice demands. That is, people's (cultural) intuitive sense of right and wrong will kick in and redress the problem, and therefore this sense of right and wrong is based on the idea that each human is not *essentially* (in the full force of that word) different.

Taking justice or just actions as an implicit justification at work in the altruistic rhetoric, the explicit principle might be formulated as

> *Justice Principle:* others have as much dignity and deserve as much respect as self.

Related then to the Justice Principle and justification is *civic community.* By *civic community*, two meanings are meant. On the one hand, it is the idea of justice operationalized on a community scale, in which groups of people form a type of solidarity.[90] This civic solidarity is implied by the Justice Principle. On the other hand, the sense of *communitas* explicitly invoked in altruistic rhetoric, especially in A2, is less about what *morality* or *justice* demands and more about a we-are-all-in-this-together mentality, an attitude towards life and each other. That is, life is full of struggles and pains, and it is often impossible to face them on one's own. Illness in general is symbolic of that, and the need for an organ is an I-can't-do-it-on-my-own moment *par excellence.*

Altruistic rhetoric appeals to different levels of community, but all of them have an underlying commitment of humans, simply, *helping* each other. This, again, is both an attitude, in which individuals adopt this approach for themselves and for their community as a whole (the we-are-all-in-this-together mentality), and an outcome, in which there is a material effect of this attitude (people actually *are* helped). In other words, civic community is something to be promoted and performed.

Civic social community as an implicit justification can in turn be formulated into an explicit principle:[91]

> *Civic Community Principle:* individuals and society as a whole are better served with both an attitude and material effect of solidarity, of beings in struggle together.

Overall, the implicit justifications and the overarching structure of justification – the circle of normative claims – can been seen to rest on four key terms. Those four key terms can then be inductively turned into guiding principles, serving as the overarching *ethos* of altruistic organ rhetoric. Taken together, they represent an ethic of civic republicanism – virtue and inspiration as *virtus*, justice as *dignitas* and *gravitas*, *civic community* as a collective humanist *piaetas* – for contemporary US society.

Chapter Conclusion

In summary, then, as seen in arguments, stories, word choices, and where trust is invited to reside, the main rhetorical justifications for the altruistic supply system are that it is virtuous, that it is inspirational, that it enacts justice, and that it promotes and performs civic community. The structure of justification is enacting and reiterating stories and arguments that give evidence to these terms, thereby encircling the normative claim of the altruistic system as the best for increasing human organ supply. This structure of rhetorical justification serves as a normative circle of sorts, and thereby allows the underlying key terms to be turned, inductively, into the altruistic organ advocates' guiding ethic.

The crux of the status quo system then is the moral concept of altruism and its institutionalization in medical contexts. Altruism and its social cohesive function, both in personal enactment and in institutionalization, harnesses and fosters civic republicanism.

While there certainly was analysis in this section, overall the goal was simply to categorize and describe the rhetoric. This is precisely the goal of the next chapter as well, but this time for compensated organ-supply rhetoric. Once having accomplished this, I will turn to more substantive analysis of the two positions by extensively treating their counterarguments and rebuttals to each other. But first, let me describe the compensated-supply system. It is quite complicated in places and requires more detail to unpack.

4 The Case for a Market-Based Supply System

This chapter describes and categorizes the multifaceted rhetoric of advocates for a compensated-supply system of human organs. This rhetoric, at first coming largely from free-market advocates and libertarians as evidenced in scholarly journal articles and the output of certain non-governmental organizations, is becoming more and more mainstream. Given that currently no organ can be given "valuable consideration" under NOTA, the market champions seek to persuade policymakers, practitioners, and the public that financial compensation for human organs is rational, efficient, and consistent with public values.

Two relatively distinct positions have emerged in regard to compensating people for their organs. I have chosen not to treat them as fundamentally different. This could be a mistake; however, there is much shared in the two positions – especially in the structure of justification. In general, advocacy takes two routes: *market* arguments and *incentive* arguments. In the former, advocates articulate the value of an open but regulated market in human organs, in which individuals can buy and sell organs. In the latter, advocates hold that, while donors are compensated (either directly financially or through tax incentives or to their estate or other types of plans), there is not an actual market; only a centralized source (i.e., the federal government) could do the buying/incentivizing – not private individuals or institutions.

The rhetoric of compensated organ supply invites an analysis of the overarching structure of justification. Mirroring the analysis and categorization work done in chapter 3, this chapter comprises four key elements: (a) the narratives of and about the organ procurement and transplantation process that serve to rhetorically strengthen the compensation position; (b) discussion of specific word clusters and the defining of semantic space; (c) the primary arguments for the compensated system, broken down by market and incentive arguments; and (d) an examination of the role and invitations of trust, and contingencies. The culminating section of this chapter will, given the preceding descriptions, offer an overarching analysis of the position and cluster the arguments based on justifications and the underlying appeals to principles.

Stories: Black Market Anxieties, Fear, and Misconceptions

The global black market for human organs is real. But the surrounding horror stories, myths, and misconceptions produce *fear*, which drives resistance to organ donation. Indeed, researchers Kopfman and Smith found that fear constituted the biggest reason for individuals not to donate their organs.[1] Susan Morgan and Jenny Miller describe how this process of fear combines with, or stems from, significant misconceptions and myths about organ transplantation. In their words,

> The issue of organ donation suffers not so much from a lack of awareness as the popularity of a number of myths and misconceptions about organ donation. Many of these myths have not been countered by national organ donation organizations, as evidenced by the lack of nationally distributed messages about donation devoted to these issues, with the exception of organ donation websites (which members of the public must seek out on their own). Myths and misconceptions about organ donation are often inadvertently reinforced by the media, including the evening news which recently highlighted stories about China's black market in organs for transplant, as well as popular shows such as *X-Files*, which plays on some of the public's impressions of organ transplant as "creepy."[2]

This general creepiness, which legal scholar Julia Mahoney suggests might be a primal aversion of sharing essential body parts,[3] combines with the all-too-real black market to create an anxiety about organ procurement. This fear and the mitigation of its consequences form part of the basis for market advocates' arguments. The following subsections document the actual and imagined fears of organ procurement that serve as the key affective component to compensation rhetoric.

Stories do not play so vital a constructive rhetorical role for compensation advocates. As in altruistic rhetoric, stories here circulate as *models*, but in this case they serve more often as cautionary tales, models of what can and does go wrong, largely utilizing sinister black-market episodes of organ sales, markets, and theft to make this point. The implicit criticism at work in black-market narratives is that a *regulated* market would eliminate illicit sales entirely, and furthermore, that a market would alleviate distrust in medical institutions, restoring autonomy to citizens. There are three different types of stories. The first is *myths*, which circulate as folklore or urban legend but also as fictional films and other commercial horror stories. The second is *true stories*, which are essentially black-market stories that are true. Finally there are *mainstream stories*, which are true stories that circulate through mainstream media-type channels.

Myths and Horror Stories

The most prominent myth of organ sales is less about the actual sale than it is about the shadiness of black-market operations. That is, the myths are more urban legends, and though they typically circulate in developing nations, they are present in the United States as well. The primary concern is that if organs have a market value and price, then organ *theft* will rise:

> These fears have given rise to one of the most durable urban legends of all time: the one about the guy who goes to Spring Break in Florida and wakes up 3 days later in a hotel room with a hole in his side through which some-one has extracted one of his kidneys.[4]

Part of the power of these kinds of myths, which have several variations – typically making the victim a child or baby – is not that the stories them-selves are actually believed to be true or necessarily even plausible, but rather that they, in Veronique Campion-Vincent's view, allow "indirect expression of uneasiness about the gift of organs, and by extension, death," and further, that they "express distrust of a medical establish-ment;" this must be indirect expression or else it would "contradict one of our basic dogmas: that medicine is benevolent."[5] This idea is perhaps most prevalent in the version of the kidnap-and-cut myth, in which the organ is not simply stolen: "In the maimed child's pockets or somewhere on its body there is an important (or derisory) sum of money and a brief ironic note: 'Thank you for the eyes [or kidney].'"[6] Here the horror of the theft is *punctuated* by the fact that it *isn't strictly theft*: the owner, though of course non-consenting, was still *compensated*, and the victim is made a child to further dramatize the point.

Horror films make use of these sorts of myths and urban legends as well. The most serious take is *Dirty Pretty Things*, directed by Stephen Frears, in which an unscrupulous hotel manager runs an organs-for-passports scheme for illegal immigrants. The film dramatizes a seedy black-market underbelly in London, with the climax scene involving a desperate immi-grant turning the tables on the manager, drugging him and stealing his kidney instead, then selling it to the intended broker as planned.[7]

Far-fetched fictional narratives come in films like *Repo! The Genetic Opera* and *Repo Men*, both sharing the premise that someday, when organs are bought and sold, they might be purchased via monetary loan. Inability to repay the loan, in this case, would result in the repossession of the organ.[8] Joseph Roth, then-president of the Association of Organ Procurement Organizations, says that these stories are false. "There are other myths and misconceptions that are perpetrated by the media, by television, and so on, such as organs being sold for profit within the country, people being found in alleyways cut up with organs missing. Those are all myths."[9]

While dramatic films foster myths, there is just enough truth, globally, to these types of stories to require public rectification. In fact, a *Newsweek* headline from 2009 casts the issue explicitly in horror-story terms: "Not Just Urban Legend," with a subtitle that reads, "Organ trafficking was long considered a myth. But now mounting evidence suggests it is a real and growing problem, even in America."[10] The HBO-produced *Tales from the Organ Trade* (2013) documents stories of black-market organ trafficking. Hollywood drama and daily news comingle to inspire fear.

True Stories

For compensated rhetoric, there are no stories at the official level, as organs sales are illegal. An "official" story of an organ sale would be a punishable affair domestically. However, official stories are recorded in government documents. The most famous and shocking one is of the Chinese government taking the organs of prisoners. In a 2001 congressional hearing on human rights and China, the story of Mr. Qiu is presented as representative:

> Mr. Qiu was sentenced to death for tax evasion, was executed, and his body was sent to the crematory all within a little more than 1 hour. When his brother arrived to attempt to claim the body, he found blood all over Qiu's shirt. He pulled the shirt open and found that Mr. Qiu's stomach was cut open with his intestines spilling out. There was a foot long gash, and several organs had been extracted.
>
> He drove back to the court to demand an explanation ... [arguing that] no family member had been asked whether his brother's organs could be removed ... Prison authorities then said that Mr. Qiu had consented to donate his organs just prior to execution. Mr. Qiu's brother asked for evidence, but the Chinese officials would not give him any. After complaining to the central government authorities, Mr. Qiu's brother was warned to keep silent or face retaliation against him and his family.[11]

Amnesty International counts more than "18,000 executions reported" in China in the 1990s alone.[12] Further suspicion exists that the Chinese government persecuted and imprisoned Falun Gong practitioners (a religious-spiritual discipline banned in China) and other perceived dissidents to harvest their organs.[13] A story out of China finds live organ sellers standing trial in what is dubbed the "Kidney for iPad Trial."[14] Authorities claim that a Chinese teenager was recruited to sell his kidney via an online chat room, went through the procedure, and used the money from the sale to buy an iPad. The trial began in August 2012, though the teenager was unable to attend because he suffered renal failure after the transplant.[15] There is potentially more at stake in Chinese culture around kidney transplantation and sales than in the West given that, in traditional Chinese medicine, the kidney is said to house the *qi*, the vital life force of a person.[16]

Organ stories from other international locales circulate as well. For example, Brazil, Pakistan, Moldova, Israel, and the Philippines are recorded as hotbeds for organ trafficking. Frequent reports of organ sales come from extremely impoverished areas in these developing nations.[17] In Pakistan, for example, "forty percent of people in some villages are turning up with only one kidney."[18] The grotesque details of what is sometimes called the *red market* (red being blood, symbolic of human flesh) are recorded in Scott Carney's journalistic account, *The Red Market: On the Trail of the World's Organ Brokers, Bone Thieves, Blood Farmers, and Child Traffickers*.[19]

Economic desperation comingles with black-market transactions. Interviewing a man in Baseco, a shantytown in Manila, ethnographer Sallie Yea noted that what was fascinating was not *that* the man participated in the organ market, but the *jealousy* from his impoverished friends: "Nearly every participant in the study had something to say about his friends being jealous that he was able to sell a kidney, or asking how they could also arrange for one of their kidneys to be sold, or relating that they sought out a broker on their own to sell a kidney."[20]

The black-market stories constitute a split narrative. On the one hand, the association of selling human organs with the *grotesque* matches what Kenneth Burke calls a frame of rejection (as opposed to frame of acceptance).[21] In advanced economies such as the United States, the stories of desperate people in slums selling their kidneys evoke both a grotesque image and sadness for their plight. On the other hand, compensation advocates document the practices to bolster claims of the willingness of people to buy and sell, which underscores the need for transparency in bringing market transactions into the foray.

Mainstream Stories

Unless operating as horror stories from developing nations, mainstream stories are rare for celebrating compensated individuals. Again, this makes sense given the illegality of the process or the general cultural taboo against transplant tourism. Here are three exceptions.

The Big Donor Show, which ran in the summer of 2007, was a reality-style television show. Lisa, a thirty-seven-year-old woman dying of a brain tumour, was to select "one of three needy contestant-patients" to receive her kidneys upon her death. The show really was all a hoax, a media stunt designed to attract attention to the shortage of organs. All the participants, including Lisa, however, were all actually in need of kidney transplants. Though this event took place in Holland, the recirculation of it by Sally Satel in the introduction to *When Altruism Isn't Enough* puts it into North American society. Satel marshals it for her case for financial incentives, though the show itself doesn't necessarily imply as much.

In a high-profile black-market human organ trade story in the United States, Levy Izak Rosenbaum, a Brooklyn resident, pled guilty in October 2011 to being an organ broker. The scheme seemed to have clients pay Rosenbaum approximately $120,000 for a kidney, which Rosenbaum often procured from "vulnerable people in Israel" for approximately $10,000.[22] Additionally, as " ... part of his service, he also helped donors and recipients invent a cover story to trick hospital staff into thinking the donation was a purely altruistic exchange between friends or relatives."[23] In July 2012, Rosenbaum was sentenced to two-and-a-half years in prison and to forfeit the $420,000 he made from these transactions.[24]

Eric De Leon represents an even more direct financial compensation story to circulate in the United States. De Leon, a California man in need of a liver, mortgaged his family house and travelled to Shanghai for his transplant. Upon returning to the United States, however, he was "stunned" to find himself "reviled as a public figure," maligned in the *San Francisco Chronicle* as an "American vampire" guilty of "moral depravity," according to Taylor and Simmerling.[25] Here, the story of someone buying an organ is told as a horror story of its own.

Overall, stories do not play as vital of a constructive role for compensated donors. In fact, they play a negative role, either showing how public sentiment needs to change regarding organ sales or revealing public anxieties about how problematic compensated-system arrangements can be. In other words, these are stories that compensation advocates either need to *overcome* to make their case, or to *exploit*, including and especially the fears and anxieties surrounding black-market narratives.

The implicit criticism at work in sinister black-market narratives is that a *transparent, open* market would eliminate the black market entirely, and furthermore, that a market itself can help alleviate distrust in medical institutions in terms of access and equality.

Language and Word Choices

There are several words and phrases that power compensation rhetoric. Analysing the clusters of key terms aids in understanding the motivations and fuller discursive positions of the advocates. For compensation arguers, the language and word choice slightly differs depending on whether one is a market or an incentive-only advocate, though some arguers fail to distinguish the lines so clearly.[26]

One of the most common terms for all compensation advocates is *motivate* or *motivation*. For example, Sally Satel, whose book is published by the American Enterprise Institute (a think tank devoted to free-markets expansion predicated on the concept of liberty), writes that incentives should be offered to "motivate individuals to donate kidneys."[27] One advocate says that compensation is like "an encouragement, like an automobile discount."[28] Here the gift element, the altruistic element, is retained: people are still *donating* their kidneys.

Some advocates say that the current system is good, and that altruism is a superior motivating scheme, but that simply it isn't enough: it isn't meeting demand.[29] But others go further, suggesting serious flaws in the current altruistic system. For specifically market-oriented proposals, *seriousness* and *transparency* become key words. The idea that the status quo altruistic system is cumbersome and inefficient is one that Michele Goodwin tackles head on. She calls the altruistic supply system in particular the "transplant game," which is meant to juxtapose conceptually a game with the seriousness of medical transplantation, further saying that as a "capitalist economy and democracy, we often turn to markets to resolve social crises."[30] The idea that the altruistic transplant system is a *game* is evidenced, for Goodwin, by the politics of making it onto the official transplant list in the first place, which she suggests favours wealthy white people.[31] In general, the point is that the list is designed to favour those who have a "greater social worth."[32] For her, a market, with greater transparency in the judgment aspect of who gets what, will be both more efficient and fair.

That such manoeuvring goes on in the altruistic system causes some advocates to recoil at the very name of *altruism*. For example, Richard Epstein calls the current practices a "veneer of altruism."[33] By calling the process a *veneer*, audiences are rhetorically invited to see past it, to look deeper, and to find out what is *really* going on in the system.

Most important, language as shaping arguments and perception is consciously a part of compensation advocates' strategy. For the most part, their rhetoric is more carefully constructed and their arguments tend to emphasize the logical (*logos* over and above *ethos* and *pathos*). For example, Goodwin suggests that critics of market-mechanisms think that "market language" applied to humans is a mistake – "the language of property" being inapplicable to the human body.[34] But Goodwin counters by saying that "language can change, be flexible, malleable"; the language "of compensation can become the language of donation."[35] There is a host of logical arguments offered by advocates, discussed further below.

The two best examples of advocates consciously making language-shaping choices are found in references to *maintaining the status quo* and *ethics*. In regard to the former, advocates of change make their appeal by indicating that market strategies would not be a major change at all, that things will remain, largely, as they currently are. Consider Arthur Matas making his case for incentives:

> The best way to increase the supply of kidneys without drastically changing the existing allocation system is to legalize a regulated system of compensation for living kidney donors. Such a system could be established using the infrastructure already in place ... [the] only change required ... is some form of payment for donors.[36]

The idea that markets or financial incentives are unethical is countered and fought by advocates, who retain the use of moral/ethical language within proposals. (The centrality and thrust of this element is discussed in detail in chapters 8 and 9). That is, to concede the very word *ethics* or *value* to the other side is thought to damage the case.

The language strategy, then, is to either deny that there are ethical concerns at all or to claim an awareness and incorporation of morality into the position. In regard to the former, Joshua Miller, president of the American Society of Transplant Surgeons, says flatly, "I personally see no ethical issue," when speaking of limited financial incentives.[37] In regard to the latter, there is an effort to have the compensation policy comport with social norms and significant ethical values. Benjamin Hippen and J.S. Taylor's conclusion to an article defending compensation makes it clear that they see themselves as "struggling to advance a morally informed practice of transplantation" and to maintain "public trust."[38]

Conscious language choices guiding advocacy appear in the distinction between *incentives* and a *market*. In a market, products are paid for, whereas the language of incentives is designed to motivate. The distinction is that in incentives, one's interests are being (re)aligned, and therefore actions will follow. This is not payment for the organ but for the interest, for the decision, for the action – a nudge. This type of distinction is made explicit in a document appended to the *Assessing Initiatives* hearing: "It is very important that the Position Paper uses the word *compensation* when defining the nature of any form of monetary payment."[39] Though the actual word choice is different, the goal is to distinguish between compensation and outright payment, in line with my (I think clearer) distinction between incentivizing the *choice* versus paying for the *organ*.

Overall, then, there is some commonality in terms used for compensated arguers. The most common element is the attempt to deploy similar *language*, similar terms of appeals (e.g., *ethics, status quo, altruism*) but to align them to support a different system. As for key word-choice differences, the market language in particular emphasizes *efficiency* and *transparency*.

Primary Positive Arguments

Two relatively distinct positions have emerged within the notion of compensating people for giving their organs. There is ambiguity between the *market* (M) and the *incentive* (I) approaches. The structure of this section is as follows: claims will be listed and numbered, and then discussion will follow of variations of that claim as it is made in public discourse and academic literature. There are five primary positive market arguments (M1 through M5) and four incentive arguments (I1 through I4).

Market Arguments

The following arguments are not to be read hierarchically. That is, they are not in order of most to least powerful. But the first three arguments, M1, M2, and M3, appear often and seem to be the most resonant.

The first argument to consider is

M: Markets Are Amoral

This is a general argument about markets and is not necessarily specific to organ supply or allocation. (How and why this argument works and resonates, especially in the era under review will be more fully explored in subsequent chapters.) The idea here is that given the complexities of pluralistic societies and competing comprehensive doctrines and visions of the good life, markets operate as an amoral, or neutral, way of navigating – even adjudicating between – conflicting moralities.

A simple example illustrates the claim and role of market amorality. Businesses, beyond just maximizing profits for shareholders, will occasionally decide to also *do good*. That a room full of shareholders will unanimously agree on what that good *is* is unlikely. Or even if they do agree on what is good, they will likely disagree on the hierarchical arrangement. Hence, Milton Friedman claims that the task of business, and its underlying moral position, is simply to maximize profits and let individuals rank and value their own ends. This is sometimes called the Friedman Doctrine.[40] So in the case of human organs, the moral permissibility of the act is not decided by the firm (in this case, the state), and individuals are free to pursue – or abstain from – the matter in accordance with the dictates of their individual conscience or doctrine.

Another animating idea holds markets to be neutral and amoral because they are simply tools; that is, merely instrumental. Benjamin Hippen, a prominent proponent of the market system for organs, puts the matter clearly:

There is nothing morally salutary about market relations in themselves. Rather, markets are instrumentally valuable in permitting persons with diverse, conflicting moral commitments to meet and interact on the basis of mutual assent and peaceable negotiation, just as abstaining from certain market relationships can be equally demonstrative of one's moral commitments.[41]

Mark J. Cherry articulates a similar position in his *Kidney for Sale by Owner*. The problem of morality and ethical content is precisely their universalizing, which confounds the pluralistic and democratic (i.e., tolerant) impulse of US society. "Moral content is gained at the price of universality," writes Cherry. "Securing a particular ethic requires specification of premises and content that will not be acknowledged among moral strangers."[42] That a moral point of view will not be universally shared, then, is a premise of (modern) US society. Therefore the enactment of a morality – of *any* ethic – is to the exclusion of another. There are some flaws in this line of thought (to be explored in section III), but the overarching point here is that markets do not presuppose commitment to a certain, singular ethical vision. While markets are not compatible with all moral views, they are not incompatible with a significantly wide variety of values.

Another major argument in favour of an open market in human organs is

M2: A Legal Market Will Eradicate the Black Market

More basically, the "dark side of organ procurement – the underground, private system – is driven by demand. That demand is unmet by altruism, and thus spreads elsewhere."[43]

The point here is simple: there is a portion of the population who, rather than wait on the transplant list, turn to the black market to purchase an organ or negotiate a transaction. Worldwide, the World Health Organization estimates that as many as 10 per cent of kidney transplants from living donors were done with organs illegally obtained.[44] Roughly ten thousand kidneys are obtained on the black market each year, which translates to a kidney being "sold every hour."[45]

But one complication is that, while only Iran has an actual open market in human organs,[46] many countries do not hold private organ transactions illegal as such. This spawns something like medical tourism or what is sometimes called "transplant tourism,"[47] as was seen with the California man above. So while financial transactions involving organs in the United States is a black market, being conducted abroad in certain countries renders the action often only a grey market. That said, many of these transactions are not just arranged in the United States (though on-line stations and servers in the United States are still legal grey areas),[48] but the operations occur there as well.

That is, operating online and therefore in "international" law, organ brokers charge high fees – for example, $160,000 for a kidney, $290,000 for lungs – in the transplant tourism scheme.[49] The issue here is not just that the actual donor sees only a fraction of that (with reports ranging from $800 to $3,000) while brokers net around $50,000 after expenses,[50] but that the brokers help to arrange the transplantation in the United States, pointing to doctors or medical institutions who are "either complicit in the scheme or willing to turn a blind eye."[51] In what is being billed as the "first legally proved case of organ trafficking," as previously discussed, Levy Izhak Rozenbaum pleaded guilty to organ brokering in the United States in October 2011, following his arrest and those of forty-three others in New Jersey (including several rabbis and the mayor of Hoboken) in 2009.[52]

A legal market in human organs, then, can be seen as not just removing these clandestine operations because they are morally *suspect*, but also as ensuring that transactions can be properly monitored, assuring some basic level of equality in payments and a more transparent path of organ procurement. A market system makes the organ system transparent and efficient. That is, here is the possible eradication of those situations in which an organ donor receives hundreds of dollars and a middleman receives tens of thousands, and also, hopefully, the eradication of more drastic means of procurement (theft or physical coercion).

Such a narrative resonates in the United States due to previous cultural narratives about Prohibition and the War on Drugs. As Taylor and Simmerling put it,

> The remedy to the corrupt and unregulated system of exchange that poses such agonizing dilemmas to very sick people is its mirror image: a regulated and transparent regime that is backed by the rule of law and devoted to donor protection.[53]

Furthermore, a black market forces US society to deal with the costs of organ donation. L.D. de Castro asserts that the black market "proves to us that even when donors are not being paid for their organs there are actual costs that society merely continues to ignore."[54] An open (or regulated) market will remedy this, advocates assert.

The third argument equates the human body with ownership in a legal and jurisdictional sense:

M3: My Body Is My Property

Property rights are fundamental in the West and much of the world. One's body may be defined as one's inviolable property. This line of argument has precedent in legal scholarship relating to organs and tissue.[55] There is an analogy to abortion, where pro-choice advocates' slogan, "Keep Your Laws Off of My Body," captures the message succinctly, prompting a change in the legality of bodily infringement/prohibition.[56] Pavle Mircov, a Serbian man attempting to sell his kidney to help feed his family, puts the matter clearly: "It's my body, and I should be able to do what I want with it."[57]

If my body is my property, then how (in a nation whose law books are full of protections for personal property) is the buying and selling of my body/property at all legally prohibited? This is more than just a rhetorical question for advocates. It is more clearly seen as a call for consistency in the law, in which arguments have deep roots but need not stem back to the rhetoric of founding fathers such as John Adams – "The moment the idea is admitted into society that property is not as sacred as the laws of God ... anarchy and tyranny commence" – nor to the Fifth Amendment.[58] Rather, the call is for consistency in the law with regard to the *body* as property. (This will be discussed in more detail in chapter 8.)

More clearly, other bodily activities and processes, such as abortion, sex/prostitution, ova and sperm, surrogacy, and blood plasma, enjoy legality in the United States.[59] As Gerald Dworkin says, "We accept the legitimacy of the sale of blood, semen, ova, hair, and tissue. By doing so, we accept the idea that individuals have the right to dispose of their organs and other bodily parts if they so choose."[60] A landmark case regarding human organ sales was decided by the Ninth Circuit Court of Appeals December 2011. The court ruled that bone-marrow donors can be now compensated, explicitly saying that NOTA does not extend to bone marrow (by defining marrow as not an "organ").[61] Though there are obvious dis-analogies between highly regenerative things, such as sperm, and a non-regenerative kidney, the health-threat distinction between giving up a kidney and carrying a baby full term (especially one that needs, say, an emergency caesarean section) are less clear.

Perhaps the most troubling element to classic liberals (especially of the conservative political and libertarian bent) of the inability to sell one's organs is that if the organs are not properly considered *private* property, then what kind of property are they? If they are public property, one's organs might be subject to whatever government agencies regulate public domain. That is, there is the twofold notion here of incorporeal rights (that I have the relational right *to* my property) and the corporeal right (that *this* is my property). Somehow my body, in terms of reproduction, sex, blood, and marrow, is mine, but in terms of organs – and nothing else, it seems – it is not. To advocates this seems not just a strange argument (in the incorporeal sense of right), but a sort of frightening thought for the corporeal sense of property rights: are my vital organs then the property of the state?[62] Among certain reactionary crowds, the images of the Falun Gong might appear as harbingers of a day when their own government does not morally approve of them and comes for their organs.

Advances in science, biotechnology, and medicine make commercial uses of the body possible. Previously, organs had little use outside an individual, and therefore little monetary value.[63] So from a perspective different than that of donors and recipients of organs, the broader picture of the monetary value of an organ comes into focus as the linchpin in the "biotechnology university industrial complex."[64] As a result, a lot of money changes hands in the name of *research*.[65]

Another argument, then, has taken shape:

M4: Market-Mechanisms Are Already Embedded in the "Altruistic" Transplant Scheme

This claim comes most forcefully from Goodwin: "Market transactions are deeply imbedded in the transplantation scheme and will likely further expand. Thinking otherwise would be naïve ... "[66] The case is made in a variety of ways, the most obvious being that which Richard Epstein motions towards in claiming that doctors and hospitals make thousands and thousands of dollars performing transplants: "Needy individuals are free to pay thousands of dollars to transplant surgeons and hospitals, but nothing to organ donors."[67]

Goodwin argues for less obvious markets and financial transactions already present in medical systems and practices. She notes that "hundreds of tissue banks throughout the United States, with very little oversight, buy, retrieve, store, experiment with and broker human tissues and body parts."[68] Furthermore, the Los Angeles County coroner's office, for example, has been documented as selling corneas (at $250 a pair) to Doheny Eye and Tissue Transplant Bank.[69]

These body banks, so to speak, are not the only entities in the body-parts market. Biotechnology firms collect human materials for research and development. Investigation into one firm, Regenerative Technologies, found that a single cadaver can bring in "more than $220,000 in products."[70] This is part and parcel of the fact that biotechnology is a multibillion dollar industry, and that many of these companies, such as Olympus, Cryolife, and Regenerative Technologies, are or were publicly traded.[71] This level of money involved in human organs, body parts, and transplantation lead Goodwin to conclude that "within the domain of the organ transplantation process, organ donors are frequently the sole gratuitous participants."[72]

In a market view, many people are making money off of a transplant – the surgeons, the hospital, the body banks – and so the United States and other market-prohibition countries hardly have altruistic transplant systems. Rather, there is a booming transplant industry, and one that, in some of the most sceptical views associated with this type of argument, thrives on and therefore exploits the good will and altruistic donation of individuals for profit. While M4 in general is marshalled by advocates of a market in order to increase supply, it can more specifically be seen as a sort of reckoning of an imbalance in monetary flow under the status quo system. Once equity is restored, more trust in the organ transplantation process will follow.[73] Or, not to put too fine a point on it, Cherry asks ironically, "Why should we compensate organ donors when we can continue to take organs for free?"[74]

Another positive argument for market advocates relates to the standing of the individuals doing the exchange, and can be formulated as

M5: Market Mechanisms Make the Organ Exchange Symmetrical

In this argument, it is precisely the elevated and noble language used to characterize donors, discussed in chapter 3, that forms a *weight* on recipients. The gift exchange paradigm, as discussed in Marcel Mauss's famous study,[75] is applied to organ donation in Renee Fox's and Judith Swazey's touchstone work.[76] The idea is that the organ gift is wonderful in one sense but virtually impossible to reciprocate in another sense (with reciprocation being the implicit expectation in the Maussian gift exchange paradigm). The inability to reciprocate, then, hangs on the recipient as weight, as a debt. This "tyranny of the gift," as Fox and Swazey famously call it, in practice and real human relations, is significantly complicated.[77]

Sally Satel, a prominent market activist, describes the inability to have a next of kin or friend to provide her needed organ as a *relief*:

> Three friends offered to donate but backed out. Frustrated at first, I soon found myself oddly relieved. I dreaded the constricting obligation that would surely come with accepting such a sacrifice. I wished I could buy a kidney just to avert the emotional debt.[78]

As if giving voice precisely to what Satel describes, Hippen says that " ... the 'tyranny' of a gift-relation arises, at least in part, from the curtailed options available to donors and recipients under the current system of procurement and allocation."[79] That Satel and others are *locked* into the gift-relation is itself another constriction. The argument here is that market mechanisms limit this debt (or at least lessen the feeling of it), given that there is more parity in the initial standing between donor and recipient. That is, in the initial standing, there is not a desperate person searching for an organ, relying on a *miracle* of altruism, on the very gift of life. Similarly, if properly presented, advocates argue there will not be a desperate person seeking cash, for the market will determine an appropriate value for the organ based on scarcity. Cherry describes a phenomenological difference of gift and commercial relations. The former is "marked by altruism, personal concern for the other, love, and in some cases, intimacy;" but though the latter is not similarly marked, it is still "constrained by honesty and agreement."[80] The most fundamental difference is that in commercial relationships, "one gets what one deserves in terms of what one has agreed to," whereas in gift relationships, "one gets what one does not deserve."[81] The implication is that some amount of symmetry be present to help already suffering patients maintain some sense of self-possession. Thus, each person in the exchange has something that the other wants, and each is able to negotiate an acceptable exchange. In advocates' rhetoric, this provides parity in the exchange and alleviation of otherwise too great a burden on the part of those in need of an organ.

Incentive Arguments

The difference between markets and incentives is, again, that the former finds a transparent market for organs in which the market would dictate price, supply, and allocation, whereas the latter only offers incentives (ranging from modest payments directly to donors to tax breaks, to insurance, to scholarships) and thus applies only to *supply*. The current Organ Procurement and Transplant Network (OPTN)/United Network for Organ Sharing (UNOS) system would remain in place for allocation, and the incentives would be offered directly by the government (even if private donations and non-profits could contribute to the fund). So there are these important dissociations: only the government may compensate, and the introduction of financial or other incentives relates only to procurement – not allocation. So no one, not even indirectly, can buy an organ – only the state can.[82]

These matters of dissociation, in one sense, could be isolated as official arguments for the program, as a way of articulating it as a sort of *third* way between the two poles of an altruism-based organ market. It can even serve as an argument in precisely that language:

I1: Financial Incentives Are the Solution to the Stalemate, the Best Way between Altruism and Market Systems

"The only thing that stands in the way of retrieving these organs and saving many thousands of lives each year is a *failure of the collective imagination* – a failure to devise a policy that, while respecting traditional social norms, provides an increased incentive for cadaveric organ donation."[83] These words are from a letter to Congress signed by a range of advocates, from priests to law professors to surgeons to UNOS board members, who present financial incentives as an imaginative and socially agreeable middle position. It is the "most viable compromise between using the power of market forces to satisfy human need while at the same time recognizing the widespread reluctance to having human body parts being treated, undignifiedly, as commodities."[84] That strong anti-market advocates such as Francis Delmonico and Nancy Scheper-Hughes also support limited incentives, such as funeral expenses or life and disability insurance, indicates to some degree the third-way element of this process.[85]

Perhaps the most striking evidence in support of financial incentives for organ donation is the public support for it. An NPR-Thomson Reuters Health Poll from 2012 indicated that as many as 60 per cent of Americans would be in favour of some sort of financial incentivization.[86] Though the sample size was small (three thousand participants) and the questions were varied, this does seem to indicate a shift in attitude coming, if not already here, with regard to incentives and human body parts.

From a slightly different perspective, chair of the 2003 *Assessing Initiatives* hearing, James C. Greenwood (R-PA), claims that "no one that I am aware of is advocating a policy that would actually pay someone to donate a kidney while they are alive, I think [that] is ethically abhorrent to all of us."[87] Greenwood seemingly means that no one at the hearing was advocating such a policy, for of course there are many advocating precisely that, as discussed above. The point here is the conviction with which he rhetorically disentangles incentives from a market, believing the former to be acceptable and the latter to be "ethically abhorrent."

This attempted disarticulation, or lack thereof, was at the core of a 1993 white paper entitled "Financial Incentives for Organ Donation: A Report of the Payment Subcommittee OPTN/UNOS Ethics Committee." The paper concluded that once financial compensation and financial incentives are disentangled in the public mind, such a practice might be ethically acceptable, and in 2006, the OPTN/UNOS Ethics Committee undertook such a clarification, with results still pending.[88]

Private firm proposals, such as Project Donor, which was the main proposal under review in the 1999 *Putting Patients First* hearing, outline an incentive proposal. Developed by Eugene C. Epstein and Alan W. Boessmann, the proposal imagined a $10,000 insurance benefit to a donor-specified beneficiary.[89] A similar proposal was drafted and advocated by the wealthy businessman Richard DeVos, himself a heart transplant recipient. His proposal was under review in the 2003 *Assessing Initiatives* hearing, and is similarly designed (a $10,000 tax credit). The US government would provide the funding, a fiscally acceptable source given that transplants would result in a net gain, a net savings, as compared to dialysis.[90] Sanctioned or appointed non-profit institutions could also offer the benefit.

While there is no national policy on this front, since then, seventeen states in the United States have adopted some form of financial incentive, the most common being a $10,000 tax deduction, with only Iowa having anything close to the proposals above, which is a $10,000 tax credit.[91] The difference between a deduction and a credit is significant, given that, according to NPR, the deduction translates to roughly $1,000 for the typical American household; this means that the live-donor version hardly even covers the cost to volunteer for the act.[92]

The overarching point is, simply, to get more people to sign the donor cards, to register to become a donor. The money, then, is simply an *incentive* to register as a donor, and almost all of the incentive proposals have focused on deceased donation (donations of one's organs from one's cadaver). The language, and a large amount of the intention, then, is retained from the altruistic system, as discussed under "Language and Word Choices," above.

That such an incentive would actually increase organ supply/donor registry is of course unknown. As DeVos put it, the thought of how to increase donation, especially among young people, led him to say "Throw some money at it. I know that's not very sophisticated, but I say let's test it and find out."[93] That incentives do work in a general sense, however, is a second argument here:

I2: Behavioural Financial Incentives Work Well in, if Not Outright Structure, US Society

The argument is consistent with the notion that, indeed, altruism is a *better* (at least morally purer, whatever that means) way to proceed. However, on its own, altruism does not seem to be *enough* of a motivation for many people in any domain, not just organs. In DeVos's words, "I love the altruistic idea of giving it. I wish everybody in America would work for the love of work. But they seem to get moved by getting a little incentive."[94] That individuals perform work (i.e., sell their labour) for something that is other than their *dream job* is itself an instance of financial incentives at work, and given that almost nobody has the job that they'd "do for free," so to speak, financial incentives are a basic part of nearly everyone's life.

Economic incentives are an integral part of daily US life and also provide a rational basis from which to coordinate social action. As Megan Clay and Walter Block argue, "To allow economic incentives to apply to so important and scarce a resource is to do no more than bring rationality to it, the same sort we as a society rely upon to obtain food, clothing, shelter and other products necessary to life."[95]

Market advocates attack altruism as a singular motivation. The line of altruism being the best or a better motivation can be seen, in its most radical instance, as entirely antithetical to the current structures of US society. This set of arguments need not be a Marxian anti-capitalist one, as Clay and Block think,[96] but instead is rather consistent with critiques levelled against welfare liberalism and its famous articulations in John Rawls's Difference Principle and his notion of justice as fairness.[97] The critique is that certain welfare liberalist views, pushed to their logical conclusion, (morally) prohibited individuals from accepting salary increases for more productive work, thereby letting the system reabsorb that extra productivity to benefit the least well-off in society.[98] This type of critique will be explored more in chapter 8, but suffice here to highlight the overall point that in US society, financial incentives are used to motivate behaviour, at a minimum, and perhaps even the stronger claim that *most* social and economic relations are structured according to the incentive paradigm. A stronger rhetorical element is the way in which rationality is aligned with markets; and furthermore, notice, critically, the way in which instrumental rationality is used a synonym for rationality writ large.

A more concrete connection of incentives exists than the more abstract claim of the incentive paradigm as structuring capitalist democracies. A particular and localized example of financial incentives at work in US society beyond pay for labour brings about the third argument for the incentive advocates:

I3: We Already Incentivize Donation

The facts of incentives such as driver discounts operate as a sort of consistency call on the part of advocates. For example, in Georgia, registering as an organ donor would save one $5 on their driver's licence renewal.[99] In Pennsylvania, a pilot program was run in which the state donated $300 towards funeral expenses.[100] This type of incentive was adopted by Maryland and Texas.[101] Less direct financial incentives exist as well, such as the U.S.'s Health Care Finance Administration making donation registration a "condition of participation in Medicare and Medicaid," which is, as Greenwood puts it, "a huge financial incentive. I mean, make no mistake about it, you will do this or we will withhold maybe millions of dollars from you. That's certainly the use of a financial incentive."[102]

Furthermore, the size of incentive matters to advocates. That states within the United States incentivize donation currently with a few hundred dollars is important, as is advocates' proposals to increase that incentive – but not too much. For example, the aforementioned letter to Congress signed by an impressively diverse range of advocates says that a figure of $5,000 is the right amount. It is "large enough so that the family members do not feel as though the memory of their loved one is being insulted or their loss trivialized" nor that they are being taken advantage of, "especially in the hospital environment, where surgeons and top hospital administrators are known to make high six-figure salaries."[103] Therefore, the amount is "a round and respectful sum that tangibly conveys a sense of the grave importance we as a society place upon the decision the family is being asked to make."[104]

Many states passed legislation between 2004 and 2008 to enact some form of tax relief for organ donors. Data that suggest the tax incentives for organ donation are not actually raising supply thus far become highly relevant to issues of size, amount, and kind of compensation.[105]

In other words, the tax incentives are not working. But that doesn't bother some advocates. That is, to certain incentive advocates such as Howard Nathan, president and CEO of the Coalition on Donation, the incentive is less about the actual *money* than it is about the publicity and conversation that such an announcement and practice of incentives would stimulate. He "doubts that the benefit" will really have "an immediate or noticeable impact on consent rates" but that over time, "the discussion regarding the availability of the benefit may lead more people to be familiar with the concept of organ donation."[106] This is interesting because the incentive advocate walks a quite fine line here: the incentive, in this view, is less about actually motivating behaviour than it is about continuing to raise awareness about organ donation, and some amount of tax break or funeral benefit or whatever is therefore welcome on such grounds.

The final positive argument is that

I4: Incentives Make the Most Sense Financially

As already discussed in the General Economic Argument in chapter 1, the cost of, say, dialysis, especially long term, far exceeds the relatively high short-term but fixed cost of transplantation. Therefore, insurance companies, and especially the government-run operations Medicare and Medicaid, stand to save a substantial amount of money if transplantation can be increased and become more prevalent. This much is common ground among all advocates in the debate.

The incentive advocates, however, say that the government should take some of that money and put it towards incentivizing people to donate their organs. Giving donors a $10,000 amount still results in significant net savings for the federal government in health care costs. Furthermore, the government has already been spending pools of money on public awareness-raising efforts such as campaigns and educational programs, and yet there is not just a shortage but that shortage is actually increasing. The money, advocates say, should be reallocated.[107]

Trust and Contingencies

Market arguers trust in self-reliance (as autonomy) and markets to fairly and justly govern organ transplantation systems. That the current system is either not making it happen (*other* people are not donating, not pulling their weight) or that the notion of altruism makes those in need overly dependent on (the goodness of) others is evidence of trust and pursuit of autonomy and self-reliance, while pointing to flaws in the judgments and practices of institutions (medical and government) indicates trust and pursuit of markets to govern. The distrust in medical and government institutions is seen in the urban-legend myths as well as many advocates' arguments and language. In the market view, other people and institutions are not as trustworthy as oneself or a transparent market.

So, just as altruism arguers have done, market arguers too have invited trust in people, but in people to make decisions for *themselves*. This way, individuals will not have to turn to God (e.g., Caitlyn's story) nor Air Force One (e.g., Ashley's story) nor media spectacle (e.g., the *Donahue* story) for solutions to their organ problem. Instead, individuals can take matters into their own hands and deal with other individuals who are similarly self-possessed. Autonomy features strongly in market advocates' rhetoric.

For strict incentive arguers, trust resides in *market mechanisms* and *institutions* together. The use of the market mechanism of payment, of using money to motivate and constrain behaviour, is evident in the financial-incentive element, and thereby indicates a diminished level of trust in individuals to "do the right thing" – given that, currently, not enough individuals are. But the maintenance of the status quo infrastructure (OPTN/UNOS/OPOs) *once* the organs have been collected indicates that trust is still maintained, or invited, in institutions.

Contingencies are dealt with by market advocates in the plain manner of neoclassical economists: the market will decide the right price, and if there is still a shortage in organs, the price will go up, thereby stimulating those able to supply. Incentive arguers, largely, view their plan *as* the contingency plan, as many advocates from both the altruistic and market side see either the material problems (the shortage) or ethical (proper human protections) or political difficulties (passing such legislation) in their approaches.

Justifications and Principles

The three key justifications for market-based rhetoric are *autonomy, efficiency*, and (*rational*) *consistency*. These compact terms serve as grounds for compensation advocates' claims for a market system as best for increasing human organ supply. I have moved from the concrete up to the more abstract, starting with the stories and arguments and word choices, showing how these can be condensed and succinctly captured in key justificatory terms. The justifications will be explained more clearly, and then they can, in turn, serve as guiding principles for compensation rhetoric.

Autonomy is seen as a justification for compensated organ systems in a basic sense.[108] That individuals have autonomy is implicitly appealed to as a justification in several key ways. The most obvious, perhaps, is in M3, in which individuals are viewed as owners of their bodies, and therefore able to do with them as they see fit. But M1, in which the amorality of markets is presented as a *solution* to the problem of ethical pluralism, is also inherently an appeal to autonomy, to individuals being able, under the fact of pluralism, to make their own moral choices. Furthermore, M5 rests on autonomy as well, in which a market acts as a *leveller* of distinctions in standing and – following the language choice discussion by Goodwin – social worth. That is, when background conditions are acceptable, a market not only implies but also constructs and affirms the autonomy of individuals.

Taking autonomy as an implicit justification at work in compensation rhetoric, it can be turned into an explicit principle:

> *Autonomy Principle:* individuals are free and equal in sociopolitical standing and therefore can negotiate and exchange according to their own moral system or conscience

The second key justification for compensation rhetoric is *efficiency*. That efficiency can serve as a justification for an action is documented in Boltanski and Thévenot.[109] The obvious usage is in terms of explicit market advocates, in which markets are deemed to be the most efficient way to collect and allocate goods and services. That markets most efficiently organize and coordinate societal relations is evidenced in the ubiquitous usage and the overall penetration of market mentalities into daily US life, from labour, shelter, and food to even expressions such as *time is money* or *money talks*. But efficiency is also an implicit justification for incentive advocates in their insistence that financial incentives are sufficiently motivational. That is, that money motivates people to act, as evidenced in I2, and that it does so quickly, is another way in which efficiency operates as a justification. The language choice of *effectiveness*, of money and markets working well in US society, also underscores this point.

Efficiency, as an implicit justification at work in compensation rhetoric, can be turned into an explicit principle:

> *Efficiency Principle:* money and other market mechanisms are the best way to organize and coordinate social behaviour and solve collective problems

The final key justificatory term is *consistency*, or even *rational consistency*. There are several different ways in which consistency serves as a justification for compensation rhetoric. The first is in the sense of *legal*, and therefore *logical*, consistency. This is evidenced clearly in M4 and I3, in which the advocates make outright consistency calls between currently legal bodily commercializations and organs. It is also evident in M3, in which it stands to reason that if my body is my property and has the same property rights as other properties under US law, including the afore-mentioned bodily ones, such must extend to organs, and anything less results in inconsistently rational governance.

The second sense in which consistency is justificatory for compensation rhetoric is, as glimpsed in M4, that the altruistic system is not entirely *altruistic* at all. Epstein and Goodwin's word choice of the veneer of altruism makes this clear, and the subsequent arguments substantiating the claim that everyone is paid (and paid handsomely) in transplantation *except* the donor make compensation for donors justified on grounds of consistency.[110]

The final sense of consistency relates to the notion of transparency. Here the maintenance of the altruistic system is predicated on things such as social responsibility and public benefits and social norms (as was discussed in chapter 2). But positions such as Goodwin's assert that it is the current institutional arrangements and structures that have violated public trust, and that they operate largely without public oversight or knowledge. In her and other advocates' view, then, the call for transparency in the system is really a call for consistency, of actually upholding the public interest and shared norms.

Having made consistency explicit as a key justification for compensated advocates, it might be expressed as

> *Consistency Principle:* arguers and institutions, especially law, need to be consistent in permissions and prohibitions

Overall, the implicit justifications and the overarching structure of justification – the circle of normative claims – can been seen to rest on three key terms. Those key terms can then be inductively turned into guiding principles, serving as the overarching *ethos* of compensation rhetoric. These terms – autonomy, efficiency, consistency – are characteristic of the theory and practice of neoliberalism.

Chapter Conclusion

Overall, now we have detailed the relationship between fear and horror stories, the black market, and neoliberal political economy. While there are key differences between market and incentive advocates, three key justificatory concepts – autonomy, efficiency, and consistency – animate both.

In summary, then, as seen in arguments, stories, word choices, and where trust is invited to reside, the main justifications for the compensated-supply system are that it promotes and maintains autonomy, that it is efficient, and that is logically consistent with US law and social norms. The structure of justification serves as a normative circle of sorts, and thereby allows the underlying key terms to be turned, inductively, into the compensation advocates' guiding ethic, consistent with and characteristic of neoliberalism.

The crux of the market advocates' case is built around the rationality and increasing prevalence of market mechanisms in daily life, with the affective backing of black-market anxieties. The reduction of morality to subjectivism/individualism under the conditions of values pluralism in contemporary liberal democracies, combined with the status quo dominance of global capitalism as a structuring principle, is also essential to compensation rhetoric and will be explored more fully in the next chapter.

Now that the description, categorization, and ordering of the rhetoric have been done for both positions, the study turns to more substantive analysis of the arguments and the context in which they occur. Right now, this is the picture that should be in focus: there are *valid* arguments on both sides and strong objections to each. A form of rhetorical rationality leaves us here, simply: once we have sufficient claims, grounds, and warrants, reasonable people can disagree. But how does one press beyond this? And is that all there is to rhetoric and rationality?

In short: we have, clearly, competing justifications for belief, policy, and action. Now what?

The next chapter addresses this broader problem of conflicting normative justifications in pluralistic constitutional societies and traces its critical-historical development: that is, how we do moral deliberation under conditions of ethical pluralism, and how we got here.

SECTION THREE

Morality, Neoliberalism, and the Prospects of Reasoning Together in a Democracy

5 The Neoliberal Graft: Medicine, Morality, and Markets in Liberal-Democratic Regimes

Moral disagreement is a significant feature of contemporary life in liberal democracies. In one view, the process of moral argumentation itself lends (if not fully licences and legitimates) the outcome of the public debates; that is, reasoned deliberation results in deliberative judgment, and collective deliberative judgment via the public sphere is the lifeblood of democracy. Publics sort out conflicts in desires and beliefs resting in comprehensive doctrines, principles, practices, institutional systems, and political parties. Everyone is entitled to her own opinion, of course, and those opinions can be counted and totalled (e.g., voting for results). But public processes continue in aspiration for reasoned deliberation and follow something like public reason so that the vote is not a matter of individual whims and subjective preferences.

But there is another kind of moral disagreement, and that is one over what constitutes and establishes a reasonable and just society itself. That is, there is also moral disagreement over the basic structure of society.[1]

The aim of a just society is both to distribute goods and resources in the right way and to value things in the right way.[2] But *right way* is, of course, a normative claim and therefore subject to debate and disagreement. Joseph Stiglitz writes that "communities have to follow some rules" in order to have people live together, and the rules "must be – and must be seen to be – fair and just ... must reflect a basic sense of decency and social justice."[3] But sometimes the disagreement is over exactly those moral terms – the right way to value something, basic senses of decency, and what it means to be fair and just.

One of the most pervasive challenges to the traditional basic structure of democratic society in the last several decades has been neoliberalism. I will use *neoliberalism* to describe the set of policies and practices associated with individual choice, deregulation, privatization, small government, and reliance on market logics to solve both market and historically non-market problems that has its roots in 1970s monetary policy shifts and which hit mainstream viability in the 1980s and 1990s in the West.[4] The motivation driving neoliberalism is simply that what we need to all share together, what needs to be agreed upon, is to be as minimal as possible, and that we should maximize what we all, necessarily, share a need for: money. It is, in short, the Friedman Doctrine (discussed in the previous chapter) for all of society and not just businesses.

Furthermore, neoliberal rhetoric insists that the complexity of judgment making across ethical, religious, and political lines requires a bare-bones, lowest-common-denominator form of collective interaction (i.e., frugal government), and that is provided via instrumental market rationality, given the necessity of money and monetary increase as *the* basic shared premise of citizens. Neoliberalism has increasing resonance in the popular imagination, policy, and laws in constitutional democratic societies such as the United States, and this chapter seeks to give an account as to why. To put the matter clearly: this chapter is an account of *how neoliberalism grafts its way onto all discussions of value* in the current era.

Scholars are aware of the increasing neoliberal ethos of the recent era. For example, Michael Sandel writes, "One of the most striking tendencies of our time is the expansion of markets and market-oriented reasoning into the spheres of life traditionally governed by non-market norms."[5] Debra Satz notes that "markets are not only spreading across the globe, they are also extending into new domains ... [f]or many people, market institutions are assuming the role of an all-purpose remedy ... "[6] Salmaan Keshavjee highlights neoliberalism as "an intellectual and political movement that defined the late twentieth century," where "the market has become the arbiter of all things social and moral," tracing, in particular, neoliberalism's development and impact in global health care policies and practices.[7]

Looking at our bioethical question of human organ procurement, where the contemporary altruistic regime, based on the 1984 NOTA prohibition on selling human organs, is challenged by market alternatives, James Childress writes that compensated and market proposals for organs "have in part reflected the 1980s style of competition, markets, and deregulation"[8] – in short, neoliberalism. While there has been, historically, overwhelming resistance to incentives or buying organs in both the transplant community and the public,[9] this resistance seems to be lessening.

To reiterate two claims from the previous chapter, a 2012 NPR-Thomson Reuters poll found that 46 per cent of Americans viewed tax credits for organ donations as acceptable, and 41 per cent viewed cash for organs as acceptable. A 2015 study found that 51 per cent of US residents found payment for organs acceptable, and when a process of explanation about the organ shortage and potential for market mechanisms to alleviate this shortage occurred, more than 70 per cent found such a payment process acceptable. So, while attitudes towards organ donation are still extremely positive, public and professional attitudes towards incentives and compensation, once anathema to all but the most economically liberal, are also becoming more positive.

This chapter has two goals. The first is to provide an explanation for this shift in public opinion on cash for organs and other neoliberal justifications in medicine and beyond; that is, to give an account as to why neoliberalism is increasing in rhetorical and practical effect. The second goal is to explain why a moral question in the contemporary era – why *any* moral question – is *so hard*, from a consensus perspective, to collectively answer. That is, let us consider that there are two main ethical questions for a society to answer in collectively binding judgment:

Q1: Is this action morally permissible?
Q2: Should society (legally) allow it?

In a general sense, one can think of ancient philosophy, particularly in its Greco-Roman variation, as forcing Q2 to be answered based upon the deliberative judgment outcome of Q1: deliberate first on whether an act is morally permissible, and then structure the law accordingly. Modernity, particularly in the liberal-democratic tradition, has forced a wedge between the two questions, and often for good reason: at some level, categorical moral content of the collectively binding variety can, and almost always does, run afoul of someone else's moral vision, and liberal democracy holds ethical, and especially religious, pluralism dear, seeking to preserve individual rights to moral visions as much as possible. Historically, tension exists with regard to just how much individual rights to competing moral visions and practices are possible while still maintaining a foundational, shared overlap of collectively binding moral content. The contemporary ascendency of neoliberalism places tension not on how much we can share, but rather on how much categorical moral content *in general* is possible in ethically pluralistic societies such as Western liberal democracies.

Questions of the good (Q1) are disarticulated from questions of what one has a right to do (Q2). Once Q1 and Q2 have become thoroughly disconnected based on justifications of moral individualism and private conscience, the ability to have any categorical moral content is diminished. That is to say, the ability for deliberative judgment on Q1 to collectively bind citizens via Q2 decreases significantly and might even be impossible altogether. That, in a nutshell, is the argument I will present.

The first section of this chapter will recap the current public policy of altruism in organ procurement and the neoliberal challenge to it as a concrete case example. The second section looks at the key theoretical issues involved in moral disagreements in liberal democracies more generally, highlighting the tensions of the concept and use of public reason in deliberative contexts. The third section offers a brief critical-historical background as to how we got here and why. The fourth sketches the beginnings of an argument about neoliberal mechanisms and justifications as an all-encompassing regime for liberal democracies, with market logics pervading into historically non-market arenas, coining the phrase the *economization of everyday life* as a trope for the grafting of neoliberalism onto all discussions of value in modernity. A conclusion section speculates on resistance to neoliberalism and just how hard that is under current sociopolitical conditions. While there are normative arguments to follow, it is hoped that the description of the current situation in liberal democracies such as the United States accurately gives voice to the fundamental questions of why neoliberalism ascends in both public policy and rhetorical effect, and tells a story that is hopefully recognizable to both critics and proponents of neoliberalism.

By the end of this chapter, the importance of a distinction between first- and second-order judgments as a means of settling disagreement in heterogeneous epistemic societies will be established, as will recognition that *some moral categoricity is required* to pursue just societies, and ultimately an account and emphasis of the philosophical, political, and hegemonic power of neoliberalism will be narrated.

Public Policy: Altruism and Neoliberalism

Let me recap a working distinction between altruism and neoliberalism as value-laden theories undergirding law and public policies. Richard Titmuss published his famous and influential study of the gift relationship in medical contexts shortly after the adoption of the Uniform Anatomical Gift Act in 1968, arguing (in 1971) empirically and philosophically that the non-profit, altruism-based blood donor system in Britain yielded better results in terms of quality and quantity than the then-for-profit market-mechanism system in the United States. Titmuss's case has been influential in persuading a number of bioethicists and lawmakers that "commercialization ... has serious destructive effects, ethical and non-ethical, on the whole of a society."[10]

A key part of the altruistic argument is that the ways "in which society organizes and structures its social institutions ... can encourage or discourage the altruistic in [people]."[11] The establishment of altruism then as a communal concept backed by public institutions is what allows Jeffrey Prottas to say, in the mid 1990s, that organ transplantation in the United States is characterizable as a continuum: on one end, "the development of highly advanced biotechnology" and, on the other end, "widespread public altruism," with "public policies designed to allow technology and kindness to support one another" in the middle.[12] The establishment of the organ procurement process – the technology, the medical practices, the organizations, institutions, and laws – was built around, and in turn continues to self-justify, a public notion of altruism.[13]

Neoliberalism, however, asserts the centrality and priority of individual rights, privatization, and free markets in and around notions of human well-being. Ideas such as "private property rights, free markets, and free trade" and "deregulation, privatization, and withdrawal of the state from many areas of social provision" characterize the view, as does the policy trend in Western countries such as the United States from the 1970s forward.[14] The political economic element of neoliberalism is vital to understanding societal shifts, of course, but the most salient element for my argument is the related ethical dimension of neoliberalism – namely, moral individualism. That is, neoliberal ethics are a type of moral individualism in which morality is a private, personal affair. The public policy element of a neoliberal ethos runs on the twin engines of moral autonomy and efficiency.

The clash is clear, then, from the perspective of public policy, in which a legally binding judgment is to be made for an ethically diverse populace. The nature of public policy in general is collectively binding and monistic, whereas the nature of neoliberalism in economics and ethics is individual and pluralistic. But the line between categorical public policy and individual moral choice is not always so clear, however, and often needs to be redrawn. The idea of categorical, collectively binding policies against murder, for example, should strike most as obvious and necessary, as should the idea of preservation of individual conscientious objections to otherwise standard and routine medical practices. That something like domestic abuse could be thought a private, individual affair outside the purview of publics indicates the need, from time to time, to shift public/ private distinctions in terms of ethical and policy judgments.

Moral disagreements in liberal democracies, then, often turn on an individual's values hierarchy and its clash with a fellow citizen's values hierarchy. In cases in which a public policy *needs* to be set, to be decided, how is the matter to be resolved? In other words, in the case of competing goods or even ethical systems something must, in the end, *override*, and in the contemporary, owing to the modern condition (discussed more below), the override is ultimately given to an individual's conscience.

But diverse and pluralistic societies with differing epistemic justifications require *some* common epistemic ground to make rational decisions.
When citizens argue in public about publicly relevant matters, there
needs to be some combination of reason-giving and reason-assessing
that is shared to determine what counts as a *better* argument. Otherwise,
it seems we are stuck with mutual, incompatible difference – and
potentially a legal guarantee and political arrangement assuring – not
assuaging – such incompatible fundamental disagreement of medicine
and beyond. Or, as Ezekiel Emanuel glaring puts it: "In liberal political
philosophy there is not even a *theoretical* way of resolving the pressing
medical issues."[15]

Values and Justification

Liberal theory contends, in short, that the public use of reason is meant
to offer a reasonable way of managing ethical pluralism. One way to think
about the work that public reason does is via the concepts of the right
and the good, in which ethical questions (what is good, is this good?)
interact with questions of rights (is there a right to act or think this way?).

The relationship, and priority in the relationship, of the right and
the good is at the core of modern social, political, and economic
organization. The distinction between first- and second-order judgments
is precisely the animating mechanism behind the liberal conception of
public reason as most forcefully outlined by John Rawls but shared by
scholars like Robert Audi, James Boettcher, and Paul Weithman in what,
following the latter, is called the *standard approach*.[16] In brief, the key
distinction in the standard approach to public reason is between one's
content-full, direct judgments of right and wrong and what is allowed to
count as a justification in determining one's first-order judgments. That
both are necessary to public reason is uncontroversial; a society must
have some mechanism for adjudicating between competing first-order
judgments. The matter turns, clearly, on what the proper relationship is
between the two, who decides, and how.

One way to understanding competing justifications is also as competing *orders of worth*.[17] The search is for principles and reasons to guide
behaviour and justify actions in deliberative engagement. Deliberation
"finds its modern expression in the imperative to justify, as it is manifested in a universe comprising several common worlds."[18] What is most
fascinating and relevant about Luc Boltanski and Laurent Thévenot's
model of justice and assumed human capacities is that it shows how
humans "encounter the sense of injustice that is aroused when different orders of justice are confused."[19] The pursuit of a shared higher

common principle – in this case, of justice – is the convergent aim of public deliberations.[20]

The previous two chapters ended with principles of justification for the advocates' respective views. When detached from their positions, all members of contemporary US society likely recognize the justifications, at some level, as powerful. That is, the Consistency, Efficiency, and Autonomy Principles, as well as the Virtue, Inspiration, Justice, and Civic Community Principles, are all, at some level, rational justifications for certain beliefs and actions. This is how rational disagreement among peers, even epistemic peers, happens in constitutional democracies. But as is evident, while maybe endorsable to all rational citizens at some level, these principles are mutually exclusive in the case of human organ procurement – as is the overarching question of allowing a market mechanism and incentives into the procurement process (i.e., it can only be allowed or disallowed).

Hence, there are two questions in justifications or orders of worth more broadly as we deliberate on the cases of altruism-based approaches to human organ procurement and market-mechanism challengers. The first is, Which case (and its corresponding justifications and principles) is, or ought to be, more persuasive? This is the subject of subsequent chapters and ultimately a deliberative question for society at large, of which this book seeks to be but one voice. The second question, though, is, *How would we choose* which case *ought* to be chosen? Here I am providing a particular critical-historical context showing just how historically conditioned and philosophically deep that question is. In one sense, *that* there is something to choose here is itself relatively novel, and this chapter shows how this element of choice, combined with emphasis on (a certain kind of) rationality, explains why a market-justification model both appears and *makes sense* (in one logic) in the contemporary moment.

Publics, Reason, and the Enlightenment Dream

The notion of a shared space in which people reason with one another about the things that pertain to the entire community has a long history. Whether that space is literal or conceptual, who exactly the community is (small groups, city states, nations, empires, humanity), and what things are or ought to be community concerns, are all variously contested. But the idea of reasoning together in public is core to this book, just as the idea has been important for many societies over the past two millennia or so. I will chart a narrow and specific trajectory of publics and reason in community, as it changes significantly from Greece to Rome to the Modern West and contemporary US society. The goal is to show how these transformational shifts explain the rise and increasing resonance of neoliberal rhetorics.

There is a robust tradition of reason being used in public in antiquity. Though it is largely interpersonal and less concerned with the *polis* per se, the Socratic Method is one of interactive dialogue and not isolated reasoning. Isocrates, as a figure both literally and figuratively between Plato and Aristotle, deemed reason a practical affair aimed at judgment, and speech as the means of moving towards the "best course" of action, supported by honour and justice.[21] Of the three types of rhetoric, Aristotle is most clearly concerned with the deliberative genre, in which citizens reason together to decide a course of action. Aristotle holds the *vita activa* as the second-best possible life choice after only the *vita contemplativa*.[22] The intellectual virtues of contemplation, of the life of mind, were the zenith of human life, but active engagement in politics, in the affairs of the city and community, were the highest ideal for non-philosophers.

The Romans switch the priority to the *vita activa* – as the Isocratean-Ciceronian paradigm of rhetoric, conceived of as reasoning in and for the public as a defence of justice and virtue[23] – as the pinnacle of possible lives. *Vita activa*, as the public life, concerning politics and action for the community, reigns as the supreme ideal for a millennium or so.[24] The orator is one of the most powerful and important figures of the epoch, and the treatises of the era are devoted to training great orators – notably, not philosophers.[25] Cicero writes in *De Oratore* (I.vii.30) that the art of rhetoric, conceived as that of the artistic use of language to move minds to action in favour of justice in public oratory, is the most important: "In every free nation, and most of all in communities which have attained the enjoyment of peace and tranquility, this one art has always flourished above the rest and ever reigned supreme."[26] Furthermore Quintilian's *Institutio Oratoria*, largely a synthesis of rhetorical and practical philosophical thought, makes a key contribution to education in that it outlines a program of study for the raising up of orators beginning, literally, from "the very cradle of speech through all the stages of education which can be of any service to our budding orator til we have reached the very summit of the art."[27] The very summit of the art is the engagement of reason and oration as the *vita activa*, and it serves as respite from a potential danger that the intellectual virtues hold for the philosopher and *vita contemplativa*. This is captured in one of Quintilian's most memorable lines (*Inst.*, 10.5.17–18): "The danger is that, coming out of shadowy retreats in which they have almost grown old, they may shrink from the bright sunlight of real conflict."[28]

The revival of the rhetorical tradition in the Renaissance and Early Modern period focuses mostly on *vita activa* component as well, despite significant interest and advances in natural philosophy. That said, there was a sense in which the anti-philosophical tendencies of the Romans, especially Quintilian,[29] is reoriented in the Early Modern period, due to both the rise of the scientific method and a growing preference for the plain-speak of the Attic as opposed to the Asiatic philosophers. The priority of *vita activa* is, once again, completely reversed in the Enlightenment, in which reason, public reason in particular, is anti-rhetorical.[30]

The Enlightenment view of public reason and public life finds reason not being multisided but univocal. In this way, Kant was emblematic: he thought that rhetoric, in the form of oratory, was a way to "move men like machines to a judgment that must lose all its weight with them upon calm reflection."[31] Public reason, then, was not synonymous with oratory or rhetorical engagement, even in and for the *polis*.

Rather, in the Modern era public reason emerges as a particular *kind* of reason. Public reason is not simply individual, private reasoners coming together to discuss and deliberate in public on collectively binding matters. This conception of reason serves as a check on and against individual reason and attempts to transform private reason into something at once more general and more *rational*. In short, public reason is a specific, rule-governed way to reason about publicly relevant matters: public reason is a particular conception of *what counts as epistemically justified*.

The key to public reason is epistemic justification, for what is created via modern public reason is a social or public epistemology tested against social knowledge.[32] That which is considered (normatively) justified is that which fulfils the demands and precepts of public reason. In this way, public reason is less about the giving of reasons per se than it is about which reasons count and which ones do not. The purpose, to be clear, is to settle disagreement. The distinction between public and private, between the reasons that count and those that do not, is a "threshold of controversy."[33] So on the one hand, public reason is, and basically ever will be, controversial. On the other, however, the idea of an epistemic account that is binding on all citizens seems a worthy goal; after all, *truth, knowledge,* and *facts* ought to be the answers to have for, or the aims of, most (all?) questions.

Epistemic common ground then is largely the purpose of public reason. As is immediately apparent, citizens do not have nearly as widely divergent epistemic grounds as some poststructuralist writers seem to think. Consider a claim such as "there are seven billion people on this planet." While it might be arguable ("there are 7,000,500,391" or any other variation of numbers), it is an empirical claim recognizable as *having* an exact answer (assuming agreement on the definition of *person*), even if we do not know exactly what it is. Furthermore, on such an empirical question, most Western societies are confident in dispelling or arguing against, or even outright blocking altogether, views to the contrary, and the grounds for as much are simple: we do not often argue about facts.[34]

The matter turns, of course, on what constitutes a fact and how one would know one. Citizens do not have insignificantly overlapping inferential norms on this matter. But there are differing norms at times, and of course different interpretations of shared factual evidence, differing judgments made about recognized knowledge, and so forth. Given as much, what ought to be considered epistemic common ground for public matters such as laws and (in the case of this study, health) policy?

The key offering of epistemic common ground in the constitution of reasons comes from Kant's "An Answer to the Question: What Is Enlightenment?" Kant distinguishes public and private reasons, finding that the reasons that matter and hence those that are to guide civic life are those that are public: "The *public* use of reason must at all times be free, and it alone can bring about enlightenment among men [sic]."[35] These public reasons are universal, the reasons that would count for all – "before the entire public of the reading world."[36] Furthermore, it is the use of public reasons in civic life and institutions that brings about enlightenment.

Kant's public reason is not a neutralized scientism. Kant sought to establish ethical conduct and the content of morality as a cognitive enterprise, with morality being within the scope of reason, both built on and nourished by reason.[37] This is the explicit goal of his *Grounding for the Metaphysics of Morals*, there seeking to establish "whether or not there is the utmost necessity for working out for once a pure moral philosophy that is wholly cleared of everything which can only be empirical and can only belong to anthropology" (§389). The elements of the empirical and anthropology he mentions are attempts to keep morality from being reducible to sociocultural processes, trying to push beyond as much to the realm of pure practical reason. This is possible because pure reason and practical reason are both sites of exploration with different applications of reason, brought together under a unifying header: "the supreme principle of morality" (§392).

The supreme principle is Kant's Categorical Imperative: "Never act on any maxim except such as can also be a universal law and hence such as the will can thereby regard itself as at the same time the legislator of the universal law" (§434). With this guiding, human beings, who are invested with dignity and thus are not to be ever treated as means (or be labelled with a "price") but only as ends in and of themselves, will form an ideal society, establishing an ideal place: the Kingdom of Ends (§433–7).

Kant's version of reason is governed not by God or a metaphysical system per se but operates according to law. In the same way that Newton did not create the Law of Gravity but simply discovered it, so Kant has discovered the Categorical Imperative, discovered as being in accordance with not the Laws of Nature but the Laws of Freedom.[38] Thus, as autonomous, rational agents, humans must recognize the validity and necessity of the supreme moral principle.

Two important things are achieved in Kant's formulation of public reason. The first is the strong connection between reason and morality, and that public reason was an attempt to make *politics* rational according the precepts of morality. As Habermas puts it in his *Structural Transformation of the Public Sphere*, "The critical process that private people engaged in rational-critical debate brought to bear on absolutist rule, interpreted itself as unpolitical: public opinion aimed at rationalizing politics in the name of morality."[39] The task of politics, as the exercise of power to enact collectively binding (moral) law on a diverse citizenry with a pluralism of beliefs, is guided fundamentally by non-political processes – that is, processes unrelated to power. Reason and morality, like science and empirical facts, are neither responsible to nor assuaged by political power.

The second achievement of Kant's formulation is that public reason is something *constructed* by citizens for their own usage. Now, the constructivist element here is controversial, in the sense that how Kant constructs public reason is not synonymous with what many social scientists and humanities scholars mean by "social construction" (in that he made it up, and might have made up virtually anything he desired or could have gotten interlocutors to go along with). Rather, what is important is that he constructed public reason *based* on foundations that were not, in his view, social constructions (reason, truth, morality, etc.). How to interpret Kant or Kantian "inspired" constructivists is not part of the task here.[40]

The overarching point is to draw attention to the strict Enlightenment-modernist notions of public reason and suggest a tie back to not just Kant's melding of public reason and morality but also to the rhetorical tradition of antiquity. In James Murphy's words, when Poggi Bracciolini and other Renaissance humanists rediscovered a complete manuscript of Quintilian's *Institutio* after it had been lost for nearly six centuries, the era was afforded the ability to re-view "rhetoric as social system built around a respect for civic life."[41] This has been the main goal of this section: to draw the emphasis on reason in public discourse as part and parcel of vibrant social systems, having both a civil and political raison d'être.

That said, social systems have changed significantly since antiquity and Enlightenment modernity, and one of the ways they have changed is in the relationship between reason and epistemology in public discourse. The most relevant issue of this discussion to the organ procurement debate is that of informal epistemic grounds in public reasoning and moral disagreement.[42]

In other words, some epistemic common ground is necessary in public deliberation. When citizens argue in public about publicly relevant matters, there needs to be some combination of reason giving and reason-assessing that is shared to determine what counts as more relevant – and more importantly, as *better* – arguments than others. One way to get such common ground is a distinction between first- and second-order judgments as a means of settling disagreement in heterogeneous epistemic societies.[43]

The Right and The Good: First-Order and Second-Order Judgments

The relationship, and priority in the relationship, of the right and the good is at the core of modern social, political, and economic organization. This discussion requires clarification between an inclination and a judgment. An inclination is an immediate, almost gut-level response to a given stimuli. So, someone asks if you want to go to the mall, or what you think of the prime minister, there is typically an immediate response: "I want to go," or "I like him." If the conversation is to continue, or disagreement ensues between interlocutors, reasons are called for to justify the inclination, and many, many unproductive hours are spent arguing and rationalizing (in the derogatory sense of the term) in this way.[44] Let's call these first-order inclinations, distinguished from a first-order judgment.

First-order judgments, by contrast, are reflective endorsements and arrived at after sustained reasoning with one's emotions, intuitions, and contrary views. In matters of public reason, that first-order *inclinations* are given no priority is common ground. Few would advocate first-order inclinations as truth tracking and/or worthy of respect. That said, what scholars of the Rawlsian variety seem to indicate is that, to some degree, first-order judgments are not all that dissimilar to first-order inclinations. There are certain second-order judgments that set up a normative distinction between first-order judgments that make certain ones akin to inclinations. This level finds two metanormative views competing: one in which the prioritizing of first-order judgments over certain other moral principles (e.g., public reason) is always a mistake, and the other that first- and second-order judgments are always entwined.

The distinction between first- and second-order judgments is precisely the animating mechanism behind the liberal conception of public reason as most forcefully outlined by Rawls but shared by scholars of the "standard approach" to public reason. In brief, the distinction is between one's content-full, direct judgments of right and wrong and what is allowed to count as a justification in determining one's first-order judgments. Again, that both are necessary to a public reason is uncontroversial; a society must have some mechanism for adjudicating between competing first-order judgments. The matter turns, of course, on what the proper relationship is between the two, who decides, and how. The language of *the right* and *the good* is often in play here, in terms of one's vision of the good life and what rights one has to pursue and limit it.

The standard view of liberal public reason posits strongly the priority of the right over the good.[45] This is understandable, for in liberal-democratic societies the state is not in the business of determining *eudemonia* but rather allows individuals the inalienable right to life, liberty, and the pursuit of happiness, as the famous expression goes. The moral authority for this in the common era is not the endowment of as much from the Creator but rather a narrow political conception of fellow citizens as autonomous moral agents. The entailment of this is that citizens, in order to enjoy such political moral freedom themselves, must in turn grant as much to their political and literal neighbours under the ethos of reciprocity and the moral duty of respect for autonomous moral agents, all substantively free and equal under a well-ordered and principled constitution. This much is relatively uncontroversial in constitutional democracies, for living together in a socially heterogeneous yet collectively binding political environment requires commitment to what has been called the "duty of civility,"[46] "an ethics of citizenship,"[47] "civic virtue,"[48] and "constitutional patriotism"[49] and what I've called an "ethics of public reason."[50] Here it will be called the Civic Restraint Principle (CRP):

> *Civic Restraint Principle:* citizens being of free and equal standing before each other and the state entails mutual restraint on imposing their first-order judgments (too far) across a democratic society

That something like the CRP is necessary for heterogeneous liberal-democratic societies is relatively uncontroversial.

The controversial part is *where* in one's hierarchy of values, of moral duties as citizens, one is to place the Civic Restraint Principle (and how to interpret the *too far* parenthetical clause, though I won't say much more about that). It is that the CRP is the fundamental component of public reason – in that adherence to as much is what *makes* it public as opposed to non-public reason – that leads to the paradox of public reason: public reason is that which is to guide collective decision-making *on first-order judgments* and yet it is conceived as restricted from making substantive judgments precisely in this way.[51]

Citizens chafe at the idea, because, as Rawls puts, they ask, "Why should citizens in discussing and voting on the most fundamental political questions honor the limits of public reason?"[52] Following Rawls, Allan

Gibbard (whose views are discussed in the next chapter) calls something like the CRP an "accommodation norm" that communities of judgment rely on given disagreement, and that many of us readily recognize that this is really a "second-best virtue."[53]

The CRP is seen clearly in the case of abortion, in which there is fundamental disagreement over the moral status of the fetus. There is often no disagreement across the scientific facts – at what stage the fetus has fingernails, a heartbeat, hair, etc. – but rather over the ontological question of personhood, which is a question not settled strictly by scientific enquiry and hence prone to protracted and perhaps even intractable debate.

The strong pro-life citizen is asked by the standard view of liberal public reason to bracket her ontological convictions. The bracketing is meant for beliefs that are part of a more comprehensive doctrine, and a strictly political conception of justice is meant to be in-between, as a form of overlapping consensus among otherwise heterogeneous comprehensive doctrines.[54]

To neoliberal organ market advocates, citizens being free to sell their organs does not mandate that all must sell their organs – you are free to sell your organs or free to give them away – whereas, conversely, it is the altruism camp's moral theories of the good that are imposed on and across society (i.e., one can give them away only, no matter what your individual moral theory of the good is).

The standard view of public reason explicates a kind of constitutional patriotism and establishes, essentially, the primary second-order virtue for constitutional democracies. In this view, citizens reason together to decide binding politics, law, and policy. But it is the distinction between political commitments and comprehensive doctrines that is puzzling, as it assumes that citizens can stand outside their comprehensive doctrines and then make judgments.

There is really no such thing as a solely political, non-comprehensive doctrine conception, for it is necessary that some moral theory informs one's hierarchical rankings, including where to put the CRP.[55] Furthermore, the discrepancy between political conceptions and comprehensive doctrines places the question of truth as necessarily secondary to CRP. To be clear, the CRP is indeed both a virtue and a moral requirement for liberal democracies. The issue turns on what weight to give it.[56]

The question is not whether it is really fair to ask the strongly pro-life citizen to bracket her individual choice on the matter, nor whether the citizen actually will (she won't); the question is whether she should. The standard view is going to say, of course she should; but critics rightly question then what role truth can actually play in such a society. It will be taken as uncontroversial that no one wants to live in a society in which truth is irrelevant or unnecessary.[57] But there is this persistent problem of disagreement over what is true and the epistemic dimension of how we would know and/or convince others of it, and so public reason en route to a political conception of justice is designed to be functionally pragmatic, to solve such impasses of disagreement on truth.

In the standard view of public reason, the limiting comes from the CRP, which bars citizens from appealing to "the whole truth."[58] The notion is of public reason as mediating between inclinations, as discussed at the outset of this subsection, and the whole truth. If a society is composed on grounds of the former, a majority will rule as aggregation of inclinations and preferences, and if the latter, comprehensive doctrines crowd an overall ethos of citizenship and *communitas* in an otherwise morally pluralistic world. So, in the end, both views are "similar in that neither recognizes the duty of civility" – that is, the CRP: "The first view is guided by our preferences and interests, the second view by what we see as the whole truth."[59]

This should strike one as bizarre. As Dennis Thompson puts it, "Refraining from telling the whole truth – deliberately ignoring reasons that are relevant to reaching a well-grounded decision – seems more like a vice than a virtue. It is like swearing to tell the partial truth, and nothing but the partial truth."[60] Put differently, Habermas's critique of this view is that in eschewing reason and truth for reasonableness in the political liberal sense, the notion ends up being "too weak to characterize the mode of validity of an intersubjectively recognized conception of political justice, or it is defined in sufficiently strong terms, in which case what is practically reasonable is indistinguishable from what is morally right."[61]

Critics like Michael Sandel press the strangeness of the CRP dominating public life even further. He notes that the priority of the right over the good is *not* necessarily about having the matter backwards. As he puts it, "The question is not whether rights should be respected, but whether rights can be identified and justified in a way that does not presuppose any particular conception of the good."[62] The answer is an unqualified *no*. Continuing with the abortion example, by justifying the legalization of abortion not on first-order judgment grounds ("it is not a person") but on liberal public reason and CRP under an overarching ethos of citizenship, the United States does not have anything that looks like *neutrality* towards competing visions of the good life.

Prima facie, it *seems* as if the United States does have neutrality towards the good life: one is free to choose to have an abortion, and one is free to choose not to, and so, indeed, the state is neutral in terms of the substantive content of morality, in terms of first-order judgments. But that is not the case, for US society has strict laws against murder. The United States does not let someone kill another person without cause *no matter the informing comprehensive doctrine/competing vision of the good life.* Murder is not a non-public issue, and so the question of abortion is not a question of public or non-public justifications per se but rather sits squarely on the first-order judgment of personhood. Therefore, by making abortion legal in the United States, the state has tacitly endorsed the moral permissibility of the act. While to permit is not necessarily to endorse, the strictures of prohibition on murder indicate that the state has at least acknowledged that abortion is of a lesser degree of moral seriousness than murder. Sandel puts the matter straightforwardly: it is "not possible to decide [abortion] without taking a stand, implicitly or explicitly, on the moral status of the fetus ... Liberals would do better to engage their opponents on the moral merits, rather than retreat to an unconvincing neutral ground."[63]

What is particularly important about Habermas's and Sandel's critiques is not just their efficacy in showing the impossibility of untangling the good from the right in terms of the state and collectively binding law-making and decision-making in a deliberative democratic context, but also that *nearly everyone endorses limits* to the CRP. In Gibbard's words,

> We can ... explain norms of accommodation as norms of the second-best, as norms for coping with deep and perilous disagreement [... and then we ...] can then tell consistent stories locally and globally ... Still we can admit openly, on occasion, that these norms are not directly the ones that matter. We can admit that we appeal to them for want of a better alternative.[64]

Even those who subscribe to versions of the standard view of public reason recognize its limitations and the second-best element. But if one also recognizes that the practice of CRP in civic life is one that does not always reign supreme – that is, given that there are many collectively binding categorical pronouncements – then one runs into a problem even deeper than one of weighing and ordering one's value hierarchy. In other words, there is an even deeper problem here than the paradox of public reason, and that is the now familiar critiques of liberalism as an *impossible* enterprise, in which advocates and citizens simply use the language of public reason, equality, and the CRP and then "smuggle" in their preferences and convictions under these guises.[65]

A potential fix here is one offered by critics such as Sandel and articulated under the ethos of public reason by Habermas in which citizens provide each other with reasons, are epistemically demanding, and also self-reflexively engage so as to promote epistemic humility.[66] The purpose, in my view, is that public reason is necessary, and deliberative politics an ideal and practical activity when we are working together to find the truth. This is not, contra the standard view, distinct or antithetical to liberal democracy, but rather a liberal democracy predicated on life, liberty, and the pursuit of happiness *presupposes* as much. Selling women into sexual slavery, for example, is antithetical to liberal democracy, and morally wrong.

Public reason, then, is not solely a rights-based conception but rather an interplay between rights and goods. Recognition of this fact, however, does not alleviate disagreement nor conflicting justifications and how to adjudicate among them.

This section argued for the *need* of a public reason and the endorsement of the CRP, and, more substantively, that the CRP is not, nor should it be, the primary political or non-political principle in democratic societies. In short, then, the standard approach to public reason in liberal democracies and its attempted disarticulation of law and morality is found wanting. But even if one disagrees with the connections I've offered between public reason and the cooperative search for truth in liberal democracies and instead recognizes and values something like the CRP as the best that we can do, it should be recognized that the right and the good are deeply entwined.

In other words, the questions

Q1: Whether financial compensation for organs is morally permissible, and
Q2: Whether a society should allow it

are entangled more significantly than a standard view of public reason will allow. And the wedge between these two questions is further pushed in, and thus the space widened, by a neoliberal ethos.

Overrides

So if the CRP is not the deciding principle in matters of moral disagreement, then what is? It is here that the notion of overrides arises. The general form of overrides is straightforward: Situation S requires Action A according to Principle P, and Situation S requires Action B according to Principle R. Given this difference, which principle ought to override, which principle is *the* decider? The details and agents of the situation matter, and so the abstractness of this formula is slightly mistaken. But the idea is that something must win out in the end, and people typically have some sort of baseline conclusion for these types of situations: Well, in such cases I always go with my gut; we've got to go with what reason dictates; the best answer is the one closest to Biblical interpretation; and so forth.

The point is that when citizens face a moral dilemma, which is already challenging enough, they are typically further caught in a bind between their first-order and second-order judgments given, if not a public reason per se, at least the conception of themselves as citizens in a value-pluralistic society.[67] If we accept that the CRP must be in the value hierarchy of citizens but not at the very top, not as the override in matters of moral disagreement, what reasonable way can a society organize itself to be moral and adjudicate ethically?

One simple way to carve the matter is that citizens have two different *types* of duties, to be called *all-things-considered duties* and *pro tanto duties.*[68] To adapt an example from W.D. Ross,[69] imagine you have promised to meet a friend for lunch to catch up on each other's lives but on the way to the lunch you are able to prevent a serious accident from occurring. In this case, you had a *pro tanto duty* to keep your promise and meet your friend, but this is overridden by your *all-things-considered duty* to prevent an accident (should you be in relatively safe a position to do so). As Roderick Chisholm puts the matter, the ethics of requirement here shifts: "The new situation not only overrides a requirement but creates a new one ... and the new requirement is incompatible with the requirement that is overridden."[70] Overrides, then, are a significant part of moral life, individually and communally.

The connection of overrides to deliberative communicative political theories is made cleanly by philosophers such as Richard McKeon or rhetorical theorists such as Thomas Farrell, who, like certain deliberative democratic scholars, theorize a society in which citizens deliberate on norms that produce discursive judgment for their society.[71] What is seen in this picture is the notion of overrides as being not just individual but social; discursive judgment according to certain norms is correct or good precisely because those norms – collectively and firmly held – are right.[72]

This is a wonderful vision of democratic society and citizenship.[73] The problem is contestation *in the norms themselves.* With the organ debate, it is precisely the justifications, it is precisely the norms by which discursive judgment is made, that are in dispute. However one wants to think about the matter – in terms of first- and second-order judgments, the right and the good, *all-things-considered* duties and *pro tanto* duties – the issue is that what is collectively and socially held (and thereby socially and legally binding) is precisely what is in dispute in most matters of moral disagreement and particularly in the debate about organ procurement.

There are public norms and duties that ought not to be violated. This is not to say that democracy and public-sphere conceptualizations lack an adequate space for dissent or coercively push towards consensus. Rather, the point is that moral overrides in the contemporary era cut all the way down. What constitutes the top spot in one's hierarchy of values or what is considered an *all-things-considered* duty is nearly always contested, and contested precisely on grounds of pluralism and liberal democracy: that might be an overriding moral concern *for you*, but it is not an overriding concern *for me*. There is a very real sense in which this is incredibly valuable: free societies need safeguards of conscience and reason-demands in dissent from majority opinion and need the ability for rational citizens to decide their moral overrides.

More to the point, the freedom (and void?) atop the individual values hierarchy makes perfect sense in the contemporary era in a way that it most likely has not in previous eras. Moral overrides as chosen by individuals according to the dictates of their conscience mean something different today than they did in previous eras in which words like *conscience* and *moral* had more fixed and collectively recognized meanings. Given this fragmentation of meaning and moral sources, the contemporary era is best characterized as having undergone an economization of everyday life.

The *economization of everyday life* is a phrase for the neoliberal encroachment of a market rationality predicated on liberty into historically non-market (hence the use of *everyday*) arenas. The next section unpacks this phrase and briefly explores how US society got to this point in history, in an effort to shed more light on just how difficult and problematic moral disagreement is in contemporary liberal democracies in general and for organ procurement in particular.

At this juncture, however, let me make the connection between market rationality, neoliberalism, and the standard view of public reason via the key notion of *choice*. It is with choice, choice in market and moral matters, that one begins to see the ascendency of liberalism and eventually neoliberalism as perhaps the defining feature of the modern condition.

That is, the very notion of overrides, especially as overrides in accordance with one's conscience, is part and parcel of the modern condition. There have been shifts in conditions of being under modernity in which secularization and reason, particularly as a moral narrative, combine with the ascendency of global capitalism in the nineteenth and especially twentieth centuries. In such a view, one sees the logic of the market as taking hold of all domains of everyday life, in which an ever-expanding range of options are available to agents and less and less is proscribed, metaphysically and materially.

Many Western liberal-democratic societies are currently headed to being (if they haven't already become) governed and sustained by the principles of neoliberalism. This is not because neoliberalism has won the ideological war against civic republicanism or against more communal reasoned-deliberation views, as if citizens believe neoliberalism to be the better basic structure of society.

Rather, in absentia of commitments to reason giving, a substantive public morality, and the paradoxes of liberalism in the standard view of secular reason, contemporary democracies really seem to have (ironically!) no choice: they are neoliberal-by-default. In the next section I'll sketch how this happened from a critical-historical perspective.

The Modern Secular Condition

It is within the modern condition that the notion of choice in moral matters not only arises most prevalently but also is rendered intelligible (as the common-sense understanding; the *of course* of conversation) to contemporary peoples. What follows in the next several sections is a sketch of the economization of everyday life – the ever-expansion of means-ends market rationality and monetization into all domains of life and limited collective citizen engagement under the ethos of neoliberalism.[74] Georg Simmel noted how money mediates among (competing) value in an abstract way, and the neoliberal version of morality and monetization takes this notion to its full conclusion: that anything and everything that is valuable is hence monetizable.[75]

Rather than rehearse the now familiar arguments of modernity as an epochal shift in social ontology,[76] the primary element for study is this: that the modern condition is one in which nearly everyone across the globe is *aware* of the discontinuities of beliefs and practices between contemporary and historical societies. This conditions existence in such a way as to make all questions, at some level, always open questions. This means, following Charles Taylor, that there is a shift in the frameworks between antiquity/middle ages and modernity in that the former are "naïve" and the latter "reflective," because "the latter has opened a question which had been foreclosed by the former by the unacknowledged shape of the background."[77] Now the reflective framework is a victory in nearly every sense, and that is not because it eliminates false beliefs or gets rid of this destructive idea of God and universality or anything of the like. Rather, the reflective frame is one in which humans accepting everything (anything?) as given and unquestionable is disrupted.

This is a victory for scientific, philosophical, and theological enquiry. The idea, then, is that the modern condition is one in which humans become (or are conceived as) self-reflexive and full of doubt: *de omnibus dubitandum*. Those with the firmest beliefs *still have some element* of if not doubt than at least *choice* in their psychology: I chose *this* and not *that*. So with a background of doubt and uncertainty, humans speak of choices and options in a way that is unprecedented historically.[78] This is, in agreement with Kierkegaard, an unqualified good and a necessary precursor to true reflective judgment.[79]

Taylor summarily says,

> We live in a condition where we cannot help but be aware that there are a number of different construals, views which intelligent, reasonably undeluded people, of good will, can and do disagree on ... It is this index of doubt, which induces people to speak of "theories" here. Because theories are often hypotheses, held in ultimate uncertainty, pending further evidence. I hope I have said something to show that we can't understand them as mere theories, that there is a way in which our whole experience is inflected if we live in one or another spirituality. But all the same we are aware today that one can live the spiritual life differently; that power, fullness, exile, etc. can take different shapes.[80]

Even though no one *lives* out their beliefs as mere theories held in ultimate uncertainty –or, as Taylor put it in an earlier work, "It is a form of self-delusion to think that we do not speak from a moral orientation which we take to be right. This is a condition of being a functioning self, not a metaphysical view we can put on or off"[81] – there *is* a backdrop of this awareness, and it is manifested most acutely, as seen throughout this chapter and our discussions so far, in moral disagreement among both social and epistemic peers in publics. The awareness of moral orderings, for self and society, as being frameworks and hierarchies that, or from which, one is free to choose, creates possibilities of invention and is always conditioned thus by doubt: that one perhaps has chosen wrongly. This idea of a self who chooses, then, is what enables and constrains the conditions for moral disagreement in contemporary liberal democracies such as the United States. This notion of self needs further articulation.

The Distanced Self and Rhetoric of "The Narrative of Moral Conscience"

Central to the idea of moral disagreement under the modern condition is the conception of a self who chooses to believe in something. The notion is that facts, ends, and theories are *out there*, and the autonomous self chooses among them. One term for this is the *unencumbered self*, which is Rawls's notion of an individual as a constitution of heterogeneous ends (i.e., not a single end *à la eudemonia*) who is free to and does hold a commitment to a comprehensive doctrine (specific moral conception and world views) and a political conception of justice. The view of an autonomous self that forms via voluntary associations and chosen ends and commitments is, indeed, a liberating conception.[82] It is also entirely a modern conception. As a critique of this view, Michael Sandel has offered his conception of the *encumbered self*, which he believes is the necessary civic republican replacement of the liberal self if we are to have thriving democratic societies.[83]

The key difference between the two might be categorized as one of *distance*, as the Rawlsian view imagines a self distanced from all specificity (as it is tied sharply with the Original Position) and the Sandelian view invites us to imagine ourselves born with social and civic responsibility. For simplicity's sake, this conception will be called the *distanced self*, because both views presuppose a self able to choose and imagine itself in certain ways, that we have a *choice* to conceive of ourselves as unencumbered or encumbered, and we have this choice because we have "confidence in our own powers of moral ordering."[84]

This, and nothing more, is what I mean to convey in this section: regardless of whether one is actually *right or better*, the modern condition is one in which we humans *conceive* of ourselves as autonomous, sovereign, and distanced.

The notion of the distanced self is thoroughly secular and modern. It gives a "sense of power [due to its connection with reason and science], of capacity, in being able to order our world and ourselves ... [and also a] sense of invulnerability."[85] The contrast here is to premodern modes of being in which a host of agents and powers within this world and beyond inspired a sense of fear, ignorance, and smallness. Why this matters is that the distanced self is one that is capable, through powers of reason and science, of legislating politically and morally. It has the freedom and power to make and use language that has ontic commitments to God, or civic humanism, or nearly anything else, or – and this is perhaps the most important and unique – the commitments can remain, generally, unidentified.[86]

The problem of the interplay between the distanced self legislating politically and morally under modern conditions is that the process ends up being paradoxical, as gestured to above in discussion of public reason: if each agent is autonomous and able to legislate for himself morally, then politically we need a way to manage and balance these competing notions within a stable and just society.

The narrative so far, then, is how the secular modern condition and the notion of the distanced self creates the need for a liberal conception of public reason that enables and constrains action. But the liberal conception of public reason collapses under its own weight in the face of rational disagreement among epistemic peers. "Didn't you know?" jokes Dmitri Karamazov, "Everything is permitted to the intelligent man."[87]

The overarching point here is that the notion of overrides *makes sense* to contemporary peoples given these epochal shifts resulting in the modern condition and the distanced self. This how we get to a stage where citizens say, "Of course you are free to pursue your own pleasures" or "I'd never tell others how to live their lives," or more colloquially and most succinctly, "You do you, and I'll do me."

In this view, all of morality reduces to choice and volunteerism and, most importantly, conscience: the notion of something within oneself dictating right and wrong and other moral evaluations. The very notion of one's conscience being one's guide is itself part and parcel of the modern secular condition; the rhetoric of "the narrative of moral conscience"[88] is perhaps *the* definitional attribute of modern morality. The notion of moral conscience is central to premodern and religious traditions as well, but what makes it particularly modern is that different speakers understand the term differently and yet there is *something* that remains consistent and categorical about conscience (and not just in the "to each his own" sense). To religious people this narrative conscience is explained as God reaching out to the distanced self, as he does to Adam in Michelangelo's fresco, and to nonreligious it is explained as nostalgia and as an eventually shakeable trace from the past.

Despite this, from Aristotelian notions of cultivating virtue to religious moral traditions *à la* Christianity, to contemporary reason-grounded nonreligious programs or sentimentalist grounded programs, the notion that the conscience is, and needs to be, shaped according to certain true dictates runs deep. Nobody knows this better, to keep with the Dostoevsky leitmotif, than the Devil.[89]

A person's conscience will sufficiently guide and/or correct someone *if* they have a rightly formed conscience.[90] But *what* a correctly formed conscience *is* is precisely what the modern condition, the distanced self, and the liberal conception refuse to fully articulate for anyone else.[91]

This way of thinking underwrites conditions of being under modernity. It is perhaps most literally presented in contemporary global capitalism. The next section shows, briefly, how global capitalism and the market economy is part and parcel of the modern condition.

The Economization of Everyday Life: The Logic of the Market

The ethics of classical political economy focuses, in one sense, on individual happiness through improved social distributions and accumulations of utilities. The simplified story of capitalism harnessing choice and self-interest to collective benefit has roots in Bernard Mandeville's *The Fable of Bees* and reaches its fullest articulation in Smith's *Wealth of*

Nations.[92] But of course the story is, at some level, oversimplified in that the classical political economists had a strong concern for virtue and figured their theories against a backdrop of the classical virtues. And Deirdre McCloskey, a contemporary defender, not only articulates the interplay of a virtue-informed background in which neoclassical economics works but also extols the virtues that capitalistic markets and societies actually create and cultivate in a multi-thousand-page magnum opus.[93]

Critical-negative versions of the history of economic liberalism as entwining with liberal conceptions of freedom as born under Enlightenment mores and philosophies are found under a guiding heading of neoliberalism.[94] The morally autonomous individual, free from state and church pressures, can conduct and legislate for herself and enter into whatever contracts and negotiations she sees fit, and this (as *shown* in philosophy, they say) is *a* guiding *ethos* for law formation in the nineteenth century, and is *the* foundation for political economic policy across the developed world under global capitalism from the 1970s forward. This has led to self-interest run amok, in which wealth and power are concentrated into fewer and fewer hands under the neoliberal refrains of individual freedom and market outcomes.[95] The deeper pull accounts for the resonance of market rationality as underwriting law and governmental arts in general. It has roots in Foucault's tracing of neoliberalism in Chicago School political economy, in which market rationalization and ordering is used to understand and order non-market relationships and practices,[96] and is evidenced in significant policies and legislation in the United States and other Western nations since the 1980s.

But virtues and vices discussion aside, at this point the purpose is simply descriptive, and *both* stories, the positive and negative versions of capitalism, underscore the overarching modern condition: a distanced self as a moral-ordering creature combines with market mechanisms to reject philosophical-theological monism and economic monopoly at the same time. But again, that is just a descriptive backdrop, as the thousands and thousands of capitalists and anti-capitalists across the globe both attest, as do the atheists and religious alike, as do the deontologists and utilitarians. That is, the modern condition affirms choice – even at the level of being able to *deny* it, in the sense that one is choosing to believe from among alternatives such as free will and determinism whether God exists or not, and so forth.[97]

The point is that the description of choice *always and already affirms* the logic of the market. It is in this sense that the modern condition as the distanced self and freedom of choice with the underlying logic of autonomy, preference, and uncertainty fuses into an economization of everyday life.

To continue with the abortion example from above, citizens *are free to choose* a deontological prohibition against borderline cases or to choose according to the dictates of their own conscience whether or not the fetus is indeed a child and/or whether society has any say in the matter at all. In other words, abortion policy is not based on a monistic moral conception. Rather, the state's position encapsulates a pluralism of values *including* those positions that categorically prohibit abortion. This is the logic of the market par excellence. But with this example, unlike with our market challengers for organ sales, it is the anti-abortion advocates who call for rational consistency, claiming that countries where abortions are legal and murder is wrong are not logic-of-the-market all the way down, so to speak.

So, with organs, market advocates follow market logic under the ethos of the economization of everyday life, and altruistic advocates defend on grounds of market encroachment into the sacred or dignified and the whole host of other discursive practices from chapter 3. That is, with organs, the prohibition on moral grounds doesn't fit well with the economization of everyday life because the point is that it is not immoral *to me*, and *you* don't get to dictate morality, and after all aren't you the people who distilled everything down to subjective conscience and autonomy anyway? This is, in essence, the liberal-democratic dilemma.

The liberal-democratic dilemma is that any attempt to resolve the dilemma results in one side winning, and – most important – other sides' visions of the good life being excluded. McCloskey puts the matter clearly:

> Any monism denies the dilemmas. Thus economics of the Max U variety says: Come now, no dilemma; just do what maximizes utility. Or an evolutionary psychology of the we-brain-scientists-have-it-all-worked-out variety says: Face up to it, there's no dilemma; just do what your genes are telling you to do. Or a revealed theology of the we-already-know-God's-will variety says: Bless you, no dilemma; just do what God so evidently wishes. Or a natural theology of the early Enlightenment variety: Be calm, no dilemma; just be assured that all is for the best in the best of all possible worlds. Or the reason-loving-side-of-the-late-Enlightenment-project variety: Seriously, no dilemma; just follow the rule of reason, such as the categorical imperative.[98]

McCloskey is speaking here of any dilemma one faces, in the sense of something needing to, or necessarily, overriding and hence deciding.

Borrowing McCloskey's tone and applying the overcoming of the liberal dilemma to modern society, advocates of the standard view of public reason might harken to the CRP: "Dear citizens, you have your vision and I have my vision of the good life, and that's just the way that it is; there is no dilemma here, because you don't want me interfering with yours, so don't

interfere with mine, and so, to each his own – you do you, and I'll do me."
So the liberal dilemma is slightly different from those listed above, insofar
as it precisely embraces all of the views – the natural theological, the cognitive psychologist, the enlightenment reasoned – under one big banner.

Or so the argument goes. The problem is that, of course, it doesn't
actually do anything of the sort – that is, unless one is content to follow
through with it to its logical conclusion, as those economic liberals and
rationalists say must be the case. In this view, then, contemporary society
is, and can only *really*, *truly* be the management of pluralistic visions of
the good life, and hence it is libertarian-by-default. Following H. Tristram
Engelhardt, Jr., and Kevin Wm. Wildes, who discuss the matter explicitly
in bioethical terms, this recognizable as the Libertarianism-By-Default
Argument.[99] It runs thusly: In the absence of a universally recognized
morality (be it rational, divine, or simply agreed on), the fragmentation
of moral conceptions and reasoning leaves only the autonomy of moral
agents as the universally *recognized* source of moral authority. "If one cannot discover an authoritative moral vision to ground moral judgments,
then one must appeal to persons as the sources of moral authority."[100]

So in matters of medicine – just as in matters of social policy, law,
education, art, and anything else that isn't strictly empirically verifiable
or universally acknowledged – the governing body, and in this case the
state in particular, has *no choice but to be libertarian*. It is for want of a better
alternative that a society ends up here.

The power of this argument, filled in with critical-historical weight
throughout these last two chapters, should be felt by nearly all contemporary people: *choice, uncertainty, and moral autonomy mark the tenor of this age
in a way that they haven't marked any other in history.* Under such conditions
of modernity, the way in which sociopolitical problems, especially law
and medicine, must be managed, seems to be as libertarian-by-default.
We all value either different things or similar things differently, with the
sole exception being money. Combine that view with the economization
of everyday life, understood as the pervasiveness and agreement of capitalist and market systems, and we end up with a society in which neoliberalism has grafted its way onto all discursive value engagements. After all,
as many of these types of advocates claim, rationality *requires* as much or,
in more explicitly moral terms, *respect* requires as much. The recognition
of moral autonomy requires the normative principle of moral respect.[101]
And that means autonomy is the only thing that matters: autonomy in
the establishment of values – individual and social values. For ethically
pluralistic liberal-democratic societies, we are neoliberal-by-default: and
that is the end of the story.

Categoricity and the Challenge of Justice in Neoliberalism

And yet, at the same time, that is not the end of the story. If autonomy is the only salient moral category for sociopolitical life, in which all value is rendered intelligible in, through, and as market value, we end up with, it seems, the Neoliberal-by-Default Society. An important principle underscores the neoliberal ethos outlined thus far: "To permit is not to endorse."[102] But as discussed above, this is not actually true – or at least not in some cases, with abortion being the most prevalent.[103]

That is, in echoes of the Categorical Grip, discussed in the firing-range example in the introduction to this book, sociopolitical-legal life without *some* moral categorical content is impossible. Regardless of one's stance on abortion, the Categorical Grip is evidenced simply in the categorical ban on murder. Again, US society has no problem allowing for a categorical ban on unnecessary and unwarranted killing of another human life. That is, society is not, at least not at this point in history, content to be morally permissible: that is, neoliberal, all the way down.

And furthermore, this shows that the fragmentation of moral sources being truly incommensurable or nonoverlapping is, at least in one basic way, exaggerated: there is some underlying moral principle of human dignity at work here (with simply differences on what is and isn't a violation of it).[104] And as mentioned in introduction, there is agreement between all advocates in the debate on the General Moral Argument: that, all things being equal, human lives must be saved.

The liberal-democratic state tries to sketch parameters of acceptable behaviour by marking out relatively clear lines of right and wrong actions. Under the modern condition citizens still feel the grip of the categorical, but the economization of everyday life fights against moral categoricity as such. Neoliberalism pushes against categorical pressures and any categorical articulation from the state. Citizens feel, at least so far, that some things shouldn't be for sale, even though rational consistency in a strict sense according to the logic of the economization of everyday life demands as much.

So this, then, is its own dilemma: we have, and seem to want, a monistic response to universal problems, and at the same time we have, and seem to want, values pluralism in the principles of liberal democracy or a constitutional regime. A society must resolve moral questions, and if there *are* right answers, that is by definition *exclusive* of many (wrong) views. There is more on this point in the coming chapter, but for now the issue is flagged and the phenomena and its associated concepts and mentality in its current and historical background are documented: *a principled liberal-democratic society cannot help but violate its foundational norms – or it must be content to be neoliberal all the way.*

Chapter Conclusion: Neoliberalism, Democracy, Moral Normativity

In conclusion to this large chapter, the collapse of a shared backdrop of moral discourse, the ensuing fragmentation of morality, and the increasing economization of everyday life under liberal democracy and global capitalism make persuasive and resonant rhetoric of the normative justification of a market mechanism for moral matters. Under such conditions, one can see why a market mechanism is also desirable for adjudication, given the difficulty of moral coherence under pluralistic constitutional democracies with strong rights-based interpretative paradigms. But that a market mechanism makes more sense or is easier than alternatives does not, necessarily, make it right. One can see the ascendency of moral choice and market choice under the modern condition as being of a similar underlying logic, and one tied deeply to modernity and capitalism writ large. But modernity, and capitalism for that matter, still hold *some* things as universally binding, as absolute duties. Without as much, *without some categoricity*, society as such can hardly even exist, let alone thrive. To give up on the categorical is, in some sense, to give up on the idea of a just society altogether.

The horrors of connecting moral categoricity with flawed human institutions is well documented in history, and nearly everyone, at some point or another in their life, is a victim of bureaucratic oversight and incapacitated judgment. This is troubling for, and ought to be unacceptable to, individuals and societies. Notions of moral categoricity that invoke policies over people, abstract rules applied uniformly without understanding of context, metrics that confuse non-discriminatory with indiscriminate, ironic disproportionalities between the seriousness of a question and the (lack of) seriousness of the ensuing enquiry, and people refusing to engage in the complexity of moral normativity are indeed mistaken. The contemporary scepticism towards institutions, especially among young people, is well understood.[105]

When taken together, then, high degrees of individual rights combined with institutional scepticism – when understood against the deep philosophical problems of collectively binding moral judgments in ethically pluralistic democratic societies as outlined in this chapter, against the modern secular capitalistic order – demand neoliberalism-by-default. A civic republican pushback, or something like it, would remain elusive.

But this retreat to individuality and moral subjectivity, if not moral relativity, under the dominating ethos of neoliberal global capitalism is hardly a satisfactory alternative. The dilemma, then, is between the economization of everyday life and established, inarguable moral boundaries – or, in other terms, between means-ends rationality and moral categoricity.

The question seems to be whether, given conditions of being in the current era, moral conflict is (or is becoming) necessarily incommensurable.[106] If so, then a market model and neoliberalism-by-default processes resonates, normatively and practically, for liberal-democratic societies. But to assume incommensurability as inevitable is also to make a deeper and more problematic assumption: that there is no way to convince others of right answers, or, even more profoundly, that there are not right answers to moral questions in the first place. That I believe such an assumption is mistaken (as I'll argue in the next two chapters), however, should have no bearing on the overarching argument of morality, community, and medicine in this book, nor on this account of how we got here, and why the logics of neoliberalism and the privatization of morality have strong rhetorical resonance contemporary era.

6 Good Reasons: Metanormativity and Categoricity

In the previous chapter, it was suggested that the policy question – whether organ sales should be legally permitted – is necessarily entwined with the question of the morality of organ sales, despite the moral pluralism of constitutional democracies. One of the worries about moral discourse and democratic practice is that morality is too monistic to be responsive to the pluralistic values of a society. Liberal democracies are often premised on a separation of morality and law. The content of the Good Life (often invoked by the phrase "the pursuit of happiness" in the United States) is up to each individual. Since every articulation of a moral statement or view has the potential to run afoul of *someone's* morality, and the state, supposedly, is not in the business of deciding morality for others, reason does not seem to have much to do with moral judgments in a collective setting. Rather, reasons to judge and act morally appear to be, at best, rationalizations of subjective preferences or, at worst, coercive and dominating to minority views and dissenters. Given the shifts on social ontology and the economization of everyday life discussed in chapter 5, autonomy, thus, reigns supreme. And it is thus no surprise that we've seen the triumph of autonomy in health care and bioethics.[1]

Morality, in such a picture, is a private and subjective affair, making democracy, and in particular voting, an exercise in the aggregation of individual preferences. Substantive agreement and overlap on morality is largely by coincidence. Such a society will become more and more libertarian-by-default, especially as differing moral statements and views are held to be incommensurable. A neoliberal ethos, then, splits moral and legal/policy concerns apart.

The two questions

Q1: Whether or not selling one's organ is moral, and
Q2: Whether or not a society should allow it

have different connections in altruistic and market camps. Civic republicans essentially say that Q2 depends on Q1, whereas neoliberals argue that Q1 is, or ought to be, significantly disarticulated from Q2.

The dilemma, then, is between the economization of everyday life and categorical moral lines. If, given conditions of being in the current era as outlined in the previous chapter, moral conflict is, or will soon become, necessarily incommensurable, then a market model and individual choice, neoliberal-by-default makes the most sense. But to assume incommensurability as inevitable is also to make a substantive assumption: that there is no way to convince others of right answers, or that there are not right answers to moral questions in the first place. In this chapter, I argue that these views are mistaken.

If the fundamental ethical question of this book is whether or not financial payment for human organs is morally permissible (accompanied by the then-related question of legal status), and the fundamental communicative-deliberative question is what to do about existing ethical disagreement on that question in a constitutional democracy, this chapter is concerned with the prior metanormative question of whether or not there are right answers to ethical questions.[2] It is an enquiry into the presuppositions of discursive ethical engagement.

While it would be easy to get off-field and fast – and perhaps you might think I've already done so[3] – the purpose of the rest of this section of the book is to defend that there are right answers to ethical questions, thereby raising the *stakes* and the *expectations* for deliberative engagement in the public sphere on questions such as organ procurement. If it really is just up to each individual to decide whatever he or she wants to do morally – if morality really is reducible to autonomy, as neoliberal rhetoric suggests – it seems nearly impossible to have any *legal* prohibitions at all while maintaining any semblance of rational consistency. That is, either epistemic justifications and reasons for action are, ultimately, subjective and personal, and therefore legal rational consistency under conditions of ethical pluralism is impossible at best and a sham at worst; or there really are reasons that are better than others, and we have an obligation to deliberate and select them and build our society with them. To put it bluntly, either all reasons are at some level equal (or illusions) or they aren't, and if the former, we must be a neoliberal society, and if the latter, we shouldn't. So are there right answers to ethical questions?

To answer that question, we've got to take a deep dive into the nature of moral deliberation and reason giving. The angle, to be clear, is this: that what counts as a good reason or not forms the linchpin to either a defence of civic republicanism or the (theoretical in conjunction with rising practical) victory of neoliberalism.

In one sense, we are, indeed, losing the thread of bioethics, medicine, and organ sales. But in another sense, we need to do so in order to not be stuck with the impasse we ended with in the previous two chapters. If we are, theoretically, stuck with such an impasse, then only two things could follow: either the book ends with chapter 5 or all the arguments in section IV would be exercises in persuasion reducible to power. I'll try to avoid the consequent from obtaining by denying the antecedent, and that means, arguing that we are not – at least philosophically – at an impasse of incommensurability. So here goes.

The Overarching Argument

Generally, moral deliberation is understood to involve two major elements: (a) ridding reasoners of mistaken beliefs held due to an inadequate knowledge or understanding of the relevant facts and reasons, and (b) reconciling different ways of *weighing* reasons. This chapter is concerned with (a) and the next chapter, chapter 7, is concerned with (b).

In terms of (a), recognizing relevant reasons and facts that bear on moral deliberation, three arguments are presented in this chapter: (1) the Aims Argument, (2) the Categorical Argument, and (3) the Argument from Normative Force. In terms of (b), arguers know the relevant facts and reasons, but weigh them differently, and this different weighing results in competing moral judgments. Previewing the next chapter, there are three elements to weighing reasons: (1) telic orientation, (2) rhetorical force, and (3) the interplay of rhetorical force and normative force. A telic orientation is the *end* towards which one aims, the backdrop that one reasons against that allows better or worse reasons to take shape. The second element in weighing reasons is rhetorical force. Rhetorical force is what *moves* an agent to assent to a claim or agree with a moral theory. An argument with rhetorical force is highly persuasive, and might even change someone's moral beliefs and motivate him to act according to the content of that moral belief. Normative force exhibits strong rhetorical force if an agent responds correctly to the relevant information in the moral deliberation. What has normative force will have rhetorical force on the idea that people are moved by normativity – in particular, that a community is full of people who aim for a just society. Schematically, those are the essential features of the next two chapters.

In the current chapter, I will offer the idea of *good reasons* as the aimed outcome of public moral deliberation. I will defend moral discourse as an enterprise of reasoned judgment in a cognitive, realist sense. *Reasoned judgment* implies that the reasons given to support moral arguments are not all equal; some reasons and moral views, upon normative reflection and empirical testing, are better than others. *Cognitivists* hold that moral judgments are beliefs, not mere preferences. Beliefs are true or false, and so moral beliefs are more or less accurate at hitting what is true in the same way as, say, biological beliefs. *Realists* hold that at least some normative beliefs are indeed true; thus, humans are not seeking normative truths in vain. What a cognitive moral realism means is that morality is not an individualist affair and that not all moral theories are equal or true. There is, then, an important move of separating out the fact of pluralism – that different individuals and societies often have different moral beliefs – from pluralism as a moral theory, which is false. Good reasons are not just the reasons that I happen to have or the reasons that support my favoured outcome. Reasons become good reasons in relation to right ends. The process of weighing reasons in moral deliberations and determining which reasons have weight necessitates a collective process of rhetorical engagement.[4] That, in essence, is the overarching argument of the chapter.

Good Reasons

The primary theoretical launching point for the moral enquiry and philosophical work of this section of the book is practical reason and rhetorical theory. Put simply, the search in moral deliberation is for good reasons. What does it mean to call something a *good reason*, to say that we have *good reason* to act or to judge something in a certain way? The literature on *reasons* – what a reason is and whether it is properly basic and primitive or reducible to something else (such as desires) – is complicated and vast.[5] In much practical argument, or in the analysis of an argument, rather than focusing on whether someone's case is really, truly possessed of a reason or rationality, we implicitly accept that the statement on offer *is* a reason and then move straightaway to the assessment of whether or not it is a *good* reason.[6] But this does not seem quite clear enough. The *what counts as a reason* discussion and the *whether this is a good reason or not* assessment are not easily separated. Here we will try to clarify the relationship between the usage and conceptualization of *good reason* with insights from metaethically focused moral philosophy. The overarching search in deliberative contexts is for the reasons that matter most – what might be captured in the rhetorical terms of *dignitas* and *gravitas*, denoting the search for the weightiest, most important reasons and what the better decision is among alternatives.[7] Furthermore, determining and deciding *which reasons matter* or which are the *good* reasons is not an individual or private affair, and I take that premise to be an essentially *rhetorical* component to what otherwise could seem like a straight-ahead moral-philosophical task.

The working argument on offer is: a good reason is one that fulfils a desired end; that desired ends are understood, implicitly or explicitly, within broader narratives; and that there is a meaningful, substantive way to distinguish which are better narratives than others, supported via enquiry and analysis of right ends in moral philosophy and metaethical theory. In seeking to clarify the instantiated public moral debate about organ sales, we might also, in this chapter and the rest of the book, move towards a more robust theory of good reasons and better understand morally normative disagreement more generally.

The overarching picture of good reasons is of an Aristotelian knotting of ethics, rhetoric, democracy, and political public life.[8] In this view, ethics, community, and facts, bear on human judgments – meaning that the search for, and persuasive engagement task of, the weightiest reasons is not a private affair. While the exactness and precision of a true/false judgment is essentially impossible in moral normativity, this does not mean, as will be discussed below, that there are not right answers. That one cannot claim morally normative arguments with the same degree of precision that one can in statements such as, for example, that a triangle's interior angles all add up to 180 degrees, every time, invokes not a *failure* of rationality but simply that we are in the territory of practical reason in the Aristotelian tradition: constitutive deliberative situations where *episteme* (knowledge) is variable and often unattainable but sliding all the way down to simply *doxa* (mere opinion) is not necessary. It is the middle ground, in which deliberators enact *krisis* (judgment) based on *pisteis*, with the connotations of faith in, trust in, and conviction that, and then act accordingly.[9] Judgment stems from practical reason, the realm of reasonableness as opposed to Reason, or what Chaim Perelman calls the *realm of rhetoric.*[10] In short, I am utilizing *rhetoric* as what Bryan Garsten calls a means to alleviate and supplant the "crisis of confidence about the human capacity to use judgment."[11] In general, the strand being followed here is the art of rhetoric in the contemporary, with its roots in the Greek Socratic context in which rhetoric itself is understood as a normative practice aiming at a moral target.

Practical reason, rhetoric, and judgment connect with the pursuit of truth. This is also consistent with the Socratic/Aristotelian tradition following William Grimaldi, who concludes that "rhetoric is useful since it is through the instrumentality of the art that truth and justice are able to realize themselves in the decisions of" humans.[12] This is a particularly important insight in that it gets to both the *practicality* of the rhetorical tradition as well as the instrumentality of it *towards truth and justice.*[13]

Stephen Toulmin's philosophical work offers important conceptual lineage of *good reasons* as well. His key insight is to conceptualize *fields* of argument and distinguish between what is field invariant and what is field dependent in matters of validity, evidence, and justification. Toulmin's *The Uses of Argument* suggests that which is field invariant is the structure by which one argues: via his famous model of claim, grounds, warrants, backing, rebuttals, and so forth. The validity of the specific content of those things (what counts as evidence, what is a plausible inference, etc.) is field dependent. That is to say, many arguers, in some form or other, utilize the Toulmin model, but the standards of classifying and the evaluation of the content of the arguments will vary for "scientists, moralists, art critics, theologians."[14] Part of the goal of his project is to provide a way of using reason in a semi-standardized way (so as to not fall into an *anything goes* ethos) but without the narrow and rigid structural constraints of formal logic, as well as to map a reintegration, if not a full conflation, between logic and epistemology.[15]

In the vein of Toulmin and the historical rhetorical tradition, there is a school of thought (some of it drawing directly on Chaim Perelman and Lucie Olbrechts-Tyteca, as well as Toulmin) that I will call the Good Reasons School. The approach includes figures such as Richard McKeon, Richard Weaver, Wayne Booth, and Walter Fisher, with the term initiated by Karl Wallace.[16] Though there are differences in their thoughts, all of these scholars are particularly concerned with the relationship between fact and value and between ethics and practice, and that is what motivated them to attempt theories that combined morality and reason.[17]

That is to say, the Good Reasons School shares the motivation of rejecting the (positivist) view that there are not right answers to moral questions because of the non-scientific structure of ethical and normative proofs; in short, it is a defence of practical reason and the non-subjective analytical usage of *good reason*. As Wayne Booth puts it, we have "rediscovered what never should have been forgotten: that some values are in fact better-grounded than others, and that disputes about them can yield results that ought to be accepted by all parties to the dispute, even though they cannot be called certain or positive."[18] This middle ground between deductive reasoning and personal preference is the ground of good reasons.

But *good reason* itself is a normative concept. That is, what makes something a *good reason* is contested and contestable. Karl Wallace particularly connects rhetoric, good reasons, and ethics together. For Wallace, the *very substance of rhetoric is good reasons*. That is, rhetoric is not merely about ornamental choices but must deal with the substance of words and discourse: the way in which words are used to make assertions and statements that are essentially value judgments. This means "the materials of rhetorical discourse are fundamentally the same as the materials of ethics."[19]

More specifically, Wallace considers a *good reason* to be a "technical label that refers to all the materials of argument and explanation,"[20] and even defines a good reason as "a statement offered in support of an ought proposition or a value judgment. Good reasons are a number of statements in support of an ought proposition or a value judgment."[21] Good reasons, not formal logical poofs, are the reasons that support value judgments.

This is all well and good. But this conceptualization of *good reasons* has trouble accounting for the deliberative assessment side of reasons once they are offered in ethical controversies – the kind where the question is precisely about what *is* ethical or morally appropriate. In other words, what happens *once* reasons are given in support of a value judgment, and the reasons conflict? For example:

Arguer 1: A reason to vote for Smith is that she will legalize human organ sales.
Arguer 2: A reason *not* to vote for Smith is that she will legalize human organ sales.

It is obvious that we both *have a reason* to vote for Smith and *have a reason not* to vote for Smith if we flatten out the normativity of reason. Following Good Reasons School thinking, flattening out the normativity of reason is mistaken. That is, in the case of the above examples, it is easy enough to make the *reason for* construction intelligible by making it dependent on the subject's goals, desires, social standing, and the like. So, if you find yourself wanting to legalize organ sales, then *you* might have reason to vote for Smith, and if you don't want an organ market, it is easy enough to reject that reason. But the issue we are working towards here is, out of the two, which is the *better reason*, which is the *weightier* reason? If we elide the discussion on the nature of reasons (i.e., we don't want to say only one of the two is a *real* reason), we still might want to say that one of those is indeed a reason, but not a *good* reason. But wouldn't the answer to which one is a *better reason* depend on what our subjective preferences and goals are? In the next section, I shall suggest that it does not.

Arguing with and about Good Reasons

A way to get around the subjectivity of good reasons – that's a good reason for you but not for me – is to place the reasons and reasoning into a broader narrative. So now we can return to the question of whether we have good reasons to vote for Smith or not by placing the reasons into a broader narrative. The core idea here is that a narrative focuses our attention on *ends* and offloads discussion of what matters and why, what makes for a better reason and why, based on the assessment of the *reason for* construction *within* a narrative about aims and ends. The reasons then serve in support of achieving some desired end; they count in favour or against the end implicit or explicit in the narrative. If it is implicit, there is often miscommunication or arguers talking past each other. Making the end explicit helps clarify that the disagreement is rarely in the reason itself but rather in the *end* that the reason supports (or does not support).

One significant feature of this book is to make more explicit the broader narratives of the opposing rhetorics in human organ procurement debate. Humans reason in order to *choose* among competing narratives. This is not to say that all stories are equal but that, in keeping with the good-reasons tradition, "some stories are better than others, more coherent, more 'true' to the way people and the world are – in fact and in value."[22]

Just like a *good* reason, the idea of a *better* story makes intuitive sense. But also, like a *good* reason, *better* is a contested term – better than what, better in what way? On what grounds? One can, usually, only assent to the proposition that A is better than B if one is given a reason, or at least an articulation, as to why. That we do tell stories and have a logic of good reasons embedded within our narratives might be descriptive; but in much scholarly theory, what capacity is there for *choosing* which narratives make sense, ring true, etc.; in other words, what makes something *better*? Why is it better to prefer reducing income inequality than preferring to keep more of one's earnings? Why is it better to favour neoliberal policies over civic republican ones? To be clear, the answer to that question is indeed a multidisciplinary task (political economy, political philosophy, etc), but what I am after here is how to make sense of *better* in that construction, not to decide (at least not yet) *which* one *is* better. In other words, a more robust account of *better reason* is needed, and more specifically, one that does not as easily run the risk of being conflated with agent-centred ends or moral subjectivism.

In one sense, accounting for a good reason is just accounting for the domain of practical reason or the realm of rhetoric writ large. In Wayne Booth's words, "A thoroughly articulated, seemingly impregnable system of dogmas has sliced the world into two unequal parts, the tiny domain of the provable, about which nobody cares very much, and the great domain of 'all the rest,' in which anyone can believe or do what he pleases."[23] The Great Domain of the All the Rest is the realm of practical reason, underscored by the rhetorical tradition, resting on the substance of good reasons.[24]

Consider a sceptical reply: a good reason, like any other moral specification, just means *good-for-you* or *good-in-your-narrative*. Depending on what one means, exactly, by narrative, there might be no resistance to this position.[25] Notice also how the good-for-you, good-in-your-narrative position serves well – perhaps even *performs* – the neoliberal ethos. That is, given that the broader narratives of Arguer 1 and Arguer 2 can be filled out, and in actually existing arguments sometimes is, with a more complete story of what justice, morality, political economy, and the like is or ought to be, we will then be left the task of evaluating which, overall, is the better narrative. So a good reason is one that brings about the desired end as understood in the construction of the overarching narrative. But *which* ends are to be *desired?* Surely they cannot be whatever ends a particular agent *happens* to desire. Can they?

In other words, in the above examples, the assessment of reasons is indeed tied to ends – does *this* make a reason given *that* end – but the situation, in a system of hypothetical imperatives, rests strictly on means-ends reasoning, reducible to an agent's desires. While indeed it is clear that reasons only become recognizable as *good reasons* in relation to their ability or the assessment of as much to count towards achieving the desired goal, there is an obvious conflict in calling both Arguer 1 and Arguer 2's reasons good reasons. A starker example will make the issue clearer:

Arguer 3: Given that I want to exploit poor people, I have a reason to legalize organ sales.

Arguer 4: Given that I want to exploit poor people, I have a reason to call my priest.

The key here is the two ends (the two antecedent clauses) are identical (wanting to exploit poor people), but the morally salient action (the result/consequent) diverge and, indeed, are opposites: Arguer 3 provides a proper *means* to accomplish that end, whereas Arguer 4 offers a means for subverting and rethinking the end altogether. To rephrase the difference, one line of reasoning is about the end, and the other is just about the means to bring about the end.

The issue, put simply, is this: if ends are beyond critical reproach (one either has them or doesn't, and that's all there is to it), then *good reasons* are those reasons that count in favour of or assist in achieving the desired end.

The point here to draw attention to is the idea that criticism of reasons and the usage or denial of the concept of *good reasons* must be imbued with a more substantive dimension of evaluation on the *ends,* and following the work done via the logic of good reasons in the rhetorical tradition, the distinction of *good reason,* if it is to be non-subjective or agent neutral, requires commitment to some ends, and some narratives, being better than others.

This is a line claimed often enough but the theoretical underpinning for it is largely missing. For example, Wallace and Fisher both claim that human nature points the way to truth in moral matters, that humans (intuitively? fixedly?) know what a good reason is.[26] I do not discount the lodging of truth and good reasons as fixed, to some extent, in human nature. But the concern is in *recognizing* what, or which, ethics and reasons *are indeed* the right ones. That is, good reasons seem to be persuasively and deliberatively *ineffectual* in Wallace or Fisher's view *if* the question is precisely what *is* fixed by human nature or, more relevantly, if the debate is *precisely* about what are, or ought to be, the generally accepted principles and practices of a society in accordance with non-subjective conceptions of truth, freedom, justice, and the like. Furthermore, Wallace and Fisher seem not to have anticipated the kind of moral pluralism and in particular the challenges of neoliberalism and moral subjectivism (true-for-you/live-your-truth/you-do-you constructions) present today.

There are two ways that the challenge of a neoliberal privatization of morality, or moral subjectivism, works in the current era: the first is as the preferred philosophical-substantive conclusion to the problems of ethically pluralistic societies (which amounts to nihilism), and the second is as the preferred procedural-managerial solution to the problems of ethically pluralistic societies. The focus here is on rejecting the former and leaving the latter open for now.

So, good reasons and the narrative approach need a supplement. Good reasons, to some extent, seem given, or well understood, or often taken for granted in debates. What a good reason is seems to be: *we know one when we hear one*. But controversy places these good reasons under stress, and moral disagreements in particular challenge good reasons in ethical perspectives as *wait, that's not a good reason*-type interjections. What metaethics does is move discussion of ethical controversies from the question of what is the right ethical judgment in this situation to the assumptions, commitments, theories, and strategies that inform the ethical statements of arguers.

In other words, metaethics can provide a theoretical supplement to the logic of good reasons that makes sense of evaluative terms like *better* and *good* by examining the deeper question of what, fundamentally, moral disagreement *amounts to* – what it is, what is at stake, and what can be defended. That is, metaethics is partly the enquiry into whether or not ends are in the domain of reason, whether or not ends are rationally criticizable. We are thereby working towards a more complete descriptive and normative account of the nature and practice of moral argumentation and of a theory of good reasons.

The organ debate in particular is ripe for metaethical analysis as advocates on all sides of the issue claim an *ethical* underpinning to their view.

Through metaethical enquiry, the discussion moves from specific ethical controversies and actions to the assumptions, commitments, theories, and strategies that inform the ethical statements of arguers.

Metanormative Disagreement on the Nature of Morality

Moral disagreements often hinge on differing conceptions of specific terms (gravity, good, just) but also on differing conceptions of the entire enterprise of morality. That there is normative disagreement is relatively uncontroversial in the case of how to increase human organ supply. The question, however, is this: What *kind* of disagreement is this? Since the concern is with the nature and presuppositions of moral discourse and practice, a *metaethical* theory of normative disagreement is needed to answer this question.[27] The purpose of this section is to try to understand what it is that moral disagreement comes to, and to judge what disagreement means in terms of this debate particularly and for rhetorical theory more generally. Differing perspectives on what kind of disagreement ethical disagreement *is* leads to differing models of justification. Competing views on disagreement cannot be understood on the same model. This prompts the question, then, of what the right model of disagreement is for our particular debate.

According to Charles L. Stevenson's touchstone distinction, there are two kinds of disagreements: *disagreements in interest* and *disagreements in belief.*[28] Consider this imagined exchange:[29]

MICHELE: Let's talk about labour legislation, as it's less divisive between us.

NANCY: No, I'd rather discuss organ sales. I think it will be fruitful.

MICHELE: All right, then.

NANCY: Organ sales are wrong. It is human trafficking, plain and simple. Sales exploit the poor.

MICHELE: Organ sales are not wrong, per se. Black market sales are indeed human trafficking that exploit the poor, but that is why we need a regulated market.

NANCY: Regulation is a mistake, because, human organ trafficking is actually a protected crime. And prosecutions don't actually happen.

MICHELE: The arrest of organ broker Levy Izak Rosenbaum in the "Jersey Sting" shows that they do. And Rosenbaum pleaded guilty.

NANCY: Indeed, that case is excellent exposure of the problem, but it is an isolated case that has not led to policy reconsiderations for solving the problem.

Here, a clear disagreement in interest exists in the opening lines: Michele has an interest in discussing labour rights, whereas Nancy has an interest in discussing organ sales. A disagreement in interest is not a disagreement about truth values. That is not to say that the interest-disagreement might indeed have required more sustained argument in order to induce inter-locutor agreement, but here it fell away rather easily. Now sharing a clear target, there is also disagreement in belief: that prosecutions do not actu-ally happen. This is a statement that has truth values. Given the evidence offered by Michele and assented to by Nancy, the disagreement is quickly dissolved. Prosecutions, while they may not happen often, do indeed hap-pen (or happened once). The question is, What type of disagreement is the claim that organ sales are wrong? Is it a disagreement in interest (such as, let's talk about labour) and hence has no truth values (strictly understood), or is it a disagreement in belief (such as, prosecutions don't happen)? Disagreements in belief and disagreements in interest are both common forms of disagreement, as this example hopefully makes clear; but they cannot both be assessed or understood on the same model.

The question – what kind of disagreement is moral disagreement – splits metaethical inquirers into cognitivists and non-cognitivists. Cognitivists hold that moral disagreement is disagreement in beliefs, whereas non-cognitivists hold them to be disagreements in interests. This is a key driving distinction in metaethical philosophy, and so it is perhaps the vital question to answer en route to the rhetorical theory of moral disagreement, which thereby illuminates the stakes of a moral disagreement. Put baldly, the disagreement about moral disagreement is largely an ontological disagreement: *what is the nature of morality?*

Following the Good Reasons School, I add bolstering arguments to a cognitive moral realism.[30] This means the following:

1 Moral claims, such as *selling one's organs is wrong*, are truth apt (i.e., capable of being judged true or false).
2 Some moral claims are indeed true.

Rejecting claim 1 results in scepticism about the role of reason in moral discourse and practice, particularly common in forms of emotivism and expressivism in which moral claims serve as expressions of emotions or feelings.[31] Accepting claim 1 but rejecting claim 2 often makes one an error theorist, meaning that moral claims can be judged true or false, but it just so happens that all of them are false.[32] The further question, which is perhaps *the* big question in metaethics among cognitivists, is

3 What *makes* the true moral claim true?

There are three main candidates to 3: (a) subjective relativism, in which the standards of truth are given by the individual; (b) community relativism, in which the standards of truth are given by the relevant community; and (c) objectivism, in which the standards of truth are given by something individual- and community-independent.

Aside from rejecting subjectivism, I leave 3 largely open insofar as there is a sense in which an ultimate answer to the question is unnecessary for practical reason and action. In short, I argue for 1 and 2 and, aside from rejecting subjectivism, leave 3 relatively open; that is, interpretable by public moral norms in a community relativist sense, an objective moral realist sense, and other ways.[33] Arguably, moral claims are truth apt, but the validity conditions vary among sources of authority such as self, other, community, society, humanity, or God. Moral disagreements are disagreements in beliefs, understood best through the deliberative weighing of reasons – searching for and articulating good reason – against telic orientations that are morally criticizable.[34]

This discussion of the nature of morality focuses on two leading proponents of each view: Derek Parfit's cognitivism, particularly as it is expressed in his massive *On What Matters*, and Allan Gibbard's non-cognitivism, particularly as it is expressed in his *Thinking How to Live*,[35] though other views are considered as well. This gets to the cornerstone arguments on the conflict of the nature of moral disagreement and in turn sheds light on both what is at *conflict* in the disagreements between human organ donation and sales advocates as well as what is at *stake*.

Gibbard views morality as essentially a practical affair, in which humans fix their aims. Moral disagreement, then, is a disagreement in *plans* to do certain things. In other words, morality is not a naturalistic or factual affair. Borrowing his example, Joe has the aptitude and abilities to be a concert pianist, but instead aims to be a modest gardener. Joe's aiming to be a gardener does not consist of a true or false judgment. Athena's disagreement with his choice, with his aim, is (simply) practical disagreement (like Michele and Nancy in deciding what to talk about above). She "agrees with all of his judgments of prosaic fact."[36]

Hence, a normative concept for Gibbard is simply a plan-laden concept.[37] These normative concepts coexist with natural facts and states of affairs, and both can be part of what it means to make a plan. In his view, plans "are judgments, in that they can act in many ways like beliefs in plain fact."[38] Believing and planning both contain the possibility of disagreement. This is why they *seem* to be the same thing to, for example, certain cognitivists. But for Gibbard, the distinction is not a severing, for "plans and factual propositions – the respective contents of planning and believing – stand in logical relations to each other, and embed in more complex logical structures that can mix the two."[39] So plan-laden concepts mix with natural facts and beliefs about the world to form actual plans. These plans fix an aim. On this model, moral disagreements are essentially disagreements in plans and not disagreements in beliefs over normative truths.

From the realist standpoint, Parfit challenges by arguing that fixing our aim is within the domain of reasoning proper. In short, to avoid nihilism (which is what all non-objective theories of normative truth eventually amount to, in his view) we should understand that there are facts about which aims are right, which aims are correct. As he puts it, "Normativity is either an illusion, or involves irreducibly normative facts."[40] A normative fact is a fact about what one ought to do, untethered from individual ends or goals and universally forceful (just like scientific facts). Parfit specifically challenges Gibbard's plan-laden conceptual apparatus as failing to properly account for normative action for deciding what one ought to do. Gibbard's formulation dissolves these two questions

Q1: What ought I do?
Q2: What shall I do?

into a single question: "I the chooser don't face two clear, distinct questions, the questions what to do and the question what I ought do," for settling what I ought to do means just settling what to do.[41] This dissolving, Parfit says, does indeed describe how (some) people "conclude what to do" but it does *not* give an account of what one ought to do.[42] For what one ought to do is based on not preference but truth and facts. "When we conclude that we ought to do something, we are not deciding to do this thing, but coming to have a normative belief. Though our decisions to act are often *based* on such beliefs, these decisions are not the same thing as *coming to have* these beliefs."[43] If disagreements are only disagreements in plans, then we don't really have, in Parfit's critique, a disagreement at all: we just have difference, and, furthermore, Gibbard has not given an accurate model of actual moral or normative disagreement.

So there is a dilemma: the non-cognitivist provides an account of the practical aspect of moral discourse and accommodates disagreement as a clash of interests, categorized under a rubric of mutual influence. There is a sort of intuitive pull that this is indeed what is happening in normative disagreement; we take actions to achieve our aims. But there is also an intuitive pull of the cognitivist, that if and when there is normative disagreement, the disagreement is reasonable and justifiable, and furthermore that this rationally justified view be objective in some sense so that it is not countered as simply true *for you*.[44] Or, to put the matter more bluntly: there is a problem of using practical reason to help settle what, as a community, ought to be done, and that this decision of what to do, that this action, needs to be rationally justified and not reducible to personal preference or exercises in power.

This realm of practical reason is precisely the overlap between philosophy and rhetoric.[45] The implication here is that if cognitivists such as Parfit are right, then practical reason is squarely within philosophy, and that if non-cognitivists such as Gibbard are right, then normative theorizing doesn't really belong to philosophy. My suggestion is that Gibbard is right to place focus on the persuasive aspects of normative theorizing, even if he is mistaken about the nature of moral concepts. Normative theorizing and action are properly rhetorical activities: they have a strong discursive reasoning component, which is, following in the Aristotelian tradition, both practical and rhetorical,[46] and also a strong undercurrent of autonomy and interest, which are not easily swayed by discursive reasoning. In terms of interest, moral argument is a rhetorical activity that attempts to, borrowing Gibbard's phrase, reconcile our aims.[47] But practical reason also helps settle what aims *ought* to be. That is, normative judgments are judgments in beliefs, and therefore, as the Good Reasons School suggests, some beliefs are better (i.e., closer to the truth) than others.

The most significant question for this section flares at this moment: *If reason plays such a substantive role in ethical discourse and practice, why is there so much moral disagreement?* In other words, do I really mean to suggest that one side in the organ procurement debate is unreasonable or doesn't have reason on its side, or something to that effect? To the latter, I answer a qualified no, as should be clear in the following paragraphs. To the former question, there are several answers. I will focus on two of them.

The first answer as to why there is moral disagreement is that there are mistaken beliefs held due to an inadequate knowledge or understanding of the relevant facts. This is quite common in everyday interpersonal disagreements, less common in structured public disagreements, and relatively rare in technical and academic moral disagreements.

The second answer as to why there is moral disagreement is that which is more common in public and technical disagreements: arguers know the relevant facts and reasons but weigh them differently, and this different weighing results in different moral judgments. The rest of this chapter, and the next chapter, are devoted to arguing for and supporting those two answers.

Three Arguments for Categoricity and Moral Realism

There are three main arguments made to support the view that some moral disagreements are related to unawareness of relevant facts and reasons: the Aims Argument, the Categorical Argument, and the Argument from Normative Force. Each argument is made in a subsection, but here is a brief overview of what each argument will do.

The first argument is the Aims Argument, adapted from Ronald Dworkin. The Aims Argument suggests that there is actually significant agreement among arguers – including moral sceptics (who think morality an illusion) – in what morality *aims to do*. In short, arguers all seek right answers to moral questions – even if that right answer is that there are not true answers in the moral domain. The right judgment in and about morality, however, is often thought to be one of three things: realism (moral claims express judgments that are true or false), scepticism (moral claims are always false or that morality is an illusion altogether), and relativism (moral claims are true or false relative to agent standards or community desires).[48] The second argument for moral realism, which I'm calling the Categorical Argument, suggests that there are good reasons, based on relevant facts, to reject simple relativistic and sceptical views about morality. There are necessarily standards for moral claims, and these standards are objective in a certain sense of that term, and thereby convergence is required from moral arguers. Extending this idea, the third argument, the Argument of Normative Force, suggests how moral convergence is possible in pluralistic societies.

For moral realism, the right answers to moral questions will be based on facts and reasons that transcend individual or local conventions. The effort to discover such facts and reasons are held to be inherently unsuccessful by thinkers who see questions of the good as simplistically relative in a pluralistic society. I say *simple relativism* to distinguish from sophisticated relativistic metaethical positions, and from here on in this chapter, *relativism* will be used to mean simple relativism, unless otherwise indicated.[49] Financial-compensation advocate Mark Cherry expresses the relativist assumption clearly: "Moral content is gained at the price of universality. Securing a particular ethic requires specification of premises and content that will not be acknowledged among moral strangers."[50] The idea is that any specification of a substantive moral principle will fall afoul of *someone's* moral view, and even if it doesn't, it *might in theory*. Therefore, the idea is to draw moral boundaries so as to be acceptable to all moral strangers – that is, to be consistent with the view of competing visions of the good life as the result of the distanced self and the modern condition discussed in chapter 5. Such a view is predicated on incommensurability – a view that is unfounded. A cognitive moral realism suggests simple relativistic views are mistaken.

What simple relativism conflates is the *fact of pluralism* (that there are different moral beliefs) – which is indisputable as a descriptive account – and the idea that there is *not a right answer* to moral questions *given* such differing beliefs. The mistake is especially prevalent in certain corners of rhetorical studies. To take a representative claim, consider this paragraph on values, truth, and argumentation from Thomas Hollihan and Kevin Baaske's mainstay textbook on argumentation:

> Acknowledging the role of human values in argumentation also helps make us aware that while arguments may be designed to reach the "truth," there may be more than one "truth." Our sense of what is true is shaped by our values and experiences. Thus, complex value questions are often complex precisely because there is no single true answer. Reasonable people can and do differ on issues.[51]

While reasonable people certainly can and do differ on issues, this is not necessarily due to there being more than one truth in any non-trivial sense of the term. The *non sequitur* is clear: our sense of what is true is shaped by our values and experiences (indeed), thus questions are complex because there is no single true answer (?). In the form of an example, the non sequitur becomes more readily apparent: Tim thinks two plus two is five, and Patti thinks two plus two is three, and Kelli thinks two plus two is four; therefore there is no single true answer to the sum of two plus two.

Now, we may or may not get closer to solving the equation accurately if we are told stories about Tim's, Patti's, and Kelli's experiences that led them to think the way they do (math-challenged parents; a misprint in the textbook; good math teachers), but their stories – even if they demonstrate a kind of justified, causal-reason-for-belief story – make no clear or persuasive pronouncement about whether or not there are right answers to questions in the first place.[52] In the next section, I will argue against relativism along these lines more thoroughly.[53]

The Aims Argument

The idea of simple moral relativism, as expressed in Cherry's as well as Hollihan and Baaske's quote above, can be seen in two different forms of scepticism about right answers: in one version, there is wholesale rejection of *right* as a category, and in the other, the more modest claim that it is difficult to tell among competing claims which is right.[54] In his touchstone essay, "Objectivity and Truth," Ronald Dworkin rebuts the idea that either version is decisive against objective, true, right answers, and that those labels are not just ways of talking (i.e., not just different terms for the same idea).[55] This section primarily draws on Dworkin's arguments.

Dworkin distinguishes two challenges to objectivity and truth in moral realism. The first challenge is rejection of the very categories of objectivity and truth. The other challenge is an endorsement of objectivity and truth in some arenas (e.g., science) but not others (e.g., morality and art). Dworkin believes that both views are mistaken. There is objectivity and truth, he claims, in matters of morality as much as there is in physics.

Dworkin's view isn't as straight-ahead as it might appear. He shares two key premises with those who challenge objectivity: that there is no place outside of thought to stand and judge the truth or falsity of certain propositions or doctrines, and that everything is indeed a matter of interpretation.

A familiar challenge to objectivity is that there is no God's Eye View from which to judge. Many think that this is decisive against the case for objectivity. But not only does Dworkin mostly agree with the claim, but he also accuses these practitioners of "wholesale Archimedean skepticism."[56] It is they who, falsely, claim to be outside of thoughts, outside of doctrines. That is, Dworkin claims that it is the person who says that all positions are wrong and nothing can be objectively true who has actually made the *most* (or at least as much of a) universal and objective claim of anyone else in metanormative debates.

The point is that if someone says, *all positions are false and not objective but relative to standards and beliefs,* this would entail, of course, that their position fits within that too, making it false as well. Dworkin wonders why it is that the sceptics are somehow immune to the shortcomings and biases that they accuse the others of having. If sceptics acknowledge, instead, that their position is equally relative to standards, then they aren't really claiming anything different or inconsistent with objective types: both schools believe that people are stuck in thought, with sets of beliefs.[57] The sceptic goes a step further from this and says, "and so, no one is right." That conclusion does not necessarily follow. Instead, Dworkin offers the view that we are stuck in thought with our sets of beliefs, and we are all aiming at truth.

The epistemic relativist argument says that all judgments are based on interpretations, and hence one cannot be *objective* in the discovery of facts. Discovery itself cannot be objective in the view-from-nowhere sense. But again, Dworkin seems to *agree* that matters are almost always *interpretations.* He believes that this doesn't undermine objective truth. In fact, interpretation depends on an objective truth target. This is better understood through the "no right answer thesis."[58] So, recalling the exchange between Nancy and Michele at the beginning of this chapter, there is a fundamental difference of moral permissibility on organ sales. Imagine further that this debate then spills into written exchanges, and the two people continue by citing evidence – cases, personal experience, history, law, politics, ethnographies, surveys – and use logic to adduce the truth or falsity of each other's inferences. Assume also that in their arguments, neither person has any logical mistakes. So each person claims truth, has good evidence, and good arguments.

So who is right? One needs, of course, to see the arguments, process them, live and breathe with them, and weigh them – which is what this study has done in the first several chapters and will return to in the next section. But now imagine a third person, Richard, comes along:

> RICHARD: You fools! You are both as wrong as you are right. There is no right answer to such things.

Here Richard represents the sceptic discussed above, and Dworkin wants to show just how strange a conclusion this is to draw from the simple fact that two people disagree.

Dworkin would not say that Richard is wrong. He is simply *offering a third interpretation*. That is, Nancy offers the interpretation that *organ sales being wrong* is the correct moral view, Michele holds that organ sales being allowed under a restricted market is the correct view, and Richard that there is no right answer to such questions. These three interpretations do not *undermine* objectivity; after all, if Richard is right, then indeed someone, that is to say *some position*, is right.

There are now three positions on the table: that organ sales are morally permissible, that they are not, and that there are no right answers to such questions. Dworkin presses further, asking how is it determined who is right?[59] Again, one needs to see the arguments, process them, live with them, and so forth. Interestingly, however, in this case, the *only* evidence that Richard has offered for the truth of his position is simply the disagreement of the other two. That, Dworkin thinks, is scant evidence. The other two people have robust metaphysical and philosophical disagreements, history, evidence, and the like, even if they turn out to both be wrong.

The sceptic, then, is not simply describing the situation but rather is making an evaluation. That is, it is an interpretive question whether a general statement about morality is true or false, and saying that there is no right answer, or no such thing, then is *itself* a positive judgment.

Scepticism – that there is no truth in general/certain domains – makes no sense as the default position given that it is an evaluation; it is itself a positive moral judgment. That is, if we really want to conduct enquiry and engage in argument on the matter, a default position cannot be substantive. Instead, the default position should be uncertainty.[60]

The turn here is that what the positions (Nancy, Michele, Richard) all share is an *aim of judgment* and an *aim of being right*. That debate participants, even sceptics, all share the aim of true judgment, as just suggested, forms the Aims Argument for cognitive moral realism.

The Aims Argument is fully consistent with the interpretive paradigm favoured by many rhetorical critics. Stanley Fish, in one of his most striking quotes, makes the case succinctly: "Independently of any comprehensive doctrine there is neither perception nor judgment; and therefore when someone urges a conclusion that supposedly follows from the setting aside of comprehensive doctrines, it is really a conclusion that follows from a comprehensive doctrine."[61] So disagreements over facts are, at one level, disagreements of interpretation, but that does nothing to undermine truth and objectivity once the distinction between uncertainty and scepticism is made.

Uncertainty, then, is neither a positive moral judgment nor a substantive conclusion. When two people disagree, or three, or six million, the default position should not be the scepticism that no one is right but rather the uncertainty of who or what exactly is right. So goes the case for the distinction of uncertainty and the avoidance of scepticism. The matter now turns on whether or not there really are right answers in the moral domain.

The Categorical Argument, or Ruling Out Scepticism and Simple Relativism

This section argues for right answers in the moral domain.[62] Categoricity, as a right answer to a moral question that does not depend on local conventions or individual agent goals, is frequently thought mistaken in the current era. Taking the aim of right judgments in moral matters to be established (and shared in sociopolitical domains) in the previous section, the question of whether or not there *are* right answers in the moral domain still persists. That is, the right judgment on moral matters might be that morality is bunk. There are three primary positions. The first two are that there are moral truths (realism) or that there are not (scepticism). The third position, of simple relativism, tries to split the difference between the universality of the categorical and the disappearance of the moral altogether.

Relativism, as a middle ground, at some level, is *exactly* what liberal democracy aims at, in the sense of being neutral with regard to specific content and thus de facto to the existence of moral content altogether. But at another level, as discussed in the previous chapter, this neutrality is not only superficial; it is also deeply undesirable insofar as it seems to make moral critique impossible.

Taking two moral pronouncements such as

MP1: Selling human organs is wrong, and
MP2: Selling human organs is not wrong,

one can see that they have the prima facie distinction of being categorical, of selling human organs being wrong or not. But the form of language can be misleading, and it is on this that an indexical theory of wrong typically hangs.[63] In such a view, *wrong* is indexed to something; in speaker subjectivism, for example, it is indexed to the speaker's desires. This view can be characterized as relativism in the social constructivist tradition, in which there is no such thing as either MP1 or MP2, but rather MP1, for example, *means*

> MP1*: Selling human organs is wrong according to dignity-centred categorical moral views.

So in general, then, the relativist position could be put this way:

> R: Selling human organs is wrong according to dignity-centred categorical moral views, but not according to autonomy-centred economic liberalist moral views.

R of course is objective and factual; no matter what anyone's actual first-order judgment *is* on whether or not selling human organs is wrong, R must be assented to *descriptively*. But what has happened here is that actually the normative has been fully removed; that is, the normative element is displaced by the descriptive. This means, then, that R doesn't say *anything* about the moral status of selling human organs but instead simply reports, simply describes, certain belief systems' take on the matter. This description is important for sociological enquiry, but unless one is content to reduce morality to geography,[64] the moral question has been ignored altogether. That is, either selling human organs is right, or it is wrong, and while right or wrong can be highly contextual, there is no middle position of relativism in morality.[65] The confusion comes in descriptions of moral beliefs and discourse, as they actually occur in the world, and whether these beliefs are mistaken or not. Given that rhetoric is concerned with both lived practice (*praxis*) and theoretical belief (*theoria*), and that a report of the *fact* of ethical pluralism is nonnormative, further examination is required.

The variability of moral codes across the globe, in the absence of a universally recognized moral source, seems to indicate that categorical morality is at best, a leftover ideal from a bygone era, or at worst, transparently false. At this point, it is tempting to conclude that given this, morality is purely code or agent relative, which makes it akin to scepticism: all values are unfounded and therefore equally incoherent.[66] A brief exchange between Robert Sade, then-member of the AMA's Council on

Ethical and Judicial Affairs, and Congresswoman Diana DeGette from the 2003 *Assessing Initiatives* hearings illustrates the matter succinctly, discussing why a financial-compensation study is unlikely:[67]

DEGETTE: And why?
SADE: Because there would be a great deal of feeling, as you're expressing very clearly, against it.
DEGETTE: Right. I agree. And I think appropriately so, don't you?
SADE: Perhaps. I'm willing to listen to any possibility that a group of investigators, in accord with the population that they wish to study, have agreed upon.
DEGETTE: Okay.
SADE: I'm not going to impose my values on a different section of the country.

While it is unclear whether DeGette holds a clear cognitivist view of morality given by reason in the categorical sense or a sentimentalist view of morality given by dispositions, Sade's position seems to be relativistic. The point is not whether or not Sade or DeGette is a relativist in matters of health or morality; rather, what we see in the exchange is the tension between political and moral concerns: even if Sade is, say, a moral realist, he is politically uncomfortable legislating public policy in such a way.[68] The tension is precisely one we've been calling attention to throughout the book so far. The highlight here is the degree to which the normative political relativism of to-each-her-own comports with a normative moral relativism in which morality is reducible to solely to autonomy. Though he is speaking more generally than the domain of morality, Paul Boghossian presents this as the equal-validity thesis (EVT):

EVT: "There are many radically different, [mutually incompatible], yet 'equally valid' ways of knowing the world."[69]

In the EVT, there is a combination of the descriptive and the normative; it is irrational for one to not agree that there are, indeed, many different ways of knowing the world, in the same way that one seemingly cannot reject that different cultures and communities *have* different moral codes. The normative part comes in, however, in what is concluded from this: Boghossian claims that relativism concludes that all are therefore *equally valid*, and, in the moral case, this amounts not to relativism but really to scepticism – the elimination of morality.

The danger here is that the descriptive and normative become conflated. That there are different interpretations and that one can study not just reasons but causal reasons for belief, and thereby explain (away) differences in beliefs among epistemic communities is not tantamount to saying that all are equally valid. It is here that there is equivocation in what is meant by the sociology of knowledge, in which the study of what is *believed to be true and why it is so appealing* is conflated with what *is true and why.*[70] The case is seen, generally, with the flat-earth belief, as one can explain, through evidence, why people in antiquity *thought* the earth was flat.[71] The point is that "evidence is fallible," and therefore it is "entirely consistent with a belief's falsity that it is explainable through evidential causes."[72]

So, again, if it is held that there is a difference between truth and falsity, there is strong reason to reject relativism,[73] and, in following the previous discussion, the case for categoricity seems sunk, for we would seem justified in our moral scepticism, given the modern condition of the distanced self and all of the seeming empirical evidence of moral disagreement.

But humans do not give up on serious moral talk: that we are uncomfortable saying that selling women into sexual slavery or that paedophilia is reducible to local conventions that might be different than mine indicates a push towards a rejection of scepticism. And so intuition here guides us towards this phenomenon as evidence for the opposite: that there *are* moral truths.

Even if one is unconvinced that there are moral truths at this point, in any event, this, it seems, is a decisive blow against simple relativism. Deciding what to do in the local here and now is deciding what anyone in a similarly constrained position ought to do. Some situations are less contextually dependent than others – for example, the local environment, the immediate context of people and structures, and the societal codes matter quite a bit in determining what is acceptable at a dinner table, whereas those contextual features make significantly less of an impact in judging the practice of, say, sexual slavery. The degree of sensitivity indicates the gradeability of normativity in contexts,[74] a point discussed in more detail in the next subsection.

Furthermore, and perhaps most decisively, to hold everything loosely in the moral realm, is also, in many ways to give up on *normative force*, conceived as the relevant facts and reasons that ought to move an agent, irreducible to mere persuasion (discussed more in the next chapter). Normative force is a tricky concept to pin down, especially in the relationship between descriptive reasons, motivation, and normative judgment. For now, let me flag this issue and conclude by putting the matter simply: moving from the normative to the descriptive, the normative is fully lost, and if that is acceptable, then moral discourse is meaningless and ought to be dropped. But since humans are unwilling to drop it, it seems that moral critique is possible, thus, modus tollens, there are normative truths.[75] So the argument is

If the normative is reducible to the descriptive, then moral critique is impossible,
moral critique is possible,
hence, the normative is not reducible to the descriptive.

The matter requires further scrutiny, but thus far, through the establishment of the aim of right judgment (the Aims Argument) and the rejection of relativism and scepticism as viable options (the Categorical Argument), reasons for believing the truth of moral categoricity are on the table.

The Argument of Normative Force and Moral Convergence

Moral categoricity and moral convergence, especially at the societal level, can go hand in hand. This section argues in favour of moral convergence, which is the idea that a community can, through the exchange of reasons, ideas, intuition, and emotions, align on morality and moral normativity. The arguments in this section represent the most direct rebuttal to alternative claims of moral incommensurability, that moral claims have such different standards of truth as to make comparison and convergence impossible. Many readers might find the argument in the previous section against scepticism and simple relativism persuasive, but the claims of categoricity or moral truths too strong. In this section, I argue for a nuanced understanding of categoricity and moral truth that will assuage some of those concerns through discussion of the concept of normative force.

Normative force is the relevant facts and reasons that move an agent, irreducible to mere persuasion or individual goals. The general idea, again, is that the Good Reasons School and arguers who hold that there are *better* narratives, or policies a society *ought* to enact, or *good* reasons, and hold that normative terms like *better, ought, good*, and so forth are not subjectivist or simple relativistic are on the same page as me here; truth is spoken in many ways. The goal continues to be to provide a metaethical supplement to the good reasons view – detailing specific theoretical commitments and presuppositions that are within, or consistent with, the logic of good reasons – and show how such metaethical discussion and argument leads to certain important implications for morality and moral disagreement in pluralistic constitutional democracies.

In deliberations on normative matters, the case has been made that there is the common aim of right answers to moral questions (such as organ procurement) and that there are moral truths, even if we do not yet know what they are. A key premise is that moral questions are rationally intelligible, and this premise matters for action, for making and executing plans. In this way, the issue of whether it is a moral fact or not to permit organ sales, while at first awkward, is really seen as a question of what a society ought to do, and that this *ought* is a rational, cognitive ought.

But normativity is not so tidy, especially when one turns to concrete moral questions that aren't as easily answered (hopefully) as sexual slavery. The aim in all these matters is a normative judgment leading to policy – whether the United States should or should not permit organ sales and/or financial incentives for organ giving – and *how* that judgment is made, in theory and in practice, becomes quite complicated. What makes permitting or denying incentive advocates' arguments and desired law especially complicated is that what US society ought to do is really (or more clearly, has become) two different questions:

Q1: whether or not selling one's organ is morally permissible, and
Q2: whether or not a society should legally allow it.

Again, advocates of the status quo essentially say that Q2 depends on Q1, whereas market advocates, in line with much liberal-democratic theory, say that Q1 is disarticulated from Q2. So the arguments of advocates on both sides navigate between making their cases in regard to Q1 and making their cases in regard to Q2.

While the discussion of the interrelationship between the right and the good in pluralistic constitutional democracies was one of the driving subjects of chapter 5, this pertains directly to issues of metanormativity (enquiring into the norms about the establishment of norms) insofar as *how* the argumentative case is made in regard to Q1. Advocates are looking for *facts* and *reasons* that support the position. Most of these facts can be read in chapters 2 and 3 respectively and how they fit into overarching arguments and the substantive rhetoric of each position. The key element for this section is to show how the concept of *normative force* and talk about the *reasons that matter* suggest the plausibility of moral convergence.

By normative force, I mean the relevant facts and reasons that move an agent. But normative force is neither reducible to mere persuasion nor to an agent simply *being* moved to act. Normative force might be best seen in terms of the *normativity of reason*. The idea of the normativity of reason is one of some reasons being better than others, of not all reasons being equal, and of being the reasons that ought to move agents. Derek Parfit gives a good characterization of normative force in terms of reason giving when he distinguishes between real reasons and apparent reasons.[76] If someone believes that eating a deadly poisonous insect will save his life, then he has a reason to eat that deadly poisonous insect. But this is only an apparent reason, for the belief that eating something that will kill you will save your life is *false* and so it is not a "real" reason: "But if we say that false beliefs can give people reasons, we would need to add that these reasons do not have any *normative force* in the sense that they do not count in favor of any act."[77] Normative force, then, is the reasons and facts that must be accorded attention to in moral deliberations. They are the actual, as opposed to potential, reasons that properly move an agent to a defensible, reasoned action.

Normative force is tethered to normative reasons and descriptive facts in a moral realist picture. I will explain this relationship without fully taking sides on the issue of naturalism and non-naturalism in morality.[78] That debate turns on whether or not ethical properties are natural, in the sense of being continuous with the natural world and science, or non-natural, in which normative concepts pick out normative properties that are properly not a part of the empirical natural world.[79] In either picture, morality is understood as being responsive to descriptive facts, and natural facts will often *count in favour* of some action. That a certain action will bring about the deaths of many people *counts in favour* of deliberating against and refraining from such an action.

This is not to say, however, that such facts are fully and clearly *decisive* in moral deliberations. Here's a quick example. Suppose I answer the moral question of organ procurement by saying selling one's organs on the free market is wrong. And you ask why that is the case, and I respond, "Because it exploits the poor." And we get on the same page about the meaning of exploit, and you counter with, "How do you know?" and I respond with several studies suggesting how, under transplant tourism, developing nations are serving as organ vendors (that is, as sources of "living cadavers"[80]) to the most advanced and richest of nations. It is still an open question, and it is fully logical for you to respond, "But still, does that make it *wrong?*" In principle, there are not situations in which natural facts will take you by the throat and force you to see something as wrong.[81]

This means that what matters in deliberative moments is not precisely what Reason says but rather turns on *weighing* which reasons matter most. The primary issue is that there are lots of reasons to act, including based on what fulfils desires and interests. And they are all honest-to-goodness reasons. This might be called the Face-Value View, in which "the things that we call reasons are the same things that we pay attention to in our deliberation."[82] That we ought to pay more attention to some reasons than others results in discussions of the *weight* of reasons. The distinction is marked as one of there being such a thing as weightier or *better reasons* – much in line with the logic of good reasons in rhetorical theory.

The worry here is in how to define *better*, and if the definition doesn't in the final instance turn back to desires.[83] That is, is there a difference between

> as I'm in end-stage renal failure, I want to buy a kidney, and
> as I'm in end-stage renal failure, it is rational for me to want to buy a kidney?

Put differently, given P (being in end-stage renal failure), and my desire D (to stay alive), isn't Q (buying a kidney) rational? On a simple instrumental model, given certain agent desires, the answer seems to be yes. But the question, again and again, is whether there is a strong reason in the normative sense; that is, an overriding or *more* important reason. The idea here is that if rationality is simply following the rules of logic given certain premises, few fail to be (instrumentally) rational, indeed. Hence, as Stephen Finlay puts it,

> Talk of "rationality" clearly suggests something more: it is intrinsic to the concept of rationality that it is normatively required (in a way that matters) of everybody capable of it. Rational requirements are such that, once we understand them as such, we cannot coherently or intelligibly challenge their authority over us. This seems to be all that is uncontroversial about the concept: but in that case all that it uncontroversially means to say that real reasons are rationally demanding on us is that they are reasons that matter.[84]

So the uncontroversial search is for the *reasons that matter*, and the debate is pitched precisely at the level of what matters or not. Public moral deliberation steps into this situation in the act of persuading that *this* matters, and it matters *more* than *that* (discussed more in the next section). But this is not all that deliberation does, for to leave the situation here implies that disagreement, moral or otherwise, is all merely a matter of interest. To move beyond mere interest one seeks the ground of reason, and which reasons matter most. And in this way, as Finlay continues the quote above, "The real difficulty – concerning what it is to matter – has merely been transposed into the question of what rationality is."[85] The question of normative reasons is that the relationship among reasons is about how one weighs reasons and what individuals and societies are trying to find is good reasons for action. Rhetorical engagement among citizens, as a special kind of practical reason and persuasion aimed at garnering assent, is poised to constitute this process.

Without the concept and import of normative force agents may simply reject a claim such as, "If you care to have a more just society, you ought to ban organ sales," by simply responding, "But I don't care about having a more just society," and hence, logically, the consequent doesn't follow through. A typical and correct response from the pressing moral agent here would be, "But you *ought* to care about having a more just society!" Such interactions must move beyond nonnormative instrumental reasoning in order to have moral purchase.

Substantial convergence in moral argumentation is possible, then, in situations in which agents act on beliefs because they think they are true, and that rationality, assuming that the belief is rational, underwrites their beliefs and therefore serves as a justification for action. This is not a relativist justification for action because not all justifications are indeed rational or true (as was seen in eliminating the EVT above). So, while there is much controversy and disagreement in ethics, the elimination of relativism, and the norm circularity of justification in any epistemic system, leaves, precisely, in Boghossian's words, "no option but to think that there are absolute, practice-independent facts about what beliefs would be most reasonable to have under fixed evidential conditions."[86] The argument I'm drawing on here is the simple one that in moving from the normative to the descriptive, the normative is lost. If such is acceptable, then moral discourse *is* meaningless and ought to be dropped, and that this necessarily will have an impact on our laws and how we structure our society.

But the overwhelming evidence is that society is unwilling to drop moral discourse, and so it seems that moral critique is possible. Again, moral practice and ethical critique is easier said than done in a public setting. In a nutshell, public moral argumentation is the process in which we give each other reasons as to why one's views are right, why this view is thought to be better than that one, and, most important, why someone might not have weighed the relevant reasons properly.

The key here is that if the advocates and deliberators are aiming at truth, then public moral arguers all really are, to borrow Parfit's metaphor, just "climbing the same mountain on different sides."[87] The mountain being climbed is to a better and more just society in accordance with what actually is right, what actually matters, and the like.

The element that rings out under present purposes is that the weighing of reasons is precisely what is controversial and problematic; the point is that if *better reasons* are to have any meaning beyond agent relativity,[88] there must be some categorical target out there, and some rational way of drawing moral boundaries in a collectively binding norm-constitution environment. There are indeed different reasons for actions, but the goal is to find *good reasons*, and these good reasons and their normative force motivate agents to act, with citizens converging on moral truth via rhetorical engagement.

The rejection of grounding for choosing which one is *better* among competing narratives, understood in the same way as we understand *having good reasons* or having *better reasons*, leaves a society and its peoples with the task of either subjective preferences bolstered by power arrangements reigning supreme or, and perhaps what amounts to the same thing in practice, the inability to choose at all.

The dangers of a (false) moral absolutism and the subjectivity of good reasons sit side by side, totalizing or individualizing. The search for *good reasons* and *better narratives* is properly a dialectical task (meaning rhetoric and philosophy), aiming to carve a way that supports, say, fancy social ideals like freedom and justice and democracy as substantively non-subjective, and yet is sufficiently sensitive to the complexities and challenges of seeing just what the right ends and corresponding reasons for those are in a given situation and broader narrative context. Easier said than done, but easier done in a public moral deliberative context than an isolated one – if the deliberative context is one in which reasoners are motivated to discover and possess good reasons.

On the assumption that citizens want to live in a just society with safeguards for freedom, autonomy, and the like, while maintaining that there are things that ought to be morally off limits (and therefore legally off limits), public deliberation in general and on bioethical matters like organ sales in specific might, ultimately, turn less on which reasons count as reasons than they do on *how we weigh* and *weight* the reasons. In the next chapter, I will outline a perspective of what it means to weigh reasons, focusing on telic orientation, rhetorical force, and normative force, before turning back, in chapters 8 and 9, to our instantiated debate and how arguers in organ procurement weigh the reasons that matter.

7 Weighing Reasons: Telic Orientation, Rhetorical Force, and Normative Force

Agreeing on the relevant facts and recognizing the relevant reasons in moral deliberation can still result in differing moral judgments due to weighing these reasons and facts differently. This chapter offers an explanation of how weighing reasons works. There are three elements to weighing reasons. The first and most important is *telic orientation*. A telic orientation is the *end* towards which one is aiming, the backdrop that one is reasoning against that allows better than/worse than reasons to take shape. The next element in weighing reasons is rhetorical force. *Rhetorical force* is what *moves* an agent to assent to a claim or agree with a moral theory. An argument with rhetorical force is an argument that is highly persuasive, often changing someone's moral beliefs and motivating her to act according to the content of that moral belief. The final element, normative force, plays a distinctive role in the weighing of reasons, and in what ought to be weighed as heavy and important regardless of whether or not certain people, or anyone, *does* indeed give it such weight and consideration. Furthermore, the claim is that what has normative force will have rhetorical force on the premise that people are moved by normativity, on the idea that a community's people aim for a just society.

The important turn in my argument is on *better* not collapsing into agent relativity or *mere* collective social norms. Derek Parfit's arguments are again quite helpful in articulating a cognitivist moral realism that imbues *better* with substantive normative meaning. The idea that something is *better* than something else, that *not exploiting the poor* is a better reason to ban organ sales than *individual property rights*, for example, means that it is the reason agents have *more* reason to have. The assumption here is that both you and I desire a just society, and what you've just told me is that a more just society is one that helps the poor. Assuming that is true, then I do not have a different preference here (for property rights over the poor); instead, I just have competing desires. But these competing desires are not of equal value. Rather, if *not exploiting the poor* is indeed a better reason to act, then it is the weightier reason. So this means – and this is key – that morality, in a cognitivist-realist picture, captured in terms like *justice*, gives us not just *a* reason but the most reason to have a certain desire, and to act on that.[1]

That works, at least to me, *very clearly in theory*. The problem comes in *recognizing* what reasons are the reasons most worthy of possession and what reasons matter most in the very abductive process of weighing reasons.[2] The process of weighing reasons, when done collectively and deliberatively, is a rhetorical process of inducing interlocutors to share in normative judgment. What sharing in a normative judgment entails is *recognition of gravitas* – either the weight of reasons or that one has weighed (in)correctly.[3]

Telic Orientation

What moral disagreement amounts to is a sort of collective calibration of human scales – the scales on which agents weigh reasons. The recognition of certain acts as having the moral property of wrongness is what a society is trying to find, and what advocates are trying to point out: *this* act has that property. The choice that one makes, or a society makes, about how to weigh reasons is what I am calling a *telic orientation*. Telic orientations are the ends towards which one aims.[4] Once an end is in place, structure is given to the multiplicity of reasons to act present in a given situation; it is in relation to ends that some reasons are seen to be better, weightier, than others. That is, better/worse than reasons take shape in relation to chosen ends.

The element of choice is crucial insofar as, connecting back up with chapter 5's notions of the distanced self, telic orientations are not the results of logical necessity. Rather, telic orientations are the aim of one's reasons and actions. As Gibbard detailed in his earlier book, morality works on a concept he calls *normative governance*, which is "the special kind of motivation that stems from making a normative judgment that applies to oneself right now."[5] The idea here is that *normative discussions* in community "coordinate acts and feelings"; speakers make normative *avowals* (including a wide range of expressions), thereby taking positions, and aim at achieving consensus via mutual influence.[6] So when a person voices a "complicated normative thought," he "expresses a thought that gets its meaning from its logical ties to other statements, and through them not only sense experience, but also normative governance."[7]

This view of motivation – to recommend to and influence the action of others – sounds very much in line with the rhetorical tradition; in short, motivation, and morality in general for Gibbard, are effects and affects of

persuasion. But much as Socratics charged the sophists with a lack of concern for truth and goodness and dealing only in flattery, so we anticipate
a charge here: what prevents the rise of a society that pursues only *inclinations* based on their subjective preferences and ends? Here I follow Kant,
in which deliberators are to measure inclinations against reason: "Reason
irremissibly commands its precepts, without thereby promising anything to
the inclinations."[8] Reason, then, is able to restrict acting on inclinations.[9]

But this reason is not as robust as Kant would like. To reiterate, there
is no such thing as rational necessity outside of not just accepted premises but also, outside of logic, one needs the *disposition*, the agent desire
to be rational. Disagreements then turn on differences of ends, and it is
here that the problem flared: are different ends reducible to differing
preferences, or are there *right* ends? While recognizing the importance
of disposition and motivation in the first instance, there is such a thing
as correct ends, ends that there is more reason to hold. This is *not* to
endorse these ends as *logically necessary*, however, at least not in the moral
realm, and the distinction is important;[10] as Parfit points out, if some
"act is rationally necessary when knowledge of the facts would irresistibly
move us to act in this way," then such an act fully *removes normativity.*[11]

Parfit is right that logical necessity removes normativity, and what I've
been calling telic orientation helps to clarify the relationship between
ends, moral beliefs, and reasons. One's aims and plans, indeed, are unable to be judged true/false in the same way that beliefs, and to some
degree even actions, are, but there is something much deeper going on
than mere instrumental relationality. The interplay of normative force
and the claims for categoricity I've argued this far are part of the point
here. A telic orientation is directed by more than logical deductive reason, and is instead inclusive of commitment and faith.[12] A telic orientation is, decidedly, a disposition or a desire and is based on choice, just as
Aristotle tells us in Book VI of the *Nicomachean Ethics.* But as Aristotle also
tells us, humans only have wisdom and reason present in cases where we
are hitting the golden mean *if* we have good ends – the ends supplied
by moral virtue. That is, without the disposition of virtue, which sup-
plies good ends, there is only instrumental reason, or what Aristotle calls
cleverness, and not wisdom or moral virtue. Cleverness, or instrumental
reason, will be indistinguishable as means-ends rationality; the moral
distinction is in the ends – ends that must be *chosen.*[13]

In the human condition, morality is complex and messy. This is
because humans do not discover moral *proofs*; humans make moral *judgments.* Telic orientation is a matter of substantive conviction, of faith,
though practical reason plays a strong and weighty role in deliberating
and fixing an individual's or society's ends.

Rhetorical Force

The second element in weighing reasons after telic orientation is rhetorical force. A telic orientation describes the *end* towards which one aims, the backdrop that one is reasoning against that allows better-than/worse-than reasons to take shape. *Rhetorical force* is what *moves* an agent to assent to a claim or agree with a moral theory, the measure of persuasiveness towards conviction.[14] An argument with rhetorical force is an argument that is highly persuasive, and might change someone's moral beliefs and motivate her to act according to the content of that moral belief. In addition to practical reason aiding in fixing ends, rhetorical deliberation aids in the foray of weighing reasons against telic orientations, saying, "You ought to have *this* telic orientation, and here's why."

One aspect of rhetorical force is the refusal to withdraw an ought claim despite unshared aims and ends. This is what I've been calling the Categorical Grip. So, in the case of whether or not one should slurp noodles, it is easy to withdraw the ought claim of not slurping noodles in Britain, though it might be permissible in parts of Asia, whereas it is less easily withdrawn in other examples despite local conventions or moral codes (e.g., paedophilia, slavery, etc.).

Another aspect of rhetorical force is seen in the following quote from Frank Jackson:

> Are we supposed to take seriously someone who says, "I see that this action will kill many and save no one, but that is not enough to justify my not doing it; what really matters is that the action has an extra property that only ethical terms are suited to pick out"?[15]

What Jackson in particular is arguing for here – that ethical terms pick out ethical properties, but that those properties are natural properties – is irrelevant for our purposes: what the quote highlights is the concept of *rhetorical force* at work in moral disagreements and policy debates. If someone doesn't believe that an act is wrong, pointing out that the act has the normative, non-natural property of *being wrong* is of course going to be persuasively ineffectual; that is, it will lack any rhetorical force.[16]

So, if someone says that he wants to buy a kidney, pointing out that *wanting to buy a kidney* has the property of wrongness is unlikely to induce much. But this lack of interlocutor influence does not undermine the truth or falsity of a claim; that is, being unable to convince someone of truth or falsity is not synonymous with something not being true or false.

The further idea is that based on their lack of rhetorical force, discussion of normative concepts and properties does not *add* to our discourse, and hence it is irrelevant and/or ought to be abandoned (or is abandonable). But again, humans have not abandoned this talk (and rightfully so). The question is how to interpret normative moral talk. Such talk is to be interpreted, as I've been arguing, on a cognitive moral realist theory, in which interlocutors try to convince each other of which are the better reasons to act on or base policy on given the better telic orientation. The process of convincing each other, of collective moral deliberation, is largely a process of discovering the arguments that have rhetorical force. Rhetorical force then is not necessarily synonymous with *whatever* persuades people. Rhetorical force derives its power from something other than itself, and in this case it is the normativity of reasons – good reasons, the reasons that matter most, what has the most normative force.

A society ought to try to form its basic rational structure on the reasons that matter most. So, is avoiding exploitation of vulnerable social members the most important reason? Or is this the wrong view of *importance* altogether? As in other moral terms, *importance simpliciter* does not exist. In Finlay's words, "There is no such thing as importance simpliciter, there is only importance for particular subjects ... [and] moral reasons matter (intrinsically) only for those with moral concern." But this is not a problem for practical reason, nor does it push morality towards subjectivism, scepticism, or simple relativism. As Finlay goes on to say, a morally concerned person might just be "almost everyone."[17] Similarly, David Copp's sophisticated community relationalism, unlike simple relativism, does not "rule out the possibility that *there is some moral code that is justified relative to every society*."[18] In these views, rhetorical force is variable: what will ultimately count as being decisive in the *weighing* of the reasons will *always* be a moral reason that matters to reasoners. But reasoners can be mistaken, as, again, ethics is not a matter of logical necessity.[19] In my view, the most powerful moral arguments will have great rhetorical force. But rhetorical force and normative force are not always so neatly entwined. The most powerful moral arguments are those that combine normative force and rhetorical force.

Normative Force and Rhetorical Force Combined

Good reasons, then, possess rhetorical force and normative force. Normative force comes from the relevant facts and reasons that ought to move an agent, but it is not reducible to mere persuasion. An argument can have a high degree of normative force, for example, but a low degree of rhetorical force. For example, simply quoting a statistic about a death toll is not, in isolation, possessed of much rhetorical force, whereas such a fact is still possessed of normative force. But normative force will have strong rhetorical force if an agent responds properly to the relevant information in a moral deliberation. More important, and most relevant to this book, arguments exhibiting normative force will have rhetorical force on the premise that people are moved by normativity, on the idea that a community is full of people who aim for a just society.

The theory of moral disagreement being worked through here, then, is one in which interlocutors argue for telic orientations *and* for certain moral truths, based on both natural facts and the conductive arguing process of weighing reasons. The form is a conductive argument that weighs reasons for and against telic orientation; it is in this way that moral disagreement can still exist despite assent to all of the relevant empirical facts.

The moral realm, then, is open to debate, interpretation, and revision, but is fully consistent with categorical moral realism. That is, I've argued that

a there are right ends, and
b that these are the ends that rational agents ought to have, but
c that rationality in this sense is itself normative, the result of telic orientation, not a matter of necessity, and thus
d ultimately, then, telic orientation, and agent and community choice, guide moral judgment (and hence action), but
e we gain and are led to telic orientations through public moral deliberation *and* the powers of discursive rationality via rhetorical engagement aimed at discovering normative force.

This conclusion, though arriving through a different path, has much in common with moral philosopher Ralph Wedgwood. He persuasively argues that in disagreements, it is rational to have an egocentric bias in forming beliefs and to trust more in our own beliefs than in the beliefs of others. In such a picture, both parties are being fully rational. That is, "Even if we do not respond to learning about disagreement by abandoning our original belief, we do not have to be so dogmatic as to conclude that the other thinker is irrational – although we are committed to thinking that the other thinker is mistaken."[20] Convergence is not always the outcome of moral disagreement, but it does, at the collective, publicly binding level, remain its goal, and seems a likely outcome should arguers with similar telic orientations discover good reasons – those possessed of the greatest rhetorical force and normative force.

This allows for competing rationalities and justifications. It does not go the extra normative step of claiming that in such disagreements, both parties are morally correct. Neither does it hold that both parties are simply rationalizing their inclinations and preferences. Such disagreements exhibit uncertainty, not scepticism, about moral claims and actions. More facts, reasons, and deliberation are seemingly necessary for moral convergence in a society. In the meantime, in terms of collectively binding policy, compromise might be the way to go.

In summary of this chapter, there is a double movement in moral rhetoric: in what agents are *trying to do* and what agents are *able* to do. Agents are trying, pace Gibbard, to reconcile aims, to induce interlocutors to subscribe to one's ends. But, pace Parfit, agents hold and advance these ends not because these ends are their preferences but because they think they are *right*, objective, and nonselective. But they are not right *because* they are one's beliefs, peculiar to the agendas of those who have them. There is a distinction between *believing that* and the actual *content of that belief*, in thinking something is true and something really being true. What is really true is often hard to discern in moral disagreements. The process turns on the *weighing* of reasons, which is, inescapably, a normative process. Reasons are weighed against telic orientations, and some telic orientations are found to be better than others in the context of disagreement.[21] Given as much, universal assent is unlikely, making the codification of moral truths in policy or law practically impossible. This, however, is not because society and its agents are wrong and there is no such thing as moral truths.[22] On the contrary, I have argued for exactly the opposite.

Towards A Rhetorical Theory of Moral Disagreement

Putting together the arguments of this chapter and the previous one, we might see that I've offered something like a *rhetorical theory of moral disagreement* or a theory of good reasons. I advanced a theory of morality as an enterprise of reasoned judgment in a cognitive, realist sense. What that means is as follows: *reasoned judgment* implies that some reasons and moral views are better than others; *cognitivists* hold that moral judgments are beliefs, not mere interests or preferences; and *realists* hold that at least some normative beliefs are indeed true, meaning that humans are not seeking normative truths in vain. What a cognitive moral realism posits is that not all moral theories are equal or true. The move was made to separate out the fact of pluralism – that different individuals and societies often have different moral beliefs – from pluralism as a moral theory (which is false according to cognitive moral realism). Good reasons are not just the reasons that I happen to possess or the reasons that support my favoured outcome. Good reasons are the product of arguments possessed of rhetorical force and normative force, and citizens rhetorically engage with each other in pursuit of such arguments and justifications for their society. What has normative force will have rhetorical force on the premise that people are moved by normativity – in particular, that a community's people aim for a just society.

In public deliberation, the key element is rhetorical force, in which interlocutors try to convince each other of the reasons that matter, of what reasons have *gravitas*. Discovering what reasons matter most and why is a process of weighing reasons. The public sphere produces collectively binding moral judgments. What ends up being given certain weight depends largely on the people and occasion for the weighing. This has resonance with Gibbard's notion of *communities of judgment* insofar as the main concern to communities is what a certain judgment will *cost* the community.[23] Part of public deliberative rhetoric is exactly this and nothing else – what the proposed judgment, on a law, policy, candidate, film, or whatever, will cost us.

The scales on which reasons weigh are one's telic orientation towards a deep and substantive end. The right telic orientation and weighing of reasons is often elusive, and hence requires public deliberation. Here, then, are connections: back to the introduction, where this study was offered in the spirit of deliberative democracy, and to chapter 5's discussion of public reason and values pluralism in detail. But now it should be apparent that my view of deliberative democracy is quite different in *substance* that those offered by other deliberative theorists.

Put simply, the *search* for moral truth, to be codified under law, is collective and procedurally intersubjective[24]; but morality itself is not. That is, procedurally, the deliberative democratic process of norm-constitution works the same for me as it does for almost any of the other theorists, but there is metanormative emphasis that matters in terms of telic orientation, distinguishing between norms in the rule-implying sense (procedural, legitimation types) and norms in the reason-implying sense (normative reasons).[25] The metaethical supplement to the logic of good reasons in rhetorical theory, then, also applies to the conceptualization of the deliberative democratic enterprise.

So, taken in context of discussions thus far, importance is to be placed on intersubjectivity and the cooperative public argument in the Rawlsian constructivist tradition, but that – as seen in this chapter and parts of chapter 5 – such a position is, in relation to morality, ultimately mistaken. Those who think that moral disagreement is simply relativistic or that it amounts strictly to differing preferences have not recognized or have misunderstood the *gravitas* of ethical deliberation in human communities.

In conclusion, what I have offered is an explicit defence of cognitive moral realism and how it supplements the rhetorical theory of good reasons. In this picture, deliberation is valued not for deliberation's sake, nor

is communal consensus actual normative truth. But the cooperative procedural process requires interlocutors to be "epistemically demanding"
of each other, and, in a contractualist picture, citizens owe each other
reasons for their beliefs and actions.[26] The key was to not give up too
much to intersubjectivity in matters of truth and to argue, following previous discussions in this book, that indeed an ethics of citizenship or the
liberal virtue of tolerance is vital to constitutional democracies. But such
is not synonymous with, nor over and above, first-order moral judgments.

Moral rhetoric, and public moral deliberation in specific, then, is a
threefold process of

1 discovering correct ends,
2 convincing each other that those ends are indeed correct, and
3 that engaging in public moral argumentation requires the appropriate stance of being epistemically demanding of each other,
  self-reflexive, and open to mutual influence under normative
  reasoning.

Taking Stock of Where We Are

To summarize the book so far, chapter 1 set up the problem of organ
donation and offered this project in the spirit of rhetoric in the classical
sense and within a conception of deliberative democracy. Chapters 2, 3,
and 4 described the primary arguments and key rhetorical points and
structure of justification for the major positions in organ procurement,
illustrated the conflicting reasons and principles at work in the debate
between the volunteer-based system and compensated-supply advocates.
Chapter 5 gave a background as to how and why there are such conflicting justificatory principles in contemporary pluralistic constitutional
democracies such as the United States and how and why something like
neoliberalism gains adherence and saliency. Then, chapters 6 and 7
defended that there are right answers to moral problems such as human
organ procurement, and that there is a right weighing of reasons and
principles against chosen ends. I have not said that we can know with certainty what the right answers to hard moral questions are, but I do take
to have established that, practically, public deliberation is just the search
for right answers to moral questions – even if the prudent solution is a
sort of ambiguity and latitude in terms of first-order moral judgment.
I argued that moral deliberation is understood as the cooperative search
for good reasons, and that the process of public moral deliberation
involves two major elements: (1) ridding reasoners of mistaken beliefs
held due to an inadequate knowledge or understanding of the relevant

facts and reasons, which includes recognizing relevant reasons and facts that bear on moral deliberation, for which I offered three arguments – the Aims Argument, the Categorical Argument, and the Argument from Normative Force; and (2) reconciling different ways of *weighing* reasons, which occurs when arguers know the relevant facts and reasons, but weigh them differently, and this different weighing results in competing moral judgments. This weighing of reasons, I argued, involves three components: (a) telic orientation, (b) rhetorical force, and (c) the interplay of rhetorical force and normative force. A telic orientation is the *end* towards which one aims, the backdrop that one reasons against that allows better or worse reasons to take shape. The second component in weighing reasons is rhetorical force. Rhetorical force is what *moves* an agent to assent to a claim or agree with a moral theory. An argument with rhetorical force is highly persuasive and might even change someone's moral beliefs and motivate him to act according to the content of that moral belief. Finally, normative force exhibits strong rhetorical force if an agent responds correctly to the relevant information in the moral deliberation. What has normative force will have rhetorical force, based on the idea that people are moved by normativity – in particular, that a community is full of people who aim for a just society.

The theoretical conversation in the preceding chapters offers a framework for understanding the character and nature of morality, especially in discursive publics, and can now, hopefully, help to clarify specific clashes in the human organ procurement debate. We now turn to how and why advocates weigh reasons the way that they do in the case of organ procurement, looking specifically at key questions of the scope of the market and community life, exploitation, consistency, and dignity.

SECTION FOUR

Weighing Reasons in the Organ Debate

8 The Scope of the Market: Exploitation, Coercion, Paternalism, and Legal Consistency

The next two chapters evaluate *how* advocates weigh reasons to arrive at judgments. Particularly, there will be analyses of (1) competing ends in the human organ procurement debate; (2) clarification of what is at stake in these competing ends; and (3) what survives critical scrutiny in terms of advocates' weights and ends for their society. It examines what has normative force and analyses which arguments have rhetorical force and why, trying to understand how the arguments are put together and weighed by the advocates, and what characterizes their weighing, their telic orientations, and their criticism of other positions.

Advocates' respective telic orientations are exposed via five major conflicts in the weighing of reasons: (a) the scope of the market in a constitutional democracy; (b) the question of justice and legal rational consistency; (c) problems of vulnerability, exploitation, and coercion in market systems; (d) the question of dignity in human organ sales and moral motivation; and (e) a distinction between what cannot be sold and what should not be sold. This chapter will address (a) through (c), and the next chapter will address (d) and (e).

Let me briefly characterize these five major conflicts in the weighing of reasons.

The first issue that is characterized differently by advocates is the scope of the market in a constitutional democracy. Here advocates have different visions for what the market should and should not cover in the United States. This includes two extreme positions, that of universal commodification, in which everything is for sale, and that of market rejection, in which any commodification results in reduced humanity and/or alienation *en toto*. A key stasis point here is the issue of whether one's body is one's property in a legal sense.

The second issue is that of justice and its relation to legal consistency. In short, market advocates make a partners-in-guilt argument that the denial of a market in human organs is rationally inconsistent with current

US law allowing bodily markets and hence is unjust, whereas altruistic advocates claim that to allow a market in human organs would be unjust given that it violates certain basic human rights.

The third section addresses how issues of vulnerability and coercion are interrelated and are the most robust disagreements, and also connect to the conceptualization and operationalization of *dignity*. The discussion turns on whether markets do or do not exemplify exploitation of vulnerable citizens. The issue of dignity – how dignity is or is not violated by organ sales, and, relatedly, if something like dignity ever could actually be bought or sold or violated through commodification – is the most central, and so I will isolate it and treat it separately in the next chapter.

Overall, we now have the task of evaluating how advocates weigh reasons by exposing the advocates' varying telic orientations. The interplay of rhetorical force and normative force, as established in the previous chapter, will be articulated in relation to market and altruistic rhetoric.

The Market's Reach: Organ Commodification, the Question of Property, and Market Prohibitions

The first set of arguments that advocates weigh differently is the scope of the market in US society. One reason offered by advocates for the status quo is that organ commodification stems from a problem in capitalist societies – namely, that everything in capitalist societies pushes towards commodification. This will be addressed in the first subsection. A counterargument to this view is that, indeed, everything can be commoditized, but the better language choice is property. When one thinks of one's body as one's private property, the negative implications of commodification and the association of treating oneself as chattel disappears. In the US, one is free to sell private property or to hold onto it forever. This line of reasoning is addressed in the second subsection.

The final subsection examines two notions that try to split between these two views, in which markets and capitalism writ large are not inherently problematic, but that does not mean that there shouldn't be limits to what is commodified and/or viewed as property.

Organ Commodification and the Fetish

One of the strongest voices against financial compensation is Nancy Scheper-Hughes, whose critiques of organ selling also indict the much larger sociopolitical context. She claims that

individual autonomy – that is, a patient's right to choose – has become the final arbiter of medical bioethical value ... [and that notions of] social justice ... [and] the good society hardly figure in these discussions, for bioethical standards have been thoroughly disciplined and brought into alignment with the needs and desires of consumer-oriented globalization.[1]

Her story is not just about the problems of buying and selling human organs per se but the overarching frameworks in which the arguments take place. The two frameworks are global capitalism and bioethical discourse, both of which have been disciplined to reflect individual autonomy as *the* justifying framework for moral claims, in resonance with the arguments of autonomy and neoliberal-by-default arguments we explored in chapter 5.

In Scheper-Hughes's judgment, values lag behind economics, and the conditions of modernity perpetuate this lag time. The people who are supposed to be cognizant of this lag – bioethicists – are complicit in the very problem. Bioethicists do not make *ethical* justifications but simply put together economic individualist rationales. Individual autonomy under global capitalism somehow stands apart from ethics – the notions of social justice and the good society invoked in the quote above.

One potential counter to Scheper-Hughes's argument is that it runs straight into the question of *whose justice/whose vision of the good society.* Conceptions of social justice and the good society are precisely what public argumentation contests and law tries to avoid pronouncing on too universally in liberal democracies. The more substantive a vision, the more likely some citizen somewhere will disagree with it. The troubled citizen can make a claim that the right to pursue the good life as each citizen sees fit is violated and coercively structured to preclude his view.

In fact, it is the ambiguity in the nature of just what the good life is and what social justice entails that spurs much of the market advocates' case, preferring maximal leeway to citizens in constructing as much. We could take that line here, of course, but I do not find that argument particularly persuasive unless we truly *want* to live in the neoliberal-by-default society – that is, unless we think that the neoliberal-by-default society actual *is* more just, gets us closer to the good life, and so forth. But I am sceptical, as most of section III suggests. This is not, of course, to say that Scheper-Hughes's vision is *the* correct one; it is rather to say that it is incoherent to dismiss her vision on the grounds that it coercively structures towards a substantive vision of justice and the good life.

That is, societies are always structured coercively in certain ways. Laws, taxes, and policy are all practised and structured to promote certain practices and disincentivize others. If the goal is to avoid *that* level of basic social arrangement, one is speaking, it seems, not of society but of anarchy. To be clear: the point here is that both a commodificationist and non-commodificationist about human organs do not actually disagree about whether or not laws are content-full or not – even if they think they do. As long as there *are* laws, policies, taxes and the like, there will always be some element of morality entwined in legal and social elements.

A more significant puzzle to Scheper-Hughes's argument is that her claim about who or what views are dominant conflicts directly with the market advocates' claim about which views and theories are running bioethics and medicine more generally. That is, her claim is that bioethics in general and specific serves the imperatives of neoliberalism, while most market advocates argue that the field of bioethics is uniformly and mistakenly categorical about morality. Clearly, bioethics cannot be both individualistic/hypothetical about morality and thereby eschew social justice and, at the same time, categorical in its prohibitions about one's rights in an overarching vision of a good society. While I am sympathetic to Scheper-Hughes's view that ethical practices, such as bioethics, in democracies are skewing more and more towards neoliberalism (and potentially fully aligned in clinical bioethics), in the specific case of human organs, given the illegality, the tip is towards the categorical.

But when human body parts become commodities, there are negative consequences to the social values of cohesion and justice. Scheper-Hughes's employment of *the fetish* is highly relevant. The notion of the fetish ties her argument conceptually to Marxian critiques of capitalism in which everything in a capitalist society is under the purview of the market, and hence a commodity (or able to be commoditized). This results in a fetishization of commodities – an unhealthy amount of attention and emotional and spiritual investment in things and/or the treatment of everything *as a thing* and therefore as a commodity. One need not be a Marxist to see the salient point of alienation that results from universal thinking of *thingness.*

Consider, for example, Steve Farber, a transplant recipient and compensation advocate. Here's a candid and vulnerable confession on this account:

> To human rights activists, the idea of buying and selling transplant organs is abominable. And they may have a point. My own search for a healthy kidney came to resemble a "fetishizing" of the organ. The group of intimates that formed around me was like something out of J.R.R. Tolkien's *Fellowship of the Ring*, with that kidney starring as the ring.[2]

The idea here, very much in line with Faber's invocation of Tolkien's ring – *the precious!* – is that the outcome of fetishization and commodification is not just alienation from oneself and a misunderstanding of the formation of a self and what it means to be human. The further point is that fetishization in the sense of universal commodification establishes and perpetuates a *society* that *reifies* such an alienation.

It is a double turn for the critics of commodification and market ubiquity: the individual misunderstands or misidentifies herself and what it means to be human, and her society affirms (maybe even promotes) such a view. A society that affirms members in a self-conception of their bodies as commodities is unlikely to be a good, just society. Something deeper, they reason, is missing here. The logic of capitalism pushes towards universal commodification. So according to advocates of the altruistic regime who significantly weight the problem of commodification as a scope of the market problem, we must resist the logic of capitalism. This is consistent with the civic republicanism that aims at a collective and just society that reinforces notions of personhood, identity, and value beyond monetization. Altruistic advocates argue that the self, and society, are not commodities, and that each has a role to play in mutually reinforcing the non-commodified view of what it means to be human and in community together.

The Body as Property and Rejections of Paternalism

The notion of one's body as property – rather than body as commodity – might offer a less inciting characterization of how to think through organ procurement. This section explores the alternative language and conceptual framing of the body as property. Property and commodity are related (if not identical in extension),[3] but there is a different intuition that seems to fire in discussions of body as property as compared to body as commodity. That is, the notion of oneself as a commodity typically invokes a strong moral intuition of disgust from across the political spectrum, either as a mistake in self-conception or as conjuring images of slavery (i.e., where people literally are a commodity). Property rhetoric has resonance on both the political right and left.

The language of *property* has deep resonance in many Western nations, especially the United States. The limitations of government to interfere with and/or revoke private property in the Lockean tradition appears as a Fifth Amendment protection, and much private-property discourse drives liberal-democratic conceptions of societies over and against other government models (e.g., socialism, communism, etc.).

The body-as-property view enjoys significant legal standing in the second half of the twentieth century, perhaps most notably in the case of abortion. One legal scholar puts the argument for abortion rights squarely in terms of the Fifth Amendment: while not definitive, "given the close connection the framers saw between property rights and personal rights, it should shed considerable light on how the fifth amendment ought to work to protect women's right to choose."[4] Also recall a feminist slogan that runs, "My body is my property."

Now, it would be strange for feminists to be shouting a proclamation of body commoditization: for example, "My body is just like a used car!" In other words, this is not a *celebration* of the transition from personhood to thinghood decried by critics like Scheper-Hughes. Rather, advocates mean not that *my body is like a car* (a commodity understanding) but that *my body is mine in the sense of private ownership* (a property understanding). The emphasis here is not "My body is my *property,*" but rather "*My* body is *my* property."

Market advocates tap into the private-property tradition through the invocation of body-as-property arguments. Some legal articles have employed a body-as-property defence, rooted in abortion legality, of human body parts in particular.[5] The connection between the abortion case and the organ sales case is enlightening, and cuts in non-obvious political directions, thus making for a rhetorically brilliant yoking of abortion and organ procurement: mutual acceptance or mutual rejection, but, on the property view, logically incoherent to accept one and not the other.

Consider that Judith Jarvis Thomson's argument, as one of the most famous statements on the permissibility of abortion, used the analogy of organ sales and abortion almost exactly in reverse. She invites us to imagine this scenario:

> You wake up in the morning and find yourself back to back in bed with an unconscious violinist. A famous unconscious violinist. He has been found to have a fatal kidney ailment, and the Society of Music Lovers has canvassed all the available medical records and found that you alone have the right blood type to help. They have therefore kidnapped you, and last night the violinist's circulatory system was plugged into yours, so that your kidneys can be used to extract poisons from his blood as well as your own. The director of the hospital now tells you, "Look, we're sorry the Society of Music Lovers did this to you – we would never have permitted it if we had known. But still, they did it, and the violinist now is plugged into you. To unplug you would be to kill him. But never mind, it's only for nine months. By then he will have recovered from his ailment, and can safely be unplugged from you."[6]

In the same way that feminists fought for abortion rights as a right to their body, as their property, in a rejection of (state) paternalism, *that same justification* is redeployed by financial-compensation advocates: my body is my private property, and the state cannot interfere in what I do with it, including buying or selling parts of it; I am free to choose what I want to do with my body.

The call by advocates here, then, is one of legal rational consistency (discussed in more detail below), characterized as a rejection of state paternalism of its citizen's bodies – which are, after all, private property. The view also expresses unrest with the alternative: if my body is not *my* property, then *whose* property is it? That your body somehow belongs to the community or to the state is a conception that causes citizens of nearly all political stripes to recoil.[7]

This two-handed discourse – claiming negative liberty as a rejection of the nanny state and of one's body as one's private property – resonates strongly in contemporary US society, given the discussion in chapter 5 and in particular in the post-*Roe v. Wade* sociopolitical and legal landscape.

If one accepts the body-as-property arguments, then organ sales are clearly permissible. Advocates weigh the notion of private property as a legally complete conception of selfhood that is central to liberal democracy; ergo, the permissibility of abortion and organ sales. That is, in this view, the scope of the market is wide and literally covers everything – including oneself. Your body is a property – private property, with all of its associational rights deriving from the Constitution.

If we legally view the body as property as discussed in this section, I see no rational way to block abortion and not organ sales. Either they both ought to be legal, or both illegal, but not one of each. The issue, it seems to me, is not *whose* property is the body, but that the body *isn't* property in any legally understood sense of the term.[8] The idea of viewing one's body as neither commodity nor property is at the root of an alternative, middle position between the two poles of anti-commodification and universal commodification, discussed next.

*Against Universal Commodification: Market Inalienability
and Noxious Markets*

One of the striking features of neoliberal justifications in cases as diverse as abortion and organ sales is that *everything* is viewed as a commodity or property, including the self. That is, while many critics in the United States reject the Marxian-style critique of commodification and the alienation of the self under capitalism, many of those same critics voluntarily protect themselves and what they perceive as valuable in rights-based discourse steeped in the language of universal commodification. This is evident in the body-as-property argument above as advocates reason that the premise of negative liberty in the case of private property is enshrined in the Bill of Rights, and legality of actions with one's body simply turns on arguing for a minor premise of one's body as property.

But there is another perspective that argues against universal commodification and body-as-property arguments but still employs a decidedly capitalist framework. Two related concepts make up this perspective. The first one is the notion of *market inalienability*, and the second is that of *noxious markets*. This subsection discusses how these two concepts play a strong role in altruistic advocates' rhetoric, given that each allows for limits to a laissez-faire market but neither falls into a wider indictment of market systems *en toto*.

The concept of market inalienability ties directly to the clause in the Declaration of Independence that citizens have certain *unalienable rights*. Margaret Jane Radin makes this point – and perhaps the defining statement on the issue – in a nearly hundred-page *Harvard Law Review* article.[9] The notion here is that if one takes the two poles on the political-economic spectrum to be that *everything is for sale* on the one side and that *nothing is for sale* on the other, market inalienability are those things that are not for sale in an otherwise market-based social and political economy. The quintessential example here is slavery. Under a model of universal commodification, in which everything is for sale, ostensibly even people could be bought and sold, in accordance with or against their will. She notes how human organs are an example of contested commodification in the current moment.[10]

As seen in the case of slavery, paradigm candidates for market inalienability are things generally tied to personhood and, more complicatedly, the notion of human dignity (discussed in detail in the next chapter). The idea is that with something such as slavery, it is the very *essence* of a person (their personhood, their dignity) that is violated, and that markets in such things ought to be prohibited. The key turn here is that this is a *moral* reason for limiting markets and one that, hopefully, enjoys universal assent.

Radin offers her theory of market inalienability as characterized by conceptions of human flourishing. She does not give a detailed account of what is meant by *flourishing*, other than that it is tied to notions of personhood, and that her key supplement to current literature on personhood is that "connections between the person and her environment are integral to personhood."[11] The overall picture here is that flourishing is itself socially defined, and that there is no way to settle the matter for once and for all, but that material conditions and normative arguments interplay to set democratic moral limitations on markets.

Similarly, Debra Satz offers her notion of *noxious markets*, which are those markets that deserve, for good reasons, to be limited and/or prohibited. In *Why Some Things Should Not Be for Sale: The Moral Limits of*

Markets, she details more specifically than Radin what defines and characterizes such markets. In particular, markets are analysed across four parameters: (1) vulnerability, (2) weak agency, (3) extremely harmful outcomes for individuals, and (4) harmful outcomes to societies at large.[12] Should a market possess these features or even just an abundance of one of them, it is deemed a noxious market and thus ought to be prohibited in constitutional democracies.

Briefly, each of Satz's four parameters is characterized as follows. The two most straightforward parameters relate to harmful outcomes: *extreme harm for an individual* means that the market produces "destitution" and harm to "basic welfare" of the individual, while *extreme harm for a society* means that the market "promotes servility and dependence," "undermines democratic governance," and/or "undermines other[oriented]" moral motivations.[13] These two harmful outcomes, individual and societal, are produced by the noxious market, but are more specifically sourced in two concepts: weak agency and vulnerability. *Weak agency* results when one party has incomplete information about the "nature and/or consequences of the market" or when "others enter the market on one's behalf." *Vulnerability* is characteristic of markets in a "desperately needed good with a limited supplier" or with its "origins in poverty and destitution" or whose participants have "unequal needs for goods being exchanged."[14] Using the example of slavery, one can see how it scores high along all four dimensions: vulnerability, by having its origins in poverty; weak agency, given that someone is entering the market on one's behalf; harm for the individual, as it produces/maintains the slave's financial destitution; and harm for society, in that it promotes servility and undermines (at least *liberal*) democratic governance.

There are two different weighing mechanisms at work in organ procurement rhetoric. There are those, such as Richard Epstein and Richard Posner, who are (nearly) universal commodificationists, in that almost anything can be bought and sold given clear contractual specifications. They are in favour of a variety of otherwise noxious markets – most notably, perhaps, in the buying and selling of babies.[15]

There is another kind of market advocate who adheres to a moral limit to markets in principle – that is, the general conception of market inalienability – but just disagrees that organ selling constitutes a noxious market or that human organs are market inalienable. The debate here turns sharply on the concepts of vulnerability and weak agency, as discussed above. The employment of these concepts requires more detail, particularly through the terms of exploitation and coercion, and these terms arise based on differing understandings of justice.

Justice and Legal Rational Consistency

This section explores how advocates' usage of key terms such as vulnerability hinges on differing conceptions of justice: market advocates' sense of justice as treating like cases alike, and altruistic advocates' sense of justice as requiring enquiry into the background conditions enabling the case. Both senses of justice enjoy strong intuitive assent from US citizens. Breaking down the senses further, the first is, simply, treating like cases in a like manner. So Tyler's first-time grand-theft-auto conviction and no previous record receives a certain sentence, and Gabe's first-time grand-theft-auto conviction and no previous record should receive the same sentence. If Tyler is given two years in prison and Gabe is given fifteen, we are inclined to say that something is unjust in this situation.

The second notion runs deeper. Justice means more than the formalities evident in the Gabe and Tyler case. This might be seen if Lindow is added to the story. Lindow also commits first-time grand theft auto and has no previous record, but it is because he was escaping from a torture chamber where he was being held against his will, as his parents sold him to the torturer. Now to give Lindow two years in prison, just like we gave Tyler and Gabe, seems also unjust – but it is clearly a different sense of justice, then, being invoked here.

One plausible reading is that the moral intuition to cut Lindow a break is based on a notion of grace, not justice. But there is also a notion of justice at work here, as evidenced in the plausibility of calling such a situation unjust, and that is that somehow the *background conditions* that lead to the otherwise illegal act were somehow unjust. The distinction here corresponds roughly to a sense of substantive justice, in which the underlying content and background conditions are foregrounded in deciding moral and legal permissibility, and procedural justice, in which like cases are treated alike based on concepts of equals before the (legal or moral) law. Some relevance to distributive and commutative justice – or between natural and political justice as we might find in Aristotle – has bearing here, in which relations between two individuals and broader social relations are evident (and evidently in tension) with each other, and potentially in tension with substantive or procedural justice.[16] US law is steeped in both the procedural and the substantive, both the commutative and the distributive, with many examples of each.

In terms of NOTA and the prohibition on a market in human organs, one can see advocates on each side arguing for justice, and its correlate in legal rational consistency being weighed differently due to these differing notions. Let's look at three key arguments in this way.

Human Organ Prohibitions Are Legally Inconsistent

If indeed one's body has the legal standing of property, as something like the legality of abortion might indicate, then for purposes of legal rational consistency, organ sales must also be permitted. While few advocates make this comparison directly, there are a host of even more carefully connected bodily elements with legality that drives these partners-in-guilt justifications. The main candidates here are that current US law recognizes the permissibility in buying and selling sperm and ova, surrogacy, and human hair.

Gerald Dworkin says as much: "We accept the legitimacy of the sale of blood, semen, ova, hair, and tissue. By doing so, we accept the idea that individuals have the right to dispose of their organs and other bodily parts if they so choose."[17] Add to this list the Ninth Circuit Court of Appeals ruling in December 2011 that bone marrow donors can be now compensated,[18] and the human bodily market is getting pretty large. It covers a number of different bodily elements and is becoming more engrained in contemporary society.

The rational-consistency argument insisting like cases treated alike further draws on the legal history of bodily exclusion being overturned. That is, previous bodily related markets were also met with controversy, and the concerns eventually subsided. Richard DeVos, a heart transplant recipient who testified in 2003 in favour of financial incentives for organ givers, says,

> There were lots of big headlines about all kinds of issues in the past. For example, in vitro fertilization was terribly controversial and people yelled and screamed about how unethical it is and how terrible it is. That made headlines. Today there are thousands of [women] every year who benefit from in vitro fertilization and have children that they never could have had otherwise.[19]

Michele Goodwin gives further examples of sperm and ova as "blended public and private financial exchanges in the body."[20] The call is not for people to buy and sell their sperm to one another privately (i.e., directly) but instead to have regulated and efficient markets.

One of Goodwin's major arguments for financial compensation, recall, is that market mechanisms and transactions are already deeply imbedded in the transplant process. Tissue banks buy and sell human parts, and biotech firms form a billion-dollar industry.[21] Rational consistency invites recognition of the way in which the current compensation and market-mechanism elements favour the interests of firms and *not* the actual organ givers. Legal scholar Danielle Wagner thinks this a concern of justice:

> The scales of justice are tipped away from the interests of those who donate their organs and tissues out of blind adherence to tradition and fear of taking the first step toward equity. The legislature must address this issue and provide a system of compensation before organ and tissue donors realize that their charity is lining the pockets of researchers and hospitals, and they rebel and cease donating.[22]

All in all, for financial-compensation advocates, legal rational consistency ends up being a major reason that matters, put squarely in terms of justice, and is thus perhaps the heaviest weighted of all the reasons available in the case of organ procurement. It certainly has rhetorical force.

Human Organ Prohibitions Are Legally Consistent

Defenders of the altruistic status quo thus have to explain why organs are somehow different than things such as sperm/ova, bone marrow, blood, surrogacy, and hair. The demands for consistency put pressure on altruistic advocates to rearticulate, or disarticulate, their position from current legal standings and rulings.

The first strategy is to claim that partners-in-guilt arguments (that *these* new arguments are just like *those* established and accepted arguments) do not actually make something morally acceptable. For all intents and purposes, an advocate could claim that bone marrow or sperm markets are wrong as well, affirming partners in guilt but from the other direction (all of it should be illegal). But from a legal standpoint, in particular from a *political conception of justice* as discussed in detail in chapter 5, this type of reasoning is blocked.

A second strategy is to suggest that there is something inherently different about organs. The most common claim is that sperm, blood, and bone marrow are all replenishable; once someone gives, for example, some of her bone marrow, her body replenishes and makes more. This strategy is met with contrary market claims that one's liver also replenishes itself if a suitably manageable size has been removed, and that living with one kidney is perfectly safe to one's health. Or, from a slightly different angle, that a woman's ova are not in infinite supply or that there are health risks associated with surrogacy as well.

This leaves only one strategy for arguing that the prohibition is legally consistent: to claim that selling one's organs is more like other legally prohibited markets or goods/services. For example, organ selling is more akin to sex labour or child labour than selling sperm. This is the strategy taken explicitly by Debra Satz: the primary problem with a market in human organs is the same problem with child labour and women's sexual labour. The key factors, for her, as detailed in her notion of noxious markets discussed above, have to do with protection of vulnerable populations and the background conditions in which individuals enter into contracts.

In terms of vulnerable populations, one can see the comparison to child labour. There is a moral intuition about eight-year-olds working in, say, coal mines, that strikes nearly everyone as wrong in most situations. Satz is careful to point out that there are child labour situations that do not involve necessarily involve harmful outcomes to children or society, once certain bottom-line categoricals are established (no children as prostitutes, in slavery, in bondage, or as soldiers).[23] While of course there is the element of weak agency, and children are certainly an overall vulnerable population, the point here is that some situations are so dire that a child must work to help provide for herself or family. But that is not to *morally accept* child labour. Rather, the problem of child labour is really a deeper social problem. As she puts it,

> Child labor may be understandable in parts of the world as a response to poverty. But different distributions of wealth and power would undercut the need for child labor. Much depends on whether these alternative distributions can be realized.[24]

The problem of child labour is not simply a problem of legality, in which the material conditions of a person's life and environment run against moral intuitions of acceptable labour behaviour. The problem is with the *background conditions of society.*

In terms of society's background conditions, the same analysis extends to woman as sexual labourers. Satz discusses the requisite consenting-adults-entering-into-contracts element of prostitution. But there is an underlying problem, a background condition, that makes the actual contractual engagement – even if undertaken voluntarily – morally suspect. Satz's case is not based on a notion of the act of prostitution *degrading* a woman but that it is "wrong by virtue of its contributions to perpetuating a pervasive form of inequality: status inequality between men and women."[25] The egalitarian perspective indicates the orientation of distributive justice, opposed to the contractual specifications perspective of neoliberalism. This is a differing telic orientation, predicated on differing views of justice, between market and altruistic advocates.

Human organ selling must connect to the background conditions under which individuals – even consenting, informed, and contract-signing adults – live. Prior problems of distributive justice pervade the scene. To the advocates of the altruistic model, the reasons that matter are connected to the background condition of inequality *from which spring* asymmetrical power and money relations among consenting adults. This means, then, that the issue of background conditions in which adults enter into contracts matters and requires more careful explication.

Protecting the Vulnerable: Exploitation, Coercion, and (Again) the Problems of Paternalism

Markets require certain background conditions to thrive, just as classical political economists told us. One element of agreement among market theorists in terms of background conditions is the necessity of parity (at least in principle) among participants as roughly equal in risk and reward. Without as much, noxious markets are prone to arising (as seen easily in the case of slavery, for example). Satz puts it this way: "Lurking behind many, if not all, noxious markets are problems relating to the *standing* of the parties before, during, and after the process of exchange."[26]

The contestation in the case of organ procurement turns, most sharply, on this issue: To what degree would a market in human organs impair or exacerbate power asymmetries? The most minimal common ground in this debate is that a market in human organs reifies power asymmetries. What makes this a reason that matters to altruistic advocates but not market advocates is that the former find it unacceptable while the latter find it unavoidable. That is, on the one hand, for the altruistic advocates, there is too much power asymmetry both prior to and after the exchange, and hence the result is a noxious market and the ensuing judgment is of prohibition.

Market advocates, on the other hand, think the asymmetry in such a case is more akin to low-paying jobs: these aren't jobs that any rich person would want, but that doesn't mean we should bar people from doing them, and such jobs can also provide a basic step in the ladder of upward mobility. The next three subsections detail that conclusion through careful analysis of the concepts of exploitation, vulnerability, coercion as employed in the debate of human organ procurement strategies.

Exploitation, Vulnerability, and Coercion

This section details the conceptual link between exploitation, vulnerability, and coercion in the human organ debate in particular and law in general. The concept of vulnerability has played an important role in policymaking, from economic limitations on things such as slavery and child labour, as discussed above, to the establishment and practice of institutional review boards. The essential link to law is not only that the vulnerable should be cared for but also that their precarious position poises them to be exploited. Exploitation – unfairly taking advantage of people to their detriment and one's benefit – is something that, as an abstract principle, most everyone is against. In fact, the seeming emptiness of the term has created many sociopolitical and legal problems. As legal scholar Jon Lawrence Hill puts it, "The concept of exploitation has assumed the role of an omnibus moral catch-all category, a term with as many meanings as those who use it, and which is, precisely for this reason, a most mercurial charge to which to respond."[27] This is because what counts as exploitation depends on what is fair and what isn't, which is no less malleable of a concept.

One of the most common claims against organ procurement is that it will exploit the poor. Low-income individuals would be the only ones selling their organs, thereby making poor people the organ vendors to the rich. Francis Delmonico puts exploitation this way:

> Payments [for organs] do the following: they exploit vulnerable members of society. And that degree of exploitation ... as we now know from the black market around the world of organ sales, is influenced by where they live, by their gender, by their ethnicity, by their social status. That is a reality that is well-described.[28]

Market logic applied to organ sales results in exploitation of vulnerable members, which means that the worse off in society (as determined through a matrix of income, location, gender, ethnicity, social status) serve the needs of the better off in the end. This outcome, from an egalitarian and distributive-justice perspective, in which democracy means an equal playing field among citizens, is undesirable.

Market advocates recognize the problem of exploitation and coercion. Such concerns animate emphasizing a *regulated* market. That is, the organ market would not be *unfettered* or *open* per se. Instead, as advocates such as Hippen and de Castro make clear, the concerns of exploitation are high, and *hence* oversight is necessary. As Hippen highlights, "Any system of incentives requires regulation and oversight, and it is a caricature to suppose that there is a contradiction between free exchange and the strictures of law."[29] In de Castro's words, "Clearly, [a market] will require a huge amount of effort to guard against oppressive commodification and exploitation. Considering the great number of lives that can be saved and enhanced, the effort is not likely to go to waste."[30]

Exploitation concerns relate to economic and material coercion. Should a kidney or a piece of one's liver be worth, say, $50,000, a struggling low-income person would, ostensibly, be unable to turn down such an offer. As there is a link between vulnerability and exploitation, there is also an intimate link between exploitation and coercion in terms of moral disapproval. This is why one might think differently of the case of a scalper selling a Radiohead ticket for 200 per cent more than its face value and a man who, amid a water crisis, purchases all the bottled water from Costco and resells the bottles at 200 per cent of face value.[31] Both are, at some level, cases of exploitation, but it seems that only the latter is coercive, the difference being due, likely, to the degree of necessity of the object.[32]

Given the necessity of money to survival in US society, a large amount of money for an organ would be coercive at some level to poor people. Representative DeGette put the matter squarely: "It has been against the public policy of this country to pay people for organ donations for many, many years ... and the feeling is that it would unduly put pressure on low-income individuals to do that."[33] There is unequal standing between the participants in the exchange, and the money coerces the would-be-seller to do something that she does not want to do. Furthermore, the problem here is that the benefits to the organ- buyer are greater than those to the organ seller. Risk, reward, and power are significantly asymmetrical in the exchange. Nonetheless, the need for an organ by a person in dire straits and facing death is not exactly an empowering situation, either.

Exploitation and Wage Labour

Market advocates claim organ procurement need not reduce to coercion or exploitation. To them, a legal market in human organs rids the world from the otherwise "irrepressible black market."[34] It is the *black* market that is truly exploitative. Beyond the black market, the problem of exploitation in markets – coercing someone to do something they do not want to do – is entirely unspecific to organ procurement. Rather, exploitation, conceived so abstractly, could be applied to nearly *any* market transaction in a capitalistic society. In Mark Cherry's words,

> Individuals may prefer leisure to work, or to receiving expensive medical resources for little or no personal expense; however, such circumstances do not entail either that employment harms workers, or that hospitals that require payment for services rendered harm patients.[35]

In addition to introducing the notion of *harm*, Cherry's point is that US society is packed full of instances in which people, in a sense, *have* to do things they would otherwise prefer not to do. And it strikes me as correct that in a society such as the United States, the vast majority of people are doing work they'd rather not do. In this sense, market advocates often try to indict advocates of curtailing exploitation and coercion as anti-capitalist; that is, to market advocates, the exploitation and coercion perspective only holds purchase if we take *all*, or nearly all, labour to be exploitative.

Goodwin gives the most succinct statement of this case:

> We would like to believe that our bodies exist outside the domain of alien-ability at all times. If we are honest, we realize this is not true as wage labor debunks that notion. Value is placed on our labor, skill, intellect, brawn, and beauty. Moreover, we are not free from coercion or pressure in the accepted patterns of daily alienation (i.e. doing work we would rather refuse).[36]

Exploitation, to these advocates, is not a reason that matters in the case of organ procurement. Counting it as a premise in the argument against a market in human organs, one will be *rationally* forced to follow it to its Marxist conclusion – that all labour ends up being exploitative.[37] Market advocates assume that the Marxist conclusion is so undesirable that exploitation cannot then be a meaningful category, for the introduction of exploitation into market systems will end up resulting in a rejection of market systems entirely. The rhetoric here is that exploitation, in some baseline sense of the term, applies to all market interactions, and so, either (a) freedom from exploitation means freedom from capital-ism (in a way that a certain kind of universal non-commodificationist would agree), or (b) that exploitation is not a useful or relevant word in the discussion.

Furthermore, to market advocates, to ban a market in human organs cuts off low-income individuals from an option to make money. Altruistic advocates say that market logic applied to organ sales results in exploita-tion of vulnerable members, which means that the worse off in society end up only maintaining and reifying the gap between themselves and the better off. Mark Cherry, for example, denies such, saying that what is missing is, essentially, the concept of mobility. The prohibition of the organ market "further restrict[s] options for the poor ... [and] unlike those better off, the impoverished are prevented from fully utilizing the market for their own advantage."[38] Sally Satel has a similar observation: "How is it unfair to poor people if compensation enhances their qual-ity of life?"[39] So in Cherry and Satel's view, the organ prohibition based on moral reasons – a moral paternalism – amounts to a continued eco-nomic impoverishment for low-income individuals, cutting off options for upward mobility through market mechanisms.

There is some data from organ sellers to support this view. Most of the ethnographic and interview data from organ sellers falls in line with this description from a seller in India: "On the day of the operation, I felt like a *kurbanir goru*, a sacrificial cow purchased for slaughtering on the day of *Eid.*" But, as discussed in chapter 3, this is not always the case. Sallie Yea, writing about Baseco slum in Manila, was surprised to find many individuals enquiring about how they, too, could sell their kidneys, and asking a recent seller to "hook them up" with his broker.[40] Between desperate sellers and desperate buyers, there is plenty of suffering, it seems, to go around.

If the claims of exploitation and moral coercion as present in current political-economic arrangements are correct, then we would have a serious issue in the contemporary status quo. Market advocates claim that limiting the options for work for society's worse off is not merely an economic concern but also a moral one. In short, is it possible that the domestic or global poor are not being exploited in the way that altruistic advocates think? That the right analogue is not ova or blood, or abortion, but the very direness of background conditions that altruistic advocates stress?

A Critique of Neoliberal Moral-Coercion and Exploitation Arguments

This section analyses the claim that there is both a moral and economic problem in prohibiting organ sales, taking Mark Cherry as representative of the neoliberal position. The problem, in his view, is not just the moral paternalism at work in the prohibition against organ sales. It is also that the moral prohibition itself amounts to coercion. It is the "unjustified coercion of legislative moral monism."[41] Here we see that coercion *is* a moral concept, and instantiations of it are indeed wrong. But to Cherry, it is the advocates of the volunteer system who are coercive in their prohibition, denying individuals agency to improve their lives. Here is one of his summative passages:

> The market increases the number of options open to impoverished individuals to improve their prospects while saving the lives of patients who are desperately ill. In contrast, prohibition appears to exploit the poor and sick to support particular views of moral propriety and human dignity, denying those impoverished and ill an important opportunity freely to choose how best to advantage themselves.[42]

This is a remarkable turn of argument and language. Here Cherry preserves the notions of exploitation and coercion as moral concepts that pick out wrong acts, but says that in the case of organ procurement, *coercion* picks out the practices of altruistic advocates and the supporting legal and bioethical-medical apparatus in preventing alternative view-points, and *exploitation* picks out those same people's treatment of those sick and dying of organ failures.

Cherry's reasoning is quite confusing. One recognizes what Cherry means here by *coercive*, in which a categorical morality serving across a morally pluralistic society ends up being coercive to dissenters (as explored in section III). That is, whether or not a market in human organs is a good idea is indeed an open question; but – if my arguments in chapter 6 are correct – that there are cognitive moral realistic claims is not. If there are rights and wrongs, it is strange to speak of them as coercive. That is, it would be strange to say that the claim "the force of gravity exists on Earth" is *coercive* against gravity- deniers, or to say that "we have been coerced into thinking two and two add up to four." But should there be a legal ruling about the status of gravity and basic math, it would be, at some level, coercive. So the wording is strange, but I guess it is defensible at a very basic but abstract level.

The claim that the "prohibition exploits the poor and sick" is seemingly indefensible, however. Charitably, what Cherry means by exploitation here is that the prohibition is unfair – that prohibition is unfair to the poor and sick, given that one could become less poor and the other less sick through this mechanism. But exploitation is not a concept that is *synonymous* with fairness; if a father gives his daughter $10 and his son $5, the son could intelligibly claim unfairness, but to claim exploitation would be utterly foreign.[43]

Exploitation is intimately linked with fairness, but it also has to do with advantage, with asymmetrical gain. What is it that the status quo *gains* here? Cui bono? To what purpose is this "exploitation" done? Cherry indicates that the status quo does so in order to "support particular views of moral propriety and human dignity." So the claim is that the status quo *exploits* the poor and sick so that it can maintain a particular view of human dignity.

Put baldly, the line of reasoning is that US lawmakers (and anyone else) against a market in human organs accept the poor staying poor and the sick staying sick *because* they believe in human dignity, and that they *exploit* the poor and sick in order to support this belief in human dignity. It is hard to untangle this knot that Cherry has tied. The oft-used images of morality as after the Tower of Babel seem apropos here,[44] where morality means something slightly or dramatically different to different speakers. That is, *coerce* and *exploit* have seemingly unique applications here, and yet Cherry wants them to maintain their *moral* connotation or import.

This is not a trivial semantic problem. In fact, it cuts to the heart of market advocates' – or at least Cherry's – case against market prohibitions for moral reasons. If moral terms such as exploitation, vulnerability, coercion, harm, good, right, and just are to have rhetorical force, they need to be tied to specific normative views. One is free to agree or disagree with these normative views, and normative disagreement, both the metalevel and in applied instances of law or policy, characterizes much of what it means to have a public sphere and live in a democracy. There is no problem here; it is just the messiness of moral philosophy and democratic life. The best ways and proper linking of rhetorical force and normative force has its own robustness of problems, to be sure, but what we are seeing here is the severing of normative force from rhetorical force altogether. To put it clearly, *all that public moral deliberation is, in market advocates' view, is the enlistment of rhetorical force.*

The predicament that advocates such as Cherry face is robust. The claim is that *any* conception of the good society or even specific normative concepts is against what the law can and ought to do. Normative force doesn't matter, and since only rhetorical force matters, it thus must be mitigated legally from impacting citizens' lives and commitments. In his words,

> Moral foundations and particular moral content forged through a consensus will likely form a stable structure for social policy only if it is coercively enforced upon dissenters, thus failing to respect the fundamental differences amongst persons and content-full moral communities. Endeavoring to bridge the gap among moral strangers and diverse moral communities, governments have attempted to establish a universal "moral culture" by decree.[45]

Here Cherry makes a judgment that government is not in the morality business at all. Such a justification is an ethical one – it is what I called the Civic Restraint Principle (CRP) in chapter 5 – and is indeed a fundamental part of the duty of civility and is an overarching ethics of citizenship in constitutional democracies. But Cherry claims a moral viewpoint as superior – something like the CRP – and enforces it by decree, which is precisely what he argues ought not be done. It seems, then, Cherry desires the *rhetorical force* of using moral terms but denies that (at least these) moral concepts have any *normative force.*

This is untenable. Making CRP *the one and only guiding principle* to questions of morality, politics, and law seems mistaken. Under such an ethos a society is unable to have much (any?) significant moral content. Without significant moral content, a society is a society in name only; in other words, neoliberalism all the way down, guided by the principles of autonomy and efficiency, makes it hard to picture what *community* could mean even in theory, let alone in practice. This line of reasoning is the root of much conflict and confusion in public-sphere arguments in general and organ sales in particular. The argument of moral coercion and paternalism, so made, has significant defects, assuming that any moral content is coercive and therefore false. While indeed moral discourse is rampant with disagreement, drawing the conclusion from this that therefore society ought not enforce any moral claims as law because such are coercive misses the fact that this is just what *law is*: the coercive structuring of a society towards or away from certain (moral) practices.

Morals and Markets: The Neoliberal-by-Default Society?

The turn to the relationship between the moral and the political economic became obvious in this chapter. How do advocates rhetorically construct the limits, or lack thereof, between morals and markets? With the turn to the moral, all of the problems discussed in section III rise again: what is moral, and who gets to say, and how does that run up against our liberal-democratic conceptions of negative liberty, of the distanced self and the concept of autonomy and subjective consciences? For example, some of the key controversial candidates for market inalienability are prostitution, surrogacy, baby selling, blood, sperm/eggs, and, of course, our case of human organs. In all these cases, the moral prohibition on a market is (probably) going to be met with controversy, and given this controversy, many in the twenty-first century reason that the best option for liberal democracies will be market permissibility. This argument is, essentially, what I called economization of everyday life, and it rests strongly on the ever-increasing push of individual moral autonomy, reducible to (individually infallible) conscience. The reduction to individual conscience presses against and increasingly views the state as the paternalistic state. The distanced self emerges and continues to grow in the collapse of a shared moral backdrop for a society. This latter part in particular is a Neoliberal-By-Default Society.

Charitably interpreted, the Neoliberal-by-Default Society is not one advocated for by those with few moral convictions. Rather, it is the *recognition* of the pressures of values pluralism on any articulation of morality, and in this case, on any articulation of market inalienability that prompts their advocacy. That is, at least in their view, there is just an ever-shrinking list of agreements on what should be market inalienable, and so what is and is not inalienable should be up to each person and not be a legally binding prohibition based on *someone's* moral precepts.

But the neoliberal-by-default logic here is challenged precisely at the moment where we consider that all laws are structurally coercive towards or away from certain practices, and that this necessitates serious moral entanglements. There is no way to keep the state out of the morality business, so to speak, and the claim of neutrality towards competing visions of the good life *while at the same time affirming the logic of neoliberalism* indicates the snake-eating-its-own-tail nature of the argument.

Now, to be clear, I am not – at least not yet – rejecting that the Neoliberal-by-Default Society is not a better way for ethically pluralistic democracies to engage one another and for citizens to coexist. At a minimum, we can see that differing justifications for the advocates' respective positions hinges on differing visions of the scope of the market in democratic societies. The logic of each pushes towards extremes of full commodification or full anti-commodification; that is, either everything is safely under the purview of markets and market mechanisms or nothing is.

The twin logics of moral autonomy and market efficiency form a powerful if contentious force pushing towards neoliberalism all the way down for democratic societies. But if the logic pushes towards everything being for sale and nothing being morally prohibited as long as two or more consenting adults agree, here's our question now: *Is that the kind of society you'd want to live in?*

It is a deliberative question, not a rhetorical one. We'll revisit it in the conclusion to this book.

One final interesting thing to note in this debate about the scope of the market and its relation to a society is that to a certain kind of arguer, human conceptions of self and society are necessarily yoked to capitalism, for better and worse. For the better, market advocate suggest that it is capitalism that affirms central human features of choice and agency; and for the worse, a certain kind of universal non-commodificationist advocate suggests that since the logic of capitalism pushes towards universal commodification and that the entailing neoliberalism is thus a feature and not a bug, it is capitalism that's got to go. Hopefully this chapter has offered a more nuanced analysis of the argument than those two positions of universal commodification and universal non-commodification.

While I've argued that the market advocates' case against exploitation fails, market advocates' can – and should – argue paternalism and exploitation more carefully. A better position is to claim that non-market advocates rhetorically exploit US society's belief in human dignity to justify opposition to an organ market. The argument would need to establish that markets not only comport with human dignity but that the fundamental error in the altruistic defence is in conflating dignity with anti-commodification writ large. That is, while I believe to have shown that arguments in particular about paternalism, coercion, and exploitation do not survive scrutiny, the market advocates' case is not defeated.

This will require some detail, as it seems to be, at bottom, the fundamental disagreement between market and non-market advocates in the case of organ procurement: the question of dignity and organ sales – in short, the question of human dignity and capitalism.

9 What Money Cannot Buy and What Money Ought Not Buy: Dignity, Motives, and Markets

This chapter examines how advocates of both the altruistic status quo and market challengers reason and weigh the central normative concept of dignity, with dignity meaning, as will be discussed more below, inherent worth and/or rank.[1] Key rhetorical strategies, including motivations and broader social visions, of the two positions are analysed and evaluated, and the separation of morally normative understandings of dignity from market encroachment is defended. The altruism-based policy stands firm.[2] The traditional strategies of raising donor awareness (such as via driver's licence registration), and even less typical strategies such as organ donation status options within Facebook, exist and continue to be invented. Yet the organ shortage remains.

A vocal alternative to the status quo policy of altruism is a market-based approach: pay people for their organs.[3] Paying people for organs is currently illegal, but the growing demand prompts discussion of alternatives.[4] The public debate on this matter is evidenced in a variety of media, documented most explicitly in chapters 4 and 8. For example, there are frequent op-eds in major newspapers, such as the one from a Rabbi Shmuly Yanklowitz, whose headline is the position, "We Badly Need More Donated Kidneys. Let's Start Paying for Them." There are many important issues to consider in the ethical debates of human organ procurement strategies, such as exploitation, care, thriving black markets, and so forth, but perhaps the most central one, and in particular the most centrally resistant normative argument to the pressures of market impingement, is the claimed preservation of, or need to comport with, human dignity. The relationship between preserving "human dignity" – meaning something like treating humans with inherent worth becoming of their status and rank as moral agents and/or their created-in-the-image-of-God standing – and "market mechanisms" – such as selling labour, parts, trading of goods and services, and so forth – is at the crux of the debate of how to increase human organ supply.

This chapter examines how advocates weigh the central normative question in this debate – human dignity – within and against market alternatives. The rhetorical strategies – most saliently the motivations and reasoning – of the two primary camps, status quo defenders of altruistic organ policy enshrined in US law and the economically liberal market challengers, are evaluated. The separation of morally normative understandings of human dignity from market encroachment is defended for discussions of human organ procurement strategies, putting the issue into a broader sociopolitico-economic context.

Dignity: More than Autonomy

Before analysing arguments about the relationship between human dignity and market forces in organ procurement, let me discuss the controversial concept of dignity. A certain kind of bioethical analysis focuses on the meaning of dignity – or lack thereof – and its conceptual capacity. For example, consider Ruth Macklin's touchstone article arguing that dignity is essentially useless in practice; the Presidential Commission on the Study of Bioethics' (PCSB's) *Human Dignity and Bioethics* as, largely, a response to Macklin; and Steve Pinker's critique of the PCSB document as being too theologically motivated and grounded.[5] The existence of dignity, and its relation to whole humans and/or body parts, characterized earlier debates on organ sales as well.[6] But in this chapter, I primarily want to analyse the types of arguers who affirm the centrality of (if not fully an ontological commitment to) human dignity and its relationship, confounding to or coextensive with, market mechanisms.

That is, this study follows arguments consistent with the essentiality of inherent value, represented by human dignity, to human life and practices.[7] Human dignity here means something akin to humans having an inherent worth, maybe a special rank, that is inviolable or market inalienable. To be clear: whether dignity is in actuality *stupid* or *useless* or the "shibboleth of all the perplexed and empty-headed moralists," as Schopenhauer says, is secondary to the point that *many arguers in human organ market debates utilize it* in their rhetoric (discussed in the subsequent section).[8] While this discussion can get us far afield, and quickly, let me briefly sketch the position to, minimally, get at what human dignity seems to mean and do in organ procurement rhetoric.

The grounding of the prohibition on organ sales in the concept of dignity has at least two key sources. One source of dignity as a moral grounding for public policy is the conception of *B'tzelem Elohim-imago Dei* in the Judeo-Christian tradition and the notion of humans being literally priceless.[9] The other key source, from the Kantian tradition, similarly holds that whatever is endowed with dignity is that which is beyond price.[10] Michael Rosen's book argues, historically and analytically, how the two versions of dignity coalesce into a powerful, if sometimes perplexing, operationally salient concept.[11] In the theological version, humans are created in the image of God, and hence have an inherent worth that not only surpasses market pricing but also makes them beyond animals. Though this invocation is clearly religious, Leon Kass notes that while the assertion of *imago Dei* is Biblically based, the truth of the Bible's assertion does not rest on Biblical authority:

> Man's more-than-animal status [his being "god-like"] is in fact performatively proved whenever human beings quit the state of nature and set up life under a law which exacts just punishment for shedding human (i.e., more-than-animal) blood. The law that establishes that men are to be law-abiding both insists on, and thereby demonstrates the truth of, the superiority of man.[12]

Rosen comes to a similar conclusion, saying that dignity is "expressed by behavior that marks the distinction between human beings and animals," though further noting that the Kantian image of dignity as "inviolable holiness" is "far from fully secular."[13]

The theological ghosting of human dignity is perhaps what causes the recoil from many, especially those in the empirical sciences. But something like human dignity need not be an ontological commitment, nor its source necessarily identified, in practical legal discussions. For example, while Pinker is critical of the theological elements of the PCSB dignity volume, holding sources and soul talk in abeyance, the value of dignity as an ideal, a metaphor, or key-organizing concept representing something importantly human is overlooked. Daniel Dennett, a famous, influential atheist, makes exactly such a point in his contribution to the PCSB volume.[14] Furthermore, the Roman *dignitas* and precapitalist notions of dignity as rank are being explored for their conceptual potentials, in a way that is not necessarily theological but irreducible to autonomy or voluntarism.[15]

Minimally, what is to be gleaned from the preceding section is human dignity as a concept meant to signify a special human worth, irreducible to other concepts like autonomy. There is much more to be argued, of course, but that is a different work. For the purposes of this book, having the correct conception of human dignity is secondary to the more specific analysis of whether or not human organ sales violate human dignity, meant in a more-than-animal, irreducible-to-autonomy sense. That is, human dignity as inherent worth – whether that be God given, morally required for rational agency, befitting the highest rank, or other non-reductive analyses – is all that is necessary to understanding the operational capacity of dignity in human organ market debates for this discussion.

The Question of Human Dignity in Organ Markets

Advocates in human organ procurement debates often share the same telic orientation towards the intrinsic value of human dignity (even if left relatively unspecified) but differ as to whether or not human organs sales violate it. In pivoting from a general understanding of dignity as something meaning inherent worth, whatever the *source* of that inherent worth, to its application in practice, let me follow Jürgen Habermas's connection of law and morality. He writes,

> "Human dignity" performs the function of a seismograph that registers what is constitutive for a democratic legal order, namely, just those rights that the citizens of a political community must grant themselves if they are to be able to respect one another as members of a voluntary association of free and equal persons ... After two hundred years of modern constitutional history, we have a better grasp of what distinguished this development from the beginning: human dignity forms the "portal" through which the egalitarian and universalistic substance of morality is imported into law.[16]

The concept, then, of human dignity grounds a universalist morality into public law. While we don't need as explicit a grounding of law on the concept of human dignity as in Germany,[17] valuing and prioritizing human dignity is consistent with advocates on (nearly) all sides of the human organ procurement debate in the United States. For example, Congressman Henry Waxman, speaking at the NOTA hearings, put the matter clearly: "Human organs should not be treated like fenders in an auto junkyard."[18] As both a transplant surgeon and then-president of the National Kidney Foundation, Delmonico in his 2003 congressional testimony claims unequivocally, "Any attempt to assign a monetary value to the human body or its body parts, even in the hope of increasing organ supply, diminishes human dignity and devaluates the very human life we seek to save."[19] Cynthia B. Cohen writes, "When we or our integral body parts are sold, our dignity as human beings is denied. Many other practices, such as slavery, prostitution, and the sale of military draft call-up notices, are wrong for the same reason – they deny the respect due to human beings as creatures with special worth."[20]

But many of those who desire to harness markets in service of the shortage also recognize the necessity of attention to and balance of human dignity in the matter. In a written addition to the record of the 2003 congressional hearing, a letter signed by a broad swath of bioethicists, economists, and doctors includes a proposal for financial compensation for organs that they believe "constitutes the most viable compromise between using the power of market forces to satisfy human need while at the same time recognizing the widespread reluctance to having human body parts being treated, undignifiedly, as commodities."[21]

Further arguments regarding dignity and markets will follow. For now, the idea is to establish the centrality of the concept of human dignity as meaning something akin to inherent worth and/or rank in existing human organ procurement debates.

So, in one very clear sense, especially as the quotes from Delmonico and Cohen above indicate, *the reason that matters* in judging the permissibility of organ sales is that a market in human organs violates human dignity. Human dignity is the heaviest, weightiest concern in the debate. It is the market advocate who accepts such a view that I am most interested in for the rest of this chapter.

That is, a subtle version of the debate in human organ sales accepts the prevailing description of human dignity as akin to inherent worth, and thereby glosses over the problems associated with establishing a universalistic conception of human dignity for a values-pluralistic society altogether. For these market advocates, the case turns not on what human dignity is but the belief that human organ sales do not violate it. Let's turn to that view now.

Consider the exemplar case of sales and dignity made by Sally Satel.[22] Here I'll focus on her chapter "Concerns about Human Dignity and Commodification" in her edited volume *When Altruism Isn't Enough*. Satel's rebuttal of the claim that material compensation for one's organ violates human dignity turns on disproving that "human worth is inevitably corroded under a regime of compensation."[23]

She makes her case using several rhetorical analogies: interest on loans, opera singers, life insurance, firefighters, and the military. The use of money in each of these instances was once thought to be either repugnant or immoral, historically, but US society is (now) happy to compensate in such instances. The case of interest is well known, the loaning of money and collection of interest on it being a sinful act according to the Christian church even as late as the thirteenth century. The issue of life insurance as putting a price on human life was debated in the nineteenth century and is well catalogued by Viviana Zelizer.[24] Both of these cases are significantly bolstered by Nobel Prize–winning economist Alvin Roth's article on how repugnance has acted as a restraint on markets throughout history – on interest, short-selling, cadavers for scientific research, reproduction, risk/insurance – but clearly "some kinds of transactions are repugnant in some times and places and not in others."[25] In other words, the rhetorical point is that times change, and with them social moral norms of dignity violations and market mechanisms.

The idea of paying opera singers as a moral mistake comes directly from Adam Smith, who writes that the talents of actor-players, opera singers, and opera dancers are so beautiful and socially important that payment for them is considered, "whether from reason or prejudice, a sort of public prostitution."[26] Yet, as Satel quotes Martha Nussbaum here, "few professions are more honored than that of opera singer ... Nor do we see the slightest reason to suppose that the unpaid artist is a purer and truer artist than the paid artist."[27]

The last examples, of firefighters and military, pump the intuition that while of course US society pays both of them, there is nothing that lessens the danger of the task, nor our admiration for them, by the presence of money. "Of course, one reason we admire firefighters, salaried though they are, is that they put themselves at some inconvenience or even grave risk for the sake of others. The same extends to the compensated kidney donor."[28] Organ sellers, like firefighters, should be financially compensated for their heroic acts.

Not only should admiration and financial compensation also extend to organ donors, Satel argues, keeping the act unpaid could result in an *undermining* of human dignity. She does not mean that we violate dignity by not compensating advocates but that the absence of remuneration *can* have this effect. That is, in short, is it really true, as Peter Singer says, that "commerce replaces fellow-feeling"?[29] Satel thinks not. In her words,

> Consider how angry and demoralized injured plaintiffs and combat veterans become when their claims for disability payments are denied. It is *because* they value their bodies and their functions so dearly that they demand restitution for harm. Similarly, when an insurance company refuses to pay for liver or heart transplant surgery, it is saying, in effect, that the patient's very life is not worth the money the treatment would cost.[30]

To bolster this perspective, let's add the field of education. It is well known that this was one of the primary oppositions the Socratic school had to the sophists – those sophists charged *fees* for their education. And yet today, even the most devoted Socratics among us academics still cash paycheques. But then again, Michael Sandel notes how most of Western society would find it an "indignity," or at least strange, to receive monetary tips at the end of particularly good lectures or semesters.[31]

Satel argues that payment does not actually diminish knowledge or the art or the goodness of the act in any of these situations. Buying and selling knowledge does not diminish *knowledge* any more than buying and selling the *Mona Lisa* diminishes artistic value; rather, the broader point to glean here is of rhetorical strategy. That is, it is not that an argument cannot be made that each case – of buying and selling knowledge or the *Mona Lisa* – includes diminishment, but that the two cases are rhetorically equivalent: either *partners in guilt* or *partners in vindication* (as we saw in chapter 8).

A further point is that payment can promote recognition of individuals, and that this recognition comports with human dignity. So, for example, paying Gustavo Dudamel and the Los Angeles Philharmonic does not violate their dignity but can even promote it. This is because, as she says, an "individual who acts to enhance the well-being of another demonstrates an awareness of the other's value and uniqueness."[32] In this case, one can see the lack of payment as illustrating an individual's or a society's lack of awareness of certain values and uniqueness. This type of complaint is common not just among artistic crowds but also those trying to rise up the corporate ladder as well, who often say that they want pay increases not for the money per se but for the "recognition of what they contribute to the company" or of being a "valuable asset" to the team, and so forth.

When one thinks along these lines, Satel's argument possesses rhetorical force. Charging fees or receiving payment and/or other financial compensation does not seem to diminish knowledge, art, or the goodness of acts. But it does, as two influential studies suggest, seem to replace a sense a community and mutual support with a sense of entitlement and/or NIMBY-ism.[33] Furthermore, even if civic community and solidarity are not replaced or violated by markets, there is something missing from this discussion thus far, and it is the question of motives.

Motives, Money, and Dignity

The notion of motivation is at the core of Satel's argument. Satel quotes James Childress characterizing the position of voluntary-system advocates as one supposing that "pure altruism marks the donation of organs to the community for those in need and suspect[s] that the presence of any other motives vitiates the gift."[34] This is not quite accurate regarding Childress, as elsewhere he is keen to note the "mixed motives for donating" and the deficiency in both the economic model and the unadulterated altruism model of motivation.[35] Both, then, share the view that purely altruistic motivations are a "romanticizing [of] altruism."[36] Furthermore, Satel's main point is that attempts to retain a "sense of purity" in motives is, "as we have seen ... not up to the task" of meeting organ demand.[37] That is, motivation to act is usually quite complicated, and even if we retain it or force its simplicity, it is still failing to meet demand. Furthermore, "truly selfless motivations would not be extinguished because others are enriched."[38]

Satel's counterclaim against market opponents is twofold: (a) that non-market advocates are demanding a purity in motives that is impractical, as evidenced in the fact that supply is not meeting demand; and (b) that those who do indeed act with such a purity of motive – the truly selfless – will be untroubled by market mechanisms in human organs. These are important claims. The invocation of "truly" here resonates with an anti-consequentialist take on human action. It is the kind of thing that can be applied to nearly any situation or work as a sort of motive check: if you *truly* cared about educating children, you'd do it for free; if you *truly* cared about art ... if you *truly* cared about pastoring ... if you *truly* cared about helping the poor ... and so forth.

The "truly care" question is an effective mechanism for sorting out one's motives. Would you, indeed, do this for free? For example, many creative people do use this as a test case, and the answer is almost always yes, and demonstrably so (the years of creation without any sales to speak of, and continuing to work away).[39] The mistake in reasoning here comes from what to draw from the motivation, and that is that payment itself is what somehow nullifies the positive answer to the "truly cares" question.

Pushing the inherent value issue further, opposition comes from doing an act for a consequentialist reason. This might include, then, people saying "thank you" or offering a toast to you at a banquet. The image of accepting money as an expression of gratitude would seemingly be just a difference of degree, not kind, from a thoughtful thank-you card. That is, if your motive for educating, or artistic expression, or pastoring, or hospice care, or whatever, is *only* for thank-you cards or public toast of your works, something seems amiss. Both stem from an impure motive, it would seem, and furthermore, that US society does express gratitude for teachers and firefighters and doctors through money does not violate their dignity. In fact, to assume that their payment *is* their thank you is also clearly a mistake, according to Satel: "The great teachers who enlighten us and the doctors who heal us inspire no less gratitude because they are paid."[40]

Humans act for a variety of motives, not simply one. This means that reductive dismissals of organ market advocates as promoting or resting their arguments on the figure of *homo economicus* are just as mistaken as the more general market advocate who does indeed subscribe to such a view.[41] So one thing that has become clear in this debate through analysis of the arguments addressing dignity and markets is that motives for action are complicated. One has, for example, the motive of artistic expression but also the motive to put food on the table for one's family. And all advocates considered in this corner of the organ debate share in the view that a single motive of monetary reward is insufficient. That is, if money is the *only* motivation, one has probably made a mistake somewhere. Yes, there are firefighters and professors who are in those positions for the money (both positions pay respectable upper five figures to well into six figures) or the lifestyle they afford (different schedules from corporate jobs, working with hands or minds, respectively), but those are not most of them. There are also people who are motivated to create art for financial purposes, but they typically are not very successful artistically (or sometimes even financially). Such would make the case for human organ sellers rhetorically similar.

But this walks squarely into another practical normative issue, which is that motives indeed matter, but merely a good motive cannot act as a blanket for action nor be a substantive basis for policy. The questions of moral critique and legal culpability are not reducible to questions of agent motive. Think of, for example, the various political economic plans to eliminate extreme poverty. We don't consider the *plans* beyond critique simply because the aim, the motive, of poverty elimination is a moral good. The relationship between dignity and motivation in organ sales is seen in terms of price and humanity with a case example.[42]

Let's use the case of Virtuous Man and Poor Woman:

> *Poor Woman Case #1.* Virtuous Man's son is dying from end-stage renal failure. Virtuous Man gives his kidney to his son and thereby saves his son's life. In the next hospital room, Poor Woman's son is dying from leukaemia. Surgery will fix the problem, but Poor Woman cannot afford the surgery. So she sells her kidney and, with the money raised, is now able to afford the surgery. It is successful, and she has thereby saved her son's life.

Many market advocates wonder what the supposed difference is in these cases. The difference, they think, seems to rest only on the presence of money in the case of Poor Woman and the absence of it in Virtuous Man. Mark Cherry puts the critique clearly: "It is difficult to understand how giving one's organs can be permissible but selling organs always impermissible, unless one has some view that accepting payment intrinsically involves a wrong."[43] The conclusion is that altruism advocates must think that money taints the entire organ process irrevocably, and, since it is seen that money doesn't sufficiently taint other morally respectable occupations and actions, as discussed in the previous section, there is a mismatch here. Again, to the market advocates, the rhetorical point is, partners in guilt or partners in vindication.

But this is a bad conclusion to draw from the Virtuous Man and Poor Woman case. These are both *dire* situations, and in the case of the Poor Woman, perhaps even a *moral dilemma*. Hence, these are not cases from which to build law and socially binding policy; these are borderline cases, tragic cases.

To make the matter clearer, push Poor Woman's story a step in a different direction:

> *Poor Woman Case #2.* Poor Woman's son needs a life-saving surgery that she knows she cannot afford. So, on the hospital admittance forms, and to the doctors, she lies about her ability to pay for the surgery. The doctors perform the surgery based on this lie, and it is a success.

In this case, most would not want to put much moral culpability on a woman who is so financially strapped in such a case of imminent life and death acting the way that she did. She lied, but she was also desperate, and was willing to go to great lengths to save her son. The immediate and broader sociopolitico-economic contexts and arrangements matter in morally judging the case. But while I am not sure how much moral culpability the woman has here, that is not to say that she has acted ethically.

In other words, it is not that *lying*, categorically, now ought to be permissible given this case of Poor Woman. That would be quite a silly conclusion to draw, like an inept president reading *Les Misérables* and then declaring, through executive power, that theft is now permissible under US law.

In summation, the issue of human dignity in organ sales turns on two related questions: whether the act of payment nullifies human dignity in some way, and whether payment nullifies altruistic motivation and/or provides a bad motivation to act. Many altruistic advocates simply invoke the violation of human dignity in selling one's organ without giving reasons for how and why it does. The analysis in this section, however, has indicated that a conception of human dignity, of something in humanity being inviolable due to its inherent worth, perhaps even given and endowed by God, is not actually removed by the presence of money.[44] Knowledge, artistic expression, exploration of the human condition, and so forth are all things that have an inherent worth, and the United States has markets that buy and sell these things every single day. Does that make organ sales permissible, then, according to an irreducible-to-autonomy view of human dignity?

That is, is the fact that the United States has markets in areas where there is also widespread agreement on inherent value enough to close the case in favour of partners in vindication, and permit organ sales? Not quite, as there seems to be some confusion in the debate between what money cannot buy, and what money should not be able to buy.

What Money Cannot Buy and What Money Ought Not Buy

The question of money tainting an exchange and corrupting a moral expression is one that runs deep. Does the mere presence of money corrupt certain things that we hold as valuable? Education again offers a parallel. Plato held that the presence of money corrupted knowledge. But given that many of those who participate in the education market also hold that there *is* something inherently valuable in knowledge and education that is undiminished by the market transaction for it, the two might not be in competition after all.

There is a difference in kind between knowledge and auto fenders: one of them cannot actually be bought. Information can be bought and sold, but knowledge cannot; it is there for the taking, for free – academics sell their service in equipping students to see it, to find it, etc. If that example is too controversial, consider simply the cases of love, friendship, passion, and even awards. As Satel puts it, no one can buy these things because "none of them 'functions' properly unless given freely."[45] Friendship that is purchased, like love that is purchased, does not function properly; there is something missing. Buying a Nobel Prize on eBay or buying Academy Award votes nullifies the very meaning of the award.

So the issue is not that the United States *should not* have markets in love or friendship or awards but that it actually *cannot* have them. This, it seems, is a sound argument. Does it apply, then, to human dignity, that one could not buy and sell human dignity even if one wanted to?

If human dignity is really inviolable, then it cannot be desecrated or even destroyed voluntarily. Someone does not somehow *lose* their dignity by selling their organs any more than the person who sells their body for sex has somehow sold their love; it seems to be a confusion of a part or an outcome for the thing itself. Stéphanie Hennette-Vauchez, in the dignity-as-rank perspective, puts it this way regarding *dignitas*: "Since human dignity relates more to humankind than it does to the human individual, it remains out of the latter's reach; she cannot renounce it, she is stuck with it."[46] Similarly, most in the Judeo-Christian tradition would suggest that the prostitute or organ seller (or dwarf-tosser or whatever controversial case you want to use) has not lost her *imago Dei*. However, they might want to say that the organ seller, like the prostitute, has not acted in a way as to *befit* such an *image*, such a property that they are endowed with, of dignity.

There are two mistakes being made in this debate. Firstly, there is equivocation in *giving something a price*. The confusion is in the literal and the symbolic notions of pricing. That someone sells his kidney for $50,000 does not mean that his inherent dignity has been violated and that his kidneys are, indeed, worth only $50,000. Giving something a literal price does not mean that it is not priceless in the deeper sense. A good example of this is torts and life insurance. Compensation to families in wrongful-death suits do not somehow make the dead loved one worth *only* X amount, any more than a life insurance policy dictates the value of each person: "Oh, I have a *million*-dollar policy on my wife, so clearly she has more dignity than your wife, given that you only have a $500,000 policy on her" or, just as mistakenly, "And so apparently I *love* my wife more than you love yours, in fact, twice as much!" That is, few would likely think that by accepting the life insurance claim or the lawsuit compensation that they have *exchange equivalence* for their dead loved one. There is no exchange equivalence for humans, and that is what people such as Kant mean by having dignity *as opposed* to price. No amount of money can change the fact that humans have an inherent worth or that humans are of a special status.

The other mistake stems from recognition of the fact (or in complete rejection of the fact, equally) that each individual can set his own terms and prices as he sees fit. This is the universal commodificationist or the crude libertarian, who believes that everything is based on permissibility of the involved agents and contractual specifications – in short, a view of dignity as equivalent to autonomy. In a universal commodificationist or crude libertarian picture, there is a very real sense in which moral critique is impossible, for the collapse of a shared moral backdrop and collectively binding moral judgment results in autonomous adults with equal legal standing before the law being able to do (almost) anything they want or, if not, to rightfully complain of injustice or indignity.[47] Perhaps this is the view of dignity that C.S. Lewis imagines espoused by the damned.[48] The universal commodificationist view rejects any understanding of (categorical) morality altogether. Under such a view, it seems it would just be a matter of time before nearly every act is legally permissible.[49]

So the difference between love for sale and organs for sale is, quite simply, that one cannot actually be sold and the other can. Love for sale is not actually love – it might seem like love, it might have the sex associated with love, or whatever, but it is not love, for love must be given freely. So the question of whether love ought to be for sale or not is actually unintelligible[50]; "ought" implies "can," and so love cannot be sold, making the normative question moot. Satel understands this, and she says that a kidney is able to be sold, because once "transplanted, it performs its essential functions of filtering waste from the blood and maintaining water and electrolyte balance, whether it is paid for or not."[51] But all Satel has actually highlighted here is that a kidney *can* be sold, not that it *should* be. The slip is from "can" to "ought."

Whether organs *should* be sold is still an open question, and exactly the normative question under consideration. Part of the reason that a kidney can be sold and love cannot is due to the materiality of the former and the immateriality of the latter; that is, it is not simply a matter of function but also form. One can buy and sell sex because it is material, just like auto fenders and kidneys, but the question of violation of dignity is deeper. So, has one sold one's dignity when one sells a kidney or one's body for sex? Those, it seems, are questions that only God can answer, if one is a theist, and that are prone to protracted ethical disagreements and competing normative theories of naturalism and non-naturalism from a non-theistic perspective.

What can be said in the here and now, however, is that some actions promote attitudes that enhance human dignity. This is the substantive issue, the one pertaining to the question of normative force, that shakes out among the analysis thus far of the way in which advocates weigh reasons: market advocates' case turns most sharply on the fact that markets do not *violate* human dignity, but altruism-based advocates respond, or can respond, that a good society would be one that actually *promotes* attitudes that *enhance* human dignity, not simply prevent its violation. While, in a sense, the telic orientation towards human dignity is shared, the corresponding justifications for (differing) actions hinge on differing telic views of society: whether it is a society's job to promote and enhance human dignity or whether the case is one of negative liberty.

What Do We Think Has Value and Why?

This chapter has analysed the way in which advocates weigh reasons in normative arguments to increase human organ supply. The market advocates' case turns most sharply on the fact that markets do not violate human dignity, and altruistic advocates respond that a good society would be one that actually promotes attitudes that enhance human dignity.

Previewing a portion of the conclusion to this book, there is a sense, then, in which the two are talking past each other: the market advocates want to establish the bare limits of acceptability whereas altruistic advocates seek a more vibrant and robust social civic community among citizens. But as Satz puts it, "Ultimately, these questions about the limits of markets are not merely questions of costs and benefits but of how we define our society, of who we are and what we care about."[52] That is, given that there must be a public policy on organ procurement, and that this public policy in turn ought to be based on reasonable justifications we as citizens can offer to each other based upon understandings of morality and dignity, deciding a question about organ sales and the limits of markets *just is* deciding, in part, what kind of society we want to be.

As a comment attributed to H.L. Mencken runs, "For every human problem, there is a solution that is simple, neat, and wrong."[53] But as we have seen in this chapter, the dismissal of the neoliberal case for a human organ market as morally mistaken is too simplistic, as made clear by the strong use of legal, occupational, and artistic analogies on the part of certain organ market advocates. A part of the case turns, then, on what ends arguers seek for a society in a larger sense. Recall Satel's quote: "The great teachers who enlighten us and the doctors who heal us inspire no less gratitude because they are paid." Here Satel, a strong market advocate, is cautious precisely because of the deleterious effect of community and gratitude that money often has on human relations. The endorsement of this perspective increases Satel's ethos and, more important, indicates thoughtfulness and commitment to promoting a society that doesn't let money solely define or arbitrate human relations.

It also has the effect, however, of admitting the power of financial compensation to undermine *communitas* and basic humanity. Love, friendship, passion, art, knowledge, salvation, patriotism – it is not that these things *should* not be sold but rather that they *cannot* be sold. A love that can be bought or sold is not love; sex and love are not the same thing. Sex *can* be bought or sold in a way that love could never be. The question, in an "ought"-implies-"can" formulation, is whether or not certain things ought to be for sale, such as votes, education, medicine, and human organs.

Human dignity, like love, cannot be bought and sold, period. But also like love, there are many things that can be bought and sold that will *diminish our attitude towards each other and ourselves*. The relationship in which sex is bought and sold is probably not going to have very much love in it, and the society that buys and sells human body parts is probably not going to have very much concern for human dignity. It is not the *acts per se* that remove these things, *but the acts and communicative patterns around them promote and reinforce attitudes towards oneself and others*.

Payment does not inherently diminish the virtues of one's behaviour but, in practice, it promotes an attitude that absolves oneself and society of gratitude and grace. In short, it promotes a society that lacks humanity, with humanity meaning here something akin to human dignity. To this end, notice the way Radin puts the issue: "The rhetoric of commodification has led us into an unreflective use of market characterizations and comparisons for almost everything people value, and hence into an inferior conception of personhood."[54] Radin's point is precisely about our *attitudes* towards what we value, asserting that it is our *language* that *promotes* this unreflective attitude that has resulted in an inferior conception of personhood. While more work is needed to explore this relationship, one can see the knot forming between (a) attitudes towards each other and towards ourselves; (b) the language we use to describe our practices and ourselves; and (c) the laws that coercively structure our society towards or away from certain moral positions.

My analysis so far provides another way of tying into a series of arguments on the connection between language, law, morality, and human dignity; of working an in-between position against universal commodification and universal non-commodification; of harnessing the power of market mechanisms without making all sociopolitical arrangements reducible to economics, without making all moral discourse and practice reducible to questions of autonomy. More specific arguments about exploitation and poverty – the generally asymmetrical power standing of buyer and seller in most instances of human organ sales – are essential to analyses of potential organ markets, in particular the *dilemma of commodification*, in that we seem to violate personhood in either allowing or disallowing organ sales.[55] But the distinction between dignity (as inherent worth or special status levelling up humans) and autonomy might help in this way: we likely violate *someone's* autonomy in allowing or disallowing human organ sales. However, that same violation occurs in nearly every decision (law, policy, vote, etc.) in a democracy: *someone's* moral view is (probably) offended, breached, etc., through the coercive use of collectively binding policy. Unless we are content to be universally morally permissive, autonomy cannot be our only rhetorical concept in and for public policy and our moral economy.[56] Dignity, irreducible to autonomy, provides another powerful moral resource in these debates.

In the contemporary era in which nearly everything is coming under the purview of money and markets, and part of the justification is that to prohibit markets and market mechanisms is to infringe on individual rights and to run afoul of *someone's* moral positioning and thus become anti-liberal democratic and therefore bad, there seems to be good reasons to fight the language, attitude, and practice – in short, the culture – of money and individuality dominating social and civic life – a sort of civic republican pushback against ascending neoliberalism. There is, to remix a phrase, "a high social utility in this sentiment being widespread" – even if that same author was sceptical about such "alleged coarsening effects" actually transferring "from primary to secondary objects."[57] But at this moment, in which people are encouraged to act and market themselves like a brand,[58] and brands are trying to act and market themselves like people,[59] it is harder to be sceptical of the coarsening effects of linguistic and social practices of money saturation. Simply consider social media: products, companies, and brands ask you to "like" and "follow" them, interact with them with pictures and messages, just as you do your friends and family – on platforms that make distinguishing between the two a hazy affair.

At a minimum, it ought to be clear that organ procurement strategies are about more than just the functionality and form of the organs themselves. They are, fundamentally, about the persons made up of such organs, and those persons' relationships to each other in community together, respecting and reflecting attitudes of human dignity. If this much is common ground among all advocates, then, the *reasons that matter most* to each side come in with different weights: market advocates weigh autonomy and the negative liberty/anti-paternalism reasons as the heaviest, most important reasons, whereas non-market advocates weigh promoting an attitude of dignity and social civic community as the heaviest, most important reasons. Once this clash is seen more clearly, debate might proceed more carefully, if casting a wider net.

Chapter Conclusion

Questions of markets and law are questions about the way in which we, as a society, reflect, promote, and motivate an image of human dignity – whatever that image may be, including the idea that human dignity does not exist or is stupid or useless. Questions of human organ procurement strategies, like many normative questions, are about the ethics and legality of the matter in question. But they are also questions about what kind of society we want to become, and what kind of policy matches with that (even if idealized) vision of social and legal relations. The primary debate on the table in organ sales is as much about increasing neoliberalism or increasing civic republican commitments as it is about organ procurement. Even so, we must not lose sight of the very material and urgent concern of friends, family members, neighbours, and strangers who are dying, in part because of an organ shortage that is ostensibly reversible.

Conclusion: What Kind of Policy for What Kind of Society?

And so we arrive at the end, which of course is really just a beginning. I asked some Big Questions in the introduction: are there right answers to moral questions, what does a society value and does how it engage in valuing, and what ought to be for sale and who gets to decide. Rather than write a philosophical treatise on those questions directly, I chose to do an extended case study of a single issue, human organ procurement rhetoric, and set up three tasks for this book: (1) to analyse how advocates rhetorically construct the relationship between morals and markets in human organ procurement debates; (2) to critique neoliberalism in bioethics in specific and public moral deliberation more generally; and (3a) to ask, deliberatively, and not (just) rhetorically, what kind of society we want, and (3b) to highlight that deciding relationships between morals and markets, in deciding what kind of laws and bioethical policies we want, *is coextensive with and performative of* deciding what kind of society we want. I've accomplished (1) and some of (2) and will remind of them in a summary before giving over the rest of this chapter to adding to (2) and finally turning to (3).

Before I take up the Big Questions of what kind of society we want and what we care about, recall that the fragmentation of morality and the increasing economization of everyday life under global capitalism form the basis of neoliberal rhetoric. Those two intersecting strands make the normative justification of a market mechanism for moral matters persuasive and resonant rhetoric. Under present conditions, one can see why a market mechanism is also desirable for adjudication, given the difficulty of moral coherence under pluralistic constitutional democracies with strong rights-based interpretative paradigms. This, to me, is the major challenge of the twenty-first century, now having witnessed the horrors of (false) absolutisms of tyrants and despots and living through the neoliberal economization of everyday life alike. A key task for our moral life together, it seems to me, is something like this: *to conceptually and practically keep alive public moral deliberation, to keep alive a rhetoric between privatization and totalization, where morality is not reducible to (subjective, private) autonomy nor is it synonymous with whatever the public decides it is or an absolute decree.* Now let's see what our story is so far, and how we might then contribute more directly to this overarching concern.

The Story So Far

Let's take stock of the book. After analysing the rhetorical structure and appeals of the altruistic status quo and market challengers, section II concluded by turning the arguments, justifications, and stories into a guiding ethos. The altruistic status quo represented a civic republican ethos, guided by the magic words of virtue, justice, and civic community. The ethos of market challengers is broadly neoliberal, guided by the magic words of autonomy, efficiency, and consistency. It was then suggested that there is something valuable in all six of those concepts within and to public moral deliberation, and that, at least broadly speaking, many in societies such as the United States value and recognize as much.

Given the disagreement on the underlying question (whether or not market sales should be legal), the wider recognition of the value of the informing justifications and reasons makes the matter more confusing, not less. So we then asked, in section III, how we got to a place where citizens have concern for both justice and autonomy, for efficiency and civic community. The first and most obvious answer is that these are not necessarily conflicting virtues or reasons for action. In one very real sense, arguers might be talking past each other. But given that there can be only one policy, and given that there is disagreement on what that policy should be, this cannot be the only answer. The story I told in section III essentially suggested how neoliberalism becomes not just a conceivable option but a priority or default option for liberal-democratic societies under conditions of ethical pluralism.

The broader story of how the market and market mechanisms can and should adjudicate public moral disagreements even further complicated the story. In short, if we were stuck with a sort of impasse after section II of "getting" the argument on both sides, then by the end of chapter 5 the prospects of a public deliberation aiming for moral consensus looked even worse. Incommensurability seems at present philosophically and legally supported in our sociopolitical arrangements, and therefore our society ends up, logically, neoliberal-by-default.

At a minimum, we can pause here (with the summary and the arguments through chapter 5) and see that I have offered a critical-historical and philosophically defensible explanation for how and why the questions of organ procurement – and any moral question in the contemporary era – are *so hard* to answer in public moral deliberation.

And the resulting Neoliberal-By-Default Society, whose guiding public normativity and rational justifications are almost exclusively efficiency, autonomy, and (legal) consistency, would indeed be where we are headed today because it is where we would, politically and philosophically speaking, have to end up. But the view, and thus its entailing logic, rests on a mistake. The neoliberal mistake is twofold. It is mistaken in assuming that incommensurability is the philosophical outcome of moral enquiry, and that, sociopolitically, there is no way to convince each other of right answers to public moral deliberations.

The crux of section III then is a series of arguments suggesting that what we are doing in public deliberation is searching for the reasons that matter, and that *reasons* are not subjective. This means that while we might not all recognize the same answers as the right answers, we are all aiming, indeed, at right answers to moral questions. This means that reasoning requires us to find good reasons to support our views, that some reasons are better than others, that there are reasons that humans have more reason to have, and therefore that there are justifications for some actions being better than others. This was, and is, a rather technical discussion, and its success or failure is in those chapters, working towards what I called my rhetorical theory of moral disagreement. The essential features of that theory suggest that public moral deliberation is a twofold process of discovering correct ends and then aiming to convince each other that those ends are indeed correct while requiring the appropriate stance of being epistemically demanding of each other, self-reflexive, and open to mutual influence under normative reasoning.

Let me pause here and highlight a different dimension to the rhetorical theory of good reasons and moral disagreement discussion, and note that it rests on – and is in large part motivated by – not reason but an article of faith: that people are moved by normative force and not just rhetorical force. That is, that there really are ways to convince people of right answers and that people can and will be moved by good reasons. While at some level that seems like an empirical claim (are people persuaded by X argument or not?), it is a much deeper kind of commitment, cashing out in something closer to hope than reason. I'll say a bit more about this in a subsequent section of this chapter.

So, picking up the thread, having argued that there are a variety of values working as justifications for public moral deliberation and cashing out in mutually exclusive judgments about the permissibility of organ sales, putting that disagreement in broader critical-historical and political-philosophic context, and concluding that, despite neoliberal scepticism about morality in general or public deliberation in specific, the uncontroversial search in moral public deliberation is for the reasons that matter and for what weight to give what reasons. Section IV then turned back to organ sales explicitly, and found that the debate featured disagreement on a variety of issues: the scope of the market, exploitation, coercion, definitions of justice, (legal and rational) consistency, and human dignity. The question of what human dignity is and how to promote it is what had the most normative force in the debate, and so, in the end, much of the debate turns particularly on this matter.

Given the normative force of dignity as the reason that matters most in this public moral deliberation, arguments that fail to consider the discursive and material effect of organ sales or market mechanisms more generally on a community were considered lacking. There is a significant chunk of market advocates, however, who stressed the need to comport with dignity, and so I focused on these arguments in chapter 9. The main conclusion there was the discovery that the public moral argumentation around human organ sales and altruism turned not on dignity but on a much wider question: whether it was society's job to promote dignity and altruism in its rhetoric and structural arrangements, or whether society's job was primarily one of negative liberty and just to defend against violations.

At some level, this is where we hit a fundamental disagreement. Even if we are stuck here, I hope to have told a persuasive story of how and why we got here to help us better understand both the debate and stakes associated with the debate, while gesturing at times towards some potential resources for moving past the impasse. Another way forward, however, is to more explicitly consider the fundamental disagreement of what a society's job is, of promotion of dignity and altruism versus negative liberty – that is, to treat *that* as the starting point for the debate, not the end.

So ... what is society's job? What do we want society's job to be? What kind of society do we want? And so we arrive at the end and, in some sense, at the broadest question. To decide what kind of policy we want on bioethical questions such as organ sales, or really any policy at all, we need to ask what kind of society we want to be. In situations where there must be a policy (especially a national policy), it is important to have a space where the broader and deeper discussions, prospects, and pressures of change can be articulated and challenged. The questions of what is or is not allowed to become commodified or enter into market transactions is more fundamental than simply what *can* be done and what maximizes efficiency or wins out in a cost/benefit calculus. In Debra Satz's terms, "Ultimately, these questions about the limits of markets are not merely questions of costs and benefits but of how we define our society, of who we are and what we care about."[1]

What kind of society we want, I've argued thus far, is one that has space for public moral deliberation, in which public argumentation is conceived as an organ of the body politic that is not reducible to the market and thus not for sale. A major through line in this book has been that a society with no categorical content, with no moral centre from which less important or more controversially uncertain moral visions can compete is not what the United States or many developed nations have been, but seems to be what the United States and others are becoming: the Neoliberal-by-Default Society. I've argued, and will argue further here, that what many citizens care about, even currently, is much deeper than neoliberalism and a you-do-you legal regime. The final argument I'll make in this chapter will be to suggest that deciding what kind of policy we want *just is* deciding what kind of society we want. But before I get there, let me now offer two arguments to this public moral deliberation of what kind of society we want.

In the rest of this chapter, let me argue that kind of society that we want has at least these two features: (1) robust rhetorical engagement on morals *and* markets, not just talk of one or the other; and (2) cultivation and promotion of dignity and altruism in rhetorical and structural arrangement, not merely an aim of negative liberty. I'll then try to close out, by way of summary, the entire book.

Feature 1: Rhetoric of Morals and Markets

That communities have the power to make law, to bind and loose moral authority and judgment with and over one another, is a heavy burden. And to avoid grappling with the categorical is to avoid grappling with morality. I am not alone in taking the stakes to this level – or, rather, in seeing that public moral deliberation in democratic societies has these stakes, especially in relation to medicine. Emanuel writes, "It is only in the practice of medicine that we are required to confront the meaning of human frailty and finitude and the many entwined ethical questions ... in this way, the practice of medicine is as much painstaking moral deliberation as it is biomedical technology and clinical judgment."[2]

As neoliberal rhetoric and policies increase in success and momentum, we are seeing a corresponding shift in public morality. The way in which all discussions of value now mean or quickly relate to monetary value needs to be halted; neoliberal language in dialogues about worth need to be de-grafted from the body politic. This is nowhere more evident than medicine, as the magic words for health care have completely shifted from compassion and care to autonomy and efficiency, from care to research, from treating the patient to treating the disease. Clinical encounters are on average just a few minutes, and the interchangeability of physicians and patients is seen as a feature of many hospital care systems, not a bug. One of the most prominent ways to advertise and discuss hospitals and practices is in terms of their ranking, and both the competition for patients and the reluctance to share data sets highlight a system of not just misaligned incentives but also malformed goals of what health care *is* as well. And this is to say nothing of the way in which, in the United States, we've offloaded de facto definitions of health and healing to insurance companies, having, almost literally, tied health care outcomes to one's ability to pay for them. This situation is, to say the least, disheartening.

Even though the pendulum has swung strongly to the neoliberal side, there have been remarkable benefits from markets and associated virtues. That is, competition, efficiency, autonomy, and other neoliberal hallmarks bring, and continue to bring, significant and wonderful features to contemporary human life. We could arguably accord advances such as the saving of hundreds of million of lives with antibiotics, significant rises in life-expectancy rates, and a general rise of the world's pre-1800-level per-person real income by an astonishing multiple (minimally 10 times and not uncommonly 30 to 100 times) to the rhetoric and practice of market-tested betterment under capitalism.[3] But if it hasn't been clear already, let me put it starkly: the critique of neoliberalism implied throughout this book is not synonymous with a critique of capitalism writ large or market-tested betterment as a concept and methodology.

To reiterate, then, what we've seen in the past few hundred years in the West is that most people care about *both* morals and markets. The horrors of totalization, of supposedly categorical moral content held in political arrangements that diminish and crush human capacity, are still fresh. What we've seen in the past several decades, especially in the United States, is the pendulum swing the other way, towards individualization and privatization of morality and pretty much everything else.[4] It is that swing in social ontology and public moral deliberation, and the concerns thereof both philosophically and politically, that I've taken up much space documenting and arguing. But I want to be clear that the aim is a redressing of the dialectic, not a claim of collectivization over individualization. The goal is to redress the imbalance, the tilt of the table that slides all conceptualizations and practices of value and worth to monetary imperatives and accounting.

Many market advocates are modernist dogmatists in the sense described by Wayne Booth: more than just claiming the established, and in many senses quite true, separation between the normative and the descriptive, much neoliberal rhetoric subscribes to the further claim of the impotence of reason in all moral matters, period. This is a slightly different than the Hobbesian and Humean style of scepticism about the rational objectivity of moral realism. As Booth puts it,

> It never occurred to Hobbes, "the atheist," or to Locke or Kant, that *all* norms are irrational or nonrational. Hume, the skeptic, had no serious trouble establishing the possibility of a rational "standard of taste," both in ethics and aesthetics ... It is really only in the last seventy-five years or so that the fact-value split became a truism *and* that the split began to entail the helplessness of reason in dealing with any values but the calculation of means to ends."[5]

This is not to say that market advocates do not have reasons for their view, or even good reasons for their views at times. Rather, it is to say that many neoliberal advocates end up, largely, dodging the fundamental questions of the moral life of a society, and hence their position can be seen, very literally, as *anti-deliberative*. In short, market advocates who appeal to modernist dogma about *is* and *ought* as a way of avoiding substantive debate are failing, in some sense, to fully participate in moral life altogether, let alone the life of their community. That is to say, they fail to actually participate in moral discussion, instead critiquing the entire enterprise of *moral discussion* as flawed. Some practices and systems might indeed be worthy of such a gigantic swipe; in a constitutional democracy, reasoning together in public moral deliberation cannot be.

Deliberative engagement and reflection are integral parts of morality. This is not necessarily to say that something like reflective equilibrium or communal consensus are what *make* something morally right or wrong. Rather, the point is that it is in normative discussion that interlocutors submit moral claims to each other and argue back and forth – in other words, in which they test their claims and hypotheses in an effort to discover the best answers to moral questions. The goal, in short, is to provide a reflective space to deliberate and weigh together the reasons for action, and to then practice such deliberative engagement. Neoliberalism hijacks the very practice of and space for public moral deliberation.

The stakes of avoiding public moral deliberation are high, as the connection between ethics, law, society, and economics is a tangled knot. Isolating each – as certain neoliberal theorists, politicians, religious fundamentalists, political philosophers, and economist often do – causes problems for societies. Extending the famous Keynes quote,[6] Parfit notes, "Many economists, we can add, think in ways that show them to be the slaves of some dead philosopher," for indeed economists are "not chiefly to blame" for believing that their professional work is predicated on a fact/value dichotomy.[7] As he continues,

> It was philosophers who first claimed that reasons are given only by desires, that all rationality is instrumental, and that no values are facts, because there are no normative truths. Given our increasing powers to destroy or damage the conditions of life on Earth, we need to lose these beliefs. It is not wealth that matters, or mere preference-fulfillment, but happiness, justice, and other things that can make our lives worth living.[8]

The point, for our purposes, is not that Parfit has the answers we seek nor that I have provided them here in this book. Rather, it is to highlight just how powerful and dramatic the shift is (or would be) to a fully neoliberal-by-default society, in which the fundamental basis for common life is the establishment and maintenance of mechanisms that facilitate moneymaking and the autonomy of desire.

Clearly, pushing back against neoliberalism hardly requires a rejection of libertarianism (in most of its forms), and certainly not a full indictment of the capitalist system. That is, while a society's language is vital to its constitution and vibrancy, as I am arguing in this section in particular, it is not the case that mere talk and invocation of markets in general necessarily degrade human dignity, let alone market practice.[9] Egalitarian approaches and virtue-market approaches both offer alternatives. Both preserve, in a general sense, a comportment of morals and markets as opposed to views that place the former in subservience to the latter.

That is, the idea that markets bring about and contribute to a virtuous society is not one that needs to be roundly dismissed. Drawing on the work of Adam Smith and the best contemporary defence of the Smithean market virtues in Deirdre McCloskey, markets are not simply a way of sociopolitical organizing or collective problem solving under pluralistic conditions. Rather, there are very real ways in which market systems inspire, and sometimes even enact, virtues – the four pagan ones (wisdom, temperance, justice, fortitude) and the three theological ones (faith, hope, love). Together they constitute the bourgeois virtues. In McCloskey's hands, market systems are powerful, even beautiful. Here's how she breaks it down.

The "leading bourgeois virtue is the Prudence to buy low and sell high," she admits. "But it is also the prudence to trade rather than invade."[10] Temperance is about saving and accumulating, but it is also about educating oneself, listening to customers, and searching for solutions. Justice is about private-property protection breaking down privilege, about honouring contracts and paying for good work, and about not being envious of one's neighbours' successes. Fortitude is what spurs innovation and new business, and the try-try-try again attitude. Love is seen as taking care of one's own and fellow citizens and workers, faith is the honouring of community and tradition, and hope is the imagining of a better product but also that there will be better days ahead and purpose in the here and now. In short, this is an eloquent and important explication of the Smithean vision and argument for market systems. What is essential is the emphasis on community, common good, morality, care. The choice is not between these goods (formal as they might be) and unfettered market capitalism.

In terms of what kind of society one wants to live in, few non-ideal – that is, real, practical, taking humans as they are, functioning and functional – societies are better than a market system approach steeped in virtue ethics. In McCloskey language, the rhetoric of Max U applies to markets and morals now, to the near universal exclusion of other approaches or virtues. This is not lost on her: "Forgetting Smith in a commercial society has orphaned the virtues. It is the ethical tragedy of the modern West."[11] That is, from the 1970s forward, the cultivation of virtues in individuals, institutions, and social structures has become less and less a part of US society while neoliberal rhetoric and policies have proliferated.

So, what kind of society citizens ought to have is going to require, it seems, something different than what the United States and other developed societies are. But the rhetoric of autonomy versus the rhetoric of community, utility versus virtue, instrumental versus categorical morality, distributive versus commutative justice must stop. There are many theories and projects that can help us think through this, and I hope this book contributes to this larger conversation.[12]

In thinking through the discourse of morals and markets, of the rhetoric of our moral public deliberation, a society that *talks* about having the utmost respect for human dignity, understood as a dialectic between categoricity and community is important. That is, between the twin pulls of categorical justice on the one hand (e.g., prohibitions against sexual slavery) and justice as fairness in a pluralistic sense on the other (e.g., that not everyone shares the same first-order moral judgments), we must think through our Categorical Grip scenario and our Family Heirloom scenario.

How we talk about our society, and how we talk about what kind of society we want to be, matters. The language of community, of morality, of autonomy and choice, and dignity are *all* vital. In a reassuring move, in the organ procurement debate most advocates from each of the camps tried to preserve this language. That is, altruistic advocates still tried to respect and engage with the notions of autonomy and choice and market advocates tried to respect and engage with notions of dignity and avoiding exploitation. This is important and a good marker for most advocates. Not all debates are so characterized.

To put the matter more bluntly, at this point I am content to suggest that there is *something* good in *simply retaining the language,* in simply communicating with each other using terms such as morality, autonomy, and dignity, *even though* there is much controversy about their substance. In short, the kind of society to live in, I think, is one that *argues about morality* – even if those arguments are fierce and at some level intractable, and even if sometimes public morality deliberation generates the wrong answer. That is, a society that argues about morality is a *better* society than one that says, simply, *there is no such thing as morality,* or, almost equivalently, *it is all relative,* or, as so many like to say now, *you do you.* Communicative patterns matter. To that end, constitutional democracies should speak of and argue about morality and – not or – markets, collective democratic deliberation and – not or – moral categoricity, normative force and – not or – rhetorical force. The dialectic of categoricity and community, here in the early twenty-first century, needs to retake centrality in our political arrangements and public moral deliberations.

Compromise, Incentives, and Disincentives

The focus of this book has not been on the strategic, practical question of how to get more organs but rather on the discursive side, on the philosophy and rhetoric of advocates in public moral deliberation on that question. It is worth, briefly, discussing what a potential compromise position looks like, given that many readers might be interested in concrete, logistical procurement, and to do so in consonance with the theme of morals and markets just discussed.

A key stasis point of altruistic and market advocates is the question of dignity, reasoning, on the one hand, that dignity is violated by selling one's organ, versus reasoning, on the other hand, that dignity is enhanced through reward and that the autonomy of all involved, including the poor, is promoted. Those are the primary reasons that matter as market and altruistic advocates weigh reasons. My contributing discussion found all three of these arguments – dignity being violated through selling, dignity being enhanced through compensation, and the promotion of autonomy as enhancing dignity – to be wanting. If part of the conversation, though, is that democracy is best understood as everyone's *second choice* for political arrangement, then let's look, briefly, at a compromise position.

A primary element of incentive advocates' case is their *aim*, residing between that of altruistic and market advocates. Advocates maintain, to repeat a quote, that incentivizing organ donation is the "most viable compromise between using the power of market forces to satisfy human need while at the same time recognizing the widespread reluctance to having human body parts being treated, undignifiedly, as commodities."[13] The position is presented precisely in terms of dignity: the use of limited financial incentives "comports with human dignity and constitutes the tiniest imaginable step toward utilizing the power of financial incentives to bring supply ... to meet demand."[14]

The harnessing-of-market-forces element is clearly seen in that the project results in a quasi-market in human organs. How incentives do not violate human dignity and treating organs as commodities is the tricky part. Details matter for the proposed cases, and I won't go into them here. At a minimum, necessary key features needed would include that the market would be highly regulated, with only one buyer (the state), and for the purposes of procurement only.[15] Furthermore, the incentive is understood to be for the choice to donate, not for organs directly. The financial compensation is for the act of signing the card, or, in the case of live donation, a removal of disincentives. At this point, for more on the details, philosophically and logistically, let it suffice to direct to Andrew Michael Flescher's discussion of how we can "make altruism practical" in his *The Organ Shortage Crisis in America*.[16]

Finally, the notion of incentives also speaks to the complications of multiple motives discussed throughout this study. That is, if what it takes to motivate some people to do the right thing is financial incentives, then so be it, and to insist on only a pure altruistic motive as acceptable only costs potential organs and therefore human lives, as, in the memorable words of transplant surgeon Amy Friedman, patients "wait with dignity for the life-saving organ that never comes."[17]

The incentive paradigm resonates with contemporary US society insofar as money drives much of human life; many of us, if not must of us, do work we'd rather not do. Based on an ethics of citizenship, in an incentive-disincentive compromise, each side recognizes the values pluralism that characterizes contemporary society, and both are willing to forgo their complete and ideal picture. It is at least a realistic political option, taming the moral outstrippings of the neoliberal side and the idealisms of the civic republican side.

Still, organ supply is not meeting demand, and the attribution of this to a *failure in our collective imagination*, as it was put,[18] is all the more potent given the major attempts to boost organ procurement since the writing of that statement in 2003. That is, in the past decade or so, there have been a number of alternatives and proposals, including the tax incentives and massive campaigns, most notably school curriculum additions, Facebook profiling, donor chains and voucher systems, and there is still a major gap between supply and demand. The push for artificial organs, though hardly without ethical questions and demands under increasing biomedicalized biotechnologies, is perhaps, empirically, our last hope.

The ethical challenges to artificial organs, while not insignificant, are dwarfed in comparison to rapidly emerging ethically fraught biomedical possibilities. Compared to germline genetic intervention and extensional and transhuman biotechnologies, moral debates about market mechanisms and neoliberal rhetoric in health care seem almost quaint. But notice how public moral deliberation in general, and bioethics in specific, as reducible to, simply, concerns of efficiency, financial cost-benefit, and moral autonomy make such bioethical decisions *almost moot*: after all, in such a picture, who would get to decide what healthy and flourishing mean if not the individual, with an alignment of economic systems and imperatives to support that biomedicine is but physicians as (now almost literally) engineers for hire? If this outcome is unsatisfactory, then rearticulating and rethinking (recommitting?) our aims and ends of public moral deliberation seems necessary in general; and, more specifically, a renewed discussion of the aims and ends of medicine – what the spirit of medicine is – also seems necessary. This book has, in some small way, contributed to both projects already, and now let me push a bit further.

Feature 2: Rhetorical Orientations of Dignity, Altruism, and Hope

In addition to wanting a society that argues about morals and markets, I suggest that we also want a society that promotes dignity, altruism, and hope, and not just an aim of negative liberty. While a defence of that position would be another book (or three), I am going to limit the discussion here not for space reasons but because I genuinely believe that the majority of people in constitutional democracies *already agree* with that premise, and that they just might need a little *reminding* of what they value. In the rest of this chapter, I mean to perform the interplay of normative force and rhetorical force in support of a particular orientation for public moral deliberation.

Public Moral Deliberation on What Matters and Why

Altruism and dignity, given the foregoing discussion of how and why we can and do cultivate them in the public morality of a society in general and its medical practice in particular, have the potential to become normative by the virtue of their promotion in a reflective public. That is, the very fact that the process of moral deliberation is public, and that certain institutions, habits, and practices have cultivated altruism and dignity, might be enough to carry weight in a public moral deliberation. *We historically have cared about this* or it is part of *who we are* become performative arguments, aiming for interlocutor consent and demonstrating a coherent, consistent identity.

In this way, an internally coherent narrative about one's society is deployed, or can be strategically deployed, to maintain certain values. While this might be obvious enough in one sense, what is important to note here is the way that locutions like *this is who we are* can do *more* than induce (or create) sociality, fellow-feeling, public spiritedness, and the like. That is, there is clearly the sociality aspect in the rhetoric, a sort of (royal?) we-ness aiming at normative consent that can be welcomed or burdensome (e.g., "remember that we Christians must turn the other cheek") or even outright paternalistic ("we don't play sports in this family"; "we don't act like that"). Rhetorical through and through, in the sense of persuasion, aiming to induce assent.

But there is also a character component in which, at both the individual level and the social level, we are deciding who we are and what we care about and why. The debt to virtue theory is obvious here, in which the key terms in a moral deliberation shift from duty or consequences to character and coherence: what kind of person would I be if I did this, and how is that consistent with who I have been, who I think I am, and who I want to be?

Individually and collectively we are prone to moral flickering (sometimes we pursue altruism, sometimes we pursue self-interest), but morality is more than social reputation and signalling as even economists suggest.[19] That is, more than just a consequential weighing of costs and rewards in the physical (theft: potential gain is money, potential cost is incarceration) or social (cost of losing family, social ostracizing, etc.), we have internal and internalized standards that we *want* to live up to.

We care about both praise and praiseworthiness, as Adam Smith reminds us, and we care about not just the appearance of honour but actually being honourable, as Plato or Aristotle might have put it.[20] Deep down, we don't really want just approval, attention, and accolades but we want to have earned them, too. The propensity for self-deception, of course, is significant, and the notion of self-conception (I'm pretty moral, I'm pretty healthy, etc.) involves trade-offs and calculations that are rarely as clear as psychological egoism or ecstatic sainthood.

Sometimes a prompt, a nudge, is enough to remind us – not tell us, not persuade us – of who we want to be. This process is no less rhetorical, but it is more of a persuasive reminder than it is an attempt to influence ends or aims. In some ways this is both strange and obvious. It is obvious in the sense that reminders, prompting, and nudges are, clearly, all around us and effectual, from reminders on your phone to physical trainers to accountability partners. But it is also strange when considering something such as honesty, "that any reminder can decrease dishonesty ... after all, people should know that it is wrong to be dishonest."[21] As an illustration, consider a study in which, prior to a task in which the participants were able to cheat, the invocation of the Ten Commandments decreased the magnitude of dishonesty – regardless of whether or not the participant was noticeably religiously committed, meaning potentially that the prompt to reflect on a standard (whatever one's standard of honesty and moral code is) sufficed.[22]

The particular turn I'm interested in here is the way in which moral situations, both in the self-reflective (me) and in public deliberation (us) alike, make for a *rhetorical moment*: that is, there is a live question on the table *even when* (if ever) we have come to strong conclusions about who we are and what we value, because the exigency requires a response. That is, even if we were completely clear individually and socially about exactly what is morally virtuous (and required, etc.), the raising of the question itself – in this case, should human organs be for sale – demands a response from us.

The Centrality of Dignity to the Moral Life

The practice of public argument and moral deliberation is important to democratic societies. But as has been insisted and problematized throughout this book, there are significant normative aims and ends that both enable and constrain discursive publics. There are substantive features to public argument and there are good reasons to support and enact them. The line between the substantive moral content and procedural practices as generating moral content can be thin at times. But the emphasis here is that morality is not reducible to just the procedural: citizen agreement on what to do does not necessarily have any bearing on whether we are, actually, doing the right thing. Put differently, there is a difference between the council of prudence and morally binding law.

In getting at the difference between council and binding law, consider again the passage in Kant's *Grounding* (§434):

> In the kingdom of ends everything has either a price or a dignity. Whatever has a price can be replaced by something else as its equivalent; on the other hand, whatever is above all price, and therefore admits of no equivalent, has a dignity.[23]

This distinction, between price and dignity, is predicated on the notion of prices being set as exchange equivalents, as evident in the quote. The common denominator of money still illustrates this otherwise mercantilist take: a basic pair of scissors and a fast-food hamburger have the same value, given that both can be purchased for a few dollars. If there is something that has no such equivalent (either in like-product or dollar value) – that is, something that cannot be replaced at any price – then one is probably dealing with something that is literally priceless. This something has a property that Kant calls dignity.

The clearest indications of moral limits to markets stem from notions of dignity in the form of vulnerability or weak agency or inalienability according to personhood. What matters here is the connection that Kant makes in the very next two paragraphs, and I will quote it at length (§434–5):

> Whatever has reference to general human inclinations and needs has a market price; whatever, without presupposing any need, accords with a certain taste ... has an affective price; but that which constitutes the condition under which alone something can be an end in itself has not merely a relative worth, i.e., a price, but has an intrinsic worth, i.e., dignity.
>
> Now morality is the condition under which alone a rational being can be an end in himself, for only thereby can he be a legislating member in the kingdom of ends. Hence morality and humanity, insofar as it is capable of morality, alone have dignity.[24]

The fundamental connection here is not humanity and dignity, as is often supposed of the Kantian-inspired picture. Rather, the key is the connection of dignity and morality. Notice the construction: dignity is in morality *and* humanity, but it is only in humanity *insofar as humanity is capable of morality*.

The matter turns keenly on what one *means* by morality. In the Kantian picture, morality issues from commands, and in particular, the categorical imperative. This is contrasted with inclinations (an agent's mere preferences), of course, but the stronger contrast is with hypothetical imperatives. That is, the hypothetical imperative links up almost precisely to market logic, in which anything can be for sale, and categorical imperatives link up with categorical prohibitions, in which no contract nor specification of details can override the standing (or moral) law. The Categorical Grip is tight – and rightly so.

Whether altruistic organ advocates, then, see humanity in particular or morality in general as having an inherent worth that is not to be violated via market logic and pricing is beside the point. What is clear is that altruistic advocates rest their case on markets having limits, that those limits are prescribed/proscribed *morally*, and that this morality is binding on *all* agents in the community. While some advocates might subscribe to the more drastic overarching critique of the corrosive effects of commodification (i.e., capitalism) on humanity, that is an extra normative step and not required. That is, moral limits to markets, as seen in previous chapters in the rhetoric of Debra Satz, Margaret Jane Radin, Ezekiel Emanuel, and Michael Sandel, to name a few, are consistent with capitalism and market systems and mechanisms in general.

Universal-commodification market advocates, on the other hand, weigh the reasons for prohibition in a way that positions *essentially all* morality as a system of hypothetical imperatives, compatible with market logic of means-ends rationality, in which there are, from a state perspective, *no* categorical ends – that is, no ends binding on all agents. In this way, market advocates *treat morality as merely counsels* of prudence as opposed to binding laws. Citizens are free to argue their particular conceptions of the good life, and offer as many hypothetical imperatives as they see fit, and all of this belongs under the rubric of counsels of prudence; it is then up to each individual to accept or deny the counsel. That, in essence, is all that morality *is*.

While I have not developed a specifically Kantian conception of categoricity, it has been argued at length in section III that categorical morality exists and that the best society will pursue categorical ends collectively. The picture is of course complicated by controversy on what exactly *are* the moral truths and *how* they bear on a certain matter relevant to discursive publics. Constitutional democracies indeed allow for pursuit of subjective conscience and deep dissent – just not in all areas across the board. In this way, then, universal-commodification advocates are mistaken in the weight they assign the reasons that matter, potentially misunderstanding what morality *is* and what constitutional democracies ought to be. Instead, certain universal commodificationists, like certain communist anti-commodificationists, aim to define a society into existence. As neoliberal rhetoric and policies increase in success and momentum, we are seeing a corresponding shift in public morality. Again, the way in which all discussions of value now mean or quickly cash out (pun intended!) in monetary value needs to be halted.

Dignity is the best way to conceptualize, and symbolize, a defence against encroaching neoliberalism. That is not because it is the proper ground for democratic public political life but because it is the basis of moral life in the first place – my moral life, your moral life, individually first, and then, *moral life* itself, in the abstract. Let me end this section with another long Kant quote:

> Humanity in our person is an object of highest respect and never to be violated in us. In cases where a man is liable to dishonor, he is duty bound to give up his life, rather than dishonor the humanity in his own person ... what matters is that, so long as he lives, he should live honorably, and not dishonor the dignity of humanity. If he can no longer live in that fashion, he cannot live at all; his moral life is then at an end. But moral life is at an end if it no longer accords with the dignity of humanity.[25]

An Existential Overlay: The Tyranny of the Gift of Life, Faith, and Hope

But, in addition to my suggestion that the problem is not markets and capitalism per se, there is a deeper, existential dimension to what decisions and choice look like. That is, while emphasis on the *public* side of public moral deliberation runs through this study, offered in the spirit of deliberative-rhetorical democracy and hence committed to third-personal and second-personal understandings of morality in categorical-community dialectic, the individual still plays the central role in both morality and social life. Bernard Williams's dictum is exactly correct: "Practical deliberation is first-personal, radically so, and involves an *I* that must be more intimately the *I* of my desires" than impartial, third-person morality allows.[26] While Williams-type views do not capture the nature of morality is its entirety, there *is something* to the highly personal nature of morality insofar as the act of judgment is concerned. It is a matter of choice. One is not only *free* to choose, one also *must* choose. Adding to both the *I* and to the *us* dimension of choice is what I will call the *existential weight of moral judgment.* This Kierkegaardian notion is an important overlay to moral conversation because in the contemporary era, moral judgment has become too light of an affair, with too narrow a set of concerns. To Kierkegaard, what characterizes a self is that it chooses, that it *wills:* "A person who has no will at all is not a self."[27] The willing self, and the will to be oneself, is, the "greatest concession, an infinite concession" given to humans; but it is also "eternity's claim upon" us.[28]

The will to be a self is, in some sense, the very gift of life; it is the human condition. To connect back up with organ donation, one of the most enduring rhetorical phrases that characterizes altruistic advocacy is the Gift of Life: by donating one's organs, you share, and perpetuate, the gift of life. However, there is a negative tension, sometimes referred to as the tyranny of the gift, that refers to both the pressures family members and close friends feel to *have* to give organs to loved ones as well as the sort of *unpayable debt* feeling that organ recipients often feel towards their donors.[29]

Putting those two concepts together in light of this discussion of the weight of judgment and eternity's claim on us, the very act of being a conscious, wilful being is a sort of tyranny, feeling like an unbearable burden. So, from an existential perspective, there is a tyranny of the gift *of life*: it is eternity's claim on us that we must have knowledge of our self before the infinite *and cannot choose to stand in any other relation*, and to then have the weight of choice on our shoulders for particular actions and judgments without always having the clearest of guidelines.[30] Even those of us who are religiously committed still live, in this sense, in a secular age, in which uncertainty and doubt – have I chosen correctly? am I sure? – pervade our social ontology.

The cleanest illustration of eternity's claim and this sort of tyranny of the gift of life in this debate is the Categorical Grip problem that opened this book. There is *something*, it seems, that longs for eternity, for absolute right answers, and to live in harmony with those answers in human community. And yet it is also seems out of reach to humans, at best, and at worst, manifested in actual human tyranny. This is because humans sit as an in-between people – not infinite and not finite, the already and the not yet. The moral domain is synecdoche for the human condition: how one ought to live is given only through glimpses and ideals, meaning that one can do no better than to live in faith and hope.

While faith and hope are theological terms, there are secular correlates. The most notable is faith as a translation of *pistis* in the rhetorical tradition, understood most particularly as *trust in* as opposed to simply *belief that*.[31] The concept of hope is similarly universal, especially in light of the previous discussion: hope is the opposite of despair. In *Negative Dialectics*, Theodor Adorno casts critical enquiry in the Kantian tradition precisely in these terms: the "secret of [Kant's critical] philosophy is the unthinkability of despair."[32] And, to add a Kierkegaardian twist to it, one must wrestle with despair – that is, recognize that the grip of the categorical is the grip of the eternal in each self – and not be crushed by it but instead to choose hope.

This living in faith and hope might sound squishy. But these concepts are meant to signal fundamental elements of the human condition and are not necessarily tied to a specific religious conception per se. Indeed, that hope and health care are linked is no surprise. Arthur Kleinman even claims that part of the physician's job is "instilling or rekindling hope."[33] While there is much more to explore in the connection between virtue theory and flourishing in its Hippocratic and Socratic context to contemporary health and medicine, a brief connection will suffice for our purposes here.[34]

Tying back into the Greek rhetorical tradition, the word faith is the translation of *pistis*, the same term that is Aristotle's term for conviction, oft-translated as proof. To further tie to Aristotle, the word for substance is *hoopostasis/hypostasis*, meaning the underlying essence (connecting to *ousia*), the stuff of which things are made. The combination suggests that faith and hope, while Ideal, are not idealistic.

The suggestion is that there is a reality, a substance, to one's hope: the Ideal City exists, seen in glimpses. But it is not here in the Contemporary City. And so, humans are caught between trying to be citizens of the Ideal City while being citizens of the Contemporary City, trying to subscribe to the ideal constitution *and* their state Constitution. This balancing act applies to anyone who has hope for and belief in an ideal constitution, and it is not a new concern. Consider Aristotle's *Politics* (III.5.1278b1–3): "As to the question whether the excellence of the good man is the same as that of the good citizen, the considerations already adduced prove that in some states the good man and the good citizen are the same and in others different."[35] Though he does not address the issue in any detail, the concern is a very modern one: the relationship between a good man and a good citizen. Drawing on other Aristotelian works, philosopher David Keyt concludes that for Aristotle, there is such a thing as a good person living in a non-ideal city, and that, most of the time, the good person will, valuing stability, go along with what it means to be a good citizen.[36] The difference is seen most strikingly in terms of education: "A good Athenian citizen will educate his sons in harmony with the Athenian constitution; a good man will educate his sons in harmony with the ideal constitution."[37]

There is a vexed contemporary relationship between competing visions of the ideal constitution, and whether or not a state's constitution ought to even try to match such an ideal constitution in the first place, as made apparent throughout this book. Organ advocates range the spectrum, and there is a clear sense in which compensation and particularly market advocates, while not unattuned to questions of dignity and exploitation, find the matching of ideal and state constitutions impossible.

Emboldened by much modern political philosophy that attempts to disarticulate the ideal constitution from the state's, by economists who claim no connection between facts and values, and certain corners of ethical philosophy that deny moral realism and hence a moral constitution altogether, advocates of market rationality and the neoliberal ethos applied to all corners of social and individual life continue to gain psychic steam and political traction.

The moral life and the ideal constitution are not matters of certain *episteme*, nor are they matters of mere *doxa*; they are matters, precisely, of faith and hope, understood, rendered, and argued for using rhetorical *pisteis*. It is a tension, an in-between position, and one that requires substantial commitment to reason giving and epistemic humility on the part of all citizens, in the cooperative search for the truth of the ideal constitution, and the best state constitution possible. An ethics of citizenship, understood as the upright citizen, requires accord and compromise in the name of stability and safety. Morality, understood as the good being, requires pursuit of moral excellence. The orientation of a public's moral deliberation creates dispositions to reason and act, and our actions and reason giving thus can and do flow from such orientations. The orientation itself is not strictly the product of rationality but something closer to hope or faith.[38]

The continued expansion of values pluralism in contemporary constitutional democracies such as the United States makes the reconciliation between questions of moral and legal permissibility daunting and seemingly insurmountable. And indeed, there are many instances in which a division is both necessary and beneficial to a stable and free society. But that all matters of legality and policy are to be seen as divorced from underlying moral positions or first-order judgments would be a significant mistake. What specifics attach to categorical morality is something that requires significant public moral deliberation, and so categoricity and community not only can but must go walking hand in hand in moral life and sociopolitical arrangement alike.

The need for public moral deliberation possessed of rhetorical force – if not the goal of *movere*, then at least rhetorical reminders in rhetorical moments – in reasoning and reflecting on what we ought to ultimately aim at (telic orientation), what we value (historically and contemporarily), and what is valuable (what has normative force) cannot be overstated. We give over such dialogue to neoliberal imperatives or, worse, fail to engage deliberatively at all, at peril to our moral lives.

Confessions

I try to imagine myself in end-stage renal failure, struggling through dialysis treatments four days a week. It sounds awful.

But I think I could do it. After all, I've been preparing for that sort of physical and moral struggle – internally and externally – for much of my life, and particularly since I began thinking about organ sales over the past ten years or so. It has also become one of my convictions that in the twenty-first century, in a world where we have become accustomed to buying and selling our way out of all problems, personally, socially, politically, and even existentially, that much of what we need are new models and new playbooks around lives worth living and a new art of dying. What we need is an *ars moriendi* for modernist global capitalism. There is part of me – surely the embarrassing egotistical part – that thinks I'd be a worthy sufferer in this sense, offering a noble alternative, an admirable candidate of mimicry in the face of imminent death. Oh, dear me, imagined here equally with grandeur and self-pitying martyrdom.

Now if I imagine one of my children or my wife needing an organ transplantation, things change. Noble talk of the *ars moriendi* disappears, as does intimations of honour and glory. Swiftly, I'd call to plead with every hospital in town and contact every surgeon I've ever met.

Failing the network-and-charm offensive, I'd want to just buy the kidney.

And I don't mean that I'd *want to buy a kidney* in some hypothetical world, where I wasn't me or I cultivated for myself a different habits and norms and aspired to different virtues. No, I mean now, in this world, in the world where I've just finished writing a book on why buying and selling organs is a mistake and promotes a flawed understanding of what humans are and what they owe in moral life more generally and to each other in human community in specific. In this world, I'd want to buy a kidney for wife.

I didn't say I *would* actually buy or even seek to buy an organ. But I would *want* to, and for nearly all of the reasons we've seen so far: the political-cultural norms of a monetary escape valve for all problems, including existential problems; the easing of the psychological and physical need for a social, moral (as opposed to a merely transactional) partner; the (assumed) psychic lessening of receiving an unpayable debt, a gift that cannot be reciprocated, thereby mitigating the tyranny of the gift, and cloaking the tyranny of the gift of life, and so forth.

This isn't flattering to me. But this section is called confessions, and not something elevated like "intellectual honesty" or more academic like "counterfactual assumptions." The point here is that, I too, need rhetorical reminders. What's wrong with the world, of course, is me.

Conclusion: End of the Beginning

By way of summary, then, *the way society is conceptualized and talked about matters*. The rhetorical weave of morals and markets, and the limits of each in a constitutional democracy respectively and on each other, is tangled, and there are not easy answers to many essential normative questions of our moral life together. But talk underscores and influences attitudes about oneself, others, and the society. Talk that uses terms such as and has aims of community, autonomy, morality, innovation, markets, dignity, and humanity ought to be the aim of public moral deliberation. Of course such talk and terms can be abused and exploited to serve unethical and unlawful ends, but at this time, there is concern that the terms themselves will disappear due to ever-increasing pressures of commodification and technologicalization, and the encroachment of market language on all areas of everyday human life. If morality is a fully privatized affair under the ethos of the triumph of autonomy over all other competing values, then all that is left of life together – of social bond, civic altruism, reasoned disagreement, and so forth – is the market and market mechanisms.

Put explicitly in terms of the organ debate, the problem of pluralism facing constitutional democracies given the modern condition and the distanced self is that the competing advocates here ought to see these two questions

Q1: whether or not selling one's organ is moral, and
Q2: whether or not society should allow it

as being fundamentally connected. If the questions are seen as divorced, a market model and moral individual choice, Neoliberalism-by-Default in the economization of everyday life makes the most sense for society. But I agree with advocates and argued myself that it is a mistake to assume incommensurability as inevitable, which often also make a deeper and more problematic assumption: that there is no way to convince others of right answers, and perhaps, even more profoundly, that there are not right answers to moral questions in the first place. The choice is not between means-ends, instrumental rationality as being the standard moral requirement of respect for a community, or categoricity in which right answers are found and agreed to be collectively binding according to the precepts of justice and morality. There ought to be talk of categoricity and community as constitutional democracies decide law and policy in public moral deliberation.

The public moral deliberation process of weighing reasons becomes the central feature of moral rhetoric, and how one weighs reasons is tied directly and inextricably to telic orientation. Telic orientation – towards what, ultimately, we aim – is not a product of logical necessity, but that is not to say that it is beyond the domain of reason altogether, just that it seeks, and needs, more than that. The concept of rhetorical force, of what is and will be persuasive in convincing interlocutors, applies at every level of discourse, but is most powerfully tied to telic orientation.

What has the most normative force in this debate is the question of human dignity. Market advocates' case turns on the fact that markets do not violate human dignity. Altruistic advocates respond that a good society would be one that actually promotes attitudes that enhance human dignity. The corresponding justifications for (differing) actions hinge on differing telic views of *society*: whether it is a society's job to promote and enhance human dignity and altruism, or whether the case is one of negative liberty.

The society that buys and sells human body parts is probably not going to have very much concern for human dignity, just as the relationship built on the buying and selling of sex is not going to have very much concern for love. The acts alone do not necessarily remove these things. But the acts and communicative patterns promote and reinforce attitudes towards ourselves and others. Payment does not inherently diminish the virtues of one's behaviour, but in practice it promotes an attitude that absolves oneself and society of gratitude and grace. In short, it promotes a mistakenly oriented society. A better society is one that has a reflective enhancement and promotion of human dignity and altruism through communicative patterns and policies.

Public moral deliberation aims at a kind of moral convergence around key themes of dignity and altruism, not because the attachment of them to our arguments will thus gain in rhetorical force or because we want honour and praise for high-minded magic words. Rather, public moral deliberation can, does, and should aim at promoting dignity and altruism, rendered in a kind of picture of human flourishing, because those are praiseworthy and valuable ideas. What makes them valuable is not that (or not only that) we care about them. What makes them valuable is that they are worthy of being cared about and pursued.

While the fundamental attitude of this enquiry is deliberative, aiming to contribute to and perform a part of public moral deliberation, explicate key tensions, and better understand the debate, normative arguments have proceeded as well, in what we might see as the beginnings of an attempt to de-graft neoliberalism from bioethics in specific and public deliberation in democratic society in general. At a minimum, hopefully it is seen that public moral deliberation on what kind of policies we want for which kind of society *just is* deciding what kind of society we want to be.

Notes

1. Organs for Sale? Normative Entanglements in the Public Sphere

1 I do not mean to push the metaphor too far, but the connection between *health* and *political life* has a long history, perhaps most notably stemming from Plato's *Republic* and *Laws*. Plato presents physician knowledge and practices of souls and bodies in the individual sense as analogous to philosopher knowledge and practices of souls and bodies in the collective city sense, healthy parts of souls and cities needing to work together.

2 Deliberative democracy is the process of reason-giving and justifying decisions with and within a deliberating public. For a succinct overview that even includes a chapter on health care deliberations, see Amy Gutmann and Dennis Thompson, *Why Deliberative Democracy* (Princeton, NJ: Princeton University Press, 2004). For more on public bioethics and democracy, see Jonathan D. Moreno, *Deciding Together: Bioethics and Moral Consensus* (New York: Oxford University Press, 1995; and Amy Gutmann and Jonathan D. Moreno, *Everybody Wants to Go to Heaven but Nobody Wants to Die: Bioethics and the Transformation of Health Care in America* (New York: Liveright, 2019), esp. 11–84.

3 Donna Dickenson, *Me Medicine vs. We Medicine* (New York: Columbia University Press, 2013).

4 Salmaan Keshavjee, *Blind Spot: How Neoliberalism Infiltrated Public Health* (Berkeley, CA: University of California Press, 2014), xxxii.

5 See, e.g., Ezekiel J. Emanuel, *The Ends of Human Life: Medical Ethics in a Liberal Polity* (Cambridge, MA: Harvard University Press, 1991).

6 The presentation here is slightly different than, say, John Evans's distinction of technical bioethics (profession), cultural bioethics (the social and political activism of bioethics), and public policy bioethics (the space where bioethicists advise on law and policy). The idea of deliberation in the public sphere is meant in the deliberative democratic sense, of citizens engaging in reason-giving and exchanges in the metaphorical space that is neither government nor civil society. It maps relatively well onto Evans's "public policy bioethics" conception. See John H. Evans, *The History and Future of Bioethics* (New York: Oxford University Press, 2012).

7 For example, in 1988, there were 5,091 organ donations, 12,618 transplants, and 15,029 on the waiting list. By 2009, there were 14,630 organ donations, 28,463 transplants, and 105,567 on the waiting list. While the waiting-list numbers climb higher, recently there has been a rising number of transplants performed each year. The

34,770 transplants performed in 2017 marked the fifth consecutive record-setting year. Statistics are updated daily by the *Organ Procurement and Transplant Network* via https://optn.transplant.hrsa.gov.

8   According to a statement made by Dr. Carlos Esquivel, Chief of Transplantation at Stanford University. See Marianne Levine, "Stanford Hospital Awarded National Gold Medal of Honor," *The Stanford Daily*, 5 Oct. 2012, http://www.stanforddaily .com/2012/10/05/stanford-hospital-awarded-national-gold-medal-of-honor/.

9   "The Kidney Project: Statistics," UCSF Schools of Pharmacy and Medicine: Department of Bioengineering and Therapeutic Sciences, https://pharm .ucsf.edu/kidney/need/statistics.

10 For a voucher system proposal, see Dominique Martin and Gabriel M. Danovitch, "Banking on Living Kidney Donors – A New Way to Facilitate Donation without Compromising on Ethical Values," *Journal of Medicine and Philosophy* 42, no. 5 (2017): 537–58. For a revised tax-credit proposal, see Sally Satel and Alan D. Viard, "The Kindest (Tax) Cut: A Federal Tax Credit for Organ Donations," *AEI's Tax Notes* 155, no. 11 (12 June 2017): https://www .aei.org/wp-content/uploads/2017/07/Tax-Credit-for-Organ-Donation.pdf.

11 Atul Gawande, "The Heroism of Incremental Care," *New Yorker*, 23 January 2017.

12 Luke J. DeRoos, Wesley J. Marrero, and Elliot B. Tapper, "Estimated Association between Organ Availability and Presumed Consent in Solid Organ Transplant," *JAMA Network Open* 2 (2019): doi:10.1001/jamanetworkopen.2019.12431.

13 There are several entire journals devoted to these areas of exploration: e.g., *Biofabrication* (founded in 2009), *Journal of Artificial Organs* (founded in 1998), and *Artificial Organs* (founded in 1977).

14 If a significant feature of neoliberal rhetoric, as evidenced in the following pages, is something about free markets and individualism being the solution to (essentially all) social and moral problems, artificial organs would represent a different (though potentially related) kind of rhetoric in which science and technology are the solution.

15 There might be some imaginative distribution solutions that could ease the tension on supply, and ultimately, if supply and demand are in equilibrium, the ethical questions are significantly quieted. Some pooling work – the formation of the South Transplant Alliance (STA), for example – pushes forward in terms of alleviating suffering through better resource pooling and distribution. The STA is, in short, a cooperation protocol between Italy, Spain, and France for human organs. Signed on 1 October 2012, it follows in the path of, and seeks to cooperate with, the Mediterranean Transplant Network. See "Transplants: New Italy-Spain-France Organ Network," *Ansamed.info*, 1 October 2012, http://www.ansamed.info /ansamed/en/news/nations/france/2012/10/01/Transplants-new-Italy-Spain -France-organ-network_7560025.html.

16 In other words, one proposed solution to the organ shortage is simply to get more donors *registered*, not convincing of the value of donation or altruism or anything of the like. The potential efficacy of this solution is evidenced through claims, such as those on OrganDonor.gov, that 95 per cent of adults in the United States support organ donation but only 48 per cent are registered as donors. https://www.organdonor .gov/statistics-stories/statistics.html.

17 Andrew Michael Flescher, *The Organ Shortage Crisis in America* (Washington, DC: Georgetown University Press, 2018).

18 Consider the art market. While plenty of wealthy people might participate in the art market only for financial reasons (ROI, as a store of value, etc.), in general the principle is supposed to be that the pieces or artists that command the highest prices are

because of their beauty or importance in art history or cultural processes or the like; the economic value is supposedly driven by some underlying other value. One of the ways we can signal the importance or prowess of a piece of art is by its price, and then raise or peg prices relationally. So, work by street-brand subcultural icons like Supreme or Banksy can now garner big-ticket prices via famous New York auction houses, which can indicate both its value as art and its place in the artworld and also might serve to send canonical works up higher as well. ("If a set of skateboards is worth *that*, then surely a Van Gogh must be worth ... ") As of course pricing and cultural authority and the like are notoriously complicated to unpack, I simply mean to highlight the intuition and practice: both the degree to which our sense of economic worth is often predicated on some other sense of value, as well as the practice of ascribing that *other* value thing *to* its price. So, your response on seeing Banksy's *Devolved Parliament* as being aesthetically trite and too politically on-the-nose is met by your friend saying, "Well, it's worth $12 million, so ... "

19 *Assessing Initiatives to Increase Organ Donations: Hearing before the House Committee on Energy and Commerce, Subcommittee on Oversight and Investigation*, 108th Cong. 1 (2003).

20 "United States Renal Data System," USRDS.org, https://www.usrds.org/2017/view/v2_09.aspx.

21 The figure for 2005 was $17 billion. Elbert S. Huang, Nidhi Thakur, and David O. Meltzer, "The Cost-Effectiveness of Renal Transplantation," in *When Altruism Isn't Enough*, ed. Sally Satel (Washington, DC: The American Enterprise Institute Press, 2008), 19.

22 As Greenwood puts it, "This country spends an enormous amount of money [on health care] ... as does the private sector ... So it seems to me that the cost/benefit analysis [is that we need to have] that donation available and [have] that transplantation occur ... from a pure dollar-and-cent perspective, I think it makes sense to do everything we can to get the organ donations going ... " (*Assessing*, 29–30).

23 The first is the most obvious and common: "express donation." The second is "presumed donation," in a quasi-opt-out sense as opposed to opting into the donation system. The third is "routine removal," which places ownership rights of an organ on society and not the individual in a social duty/contract formulation. The fourth is "abandonment," in which an unclaimed body can be harvested. The fifth is "expropriation" or "conscription," which is similar to routine removal but goes even further by suggesting that public health and public interest have a right to organs over and against individual preferences to the contrary. The sixth is "sale" or "purchase," which is also self-explanatory (Childress, *Practical Reasoning in Bioethics* [Bloomington: Indiana University Press, 1997], 284, cf. 265–81).

24 For simplicity's sake, I have chosen to focus only on organs and not HBPs more generally, and follow his lead in focusing on express donation and sale/purchase. Childress, *Practical*, 284.

25 John Rawls, *Political Liberalism: Expanded Edition* (New York: Columbia University Press, 2005), xvii.

26 This style of enquiry has many different names as a field: rhetorical democracy, deliberative democracy, public-sphere studies, deliberative theory. Key works are Jürgen Habermas, *The Structural Transformation of the Public Sphere*, trans. Thomas Berger (Cambridge, MA: MIT Press, 1989); Rawls, *Political*; James Bohman and William Rehg, ed., *Deliberative Democracy: Essays in Reason and Politics* (Cambridge, MA: MIT Press, 1997); Amy Gutmann and Dennis Thompson, *Democracy and Disagreement* (Cambridge, MA: Belknap/Harvard University Press, 1996); Gutmann and Thompson, *Why Deliberative?*; Seyla Benhabib, *Democracy and Difference*

(Princeton: Princeton University Press, 1996); G. Thomas Goodnight and David B. Hingstman, "Studies in the Public Sphere," *Quarterly Journal of Speech* 83, no. 3 (1997): 351–99; and Gerard Hauser and Amy Grim, *Rhetorical Democracy: Discursive Practices of Civic Engagement* (Mahwah, NJ: Lawrence Erlbaum Associates, 2004). See also the Robert Asen and Daniel C. Brouwer guest-edited special issue of *Argumentation and Advocacy* 39, no. 3 (2003). On the potential for a postsecular public sphere, see Ryan Gillespie, "Religion and the Postsecular Public Sphere," *Quarterly Journal of Speech* 102, no. 2 (2016): 194–207.

27   Michael Sandel, *Justice: What's the Right Thing to Do?* (New York: Farrar, Straus, & Giroux, 2009), 28.

28   Here is T.M. Scanlon: "The 'basic structure' of a society is its legal, political and economic framework, the function of which is to define the rights and liberties of citizens and to determine a range of social positions to which different powers and economic rewards are attached. If a basic structure does this in an acceptable way ... then the structure is just." (*What We Owe Each Other* [Cambridge, MA: Harvard University Press, 1998], 244).

29   G. Thomas Goodnight, "The Engagements of Communication: Jürgen Habermas on Discourse, Critical Reason, and Controversy," in *Perspectives on Philosophy of Communication*, ed. Pat Arneson (West Lafayette, IN: Purdue University Press, 2007), 103. The internal quote is attributed to Habermas's *Religion and Rationality: Essays on Reason, God, and Modernity*, ed. Eduardo Mendieta (Cambridge, MA: MIT Press, 2002), 148.

30   A public sphere, as theorized by Habermas in *The Structural Transformation of the Public Sphere*, is a space between the state (and/or noble society) and civil society in which people come together to argue, in a common language of rational-critical debate, issues of legitimacy of the state, laws, etc. The high mark for this is considered Immanuel Kant's principle of publicity, which serves as a bridge between politics and morality. In a quick gloss, the book shows how the institutionalization of the bourgeois public sphere combined with notions of instrumentality and a confusion of publicity with anything that was not private ultimately led to the disappearance of the political function of the public. Though critics of Habermas's declinist thesis as well as his rational-critical model abound (e.g., Calhoun, Benhabib), the driving impulse to raise public discourse (or to *have* a public discourse) is strongly felt.

31   The continual importance of the intersubjective element of public deliberation, of a *discursive ethic*, is evidenced by the ever-widening polarization of communities, which, through the interconnectivity of technology and increasingly partisan media outlets (blogs, cable news channels, etc.) become more and more connected to each other (i.e., to "like" minds) and less and less engaged with differing opinions. Technology in the twenty-first century has greatly increased the connectivity – literally and figuratively – of civil society, but it seems it has done so at the expense of a public sphere. The contemporary world is one in which it is becoming more and more possible to altogether avoid opinions with which one disagrees, just as, ironically, through social networking sites, twenty-four-hour news cycles and other media contributing to our hypermediated era, the boundary between what is private and what is public is being erased. For democratic societies, this is a significant and severe problem. See my "Reason, Religion, and Postsecular Liberal Democratic Epistemology," *Philosophy & Rhetoric* 45, no. 1 (2014): 1–24. Further, I connect some of these ideas to Cass Sunstein's notion of *digital enclaves* in another piece. See Cass R. Sunstein, *Republic.com* (Princeton: Princeton University Press, 2001); Ryan Gillespie, "The Art of Criticism in the

Age of Interactive Technology: Critics, Participatory Culture, and the Avant Garde," *International Journal of Communication*, 6 (2012): 56–75. For more on the connection between public-argument processes and healthy democracies, see Rawls, *Political*; Roderick P. Hart and Courtney L. Dillard, "Deliberative Genre," in *Encyclopedia of Rhetoric*, ed. Thomas Sloane (New York: Oxford University Press, 2001), 210–11.

32 Gutmann and Thompson, *Why*, 98.

33 Seyla Benhabib, *Situating the Self: Gender, Community and Postmodernism in Contemporary Ethics* (New York: Routledge, 1992), 53.

34 Jürgen Habermas, *Between Naturalism and Religion*, trans. Ciaran Cronin (Malden: Polity, 2008), 141. For more detailed discussion of this work and how it relates to public reason and religion in particular, see Ryan Gillespie, "Uses of Religion," *International Journal of Communication*, 5 (2011): 1669–86; Gillespie, "Reason, Religion."

35 "Justice is not only about the right way to distribute things. It is also about the right way to value things." Sandel, *Justice*, 261.

36 Scanlon, *What*, 5.

37 Ralph Wedgwood, "The Moral Evil Demons," in *Disagreement*, ed. Richard Feldman and Ted A. Warfield (New York: Oxford University Press, 2010), 244.

38 While metaethics is precisely a field identified by Toulmin as avoiding the substantive issues of ethics by trying to remain scientifically or mathematically analogous, I think there are significant ways in which this view is misguided. There are two things that applied ethics and case studies, as an approach, miss. The first is that they perpetuate a disentangling of theory and practice, of principles and application that is, again, both unhelpful and inaccurate to human experience. While there is a hermeneutic quality to casuistry in terms of moving between (universal) principles and (particular) application of them, there are a lot of *bad* applied ethical studies that focus only on the details of particular cases without acknowledgment of informing principles or doctrines or recognition of potential and actual competing informing standards.

In this way, then, theoretical or strictly applied ethics will be equally mistaken. Secondly, I endorse much of Toulmin's focus on Aristotle, particularly the assertion that ethical judgment is often more a matter of the kind of person doing the judging and her relationship to both others and the object.

39 Christine Korsgaard, *Sources of Normativity* (Cambridge: Cambridge University Press, 1996), 46–7.

40 To use a probably apocryphal story, a *New England Journal of Medicine* editor, at the advent of the National Commission on Human Subjects, quipped, "Now we shall see matters of eternal principle decided by a six to five vote." The quote, and its status as likely untrue or as at least currently undocumented, is found in Toulmin, "The Tyranny of Principle," *Hastings Center Report* 11, no. 6 (1981): 31.

41 The work of Jonathan Haidt is perhaps most relevant here. See his touchstone "The Emotional Dog and Its Rational Tail: A Social Intuitionist Approach to Moral Judgment," *Psychology Review* 108, no. 4 (2001): 814–34; and his most recent, quasi-popularly aimed book: *The Righteous Mind: Why Good People Are Divided by Politics and Religion* (New York: Pantheon, 2012). I address some of this work from an argumentation perspective in Ryan Gillespie, "The Role of Intuition, Emotion, and Reason in the Act of Judgment: Implications from Moral Psychology and Metaethics for Argumentation Studies," in *Reasoned Argument: Selected Papers from the 16ᵗʰ Biennial AFA/NCA Conference on Argumentation*, ed. Robert Rowland (Washington, DC: National Communication Association), 95–103.

42 Aristotle, *Nicomachean Ethics*, II. 3. 1104.b.10; in *The Complete Works of Aristotle*, ed. Jonathan Barnes, trans. W.D. Ross (Princeton: Princeton/Bollinger Series, 1995), 1744.
43 David Harvey, *A Brief History of Neoliberalism* (New York: Oxford University Press, 2007), 2–3.
44 Tom Koch, *Thieves of Virtue: How Bioethics Stole Medicine* (Cambridge, MA: MIT Press, 2012), 256.
45 Ludwig Wittgenstein, "Lecture on Ethics," in *Moral Discourse and Practice*, ed. Stephen Darwall, Allan Gibbard, and Peter Railton (New York: Oxford University Press, 1997), 66–67.
46 Though there would probably be some disagreement as to *why*.
47 Wittgenstein was, more or less, content to marvel at the puzzle whereas someone like Rawls was keen to solve the problem. For Rawls, this was achieved, mainly, by separating the Good from the Just (or from the Right), arguing that the state was not in the business of the former but rather, and (relatively) only, the latter. The details of his solution, and others, are not relevant at this juncture, being explored in more detail in section III of this book.
48 Albert R. Jonsen, *The New Medicine and the Old Ethics* (Cambridge, MA: Harvard University Press, 1990), 4–5.

2. Public Morality: Altruism, Rhetoric, and Bioethics

1 The details of this story and subsequent tradition are culled from Nicholas Tilney, *Transplant: From Myth to Reality* (New Have: Yale University Press, 2003), 9–11.
2 The tale is the subject of much medieval art, and the two brothers are the patron saints of physicians, surgeons, and transplantation in the Roman Catholic tradition.
3 See Barbara Mantel, "Organ Donations: Can the Growing Demand Be Met?" *CQ Researcher*, 21, no. 15 (2011): 346–50.
4 According to James F. Childress, between 1968 and 1983, organ sales were not illegal and "kidneys were occasionally offered for sale during that period." One of the incidents that led to the establishment of the ban on human organ sales was the announcement that an ex-physician in Virginia was operating an organ brokerage firm, focusing mostly on procuring organs from underdeveloped nations. Other incidents were the hearings and the case of Ashley Bailey, both discussed in the main text. See James F. Childress, *Practical Reasoning in Bioethics* (Bloomington: Indiana University Press, 1997), 283.
5 *National Organ Transplant Act: Hearings on H.R. 4080 Before the Subcommittee on Health and the Environment of the House Committee on Energy and Commerce*, 98th Cong. 4 (1983) (inserted statement of Ronald Reagan).
6 NOTA 1983, 3.
7 National Organ Transplant Act. Pub.L. No. 98–507. 98 Stat 2339 (1984).
8 Three example of contestation: Henry Hansmann, "The Economics and Ethics of Markets for Human Organs," *Journal of Health Politics, Policy and Law* 14, no. 1 (1989): 57–85; Lloyd R. Cohen, "Increasing the Supply of Transplant Organs: The Virtues of a Futures Market," *George Washington Law Review* 58, no. 1 (1989): 1–51; and the UNOS Ethics Committee Report and White Paper: "Are Financial Incentives for Obtaining Organs Ethically Justifiable?" Subcommittee of Incentives for Donation, UNOS Ethics Committee, May 1991.
9 A white paper entitled "Financial Incentives for Organ Donation: A Report of the Payment Subcommittee OPTN/UNOS Ethics Committee," circulated through the

bioethical and interested academic communities, despite its conclusion that only once financial compensation and financial incentives are disentangled in the public mind might such a practice be ethically acceptable.

10 A sampling: Donald Joralmon, "Shifting Ethics: Debating the Incentive Question in Organ Transplantation," *Journal of Medical Ethics*, 27, no. 1 (2001): 30–5; Francis L. Delmonico, Robert Arnold, Nancy Scheper-Hughes, et al. "Ethical Incentives – Not Payment – for Organ Donation," *New England Journal of Medicine* 346, no. 25 (2002): 2002–5; L.D. de Castro, "Commodification and Exploitation: Arguments in Favour of Compensated Organ Donation," *Journal of Medical Ethics* 29, no. 3 (2003): 142–6.

11 Sometimes this is referred to as paid organ donation, which is too oxymoronic. There are, however, many ways of slicing the pie, ranging from simply offering financial incentives to entice people to donate their organs upon death, which is a difference of degree from financial compensation for an organ while still alive. There are also differences between who is doing the compensating/incentivizing – private industry or the state or federal government – and also in terms of price, ranging from $5 to tax credits to $50,000 in compensation. These will be discussed in later chapters in more detail but are worth noting up front.

12 For example, in 2006 there was a Public Broadcasting Service's episode of *Think Tank* that featured a debate on "The Market for Human Organs." In 2008, National Public Radio facilitated and broadcasted a debate, "Should We Legalize the Market for Human Organs?" and the National Forensic League (high school debate; now called National Speech and Debate Association) topic for April 2011 was "Resolved: The United States federal government should permit the use of financial incentives to encourage organ donation."See "The Market for Human Organs?" *Think Tank*/PBS, 16 July 2006, http://www.pbs.org/thinktank/transcript1248.html; "Should We Legalize the Market in Human Organs?" *National Public Radio*, 21 May 2008, http://www.npr.org/templates/story/story.php?storyId=90632108; National Speech and Debate Association, "Past Topics: Public Forum Debate," https://www.speechanddebate.org/topics/.

13 J.D. Jasper, Carol A.E. Nickerson, Peter A. Ubel, and David A. Asc, "Altruism, Incentives, and Organ Donation," *Medical Care* 42, no. 4 (2004): 378–86.

14 Scott Hensley, "Poll: Americans Show Support for Compensation of Organ Donation," NPR.org, 16 May 2012, http://www.npr.org/blogs/health/2012/05/16/152498553/poll-americans-show-support-for-compensation-of-organ-donors.

15 Julio J. Elias, Nicole Lacetera, and Mario Macis, "Sacred Values? The Effect of Information on Attitudes toward Payments for Human Organs," *American Economic Review* 105, no. 5 (2015): 363.

16 Ludwig Edelstein, *Ancient Medicine* (Baltimore: Johns Hopkins University Press, 1967), 15.

17 Vivian Nutton, *Ancient Medicine* (New York: Routledge, 2004), esp. 53–72.

18 Lawrence I. Conrad, Michael Neve, Vivian Nutton, Roy Porter, and Andrew Wear, *The Western Medical Tradition: 800 BC to AD 1800* (New York: Cambridge University Press, 1995), 77.

19 Gary Ferngren, *Medicine & Health Care in Early Christianity* (Baltimore: Johns Hopkins University Press, 2009), esp. 86–112; Cf. Gary Ferngren, *Medicine & Religion: A Historical Introduction* (Baltimore: Johns Hopkins University Press, 2014), 202–5.

20 Ferngren, *Medicine & Religion*, 89–90.

21 See, e.g., W.F. Bynum, Anne Hardy, Stephen Jacyna, Christopher Lawrence, E.M. Tansey, *The Western Medical Tradition: 1800–2000* (New York: Cambridge University Press, 2006); Michel Foucault, *The Birth of the Clinic* (New York: Vintage, 1994).

22   An excellent account is given in Paul Starr, *The Social Transformation of American Medicine* (New York: Basic Books, 1984). Victoria Sweet memorably captures these transitional struggles in her memoir about Laguna Honda Hospital, which was – and still essentially is – an almshouse. See her *God's Hotel* (New York: Riverhead Books, 2012).

23   "Five percent of dialysis patients take their own lives, and another 7 percent commit 'passive suicide' by dropping out of treatment programs or refusing to stick to their diet." Ronald Munson, *Raising the Dead: Organ Transplants, Ethics, and Society* (New York: Oxford University Press, 2002), 114.

24   Jeffrey Prottas, *The Most Useful Gift: Altruism and the Public Policy of Organ Transplants* (San Francisco: Jossey-Bass Publishers, 1994), 52.

25   The OPO receives the information either through someone on staff at the hospital notifying them of the potential organs or by having an OPO representative on staff at the hospital.

26   The hospital plays a vital role in the process, as "OPOs may make [these] referral agreements with hospitals. The more hospitals an OPO has referral agreements with, the greater its scope and the more donors it is likely to procure." Kieran Healy, "Altruism as an Organizational Problem: The Case of Organ Procurement," *American Sociological Review*, 69, no. 3 (2004): 394.

27   Prottas, *Most*, 81.

28   In Prottas's words,
       Families are the decision-making unit in organ donation. The law vests that right in the donors themselves, to be exercised by the donor card, but in practice it is exercised by mothers, fathers, children and siblings. Personal willingness to donate one's organs tells us something about an individual's kindness but very little about the actual supply of organs. The real criterion is the willingness to donate the organs of a loved one. The donation decision is therefore not an individual one but a familial one.
       Prottas, *Most*, 50.

29   Arthur Caplan and Paul Welvang. "Are Required Request Laws Working? Altruism and the Procurement of Organs and Tissues," *Clinical Transplantation* 3, no. 3 (1989): 170–6.

30   Susan Morgan and Jenny Miller, "Beyond the Organ Donor Card: The Effect of Knowledge, Attitudes and Values on Willingness to Communicate about Organ Donation to Family Members," *Health Communication* 14, no. 1 (2001): 121–34.

31   Morgan and Miller, "Beyond," 132.

32   Richard Titmuss, *The Gift Relationship* (New York: Vintage, 1971).

33   Edmund Pellegrino, "Families' Self-Interest and the Cadaver's Organs: What Price Consent?" in *The Ethics of Organ Transplants: The Current Debate*, ed. Arthur Caplan and Daniel Coelho (New York: Prometheus Books, 1998), 206.

34   Titmuss, *Gift*, 225.

35   Prottas, *Most*, 1.

36   Prior to this, the organ transplantation system in the United States was dependent on too many locally flavoured judgments by surgeons or other medical professionals. By 1986, Prottas argues, the full institutionalization and establishment of the organ transplant system, from procurement to allocation, was complete. Prottas, *Most*, 148.

37   Bruno S. Frey and Felix Oberholzer-Gee, "The Cost of Price Incentives: An Empirical Analysis of Motivation Crowding Out," *The American Economic Review* 87, no. 4 (1997): 746–55.

38   The voting in favour/against cannot be attributed solely to ignorance about harmful effects of radiation, as nearly 80 per cent claimed that they believed local residents would suffer long-term effects. Frey, "The Cost," 749.

39 Conversely, they suggest that when intrinsic motivation is low or non-existent, monetary incentives can work. This study is now more than twenty years old, and I wonder
if this result still holds empirically in the West, let alone North America.

40 Uri Gneezy and Aldo Rustichini, "A Fine Is a Price," *Journal of Legal Studies* 29, no. 1
(2000): 1–17. The article has nearly 2,500 citations and is often included in discussions of "freakonomics."

41 The connection to classical civic republicanism is meant more as a counterpoint to
the increasing neoliberalism (as will be discussed in chapters 3 and 4) and not as a
defence of its fundamental ideals (in the Aristotelian/Greek, Roman, or French variations). That is, a surface gloss, like this one presented by John Murphy (drawing on
and quoting Gordon Wood's *The Radicalism of the American Revolution*), will suffice:

> ... [civic] republicans argue that people are, by nature, political beings who
> achieve "great moral fulfillment by participating in a self-governing republic."
> Liberty can only be realized through the active participation in government of
> "virtuous citizens," [who are those] "willing to sacrifice their private interests
> for the sake of community." ... Private interests can only be protected in an
> atmosphere which assures the hegemony of public interest. ... Cicero and Cato
> were the outstanding examples.

John Murphy, "Civic Republicanism in the Modern Age: Adlai Stevenson in the
1952 Presidential Campaign," *Quarterly Journal of Speech* 80, no. 3 (1994): 314. See
also Gordon S. Wood, *The Radicalism of the American Revolution* (New York: Knopf,
1991).

42 Celeste Condit, "Crafting Virtue: The Rhetorical Construction of Public Morality,"
Quarterly Journal of Speech 73, no. 1 (1987): 79–87.

43 Jeffrey Prottas, "Encouraging Altruism: Public Attitudes and the Marketing of Organ
Donation," *Milbank Memorial Fund Quarterly/Health & Society* 61, no. 2 (1983): 278.

44 Healy, "Altruism," 390.

45 Healy, 400.

46 Andrew Michael Flescher, *The Organ Shortage Crisis in America* (Washington, DC:
Georgetown University Press, 2018), esp. 81–110.

47 Roberta Simmons, "Presidential Address on Altruism and Sociology," *The Sociological
Quarterly* 32, no. 1 (1991): 11.

48 Simmons, "Presidential," 13.

49 Michael Flescher and Daniel L. Worthen, *The Altruistic Species* (Philadelphia, PA:
Templeton Foundation Press, 2007), 250.

50 Flescher and Worthen, *Altruistic*, 250.

51 Anders K. Ericcson, Neil Charness, Paul Feltovich, and Robert R. Hoffman, eds.,
Cambridge Handbook of Expertise and Expert Performance (Cambridge: Cambridge
University Press, 2006).

52 E.g., in Plato's *Apology* (20a–b).

53 It is easy enough to suggest that the analogy is flawed because while all of us, in some
sense, desire to be healthy, one might not want to become a professional athlete (let
alone have the talent or physical endowments for such pursuit). And so, sure, some
of us might be morally excellent heroes (saints, shamans, etc.), but most of us are
just playing weekend hoops. I am not taking on this discussion here, and I do not
even mean to invoke conversations of moral obligation, duty, and the supererogatory and such. Rather, the salient point here is that no matter what your givens are
(biological, capacity, etc.), the desire to excel (improve, grow, etc.) must be present.
That is, while the starting line is different for everyone – and I'm acknowledging that
that may influence how quickly people finish *certain* races – as soon as we adopt the
possibility of *better* (or improvement, development, learning, etc.) then we get, pretty

quickly, to the question of absolute and relative standards (a significant subject of Section III). For discussions of saints and the supererogatory, see, e.g., J.O. Urmson, "Saints and Heroes," in *Essays in Moral Philosophy*, ed. A.L. Melden (Seattle: University of Washington Press, 1958), 198–216; Andrew Michael Flescher, *Heroes, Saints, and Ordinary Morality* (Washington, DC: Georgetown University Press, 2003).

54   See Sidney E. Cleveland, "Personality Characteristics, Body Image, and Social Attitudes of Organ Transplant Donors versus Non-Donors," *Psychosomatic Medicine* 37, no. 4 (1975): 313–19; R.L. Horton and P.J. Horton, "A Model of Willingness to Become a Potential Organ Donor," *Social Science and Medicine* 33, no. 9 (1991): 1037–51; Jenifer E. Kopfman and Sandi W. Smith, "Understanding the Audiences of a Health Communication Campaign: A Discriminant Analysis of Potential Organ Donors Based on Intent to Donate," *Journal of Applied Communication Research* 24, no. 1 (1996): 33–49; Margaret Stevens, "Factors Influencing Decisions about Donations of the Brain for Research Purposes," *Age and Aging* 27, no. 5 (1998): 623–9.

55   It is worth noting that the three people who remained undecided were deemed to also have "high moral standards of altruism." But they harboured strong beliefs about life lingering on past bodily death yet still involving the body. Margareta Sanner, "Attitudes toward Organ Donation and Transplantation: A Model for Understanding Reactions to Medical Procedures after Death," *Social Science and Medicine* 38, no. 8 (1994): 1150.

56   On the "confluence" of altruism and self-regard in donors, see, e.g., Flescher *Organ Shortage*, esp. 111–37. For a nice overview of the concerns and tensions from an anthropological perspective, see Charlotte Ikels, "The Anthropology of Organ Transplantation," *Annual Review of Anthropology* 42 (2013): 89–102.

57   Peter Singer, "Altruism and Commerce: A Defense of Titmuss against Arrow," *Philosophy & Public Affairs* 2, no. 3 (1973): 319.

58   Cf. Salvador Giner and Sebastian Sarasa, "Civic Altruism and Social Policy," *International Sociology* 11, no. 2 (1996): 139–59.

59   Prottas, *Most*, 172.

3. The Case for an Altruistic Supply System

1   Alasdair MacIntyre, *After Virtue*, 2nd ed. (Notre Dame, IN: University of Notre Dame Press, 1984), 216.

2   Walter Fisher, "Narration as a Human Communication Paradigm: The Case of Public Moral Argument," *Communication Monographs* 51, no. 1 (1984): 1–22, esp. 4–9.

3   Wayne Booth, *Modern Dogma and the Rhetoric of Assent* (Chicago: University Press of Chicago Press, 1974), xiii.

4   Cicero, *Cicero III*, trans. H. Rackham (Cambridge, MA: Harvard University Press/ Loeb, 1942), 291.

5   Aristotle, "Rhetoric," trans. W. Rhys Roberts. In *The Complete Works of Aristotle*, ed. Jonathan Barnes (Princeton: Princeton/Bollinger Series, 1995), 2177. For good work connecting *movere*, epideictic and deliberative rhetoric, see Brian Vickers, *In Defense of Rhetoric* (Oxford: Oxford University Press, 1989), 1–82, esp. 54–63.

6   Cf. Susan Morgan, "The Intersection of Conversation, Cognition, and Campaigns: The Social Representation of Organ Donation," *Communication Theory* 19, no. 1 (2009): 29–48.

7   "Life Stories: New Heart Turns Sick Child into Active Girl," OrganDonor.gov, accessed 8 December 2011, http://www.organdonor.gov/lifestories/lifebaladez.html.

8   "Your Decision to Donate," Donate Life California.org, accessed 8 December 2011, https://www.donatelifecalifornia.org/.

9   *Assessing Initiatives to Increase Organ Donations: Hearing before the House Committee on Energy and Commerce, Subcommittee on Oversight and Investigation*, 108th Cong. 1 (2003), 13, 14.

10   *Assessing*, 13.

11   *Assessing*, 13.

12   *Utilizing Public Policy and Technology to Strengthen Organ Donor Programs: Hearing Before the House Committee on Oversight and Government Reform, Subcommittee on Information Policy, Census, and National Archives*, 110th Cong. 6–12 (2007).

13   *Utilizing*, 7.

14   *Utilizing*, 8.

15   For example, Mourning discussed his kidney disease often in public settings (e.g., Mehmet Oz's radio show; NPR's Weekend Edition Sunday) and told his story in his 2008 memoir, *Resilience*. See, for example, "NBA's Alonzo Mourning Touts 'Resilience' in Memoir," NPR.org, 5 October 2008: https://www.npr.org/templates/story/story.php?storyId=95387250.

16   Morgan, who underwent transplantation in December 2010, talked about his new kidney in 2011 with late-night talk-show host Conan O'Brien and daytime talk-show host Gayle King, for example. See "Tracy Morgan Interview 04/05/11," *TeamCoco*, accessed 1 April 2020: https://teamcoco.com/content/tracy-morgans-new-kidney-making-him-crazy.

17   Marcia Chambers, "Tough Questions about Transplants Raised by New Heart for 'Baby Jesse,'" *The New York Times*, 15 June 1986, http://www.nytimes.com/1986/06/15/us/tough-questions-about-transplants-raised-by-new-heart-for-baby-jesse.html.

18   NOTA 1983, 7.

19   Ian Parker, "The Gift," *The New Yorker*, 2 August 2004, 54–63.

20   Parker, 54.

21   It is necessary to note that, perhaps ironically, Kravinsky is in *favour* of a market for human organs. But overall his story, including its underlying nature and his actions, points in the other direction. One possibility arises in which Kravinsky sees a potential role for himself as broker between someone willing to buy and someone willing to sell an organ but while he was at first energized by this idea and the notoriety, the notion eventually gave way to concern for legal consequences. Parker, 61–2.

22   Parker, 60.

23   Parker gives two interesting frames to this line of thought. The first is Charles Dickens's *Bleak House*. There, the character of Mrs. Jelly is so supposedly selfless and philanthropic and so concerned about children across the globe that she fails to adequately tend to and raise her own children, and has a filthy house to boot. The second is a quote given by philosopher Judith Jarvis Thomson from an original interview:

> His children are presumably no more valuable to the universe than anybody else's children are, but the universe doesn't really care about *any* children – yours, or mine, or anybody else's. A father who says, "I'm no more concerned about my children's lives than about anybody else's life" is just flatly a defective parent; he's deficient in views that parents ought to have, whether it maximizes utility or not.

Parker, 61.

Compare a reading of Kravinsky by Flescher and Worthen. While they note the potential "dark side of altruism" in case like Kravinsky's (in which his heroic acts also bear the cost of trust and participation in marriage and family life), the centrality of moral duty in his motivations are clear, both from his public language and from personal interviews: if it is the case that *this* is a good thing to do, and if all human lives are equally valuable, morality seems to require as much of me (and every moral agent), regardless of, inter alia, kin and commitments. See Michael Flescher and Daniel L. Worthen, *The Altruistic Species* (Philadelphia, PA: Templeton Foundation Press, 2007), 31–3; 40–3.

24 Parker, 62.

25 Larissa MacFarquhar, "The Kindest Cut," *The New Yorker*, 27 July 2009, 38–51.

26 MacFarquhar, 40. Facebook has also been used to solicit and find donors. See Benjamin Duerr, "Should Patients Be Able to Find Organ Donors on Facebook?" *The Atlantic*, 15 April 2015, https://www.theatlantic.com/health/archive/2015/04 /should-patients-be-able-to-find-organ-donors-on-facebook/390144/.

27 MacFarquhar, 44.

28 Although this story has complications – the man was relatively unresponsive and didn't seem very thankful, causing much pain for Stephens.

29 Jodi Picoult, *My Sister's Keeper* (New York, Atria, 2003); *My Sister's Keeper*, directed by Nick Cassavetes (2009; Burbank, CA: Warner Home Video, 2009) DVD.

30 "My Sister's Keeper (2009)," IMDB.Pro, accessed 10 December 2011, http://pro .imdb.com/title/tt1078588/boxoffice.

31 A.O. Scott, "An I.R.S. Do-Gooder and Other Strangeness," New York Times.com, 19 December 2008, http://movies.nytimes.com/2008/12/19/movies/19seve.html. The worldwide gross figure is taken from "Seven Pounds (2008)," IMDB.Pro, accessed September 2018, http://pro.imdb.com/title/tt0814314/boxoffice.

32 *30 Rock*, "Kidney Now!" television show (National Broadcasting Company, 14 May 2009).

33 *Curb Your Enthusiasm*, "Lewis Needs a Kidney," television show (Home Box Office, 30 October 2005).

34 George Gerbner, Larry Gross, Michael Morgan, Nancy Signorielli, James Shanahan, "Growing Up with Television: Cultivation Processes," in *Media Effects*, 2nd ed., ed. Jennings Bryant and Dolf Zillmann (Mahwah, NJ: Lawrence Erlbaum, 2002), 49. See also Nancy Signorielli and Michael Morgan, *Cultivation Analysis: New Directions in Media Effects Research* (Newberry Park, CA: Sage, 1990).

35 *Assessing*, 11.

36 *Assessing*, 10.

37 *Assessing*, 10.

38 According to numbers published by Facebook itself. Facebook, accessed September 2018, https://newsroom.fb.com/company-info/.

39 Scott Hensley, "What's on Facebook's Mind? Organ Donation," NPR.org, 1 May 2012, http://www.npr.org/blogs/health/2012/05/01/151768743/whats-on-facebooks -mind-organ-donation.

40 David Schultz, "The 'Facebook Effect' on Organ Donation," NPR.org, 20 September 2012, http://www.npr.org/blogs/health/2012/09/18/161358304/the -facebook-effect-on-organ-donation.

41 "Longest Kidney Chain Ever Wraps at UW Hospital and Clinics," UW Health News and Events, 14 April 2015, https://www.uwhealth.org/news/longest-kidney-chain -ever-completed-wraps-up-at-uw-hospital-and-clinics/45549.

42 Dean Reynolds, "Stranger's Kidney Donation Sets Off a Chain Reaction of Good Deeds," *CBS News*, 28 February 2018, https://www.cbsnews.com/news/strangers -kidney-donation-sets-off-chain-reaction-of-good-deeds/.

43 "UCLA Kidney Chain," https://www.uclahealth.org/transplants/kidney-exchange /kidneychain.

44 Amy Hubbard, "Now Live-Tweeting: Play-by-Play of a Kidney Transplant," *Los Angeles Times*, 13 June 2012: https://www.latimes.com/nation/la-xpm-2012-jun-13-la-na-nn -live-tweeting-kidney-transplant-20120613-story.html.

45 For a discussion of social media and non-profit work in general, with explicit reference to Facebook and organ donation, see Alan Greenblatt, "Have You Friended Your Favorite Cause Lately?" NPR.org, 4 May 2012, http://www.npr.org/2012/05/04 /152018256/have-you-friended-your-favorite-cause.

46 Schultz, "Facebook Effect."

47 Karen Chen, "Inspired by Hélène Campbell, Ottawa Sees Increase in Organ Donor Registrations," *The Ottawa Citizen*, 26 July 2012, http://www.ottawacitizen.com/health /Inspired+Hélène+Campbell+Ottawa+sees+increase+organ+donor+registrations /6990127/story.html.

48 This has long been used as the slogan for the US official and NGO operations. One of the first campaigns was called the "Gift of Life Donor Program," and an American Liver Foundation brochure, with questions and answers, is entitled, "Transplants: A Gift of Life." And more contemporarily, for example, on OrganDonor.gov, the banner headline reads, "Donate the Gift of Life." See NOTA 1983, 336.

49 The usage of *master trope* is different here than Kenneth Burke's usage of the phrase. Instead, the suggestion is that the "gift of life" is the master trope of altruistic, volunteerist organ donation and is synecdochic for the entire rhetorical position. No engagement is meant in any substantive discussion of what tropes are or how they work. For an overview of those latter things, see Richard A. Lanham, *A Handlist of Rhetorical Terms*, 2nd ed. (Berkeley, CA: University of California Press, 1991), 154–7; John Bacon, "Tropes," *Stanford Encyclopedia of Philosophy*, accessed 1 December 2011, http://171.67.193.20/entries/tropes/. Burke's discussion of what he calls the four master tropes (metaphor, metonymy, synecdoche, irony) is found in *A Grammar of Motives* (Los Angeles: University of California Press, 1969), 503–17.

50 *Putting Patients First: Increasing Organ Supply for Transplantation: Hearing Before the House Committee on Commerce, Subcommittee on Health and Environment*, 106th Cong. 29 (1999).

51 *Assessing*, 35, 75.

52 The DVD is available free of charge from the Health Resources and Services Administration of the United States.

53 *Assessing*, 11, 14.

54 "Life Stories: Having the Heart to Survive Years of Waiting," OrganDonor.gov, accessed 8 December 2011, http://organdonor.gov/lifestories/lifewong.html.

55 This is perhaps because it wasn't ultimately their decision, due to family consent often still being required.

56 "Life Stories: The Real Heroes Are the Donor Families," OrganDonor.gov, accessed 8 December 2011, http://organdonor.gov/lifestories/lifeabrown.html.

57 *Putting*, 20.

58 *Putting*, 20.

59 *Putting*, 38.

60 *Assessing*, 25.

61 *Putting*, 54.

62 *Putting*, 19–21; *Assessing*, 44–5.

63 *Assessing*, 24.

64 Melissa Culross, "Organ Donation Becomes Part of California's Curriculum," *CBS News*, 28 September 2012, http://sanfrancisco.cbslocal.com/2012/09/28/organ-donation-becomes-part-of-californias-curriculum/.

65 *Assessing*, 46.

66 "National Donation Events," *U.S. Department of Health and Human Services*, accessed 6 December 2011, http://www.organdonor.gov/materialsresources/materialsntlevents.html.

67 *Assessing*, 34.

68 Transplant Games of America took over in 2012 as the National Kidney Foundation was forced to suspend its event, the US Transplant Games. See *Transplant Games of America*, accessed 11 January 2013, http://www.transplantgamesofamerica.org; *The World Transplant Games*, accessed 11 January 2013. http://www.wtgf.org.

69 *Assessing*, 24, 25.

70 *Assessing*, 25.

71 That military platoons are the exemplar here is mostly a matter of common/social knowledge. There is an entire field of trauma studies, evidenced most clearly in the International Society for Traumatic Stress Studies, established in 1985. The attempt to move the smaller group process of trauma and attachment to a society-level scale is seen in the notions of "cultural trauma" (e.g., the Holocaust, September 11) as applied in work such as Jeffrey Alexander, *Cultural Trauma and Collective Identity* (Los Angeles: University of California Press, 2004).

72 *Assessing*, 14.

73 *Assessing*, 11.

74 "Life Stories: The Real Heroes."

75 T.M. Scanlon, *What We Owe Each Other* (Cambridge, MA: Harvard University Press, 1998), 79.

76 A level of sophistication is necessary for later analyses in this study, but at this point it serves a simple task of explaining how we feel the moral point of view in community. Scanlon, *What*, 106.

77 This point, drawing in particular on Scanlon's earlier work, is discussed in Norman Daniels, "Health Care Needs and Distributive Justice," in *Bioethics*, ed. John Harris (Oxford: Oxford University Press, 2001), esp. 322–5.

78 Parker, 58. Again, despite his actions and moral philosophic talk on selflessness and others, which falls into a celebration of community, Kravinsky does support organ markets.

79 MacFarquhar, 46.

80 *Putting*, 55.

81 *Putting*, 55.

82 *Putting*, 66.

83 *Assessing*, 66.

84 NOTA 1983, 26. Humphrey's original quote runs,
    The moral test of a government is how it treats those who are at the dawn of life, the children; those who are in the twilight of life, the aged; and those who are in the shadow of life, the sick, the needy, and the handicapped.
    See Hubert H. Humphrey, "Remarks at the dedication of the Hubert H. Humphrey Building, November 1, 1977," *Congressional Record*, November 4, 1977, vol. 123, p. 37287; taken from *Bartleby's Respectfully Quoted: A Dictionary of Quotations*: https://www.bartleby.com/73/724.html.

85 Organdonor.gov, accessed 12 December 2011, www.organdonor.gov.

86 The four Classical Virtues (wisdom, temperance, justice, fortitude) or the three Theological Virtues (faith, hope, love), or the details of virtue ethics programs from

Aristotle to Philippa Foot are not quite what I mean here, instead meaning the most common and basic sense of the term, that someone or some action that is morally good is considered virtuous. There is of course some relevance of those systems and key terms.

87 Luc Boltanski and Laurent Thévenot, *On Justification: Economies of Worth*, trans. Catherine Porter (Princeton, NJ: Princeton University Press, 2006), 83–90, 159–64, 237–41.

88 Cf. Aristotle, Book V. iii.10–25; in *Nicomachean*, 1785.

89 Robert Veatch makes the sort of general distinction I'm making here in the opening of his essay, saying, "Liberals and others oriented toward justice in health care traditionally have had a problem with proposals to increase the supply of organs for transplant by offering financial payment or other incentives ... " See "Why Liberals Should Accept Financial Incentives for Organ Procurement," *Kennedy Institute of Ethics Journal* 13 (2003): 19.

90 That civic solidarity means citizens have certain obligations to each other is something that connects civic republicanism to contractualism/social contractarianism. For more on civic and social solidarity, see Michael Sandel, *Justice: What's the Right Thing to Do?* (New York: Farrar, Straus, & Giroux, 2009), 225–43, in particular his notion of the obligations of solidarity. Related to this notion is Sandel's conception of a self as an *encumbered self*, born into a situation and society that has demands upon you, which will be discussed in chapter 5.

91 This will have relation to, but distinguishable from, the civic restraint principle (CRP) discussed in chapter 5.

4. The Case for a Market-Based Supply System

1 Kopfman and Smith, 36.

2 Susan Morgan and Jenny Miller, "Communicating about Gifts of Life: The Effect of Knowledge, Attitudes, and Altruism on Behavior and Behavioral Intentions Regarding Organ Donation," *Journal of Applied Communication Research* 30, no. 2 (2002): 164.

3 Julia D. Mahoney, "Altruism, Markets, and Organ Procurement," *Law and Contemporary Problems* 72, no. 3 (2009): 19.

4 Ronald Bailey, "The Case for Selling Human Organs," *Reason Magazine*, 18 April 2001, http://reason.com/archives/2001/04/18/the-case-for-selling-human-org.

5 Veronique Campion-Vincent, "Organ Theft Narratives as Medical and Social Critique," *Journal of Folklore Research* 39, no. 1 (2002): 35.

6 Campion-Vincent, "Organ Theft," 34.

7 *Dirty Pretty Things*, directed by Stephen Frears (2002; New York: Miramax, DVD, 2002).

8 *Repo! The Genetic Opera*, directed by Darren Lynn Bousmann (2009; Los Angeles: Lionsgate, DVD, 2009); *Repo Men*, directed by Miguel Sapochnik (2010; Universal City, CA: Universal Studios, DVD, 2011).

9 *Assessing Initiatives to Increase Organ Donations: Hearing before the House Committee on Energy and Commerce, Subcommittee on Oversight and Investigation*, 108th Cong. 23 (2003).

10 Jeneen Interlandi, "Not Just Urban Legend," *Newsweek*, 9 January 2009, https://www.ncbi.nlm.nih.gov/pubmed/19496356.

11 *Organs for Sale: China's Growing Trade and Ultimate Violation of Prisoner's Rights: Hearing of the Committee on International Relations, Subcommittee on International Operations and Human Rights*, 107th Cong. 2 (2001).

12 *Organs*, 2.
13 James Griffiths, "Report: China Still Harvesting Organs from Prisoners at a Massive Scale," CNN.com, 25 June 2016, https://edition.cnn.com/2016/06/23/asia/china-organ-harvesting/index.html.
14 This characterization is misleading, however, as the kidney was not given for an iPad directly. Rather, the iPad is what the seller bought using the money given to him for his kidney.
15 "China 'Kidney for iPad' Trial Begins in Hunan," BBC.com, 9 August 2012, http://www.bbc.co.uk/news/world-asia-china-19197542.
16 Charlotte Ikels, "Kidney Failure and Transplantation in China," *Social Science & Medicine* 44, no. 9 (1997): 1271–83.
17 Academic accounts include Susanne Lundin, "Organ Economy: Organ Trafficking in Moldova and Israel," *Public Understandings of Science* 21, no. 2 (2012): 226–41; Sallie Yea, "Trafficking in Part(s): The Commercial Kidney Market in a Manila Slum, Philippines," *Global Social Policy* 10, no. 3 (2010): 358–76.
18 William Saletan, "Shopped Liver: The Worldwide Market in Human Organs," *Slate*, 14 April 2007, http://www.slate.com/articles/health_and_science/human_nature/2007/04/shopped_liver.html.
19 Scott Carney, *The Red Market: On the Trail of the World's Organ Brokers, Bone Thieves, Blood Farmers, and Child Traffickers* (New York: William Morrow, 2011).
20 Yea, "Trafficking," 359.
21 Kenneth Burke, *Attitudes toward History* (Los Angeles: University of California Press, 1937), esp. 34–91.
22 Samantha Henry and David Porter, "Levy Izak Rosenbaum Pleads Guilty to Selling Black Market Kidneys," *Huffington Post*, 27 October 2011, reposted on http://donatelife-organdonation.blogspot.com/2011/10/levy-izhak-rosenbaum-pleads-guilty-to.html.
23 Jonathan Allen, "'Israeli Man Gets 2 ½ Years in U.S. Kidneys-for-Cash Case," Reuters.com, 13 July 2012: https://www.reuters.com/article/us-usa-kidneys-idUSBRE86B00020120712.
24 Allen, "Israeli Man."
25 James Stacey Taylor and Marcy C. Simmerling, "Donor Compensation without Exploitation," in *When Altruism Isn't Enough*, ed. Sally Satel (Washington, DC: The American Enterprise Institute Press 2008), 50.
26 For example, Sally Satel argues primarily for incentives at times and for an outright market at other. For the former, see Satel, *When*; the latter, "Altruism + Incentive = More Organ Donation," *The Times* [online], 13 June 2010, https://www.aei.org/publication/altruism-incentive-more-organ-donations/.
27 Satel, *When*, 6.
28 Richard DeVos, in *Assessing*, 69.
29 Satel, *When; Assessing*, 74.
30 Michele Goodwin, "Altruism's Limits: Law, Capacity, and Organ Commodification," *Rutgers Law Review* 56, no. 2 (2004): 338, 316.
31 Goodwin, "Altruism's," 333–9.
32 Goodwin, "Altruism's," 340.
33 Richard A. Epstein, *Principles for a Free Society: Reconciling Individual Liberty with the Common Good* (Cambridge, MA: Basic Books, 1998), 153; Goodwin calls it this as well: Goodwin, "Altruism's," 312.
34 Goodwin, "Altruism's," 361.
35 Goodwin, "Altruism's," 404.

36   Arthur Matas, "A Gift of Life Deserves Compensation: How to Increase Living Kidney Donation with Realistic Incentives," *Cato Policy Analysis*, 7 November 2007, https://www.cato.org/publications/policy-analysis/gift-life-deserves-compensation-how-increase-living-kidney-donation-realistic-incentives.

37   Speaking, in particular, of Pennsylvania's contribution to donors' burials. *Putting Patients First: Increasing Organ Supply for Transplantation: Hearing before the House Committee on Commerce, Subcommittee on Health and Environment*, 106th Cong. 74 (1999).

38   Benjamin Hippen and J.S. Taylor, "In Defense of Transplantation: A Reply to Nancy Scheper-Hughes," *American Journal of Transplantation* 7, no. 7 (2007): 1697.

39   *Assessing*, 87.

40   Milton Friedman, "The Social Responsibility of Business Is to Increase Its Profits," *The New York Times*, 13 September 1970.

41   Benjamin Hippen, "In Defense of a Regulated Market in Kidneys from Living Vendors," Journal of Medicine and Philosophy 30, no. 6 (2005): 608.

42   Mark J. Cherry, *Kidney for Sale by Owner: Human Organs, Transplantation, and the Market* (Washington, DC: Georgetown University Press, 2005), 154.

43   Goodwin, "Altruism's Limits," 341.

44   Dominick Tao, "Worldwide Market Fuels Illegal Traffic in Organs," *The New York Times*, 30 July 2009, http://www.nytimes.com/2009/07/30/nyregion/30organs.html.

45   Denis Campbell and Nicola Davison, "Illegal Kidney Trade Booms as New Organ Is 'Sold Every Hour,'" *Guardian*, 27 May 2012, http://www.guardian.co.uk/world/2012/may/27/kidney-trade-illegal-operations-who.

46   For discussion of the Iranian market and its intersection with Islam, see Diane Tober, "Kidneys and Controversies in the Islamic Republic of Iran: The Case of Organ Sales," *Body & Society* 13, no. 3 (2007): 151–70.

47   Nancy Scheper-Hughes, "Mr Tati's Holiday and João's Safari: Seeing the World through Transplant Tourism," *Body & Society* 17, nos. 2–3 (2011): 55–92.

48   Here's a description of a southern California organ broker:

> What he is doing, he says, is entirely legal; he does not buy or sell organs but merely brings clients to hospitals that are equipped to provide them. He claims that his customers come in at the rate of one a week from all over the world, and he finds them new "engines" in a network of 15 or so transplant hospitals he has cultivated in China, India, the Philippines, South Africa, Singapore, Pakistan and South America.

See Richard C. Morais, "Desperate Arrangements," Forbes.com, 29 January 2007, http://www.forbes.com/forbes/2007/0129/072. See also Wendy Pollack, "Organ Brokers Flourish Online," Wall Street Journal.com, 11 January 2007, http://blogs.wsj.com/informedreader/2007/01/11/organ-brokers-flourish-online/.

49   The former figure is taken from Tao; the latter, from Pollack.

50   The first figures are taken from Pollack; the second two are from Interlandi.

51   Interlandi, "Not Just."

52   Henry and Porter, "Levy Izak Rosenbaum."

53   Taylor and Simmerling, "Donor Compensation," 51.

54   L.D. de Castro, "Commodification and Exploitation: Arguments in Favour of Compensated Organ Donation," *Journal of Medical Ethics* 29, no. 3 (2003): 145.

55   Russell Scott, *The Body as Property* (New York: Viking, 1981); Lori B. Andrews, "My Body, My Property," *The Hastings Center Report* 16, no. 5 (1986): 28–38; Roy Hardiman, "Toward the Right of Commerciality: Recognizing Property Rights in the Value of Human Tissue," *UCLA Law Review*, no. 1 (1986): 207–64; Danielle M. Wagner, "Property Rights in the Human Body: The Commercialization of

Organ Transplantation and Biotechnology," *Duquesne Law Review* 33, no. 4 (1995): 931–58; Linda C. McClain, "Inviolability and Privacy: The Castle, The Sanctuary, The Body," *Yale Journal of Law and Humanities* 7, no. 1 (1995): 195–242; Goodwin, "Altruism's."

56 A representative here is Jeffrey Goldberg, "Involuntary Servitude: A Property-Based Notion of Abortion-Choice," *UCLA Law Review* 38 no. 6 (1991): 1597–658, discussing the Supreme Court's view of women's bodies in *Roe v. Wade*, 410 U.S. 113 (1973) and *Webster v. Reproductive Health Services*, 492 U.S.490 (1989).

57 Dan Bilefsky, "Black Market for Body Parts Spreads among the Poor in Europe," *The New York Times*, 29 June 2012, https://www.nytimes.com/2012/06/29/world/europe/black-market-for-body-parts-spreads-in-europe.html.

58 John Adams, "John Adams, Defense of the Constitutions of Government of the United States," University of Chicago website, accessed 14 December 2011, http://press-pubs.uchicago.edu/founders/documents/v1ch16s15.html.

59 Goodwin, "Altruism's" 389, 392; see also Debra Satz, *Why Some Things Should Not Be for Sale: The Moral Limits of Markets* (New York: Oxford University Press, 2010), 115–89.

60 Gerald Dworkin, "Markets and Morals: The Case for Organ Sales," in *Morality, Harm, and the Law*, ed. Gerald Dworkin (Boulder, CO: Westview Press, 1994), 156.

61 "Bone Marrow Donors Can Be Compensated, Appeals Court Rules," *Los Angeles Times*, 1 December 2011, http://latimesblogs.latimes.com/lanow/2011/12/bone-marrow-donors-can-be-compensated-appeals-court-rules.html.

62 Cf. Hardiman, "Toward the Right," 214–23.

63 Cf. Hardiman, 228.

64 Martin Kenny, *Biotechnology: The University Industrial Complex* (New Haven: Yale University Press, 1988).

65 Here is Hardiman on the issue:

> The old common-law treatment of dead bodies never foresaw the huge commercial potential of the human body. Currently, researchers enjoy a free supply of patient tissue because the public is unaware of the economic value of the material. The public's ignorance allows researchers to disregard costs to the patient and to consider only the benefits to the researcher.

Hardiman, 227.

66 Goodwin, 383.

67 Epstein, *Principles*, 153.

68 Goodwin, 386. She notes that the Food and Drug Administration, after several decades of non-oversight, stepped in to investigate in 2001.

69 Goodwin, 327.

70 Quoted in Goodwin, 387.

71 All documented in Goodwin, 387.

72 Goodwin, 407.

73 Broken trust in the altruistic system plays a vital role in Goodwin's case. That a lack of trust actually deters donors is not a case well made in her article, but the symbolic power of the system being broken and therefore trust needing to be restored is better articulated. Goodwin, esp. 330–41.

74 Mark J. Cherry, "Why Should We Compensate Organ Donors When We Can Continue to Take Organs for Free? A Response to Some of My Critics," *Journal of Medicine and Philosophy* 34, no. 6 (2009): 649–73.

75 Marcel Mauss, *The Gift* (New York: Norton, 2000).

76 Renee Fox and Judith P. Swazey, *Spare Parts: Organ Replacement in American Society* (New York: Oxford University Press, 1992).

77 Fox and Swazey, *Spare*, 39–42; cf. Nancy Scheper-Hughes, "The Tyranny of the Gift: Sacrificial Violence in Living Donor Transplants," *American Journal of Transplantation* 7, no. 3 (2007): 507–11.

78 Satel, "Altruism."

79 Hippen, "In Defense of a Regulated," 597.

80 Cherry, *Kidney*, 107.

81 Cherry, *Kidney*, 107.

82 Surgeon and incentive advocate Arthur Matas puts the issue succinctly:

> The patient would not be paying for the kidneys; the government or insurance companies (who currently pay for dialysis) would be the payors. The kidneys would be allocated in the same way that we allocate kidneys from deceased donors today, so that everyone would have a chance to be transplanted.

Arthur Matas, "Organ Transplant Expert Answers Our Viewer Questions about Kidney Sales," *ABC News*, 22 November 2007, http://abcnews.go.com/print?id =3902508.

83 *Assessing*, 82, emphasis added.

84 *Assessing*, 82.

85 Delmonico et al., "Ethical Incentives – Not Payment – for Organ Donation." *New England Journal of Medicine* 346, no. 25 (2002): 2002–6.

86 Here's the way some of the data broke down:

> If compensation took the form of credits for health care needs, about 60 percent of Americans would support it. Tax credits and tuition reimbursements were viewed favorably by 46 percent and 42 percent, respectively. Cash for organs was seen as OK by 41 percent of respondents.

Scott Hensley, "Poll: Americans Show Support for Compensation of Organ Donation," NPR.org, 16 May 2012, http://www.npr.org/blogs/health/2012 /05/16/152498553/poll-americans-show-support-for-compensation-of-organ-donors.

87 *Assessing*, 67.

88 As of 2009, the paper still needed clarification and simplification. "OPTN/UNOS Ethics Committee Report to the Board of Directors," 2–3 March 2009, Houston, TX.

89 *Putting*, 115.

90 *Putting*, 118.

91 Richard Knox, "Tax Breaks for Organ Donors Aren't Boosting Transplant Supply," NPR.org, 31 August 2012, http://www.npr.org/blogs/health/2012/08/30 /160338259/tax-breaks-for-organ-donors-arent-boosting-transplant-supply.

92 From the story:

> Typically states offer a deduction of up to $10,000 from taxable income. For a typical family that translates to less than $1,000 in reduced taxes. But the financial burden for a living kidney donor can range from $907 to $3,089.

Knox, "Tax Breaks."

93 *Assessing*, 55.

94 *Assessing*, 74.

95 Megan Clay and Walter Block, "A Free Market for Human Organs," *The Journal of Social, Political, and Economic Studies* 27, no. 2 (2002): 232.

96 They say that for altruistic advocates, it seems that "nothing but the economic system of the Soviet Union is 'pure' enough … " Clay and Block, "A Free Market," 232.

97 John Rawls, *Theory of Justice* (Cambridge, MA: Harvard University Press, 1971).

98 G.A. Cohen, *Rescuing Justice and Equality* (Cambridge, MA: Harvard University Press, 2008).

99   *Assessing*, 21.
100 Sheryl Gay Stolberg, "Pennsylvania Set to Break Taboo on Reward for Organ
     Donation," *The New York Times*, 6 May 1999, http://www.nytimes.com/1999/05/06
     /us/pennsylvania-set-to-break-taboo-on-reward-for-organ-donations.html; Cf. *Putting*, 5.
101 *Putting*, 58.
102 *Putting*, 56.
103 *Assessing*, 82.
104 *Assessing*, 82.
105 Allison J. Wellington and Edward Sayre, "An Evaluation of Financial Incentive Policies
     for Organ Donations in the United States," *Contemporary Economic Policy* 29, no. 1
     (2011): 1–13; A.S. Venkataramani, E.G. Martin, A. Vijayan, and J.R. Wellen, "The
     Impact of Tax Policies on Organ Donations in the United States," *American Journal of
     Transplantation* 12, no. 8 (2012): 2133–40; Knox, "Tax Breaks."
106 *Putting*, 83, 84
107 *Putting*, 100–22.
108 Autonomy is not being invoked as a substantive moral concept, and therefore an
     account (i.e., libertarian versus Kantian) need not be given.
109 They, however, identify it more specifically as an element within *industrial* worlds,
     though it clearly has resonance in their *market* world as well. See Luc Boltanski
     and Laurent Thévenot, *On Justification: Economies of Worth*, trans. Catherine Porter
     (Princeton, NJ: Princeton University Press, 2006), 203–12.
110 This is similar to the argument often made about compensating college athletes.

5. The Neoliberal Graft: Medicine, Morality, and Markets in Liberal-Democratic Regimes

1 In the words of T.M. Scanlon,
   The "basic structure" of a society is its legal, political and economic framework,
   the function of which is to define the rights and liberties of citizens and to
   determine a range of social positions to which different powers and economic
   rewards are attached. If a basic structure does this in an acceptable way ... then
   the structure is just.
   T.M. Scanlon, *What We Owe Each Other* (Cambridge, MA: Harvard University Press,
   1998), 244.
2 Michael Sandel, *Justice: What's the Right Thing to Do?* (New York: Farrar, Straus, &
   Giroux, 2009), 261.
3 Joseph Stiglitz, *Globalization and Its Discontents* (New York: Norton, 2003), xv.
4 As another snapshot, neoliberalism is a theory of political economy that asserts the
   centrality and priority of individual rights, privatization, and free markets, and that
   society ought be structured accordingly around these and only such essential mini-
   mums. It is important to note, as Antoon Braeckman does, that the reorganization
   of social and political life around market mechanisms and principles is "not simply a
   revival of 18th century liberalism, but rather a mutation thereof which builds on its
   utopian dimensions." That is, much of neoliberalism, when argued for and practised
   in the positive, is indeed a utopian project. My primary interest in neoliberalism, if
   it isn't clear already, is in understanding its rhetorical and moral grounding – that
   is, in viewing neoliberalism as a moral position – even if it is a moral position sometimes taken by default for certain policymakers and citizens alike; in other words, my
   argument highlights the neoliberal utopian side while adding the practical and even
   ethically demanded in certain (mistaken) variations side. Default is very different

than utopia. See Antoon Braeckman, "Neo-liberalism and the Symbolic Institution of Society: Pitting Foucault Against Lefort on the State and the 'Political,'" *Philosophy and Social Criticism* 41, no. 9 (2015): 953.

5 Sandel, *Justice*, 265.

6 Debra Satz, *Why Some Things Should Not Be for Sale: The Moral Limits of Markets* (New York: Oxford University Press, 2010), 3.

7 Salmaan Keshavjee, *Blind Spot: How Neoliberalism Infiltrated Public Health* (Berkeley, CA: University of California Press, 2014), 138.

8 James F. Childress, *Practical Reasoning in Bioethics* (Bloomington: Indiana University Press, 1997), 284.

9 The beginning of the shift within the medical community is documented in J.D. Jasper, Carol A.E. Nickerson, Peter A. Ubel, and David A. Asc, "Altruism, Incentives, and Organ Donation," *Medical Care* 42, no. 4 (2004): 378–86.

10 Edmund Pellegrino, "Families' Self-Interest and the Cadaver's Organs: What Price Consent?" in *The Ethics of Organ Transplants: The Current Debate*, ed. Arthur Caplan and Daniel Coelho (New York: Prometheus Books, 1998), 206.

11 Richard Titmuss, *The Gift Relationship* (New York: Vintage, 1971), 225.

12 Jeffrey Prottas, *The Most Useful Gift: Altruism and the Public Policy of Organ Transplants* (San Francisco: Jossey-Bass Publishers, 1994), 1.

13 The fuller account of the institutionalization of the transplant system is given in Chapter 2.

14 David Harvey, *A Brief History of Neoliberalism* (New York: Oxford University Press, 2007), 2–3.

15 Ezekiel J. Emanuel, *The Ends of Human Life: Medical Ethics in a Liberal Polity* (Cambridge, MA: Harvard University Press, 1991), 33, emphasis added.

16 Paul Weithman, *Religion and the Obligations of Citizenship* (New York: Cambridge University Press, 2002). Cf. Robert Audi, *Religious Commitment and Secular Reason* (New York: Cambridge University Press, 2000); James W. Boettcher, "Respect, Recognition, and Public Reason," Social Theory and Practice 33, no. 2 (2007): 223–49; and his "The Moral Status of Public Reason," Journal of Political Philosophy 20, no. 2 (2012):156–77.

17 Boltanski and Thévenot's orders of worth, or worlds of worth, is a way of understanding conflicting justifications in response to the same set of claims or actions. These include *inspired* (nonconformity, emotion, passion, creativity), *domestic* (esteem, oral, trust, authority), *civic* (collective, formal, solidarity, equality), *renown* (opinion, semiotic/signs, recognition, celebrity), *market* (price, monetary, exchange, desire/purchasing power), and *industrial* (efficiency, measurable, functional, expertise). Prima facie, there appears to be a conflict between *inspired* and *civic* justifications for the status quo altruism of organ donation against the *market* and *industrial* justifications for the financial/economic arguers. See Luc Boltanski and Laurent Thévenot, "The Sociology of Critical Capacity," *European Journal of Social Theory* 2, no. 3 (1999): 359–77; and their *On Justification: Economies of Worth*, trans. Catherine Porter (Princeton, NJ: Princeton University Press, 2006).

18 Boltanski and Thévenot, *Justification*, 150.

19 Boltanski and Thévenot, *Justification*, 15.

20 Boltanski and Thévenot write that there is a shared *Higher Common Principle* (HCP) at work in argumentative engagement – the principle of coordination – that "characterizes a polity [and] is a convention for establishing equivalence amongst beings."

This is not to say that this principle of argumentation, or the Gricean Cooperative Principle of conversation, are never violated or are always assumed. Dissensus and epidiectic display are also common to conversation, argumentation, and social interaction more generally. But in matters in which there are sincere attempts at public argumentative engagement, there is a shared goal of agreement, and it is *justice*, though abstract and contested conceptually, that, at least temporarily, settles disagreement and secures assent. Boltanski and Thévenot, *Justification*, 140. Furthermore, justice, at some level, pushes towards convergence and agreement. Following Boltanski and Thévenot: "Focusing on associations capable of bringing about agreement and of being incorporated into judgments, we shall argue that the foregoing modalities refer to principles of *justice* (or of *justness*) ... As Henri Levy-Bruhl ... points out, justice has the property of bringing disputes to an end; we shall treat that property as a distinctive feature of justice." *Justification*, 34.

21   In *Antidosis*, 270:

> For since it is not in the nature of man to attain a science by the possession of which we can know positively what we should do or what we should say, in the next resort, I hold that man to be wise who is able by his powers of conjecture to arrive generally at the best course.

And later, at 271–2:

> I consider that kind of art which can implant honest and justice in depraved natures has never existed and does not now exist ... But I do hold that people can become better and worthier if they conceive an ambition to speak well ... for ... when anyone elects to speak or write discourse which are worthy of praise and honour, it is not conceivable that he will support causes which are unjust or petty or devoted to private quarrels.

Isocrates, *Isocrates, Vol. II*, trans. George Norlin (Cambridge, MA: Harvard University Press/Loeb, 1929). Connections between Isocratean philosophical rhetoric and civic life are made explicitly in Takis Poulakos, *Speaking for the Polis: Isocrates on Civic Education* (Columbia: University of South Carolina Press, 1997) and Takis Poulakos and David Depew, *Isocrates and Civic Education* (Austin: University of Texas Press, 2004).

22   The relationship is close, but in *Nicomachean Ethics* Book X (1177a.11–23) he offers a clear summation:

> If happiness is activity in accordance with excellence, it is reasonable that it should be in accordance with the highest excellence; and this will be that of the best thing in us. Whether it be in intellect or something else that is this element which is thought to be our natural ruler and guide and to take thought of things noble and divine, whether it be itself also divine or only the most divine element in us, the activity of this in accordance with proper excellence will be complete happiness. That this activity is contemplative we have already said.
>
> Now this would seem to be in agreement both with what we said before and with the truth. For this activity is the best (since not only is intellect the best thing in us, but the objects of intellect are the best of knowable objects); and, secondly, it is the most continuous, since we can contemplate truth more continuously than we can *do* anything.

Aristotle, *Nicomachean*, 1860.

23   Though of course it was not for *the public* in the more modern conception of *the public interest*, given Empire politics.

24   For more on this distinction, especially in relationship to the rhetorical tradition and its development from Greece through the Enlightenment, see Brian Vickers, *In*

Defense of Rhetoric (Oxford: Oxford University Press, 1989); James J. Murphy, *Rhetoric in the Middle Ages* (Los Angeles: University of California Press, 1974). For a treatment of the terms in modernity and a modernist reading of them in antiquity, see Hannah Arendt, *The Human Condition* (Chicago: University of Chicago Press, 1958).

25 The notion of *viva contemplativa* being continuous and unending in ways that actions are not is one of its virtues in Aristotle's thinking, whereas it is vice to the Roman rhetoricians and statesmen. Consider Cicero in *De Oratore* (III.xiii.86–9):

> The consequence is that the pursuit of facts is unlimited, and their acquisition easy if study is reinforced by practice ... [But] nobody need be afraid of the magnitude of the sciences on the ground that old men are studying them ... In fact my view of the situation is that unless a man is able to learn a subject quickly he will never be able to learn it thoroughly at all.

Cicero, *Cicero IV*, trans. H. Rackham (Cambridge, MA: Harvard University Press/ Loeb, 1942), 71.

26 Cicero, *Cicero III*, trans. H. Rackham (Cambridge, MA: Harvard University Press/ Loeb, 1942), 23.

27 Qtd. in Vickers, *Defense*, 39.

28 Quintilian, *IV: Institutio Oratoria, Books 9–10*, trans. Donald A. Russell (Cambridge, MA: Harvard University Press/Loeb, 2001), 365.

29 Consider this from *Institutio* (10.5.10–11):

> Weakness can easily hide behind the complications of persons, motives, times, places, words, and deeds, when so many ideas present themselves on every side, any one of which can be taken up. The real sign of high quality is the capacity to expand what is by nature brief, amplify the insignificant, vary the monotonous, lend charm to what has been already set out, and speak well and at length on a limited subject.

Quintilian, *Institutio*, 361.

30 The standard marking for this is Peter Ramus's division of rhetoric, which in antiquity and through the middle ages was composed of five canons (invention, disposition, elocution, memory, delivery), placing invention and disposition properly under the domain of *dialectic* and leaving rhetoric to be, then, style, memory, and delivery – simply as ornamental. The key source for that perspective is Walter J. Ong, *Ramus, Method, and the Decay of Dialogue: From the Art of Discourse to the Art of Reason* (Cambridge, MA: Harvard University Press, 1983). It should be noted, however, that the view of rhetoric as being primarily concerned with the *words* and less with relations (which was for logic) or ethics or politics (which was for theology and ecclesiastics) began as early as the thirteenth century: "Writers as different as John of Salisbury and Brunetto Latini seem to think of [rhetoric] as polishing, decorating, especially dilating, what has been already expressed," according to C.S. Baldwin, as quoted in Vickers, *Defense*, 227.

31 Though, to be clear, Kant was not against rhetoric in the sense of it being a fine art *à la* poetry. As he clarifies, in the continuation of the quote in the main text: "Force and elegance of speech (which together constitute rhetoric) belong to fine art; but oratory (ars oratoria), being the art of playing for one's purpose up the weaknesses of others ... merits no attention whatsoever." Immanuel Kant, *Critique of Judgment*, trans. James Creed Meredith, ed. Nicholas Walker (New York: Oxford University Press, 2007), 156. In terms of contemporary understanding of the ars rhetorica, the most fitting story is to be found in the quadrangle of the Bodleian Library at Oxford. The names of the arts, as respective lecture rooms, adorn the doorways: Schola Grammaticae et Historiae, Schola Naturalis Philosophiae, etc. The building has been

reconfigured for modern purposes, of course, but I cannot help but laugh at the (likely unintended) fact that the doorway adorned by Rhetoricae leads to the Bod's gift shop.

32   Thomas Farrell, "Knowledge, Consensus, and Rhetorical Theory," *Quarterly Journal of Speech* 62, no. 1 (1976): 1–14.

33   Thomas G. Goodnight, "Controversy," in *Argument in Controversy: Proceedings of the NCA/AFA Conference on Argumentation*, ed. Donn Parsons, (Annandale, VA: Speech Communication Association, 1991), 5.

34   Even in the wake of the 2016 US presidential election and public conversations about alternative facts and fake news and the like, the core disagreement does not turn, generally, on there being such a thing as empirical facts or not, just which things fit the criteria (or which ones are the facts). An analogy here might be seen in arguing about films. While many people disagree on which film is the best film, something like one person claiming something more traditionally well regarded such as *Citizen Kane* as the best film and another person claiming something such as *The Avengers* does not indicate that the two people have different *standards* for what makes the best film. In fact, I'd argue that most people have the same standards for what makes a great film but just disagree about what fits those standards. (You call *that* good acting? You thought *that* plot was intriguing? You thought *those* characters were textured? etc.)

35   Immanuel Kant, "An Answer to the Question: What is Enlightenment?" in *What Is Enlightenment?* ed. James Schmidt (Berkeley: University of California Press, 1996), 58–64.

36   Kant, "An Answer," 60.

37   The meaning of *reason* in Kant is debatable, as he was, of course, critical of both theoretical and practical reason in his critiques. To him, the goal of a pure practical reason was not paradoxical. As he puts it, "If a critical examination of pure practical reason is to be complete, then there must, in my view, be the possibility at the same time of showing the unity of practical and speculative reason in a common principle; for in the final analysis there can be only one and the same reason, which is differentiated solely in its application" (*Grounding*, §391). See Immanuel Kant, *Ethical Philosophy*, trans. James W. Ellington (Indianapolis: Hackett Publishing Company, 1994).

38   Here's the relevant passage from the preface to *Grounding*: "Material philosophy, however, has to do with determinate objects and with the laws to which these objects are subject; and such philosophy is divided into two parts, because these laws are either laws of nature or laws of freedom" (§387).

39   Jürgen Habermas, *The Structural Transformation of the Public Sphere*, trans. Thomas Berger (Cambridge, MA: MIT Press, 1989), 102.

40   To what degree constructivism means anti-realism – which means, partly, interpreting Kant's project – is a live debate. In fact, a recent volume on Kant aims to take back, so to speak, the Kantian project of practical philosophy from Rawls and Rawlsian-inspired anti-realists. In a substantive review of the work, Paul Guyer gives good reasons to worry about Rawls in particular being too strongly considered anti-realist. See Benjamin J. Bruxvoort Lipscomb and James Krueger (eds.), *Kant's Moral Metaphysics: God, Freedom, and Immortality* (Berlin: De Gruyter, 2010); Paul Guyer, "Review of Kant's Moral Metaphysics," *Notre Dame Philosophical Reviews*, 24 April 2012, http://ndpr.nd.edu/news/30472-kant-s-moral-metaphysics-god-freedom-and-immortality/.

41   Murphy, *Rhetoric*, 360.

42   Though at some level this is still thoroughly Ciceronian, for at the end of *De Partitione Oratoria* (xl. 140) there is invocation for the orator to study logic and

morality as separate subjects as well: "What readiness of style or supply of matter can a speaker possess on the subject of good and bad, right and wrong, utility and inutility, virtue and vice, without knowing these sciences of primary importance?" Cicero, *Cicero IV*, 421.

43 Whether pluralistic societies are actually *epistemically diverse* in a *normative* sense – as opposed to a descriptive sense – is a major part of chapters 6 and 7. Briefly, the matter is seen in something like this example. If there were an enclave of people in the United States who really, truly believed that two plus two did not equal four, and they meant, roughly the same things we mean by those terms in that, say, two plus four equals six, but it was based on the mistaken belief that any time two positive whole integers less than three but more than one are added together, they equal seven, we would be accurate in describing them as an epistemically different culture from the status quo Western citizen. But I think most of us would also be just as comfortable in describing their culture as *wrong* on this mathematical front. Hence, we might say something like, "They have, indeed, an alternative epistemology, but it is mistaken" and, in a normative sense, we would not call their view *rationally justified.*

44 Though, again, there is some contemporary literature, most notably empirical cognitive psychology, that suggests that this is characteristic of *all* argument. I think this is mistaken, as discussed substantively in this section of the book. See also my "Normative Reasoning and Moral Argumentation in Theory and Practice," *Philosophy & Rhetoric* 49, no. 1 (2016): 49–73; and my "The Role of Intuition, Emotion, and Reason in the Act of Judgment: Implications from Moral Psychology and Metaethics for Argumentation Studies," in *Reasoned Argument: Selected Papers from the 16th Biennial AFA/NCA Conference on Argumentation*, ed. Robert Rowland (Washington, DC: National Communication Association, 2011), 95–103.

45 For a clear articulation, see John Rawls, *Political Liberalism: Expanded Edition* (New York: Columbia University Press, 2005), 173–211.

46 Rawls, *Political*, 217.

47 Many have used this terminology, including as the title of a collection of essays on public reason and religion in J. Caleb Clanton, *The Ethics of Citizenship: Liberal Democracy and Religious Convictions* (Waco, TX: Baylor University Press, 2009).

48 Audi, *Religious*, 150.

49 Craig Calhoun, "Imagining Solidarity: Cosmopolitanism, Constitutional Patriotism, and the Public Sphere," *Public Culture*, 14, no. 1 (2002): 147–71.

50 Ryan Gillespie, "Reason, Religion, and Postsecular Liberal Democratic Epistemology," *Philosophy & Rhetoric* 45, no. 1 (2014): 1–24.

51 For a similar critique, see Micah Lott, "Restraint on Reasons and Reason for Restraint: A Problem for Rawls' Ideal of Public Reason," *Pacific Philosophical Quarterly* 87, no. 1 (2006): 75–95.

52 Rawls, *Political*, 216.

53 Allan Gibbard, *Wise Choices, Apt Feelings: A Theory of Normative Judgment* (Cambridge, MA: Harvard University Press, 1990), 243, 242.

54 Political liberalism, it should be noted, is not meant to replace nor override comprehensive doctrines. Rawls notes that citizens need more than just a commitment to the CRP: "It is central to political liberalism that free and equal citizens affirm both a comprehensive doctrine and a political conception." Rawls, *Political*, 482.

55 Cf. Stanley Fish, *The Trouble with Principle* (Cambridge, MA: Harvard University Press, 1999), 286.

56 The Roman notion of *gravitas* has relevance to how I'm using weight here. The difference is that weight, in the context above, is a subjective experience; an individual

chooses how much weight to assign a reason, so to speak. Gravitas does not map onto that conception neatly, given a more unified understanding of its meaning and import in Roman contexts.

57   I mean truth here in the most minimal and practical sense of the term, for if there is no such thing, or at least an analogous concept, laws and society itself would be impossible. I imagine a post-truth place to be one in which every single utterance is met with "Well, that's not true for me, only for you." It seems that communication, let alone a civil society, would not even really be possible in such a place. While we see elements of this at times in Western liberal democracies, the full-scale Orwellian dystopian vision is hardly analogues (yet?).

58   The quote: "Why the apparent paradox of public reason is no paradox is clearer once we remember that there are familiar cases where we grant that we should not appeal to the whole truth as we see it, even when it might be readily available." Rawls, *Political*, 218.

59   Rawls, *Political*, 219.

60   Dennis Thompson, "Public Reasons and Precluded Reasons," *Fordham Law Review* 72, no. 5 (2003–4): 2073.

61   Jürgen Habermas, *The Inclusion of the Other: Studies in Political Theory*, ed. Ciaran Cronin and Pablo De Grieff (Cambridge, MA: MIT Press, 1998), 77.

62   Michael Sandel, "Political Liberalism," *Harvard Law Review*, 107 (1994): 1767.

63   Michael J. Sandel and Thomas Nagel, "The Case for Liberalism: An Exchange," *The New York Review of Books*, 5 October 2006. To be quite clear that this exchange is precisely about justification and how that works in constitutional democracies in accordance with something like public reason, Sandel is pro-choice, just like Nagel; in other words, they share the same first-order judgment on the matter but sharply disagree about the setup of the second-order judgment.

64   Gibbard, *Wise*, 243.

65   Steven Smith, *The Disenchantment of Secular Discourse* (Cambridge, MA: Harvard University Press, 2010), 26–41. See also my discussion in "Uses of Religion" *International Journal of Communication* 5 (2011): 1669–86.

66   Habermas's view is that reflexivity is the "ethos of liberal citizenship," and is a "cognitive presupposition" that interlocutors should hold prior to argumentative engagement. Reflexivity allows for arguers to recognize epistemic blindspots (or at least the potential for them), and thus the clash of reasons in the public sphere is done with these "appropriate epistemic attitudes ... " – perhaps a better name for this is *epistemic humility*. Jürgen Habermas, *Between Naturalism and Religion*, trans. Ciaran Cronin (Malden: Polity, 2008), 6, 143; cf. Gillespie, "Reason, Religion," esp. 14–17.

67   It is worth noting that citizens have to contend with their individual and often a collective instinctual reaction as well. So there is the instinctual response, the first-order judgment, and the second-order judgment often working in the same situation.

68   The distinction is made and discussed in my "Reason, Religion," where *omnibus rebus consideratis* is used for all-things-considered to maintain the Latin symmetry. The two duties here correspond roughly to Kant's *perfect* and *imperfect* duties and W.D. Ross' *duties proper* and *prima facie duties*. I refrain from using either of those so as not to be on the hook for interpreting those authors' conceptions. See Kant, *Ethical*, esp. 30–6; W.D. Ross, *The Right and the Good* (New York: Oxford University Press, 1930).

69   Ross, *Right*, 18.

70   Roderick M. Chisholm, "The Ethics of Requirement," *American Philosophical Quarterly* 1, no. 2 (1964): 148.

71 McKeon's use of communication and ethics and Farrell's notion of a rhetorical culture channels the deliberative-rhetoric branch of classical rhetorical theory explicitly.
McKeon puts the connection between rhetoric, ethics, truth, and communication
eloquently:

> Communication can embody values, realize freedom, promote the ends of
> society, only by advancing truth and using truth. To do that it must form in
> those who participate in communication an attitude and ability to judge truth,
> be sensitive to values, to develop in the use of freedom, and to build confidence
> in the institutions of society on truth, values, and freedom. To strengthen these
> attitudes and abilities is to make men of one mind in truth; and the art of com-
> munication – which has been referred to earlier as deliberative rhetoric – is the
> art by which that can be done

Richard McKeon, "Communication, Truth, and Society," *Ethics* 67, no. 2 (1957): 98.

72 This is a channeling of Habermas, as Farrell made clear in an earlier essay. Here's the
relevant passage, with the internal quotes being from *Legitimation Crisis*:

> " ... we cannot explain the validity claim of norms without recourse to ration-
> ally motivated agreement or at least to the conviction that consensus on a rec-
> ommended norm could be brought about with reasons ... " and furthermore
> this requires interlocutors, as a communicative community affected by the out-
> come of the deliberation process, to hold firmly the belief that the "proposed
> norms are right."

Thomas Farrell, "Knowledge, Consensus, and Rhetorical Theory," *Quarterly Journal
of Speech* 62, no. 1 (1976): 7.

73 A more complete vision of this process can be found in Habermas, *Between Facts and
Norms: Contributions to a Discourse Theory of Law and Democracy*, trans. William Rehg
(Cambridge, MA: MIT Press, 1998). Robert Asen gives a good account of citizenship
from a discourse theory perspective in "A Discourse Theory of Citizenship," *Quarterly
Journal of Speech* 90, no. 2 (2004): 189–211. Robert Hariman gives a succinct overview
of these processes in his "Norms of Rhetorical Theory," *Quarterly Journal of Speech* 80
(1994): 329–32.

74 There are two major schools of thought that share a version of this argument: biopolitics in the Foucauldian school and critiques of instrumental reason in the Frankfurt
School. There is a significant connection to both these programs. The overlap with
Foucault and his lectures from 1978 to 1979 is that liberal government, as a government dedicated to the dual task of rationality and self-limitation, takes shape in the
late Enlightenment forward. Even more prevalent of an overlap is the US neoliberalism story, in which market rationality is applied to nonmarket situations and actors.
I will make some comparisons below, but as should be clear from the subsections, my
story of how and why this economization both occurs and resonates is more strongly
tied to moral philosophy and political economy than his. In terms of the Frankfurt
School, the critique of instrumental reason is part of the rationalization of society
born of the Enlightenment, which has a dialectical interplay: "Enlightenment has
always aimed at liberating men from fear and establishing their sovereignty. Yet the
fully enlightened earth radiates disaster triumphantly." In this line of thought, the
problem is that the powers of ratio to organize self and society without distortion have
resulted in a re-entwinement of enlightenment and myth. Furthermore, the concept
of reason is reduced in modern life, from law to culture, to instrumental reasoning as
the only kind of acceptable public reasoning. My story has much in common with this
story, but some of the characters are different, I endorse more market mechanisms
than they do, and I am writing more about the second half of the twentieth century

than the first. See Foucault, *The Birth of the Clinic* (New York: Vintage, 1994); Max
Horkheimer and Theodor W. Adorno, *Dialectic of Enlightenment*, trans. John Cumming
(New York: Continuum, 2002), 3.

75 Georg Simmel, *The Philosophy of Money*, ed. David Frisby, trans. Tom Bottomore and
David Frisby (New York: Routledge, 1978).

76 Key works here are MacIntyre's *After Virtue*, Taylor's *Sources of Self*, and Habermas's
Theory of Communicative Action volumes. See Alasdair MacIntyre, *After Virtue*, 2nd ed.
(Notre Dame, IN: University of Notre Dame Press, 1984); Charles Taylor, *Sources
of the Self* (Cambridge, MA: Harvard University Press, 1989); and his *A Secular Age*
(Cambridge, MA: Belknap/Harvard University Press, 2007). Horkheimer and
Adorno's famous "culture industry" essay opens with a line that encapsulates much of
the view (though from a different perspective):

> The sociological theory that the loss of the support of objectively established
> religion, the dissolution of the last remnants of precapitalism, together with
> technological and social differentiation or specialization, have led to cultural
> chaos is disproved every day; for culture now impresses the same stamp on
> everything.

The stamp is, basically, instrumental reason as the technique of domination in society to serve the interests of the most powerful. What becomes universal in society,
then, is not God nor social cohesive notions of *communitas* but the replication of
sameness via culture industries governed by the imperative of economic rationality.
Horkheimer and Adorno, 120.

77 Taylor, *Secular*, 13.

78 The issue of doubt as defining both those who choose to believe in God and those
who don't is dramatized to great effect by Dostoevsky, when Dmitri, the agnostic
between his atheist brother Ivan (whose view is similar to Rakitin) and his Believer-
monk brother Alexei, is in prison:

> You see, before I didn't have any of these doubts, but they were all hiding
> in me. Maybe I was drinking and fighting and raging, just because unknown
> ideas were storming inside me. I was fighting to quell them within me, to tame
> them, to subdue them ... And I'm tormented by God. Tormented by only that.
> What if he doesn't exist? What if Rakitin is right, that it's an artificial idea of
> mankind? So then, if he doesn't exist, man is chief of the earth, of the universe.
> Splendid! Only how is he going to be virtuous without God? ... Rakitin says it's
> possible to love mankind even without God. Well, only a snotty little shrimp
> can affirm such a thing, but I can't understand it. Life is simple for Rakitin:
> "You'd do better to worry about extending man's civil rights," he told me today,
> "or at least about not letting the price of beef go up; you'd render your love for
> mankind more simply and directly that way than with any philosophies." But
> I came back at him: "And without God," I said, "you'll hike up the price of beef
> yourself, if the chance comes your way, and make a rouble on every kopeck."
> He got angry. Because what is virtue? – answer me that, Alexei. I have one vir-
> tue and a Chinese has another – so it's a relative thing. Or not? Not relative?
> Insidious question! You mustn't laugh if I tell you that I didn't sleep for two
> nights because of it.

Fyodor Dostoevsky, *The Brothers Karamazov*, trans. Richard Peaver and Larissa Volokhonsky (New York: Farrar, Straus, Giroux, 2002), 592–3.

79 The idea here is that it is only through deep reflection and a sense of existential
choice that true judgment can be made. This is attributed to Kierkegaard given
a number of his writings, but the one at the forefront of my mind here is *Sickness*

unto Death. In this work, Kierkegaard articulates how it is through despair – with the full implication of the word *through* – that one can arrive at a saving faith in God. But the danger, he warns, is that many go *to* despair, and don't come back, so to speak. That is, the certainty of death and impossibility of overcoming it should create an existential angst that is a necessary precursor to reflective judgment. That this sickness of despair can result in radical uncertainty, of not making a choice or of making the wrong eternal choice (that the material world is all there is), is what Kierkegaard calls the sickness unto death. The salient point for the current chapter is that *doubt, uncertainty,* and *choice* are the key elements to both eternal death and eternal life. I will return to this concept and Kierkegaard in this book's conclusion. See Søren Kierkegaard, *Sickness unto Death,* ed. and trans. Howard V. Hong and Edna H. Hong (Princeton: Princeton University Press, 1980), esp. 47–67, 125–31.

80 The rest of the quote indicates the contrast with previous eras:
> But there is clearly another way one can live these things, and many human beings did. This is a condition in which the immediate experience of power, a place of fullness, exile, is in terms which *we* would identify as one of the possible alternatives, but where for the people concerned no such distinction, between experience and its construal, arose. Let's recur to Hieronymus Bosch for instance. Those nightmare scenarios of possession ... were not "theories" in any sense in the lived experience of many people ... they were objects of real fear ...

See Taylor, *Secular,* 11.

81 Taylor, *Sources,* 99.

82 In Michael Sandel's words,
> The unencumbered self and the ethic it inspires, taken together, hold out a liberating vision. Freed from the dictates of nature and the sanction of social roles, the human subject is installed as sovereign, cast as the author of the only moral meanings there are. As participants in pure practical reason, or as parties to the original position, we are free to construct principles of justice unconstrained by an order of value antecedently given. And as actual, individual selves, we are free to choose our purposes and ends unbound by such an order.

Michael Sandel, "The Procedural Republic and the Unencumbered Self," *Political Theory* 12 (1984): 87.

83 His view is spelled out in a number of works from the 1980s forward, perhaps most explicitly in his *Democracy's Discontent* (Cambridge, MA: Belknap/Harvard, 1998). For an overview, see Richard Dagger, "The Sandelian Republic and the Encumbered Self," *The Review of Politics* 61 (1999): 181–208.

84 Taylor, *Secular,* 27. He calls this view the buffered self, and his argument is historically charted throughout the book, including changes in lived conditions and elite cultures, from politics (kings to democracy), astronomy (cosmos to the universe), and moral philosophy (God to Deism to exclusive humanism) to art and poetry (the notion of "subtler languages") and music (from music tied to places and events to "absolute music" without words and specific reference). I am not choosing to endorse or deny the similar conceptions of encumbered, unencumbered, and buffered self, instead using *distanced self* to convey the central features needed for this analysis: a self-conception of humans as sovereign, autonomous, and distanced. The neoliberal emphasis on autonomy and autonomous persons should be coming into focus.

85 Taylor, *Secular,* 300.

86 Cf. Taylor, *Secular,* 359–61.

87 Dostoevsky, *Brothers,* 589.

88 For a nice overview of this conception in the form of a critique, see Stanley Hauerwas, "Whose Conscience? Whose Emotion?" *The Hastings Center Report* 22, no. 1 (1992): 48–9.

89 Discussing the power of conscience to torment a person in addition to, or more substantively than, physical punishment, the Devil laughs:

> What other torments? Ah, don't even ask: before it was one thing and another, but now it's mostly the moral sort, "remorse of conscience" and all that nonsense. That also started because of you, from the "mellowing of your mores." Well, and who benefited? The unscrupulous benefited, because what is remorse of conscience to a man who has no conscience at all? Decent people who still had some conscience and honor left suffered instead ... There you have it – reforms on unprepared ground, and copied from institutions as well – nothing but harm!

Dostoevsky, *Brothers*, 643.

90 There are at least two senses to *following one's conscience*. There is the sense that following one's conscience just means satisfying whatever one's conscience says. In this view, if one's conscience isn't pricked by an act, the act is permissible. This view is consistent with both the idea that a conscience is simply the indicator of what feels right or wrong in as subjectivist a sense as possible and that which indicates right and wrong as a moral compass, with the compass perhaps being implanted in humans by the Divine. This is the sense that I have in mind when discussing conscience. Another view of conscience, however, has to do with *why* one would follow one's conscience. In this sense, one should follow one's conscience not because it is infallible, and not because it makes one feel better, but because it is most likely to actually be the right thing to do. This is a more complicated view and would require much more space to adequately unpack and address.

91 In Kantian terms, it is the Autonomy Formula – and only the Autonomy Formula – that forms contemporary conscience. The idea is to think of "the will of every rational being as a will that legislates universal law" (§431; cf. §440). That is, as outlined in *Grounding*, Kant's three formulas – the Humanity-as-End Formula, which is the Categorical Imperative in terms of never treating humans as means but only as ends (§429), the Autonomy Formula, and the Kingdom of Ends Formula, in which humanity treats each other as ends to bring about an ideal kingdom (§434) – have a rational unity among themselves. Each one leads to and implies the other. Wrench free Autonomy of each individual able to legislate for themselves from the backdrop of the Categorical Imperative and perfect and imperfect duties, and one ends up with a strikingly different situation – the economization of everyday life. See Kant, *Grounding*, 36–42, also 44–5. The same wrenching occurs of eudemonia from the Greek virtue context, or of capitalism from its virtue context, as discussed below, and that Kant seemingly wrenches something like the Categorical Imperative or Kingdom of Ends from its Christian context is also worth noting. Wrenching all the way down.

92 As the famous Smith passage goes:

> It is not from the benevolence of the butcher, the brewer, or the baker, that we expect our dinner, but from their regard to their own interest. We address ourselves, not to their humanity but to their self-love, and never talk to them of our own necessities but of their advantages. Nobody but a beggar chooses to depend chiefly upon the benevolence of his fellow-citizens.

Adam Smith, *The Essential Adam Smith* (New York: Norton, 1986), 169.

93 The outline for the series is in the back of the first instalment: Deirdre McCloskey, *The Bourgeois Virtues: Ethics for an Age of Commerce* (Chicago: University of Chicago Press, 2006), 509–14, though it ended up being a trilogy.

94 Again, Foucault doesn't account for the moral import that I have been tracking. But his lectures have strong relevance: the shift from *raison d'État* to self-imposed limits of governmentality and governmental reason in the nineteenth century hits its strongest head in post-World War II Germany and America. Though the two neoliberalisms are distinct, they share a "a critique of the irrationality peculiar to excessive government, and [desire a] return to a technology of frugal government." The notion of frugal government is Foucault's encapsulation of the "reason of the least state," of the state being that which limits itself, or has in mind the notion of limiting itself and not overstepping its exercise of power and authority. While Foucault puts this as Benjamin Franklin's expression, the clearer correlate for US society I think is the Jeffersonian motto, "That government is best which governs least." (NB: I say Jeffersonian because the quote is usually attributed to him, though there is, to my knowledge, no confirmation of this in his writings.) For the quotes, see Foucault, *Birth*, 322, 37.

95 Three key outlines of the view are Harvey, *Brief History of Neoliberalism;* Jean and John Comaroff's *Millennial Capitalism and the Culture of Neoliberalism* (Durham, NC: Duke University Press, 2001); Wendy Brown, *Undoing the Demos* (New York: Zone Books, 2015).

96 The main source for these claims is found in Foucault, *Birth*, 239–65, though, in a way, his whole lecture series argues for this.

97 I understand that this is slippery analytic territory, as one is, from either the free will or determinist perspective, not *free* to choose either of those things, metaphysically speaking: either free will exists or it doesn't, regardless of the phenomenological and psychological variants and appearances. The point is simply at the phenomenological level: in a general sense, society is *structured as if* we have choices like this.

98 McCloskey, *Bourgeois*, 357.

99 H. Tristram Engelhardt Jr. and Kevin Wm. Wildes, "Postmodernity and Limits on the Human Body: Libertarianism by Default," in *Medicine Unbound: The Human Body and the Limits of Medical Intervention*, ed. Robert H. Blank and Andrea L. Bonnicksen (New York: Columbia University Press, 1994).

100 Engelhardt Jr. and Wildes, 65.

101 Boettcher puts the matter quite clearly:

> Respect is not simply a political value that needs to be maximized up to a certain threshold. Nor is its significance reducible to favorable political consequences such as additional trust and civic friendship. Respect is also a normative principle according to which we should properly recognize the moral *standing* and *authority* of our fellow citizens as entitled to good reasons for our exercise of power over them on fundamental political questions.

Boettcher, "Moral Status," 169, emphasis original.

This is the key point: what could ever end up being prohibited under such an ethos, as the logic pushes to ever expansion, much like the logic of the market under global capitalism? See also Childress, *Practical*, 289–95, for discussion of the libertarian-by-default issue.

102 Engelhardt Jr. and Wildes, 68.

103 Again, it is important to note that the state does not morally endorse abortion per se, but its permitting of the act indicates that it is of a lesser moral degree of seriousness than murder (for which there is a categorical ban), and hence it doesn't remain fully *neutral.*

104 Childress gestures at this point as well, in explicit reference to Engelhardt Jr. and Wildes. Childress, *Practical*, 289.

105   A Pew study documents that millennial-generation adults have low social trust, and, in particular, scepticism towards institutions. See "Millennials in Adulthood: Detached from Institutions, Networked with Friends," March 2014, Pew Research Center: http://www.pewsocialtrends.org/2014/03/07/millennials-in-adulthood/.

106   Incommensurability is the notion that two theories (or even things) are incomparable and incompatible due to meaning changes and referents, often amounting to two different things being neither equal nor superior/inferior. Taken in wide scope, the view is characteristic of Thomas Kuhn and Paul Feyerabend, and is the subject of a significant amount of literature. A good overview of the incommensurability in its widest scope and its shortcomings is found in Michael Devitt, "Against Incommensurability," *Australasian Journal of Philosophy* 57, no. 1 (1979): 29–50. For incommensurability and values, in which the refusal to make a judgment between two things is (rightly) recognized as a kind of incommensurability, see Joseph Raz, "Value Incommensurability," *Proceedings of the Aristotelian Society* 86, no. 1 (1985–6): 117–34.

6. Good Reasons: Metanormativity and Categoricity

1   Cf. Jonathan Moreno, "The Triumph of Autonomy in Bioethics and Commercialism in Health Care," *Cambridge Quarterly of Healthcare Ethics* 16, no. 4 (2007): 415–19.

2   Furthermore, there is not such a stark contrast between ethics and metaethics as is sometimes claimed. Here I agree with Bernard Williams:

> The distinction between the ethical and the meta-ethical is no longer found so convincing or important. There are several reasons for this, but the most relevant here is that it is now obvious ... that what one thinks about the subject matter of ethical thought, what one supposes it to be about, must itself affect what tests for acceptability or coherence are appropriate to it.

Bernard Williams, *Ethics and the Limits of Philosophy* (Cambridge, MA: Harvard University Press, 1985), 73.

3   Those readers who find this sort of metanormative enquiry tiresome *and* are already convinced that some reasons are better than others and that there are right answers to ethical questions might skip to chapter 8. For me, I find this discussion vital to those who hold the view or not, and I can think of no better defence than these Wayne Booth lines:

> The only excuse I can offer for tackling a problem that is bigger than I am is that these are, for many of us, matters of life and death – sometimes even literally deciding choices about suicide and murder. We all must answer, consciously or unconsciously, the question of whether values are objective, and we should therefore try to answer it well rather than thoughtlessly to repeat fashionable doctrines.

Wayne Booth, *Now Don't Try to Reason with Me: Essays and Ironies for a Credulous Age* (Chicago: University of Chicago Press, 1970), 362.

4   *Gravitas*, meaning gravity, importance, and *dignitas*, meaning prestige and worthiness, combine to indicate an underlying *important weight of seriousness*. The emphasis here is of gravity and dignity representing a material and moral pull on reasoners.

5   One of the debates at issue is whether a reason and reasons are the fundamental component of normativity (Scanlon; Skorupski) or whether desire, in the Humean theory, is properly primary (e.g., Schroeder) or that ought ontologies are preferable and non-reducible to reason ontologies in normativity (e.g., Broome). In general, perhaps the character and properties of reason itself being so mysterious make for the challenge here. At a minimum, it seems to be shared, as I will share as well, that the idea

of a reason is something that counts in favour of (Derek Parfit, *On What Matters, Vol. 1* (New York: Oxford University Press, 2011), 31; T.M. Scanlon, *What We Owe Each Other* [Cambridge, MA: Harvard University Press, 1998], 17). I am sympathetic to the idea (though am not fully prepared to defend it) of reason and normativity going hand in hand, as in Joseph Raz's phrasing: "The normativity of all that is normative consists in the way that it is, or provides, or is otherwise related to reasons." I take, as in (rhetorical) practical reasoning, that emotions, attitudes, and dispositions relate to rationality, and that normative disagreement is disagreement in ends and not reasons per se. See John Skorupski, *The Domain of Reasons* (New York: Oxford University Press, 2010); T.M. Scanlon, *Being Realistic about Reasons* (New York: Oxford University Press, 2014); Mark Schroeder, *Slaves of the Passions* (New York: Oxford University Press, 2007); John Broome, "Reason versus Ought," Philosophical Issues 25, no. 1 (2015): 80–97; Joseph Raz, *Engaging Reason: On the Theory of Value and Action* (New York: Oxford University Press, 1999), 67.

6 Even I did this in my article "Normative Reasoning and Moral Argumentation in Theory and Practice," *Philosophy & Rhetoric* 49, no. 1 (2016): 49–73.

7 There is much overlap here with contemporary moral philosophy, with the literature full of discussions of modifiers, context, conditions, commitment, and requirements. There is significant and rich potential for rhetorical deliberation work, particularly with those who indeed see moral discourse as the discovery and persuasion of the reasons that matter (e.g., Stephen Finlay, "The Reasons That Matter," *Australasian Journal of Philosophy* 84, no. 1 [2006]: 1–20); or as precisely a process of weighing and weight (e.g., see the edited volume by Errol Lord and Barry Maguire, *Weighing Reasons* [New York: Oxford University Press, 2016]).

8 It is with that knot that I'm positioned in the Aristotelian tradition (see Book I of the *Rhetoric*, 1356a.7–8; 1926, 19).

9 Eugene Garver captures the intimacy between pistis and rhetoric when, in the introduction to his excellent book, he writes that his entire study can be thought of as exploring all the connotations of pistis for rhetoric: " ... proof, argument, reasoning, persuasion, belief, trust, faith, conviction, obligation, and confidence. These essays are a meditation on the connections amongst those terms." See his *For the Sake of Argument: Practical Reasoning, Character, and the Ethics of Belief* (Chicago: University of Chicago Press 2004), 3.

10 Aristotle uses practical reason and the concept of reasonableness, as does Stephen Toulmin. For example, Toulmin's whole 2003 book *Return to Reason* (Cambridge, MA: Harvard University Press, 2003) is about redressing the balance between reason and reasonableness. Chaim Perelman calls this the realm of rhetoric, as seen in his touchstone work with Lucie Olbrechts-Tyteca, *The New Rhetoric: A Treatise on Argumentation*, trans. John Wilkinson and Purcell Weaver (Notre Dame, IN: University of Notre Dame Press, 1969), and uses the phrase directly as the title of a shorter version of that work (*The Realm of Rhetoric*, trans. William Kluback [Notre Dame, IN: Notre Dame University Press, 1982]).

11 Bryan Garsten, *Saving Persuasion: A Defense of Rhetoric and Judgment* (Cambridge, MA: Harvard University Press, 2006), 115.

12 William Grimaldi, "Rhetoric and Truth: A Note on Aristotle 'Rhetoric' 1355a.21–24," *Philosophy & Rhetoric* 11, no. 3 (1978): 173.

13 This view of Aristotelian rhetoric thrived in the middle part of the twentieth century, both directly and indirectly, as philosophers like Perelman and Toulmin sought an alternative to the confining philosophical enquiry of logical positivism, or "deductive inference," as Toulmin calls it. This is especially important in that both Perelman

and Toulmin were former practitioners of analytic positivism, whereas others associated with the "new" rhetoric (e.g., Kenneth Burke, Wayne Booth) did not have this first-hand experience. This is not to say that Toulmin and Perelman *rejected* analytical philosophy in the positivist tradition; rather, they simply saw it as a category mistake in certain matters. As Perelman writes, analytic reasoning and dialectic reasoning (which he credits to Aristotle, as *apoedixis* and *dialektike*), in which the "former deals with truth and the latter justifiable opinions," are not separate activities or different methods but different fields of thought. "Each field of thought requires different discourse; it is as inappropriate to be satisfied with merely reasonable arguments from mathematicians as it would be to require scientific proofs from an orator" in *Realm of Rhetoric*, 3. I try my hand at some connections between dialectic, rhetoric, (meta)ethics, and judgment in Ryan Gillespie, "The Normative Relationship between Rhetoric and Judgment: On Pistis, Krisis, and Moral Inquiry," in *Rhetoric in the Twenty-First Century*, ed. Nicholas Crowe and David Frank (Newcastle Upon Tyne: Cambridge Scholars, 2016), 39–52.

14 Stephen Toulmin, *The Uses of Argument* (Cambridge: Cambridge University Press, 1958), 10.

15 This becomes even clearer in later Toulmin works, specifically *Return to Reason*, in which the division between, say, Humean desire or Cartesian rationality is seen to meld into a single practice of philosophy, into a "way of life," based not in abstract reasoning but in the situated world of "where" and "when." Toulmin sees the reasonable as the domain of neither philosophy nor rhetoric, for philosophy and rhetoric are not at odds with each other (this was the result of the invention of the disciplines and the pretences of an objective, scientific logic); more importantly, he is not to be read as advocating *only* reasonability; rather, what is to be hoped for is a "proper balance between Theory and Practice, Logic and Rhetoric, Rationality and Reasonableness." See Toulmin, *Return to Reason*, 13.

16 A sampling: Richard Weaver *The Ethics of Rhetoric* (Davis, CA: Hermogoras Press/Routledge, 1953/1985); Karl Wallace, "The Substance of Good Reasons," *Quarterly Journal of Speech* 49, no. 3 (1963): 239–49; Wayne Booth, *Modern Dogma and the Rhetoric of Assent* (Chicago: Chicago University Press, 1974); Walt Fisher, "Toward a Logic of Good Reasons," *Quarterly Journal of Speech* 64 (1978): 376–84; cf. "Narration as a Human Communication Paradigm: The Case of Public Moral Argument," *Communication Monographs* 51, no. 1 (1984): 1–22. For a sort of overview, see Paul Bator, "The 'Good Reasons Movement': A 'Confounding' of Rhetoric and Dialectic?" *Philosophy & Rhetoric* 21, no. 1 (1988): 38–47.

17 For example, in his 1953 book, *The Ethics of Rhetoric*, Weaver writes that "an ethics of rhetoric requires ultimate terms" – terms which are atop the signifying chain of value – "be ultimate in some rational sense," 232. In *Modern Dogma*, Booth attacks what he considers the modern dogma of academic discourse, including and especially the fact/value split en route to a "discovery of good reasons, finding what really warrants assent because any reasonable person ought to be persuaded by what has been said." This is not at the exclusion of truth (if philosophy is defined as enquiry into truth), because "to talk of improving beliefs implies that deliberators are seeking truth, since some beliefs are 'truer' than others" – so, then, the differences between warranted belief in shared discourse, or differences between philosophy and rhetoric, are not so "sharply definable," xiii.

18 Booth, *Modern Dogma*, 147.

19 Wallace, "The Substance," 244.

20 Wallace, "The Substance," 248.

21 Wallace, "The Substance," 247.

22 Fisher, "Narration," 10.

23 Booth, *Modern Dogma*, 85.

24 The resuscitation of reason to normative and other domains unsettleable by a thoroughgoing scientific reasoning in general and to ethical enquiry in particular, already occurring at the time of Booth's writing in 1974, has undergone significant improvements and changes over the last few decades. The logic of good reasons allows for the maintenance of some values being better grounded than others. This is hardly the domain strictly of rhetoricians, and in fact the Good Reasons School largely rejects a philosophy/rhetoric dualism: there is little legitimacy of and efficacy for "maintaining a theoretical distinction between dialectic and rhetoric ... and such a duality [is] unnecessary in practice and probably counterproductive." Bator, "Good Reasons," 46.

25 The idea here is that at some level, indeed all reasons are good reasons-in-a-narrative, and that this is exactly true. In another sense, such a view, too narrowly understood, is quite false, as articulated in the main text.

26 For example, Wallace writes,

> What a good reason *is* is to some extent fixed by human nature and to a very large extent by generally accepted principles and practices which make social life, as we understand it, possible. In a word, the concept of good reasons embraces both the substance and processes of practical reason. One could do worse than characterize rhetoric as the art of finding and effectively presenting good reasons.

Fisher writes, in accordance with the classical tradition beginning with Plato, that people have a "natural" tendency to "prefer the 'true' and the 'just.'" See Wallace, "The Substance," 248; Fisher, "Narration," 9.

27 As further clarification, the distinction is between normative ethics (e.g., what is the right thing to do?) and metaethics (e.g., what does *right* mean?). Again, the idea is to move discussion of ethical controversies – such as organ donation strategies – from the question of what is the right ethical judgment to the assumptions, commitments, theories, and strategies that inform the ethical statements of arguers.

28 Charles Stevenson, "The Emotive Meaning of Ethical Terms," in *Moral Discourse & Practice: Some Philosophical Approaches*, ed. Stephen Darwall, Allan Gibbard, and Peter Railton (New York: Oxford University Press, 1997), 79.

29 Though this is not an actual exchange, this might be what Nancy Scheper-Hughes and Michele Goodwin might say to each other (save the opening two lines) given their work most relevant to this brief bit: Goodwin, "Altruism's Limits: Law, Capacity, and Organ Commodification," *Rutgers Law Review* 56, no. 2 (2004): 305–407, and Scheper-Hughes, "The Rosenbaum Kidney Trafficking Gang," *Counterpunch*, 30 November 2011.

30 *Moral realism* is used differently by different speakers, even in the philosophical literature. Stephen Finlay distinguishes four dimensions to moral realism: the semantic (whether or not moral claims have attitude-independent truth values), the ontological (whether or not moral claims aim to describe moral facts involving properties), the metaphysical (whether or not moral properties are attitude-independent in nature), and the normative (whether or not moral properties have attitude-independent authority). I will be defending a view here that is consistent with certain different mixing and matching along those dimensions and will not be weighing in on all of those areas. Stephen Finlay, "Four Faces of Moral Realism," *Philosophy Compass* 2, no. 6 (2007): 829–49.

31 Emotivism holds that moral utterances are not propositions or claims but rather are senseless (adhering to verificationism; instead moral utterances are expressions

of the speakers' emotions. This is largely the view of moral discourse in the middle part of the twentieth century of Anglo-style philosophy, typified perhaps in A.J. Ayer. Expressivism holds a similar rejection of the surface syntax of moral claims, in which saying something like *selling organs is wrong* amounts to something like saying: selling organs – boo! Contemporary expressivism is quite sophisticated, with Allan Gibbard, who is discussed below, being a prominent theorist.

32 For example, see J.L. Mackie, *Ethics: Inventing Right and Wrong* (New York: Penguin, 1977).

33 As will be made clear later, there is a type of relativism that is not just compatible with my theory worked out here but that I actually, at some level, endorse.

34 Furthermore I will not be taking a stance on the priority of the relationship between reason and desire, only that reason plays a substantive role in fixing ends.

35 I am aware that Gibbard has much to endorse in cognitivism and seemingly prefers to refer to his view as expressivism and not non-cognitivism. The distinction I am making between the two, however, is simply regarding whether moral statements have truth conditions (on a traditional correspondence theory) or not. On this, Gibbard can be seen as a non-cognitivist. Allan Gibbard, *Thinking How to Live* (Cambridge, MA: Harvard University Press, 2003); Parfit, *On What Matters, Vol. 1 & 2.*

36 Gibbard, *Thinking*, 223.

37 See especially his discussion of plans versus concepts, *Thinking*, 29–33.

38 Gibbard, *Thinking*, 137.

39 Gibbard, *Thinking*, 68.

40 Parfit, *Matters, Vol. 2*, 267.

41 Gibbard, *Thinking*, 9.

42 Parfit, *Matters, Vol. 2*, 386.

43 Parfit, *Matters, Vol. 2*, 386. Emphasis added.

44 This might be slippery to some, but I hold to the classic view (or antiquated, from a critics' perspective) of an interrelationship between truth, beauty, and goodness. If a contemporary metaethical theorist, perhaps such as Gibbard, denies that he is interested in talking about plans or aims being true-for-you or good-for-our-community, then not only are we not talking about the same thing but also I question the value of his contribution to understanding moral discourse. I do think that Gibbard is up to something like *explanation* at least of true and good in terms of aims in *Reconciling Our Aims: In Search of Bases for Ethics* (New York: Oxford University Press, 2008).

45 In many ways, this is another variation on the Socratics versus the sophists debating something like Protagoras's claim that man is the measure of all things, applied to the case of morality. William Frankena closed his book *Ethics* by saying, "Morality is made for man, not man for morality." This is slightly cryptic, even if one understands the allusion to Mark 2:27 ("The Sabbath was made for man, not man for the Sabbath") – which Jesus offers as his concluding thought on why it was morally permissible for David to eat the consecrated bread otherwise restricted for the high priest. This prompts an issue of the generalizability: can we substitute law in place of Sabbath in that quote? Morality? The answer to that question is for theologians, but the issue here is that it raises what Kant calls a *natural dialectic*: if morality is made for man, there is the "propensity to quibble" with the strict laws of duty established by reason and to make them "more compatible with our wishes and inclinations," which for him is a corruption of morality (*Grounding*, (§405). See Immanuel Kant, *Ethical Philosophy*, trans. James W. Ellington (Indianapolis: Hackett Publishing Company, 1994), 17.

46 This is debatable, as there are conflicting readings of what Aristotle is up to in general and the place of rhetoric in his overarching theories of reasoning in specific. Again,

I buy Eugene Garver's perspective, as argued for in *Sake*, succinctly in the concluding chapter, "Rhetoric and the Unity of Practical Reason." Garver, *Sake*, 175–202. Similar views are found in William M.A. Grimaldi, "Rhetoric and the Philosophy of Aristotle," *The Classical Journal* 53, no. 3 (1958): 371–5; and Alan G. Gross and Marcelo Dascal, "The Conceptual Unity of Aristotle's Rhetoric," *Philosophy & Rhetoric* 34, no. 4 (2001): 275–91.

47   Gibbard, *Reconciling*.

48   As will be discussed, this is a view of relativism – a sort of simple or naïve relativism. There are sophisticated versions of relativism that are compatible with my theory. NB: I move from rejecting agent-based standards to community desires, thereby leaving open, to some degree, community standards as a plausible and perhaps correct view.

49   *Simple moral relativism* contrasts sharply with quite sophisticated versions, some of which, such as those held by David Copp and Stephen Finlay, are discussed below. These latter versions of moral relativism differ from the former insofar as sometimes the relevant standard of a moral claim (i.e., what a moral claim is relative to) can be humanity writ large. Furthermore, these views hold a significant place for substantive discussions of truth.

50   Mark J. Cherry, *Kidney for Sale by Owner: Human Organs, Transplantation, and the Market* (Washington, DC: Georgetown University Press, 2005), 154.

51   Thomas A. Hollihan and Kevin T. Baaske, *Arguments and Arguing: The Products and Process of Human Decision Making* (Prospect Heights, IL: Waveland Press, 1994), 9. Notice also the transition from *truth* in scare quotes to its usage without them in the final instance. The passage is changed in the second edition of the book published in 2005.

52   The example could be complicated if, when we add responses from Steve, James, Billie, Daniella, and Paul, we get five further different answers to the same equation. But nothing about the fact of disagreement (between two or eight or eight thousand people) necessarily points to right answers being impossible or non-existent. Imagine how quickly the story changes when I add that both Marvi and Jim, the teachers, reason together that two plus two is four; and that all the other people mentioned thus far are kindergartners. I don't mean to prematurely invoke epistemic authority, consensus, normative reasoning and other complicated issues; the point on offer is meant to pump basic intuitions of there being such a thing as right answers.

53   See also my "Normative Reasoning and Moral Argumentation" article, where I argue strongly against the conflation of the fact of pluralism and pluralism as a moral theory.

54   Strictly speaking, Cherry does not seem to be an advocate of moral relativism per se but instead takes the empirical fact of relativism as therefore requiring certain second-order judgments (from society and law, not individuals per se). Similarly, Hollihan and Baaske's second edition, as noted, seems to move to a more descriptivist account of values in argumentation. But both views are representative in the sense that they claim, *in practice*, equal validity among competing visions of the good, which is largely what I'll be arguing against in this section. It was explicitly set up and discussed at the end of chapter 5 as well.

55   Ronald Dworkin, "Objectivity and Truth: You'd Better Believe It," *Philosophy & Public Affairs* 25, no. 2 (1996): 87–139.

56   Dworkin, "Objectivity," 95.

57   This might not be exactly Dworkin's position, insofar as he might hold that there is no *standards* element to objectivity. But this is my view, in which all claims are relative

to some standard (even if that standard is God or Nature or whatever). Take the familiar substance/appearance example of a stick bent in water. We are content to say that the stick appears bent (and it is true that the stick *is* bent *from my perspective*), but it is really, substantively, not bent. But in the latter, it is substantively not bent from some better perspective (and that is given to us, in this case, by scientific enquiry into the nature of objects, light, water, etc.). Whatever you want to call that latter thing – for example, the way the world is – is still a perspective in the sense that what humans are doing is using methods to gain the best perspective, the illusive view-from-nowhere. Where I part company from that view (and perhaps Dworkin, I'm not sure) is that this view is unachievable – humans are never in a position to say "really, truly – that is unchangeably – the way the world is," because future data might lead to revised judgments. The difference is crucial: the stick is not bent, and we are so sure of this we call it a fact, the way the world is. But it is possible at least (it seems) that some future evidence might reveal something different, or that we have been interpreting the evidence of light particles or waves wrong, or whatever. In that case, I am comfortable saying that we had a good interpretation – one that maybe holds for millennia – that is still nonetheless an interpretation (of data, of the world), because the way the world really is differs from what we said was the way it is.

So I maintain, with objectivist-types, that the view of the way things really are a) *exists*, and b) *must* remain our goal, but that c) our statements about as much are always, no matter how irrefutable in any given moment (or epoch) of time, provisional. However, I have no problem binding the nature of this view into specific periods and moments (i.e., bounded rationality) and hence have no problem calling certain things, for which we have lots of evidence and confidence in our interpretations, facts, and that many of things we call facts – perhaps even almost all of them – might even indeed be exactly how the world is.

58 Dworkin, "Objectivity," 89, 129. What follows in the main text is my version of his argument.

59 Dworkin, "Objectivity," 131–2.

60 Here is a powerful quote expressing this view:

> It is common for philosophers to ridicule, as woolly or inconclusive or dogmatic, the arguments of people who believe that one position in some deep controversy has the better of the case. They say these partisans overlook the obvious truth that there is no "fact of the matter," no "single right answer" to the issue in play. They do not pause to consider whether they have any substantive arguments for that equally substantive position, and, if they do, whether these might not also be ridiculed as vague or unpersuasive or as resting on instincts or even bare assertions in the same way. *Absolute clarity is the privilege of fools and fanatics.* The rest of us must do the best we can: we must choose amongst the three substantive views on offer by asking which strikes us, after reflection and due thought, as more plausible than the others. And if none does, we must then settle for the true default view, which is not indeterminacy but uncertainty.

Dworkin, "Objectivity," 134–5, emphasis added.

61 Fish, *Trouble*, 286.

62 For a similar unfolding of this argument in a different context, see my, "Normative Reasoning."

63 Such as those offered by, for example, David Copp, *Morality, Normativity, and Society* (New York: Oxford University Press, 1995); Stephen Finlay, "Oughts and Ends," *Philosophical Studies* 143, no. 3 (2009): 315–40; and Paul Ziff, *Semantic Analysis* (Ithaca, NY: Cornell University Press, 1960).

64 To be clear, there is a sense in which I endorse the view that the relevant ethical standards are the beliefs and practices of the relevant community. This is different than the *preferences* of the relevant community, and, furthermore, the *relevant* community in some situations is *all of humanity*. In contrast, that morality is reducible to community preference is quite a popular view, with versions of it, essentially, being the logical outcome of certain forms of contractualism, intersubjectivism, and social-intuitionist accounts, if no mechanism of an all-of-humanity-being-relevant is built into the theory. For example, in a response chapter, Jonathan Haidt and Fredik Bjorklund bite this bullet, in a way, by saying that under Nazi rule, a good Nazi citizen would indeed be "a virtuous person." See Jonathan Haidt and Fredik Bjorklund, "Social Intuitionists Reason, in Conversation," *Moral Psychology, Vol. 2: The Cognitive Science of Morality: Intuition and Diversity*, ed. Walter Sinnott-Armstrong (Cambridge, MA: MIT Press, 2008), esp. 252–3.

65 I do not take this to tell against end-relational relativistic views but more simple constructivist-type relativism. I think, as cited above, end-relational theories, particularly Stephen Finlay's, capture the semantic level of the complicated nature of moral discourse strikingly well, if not exactly spot on. The part where we disagree, as discussed briefly below, is whether or not there are indeed correct moral ends, cognitively rendered, for questions of what agents and societies ought to do.

66 Again, this is a bit of an overstatement against nuanced and complicated relativistic views. The claim is essentially Parfit's, even and especially against Gibbard and Mark Schroeder, but why I back off is that sophisticated relativist-type views are clear that there might be some moral code that is justified relative to every society. In that sense, and indeed if that is the case, then I am merely speaking differently; the type of thing that would be justified relative to every society is what I would call a moral truth, discussed more in the next section.

67 *Assessing Initiatives to Increase Organ Donations: Hearing before the House Committee on Energy and Commerce, Subcommittee on Oversight and Investigation.* 108th Cong. (2003), 71.

68 To be clear, one might read Sade's response differently, in that there is a distinction between a categorical moral realism and *imposing* a categorical moral realism. And in fact, the distinction might be exactly one that a good divine-command theorist who is also a good liberal-democratic citizen might subscribe to. The problem here, however, is that at least in the United States, that is *not* how US liberal democracy works *in practice*, as argued for in chapter 5 extensively. That is, murder is wrong, and against the law, and the United States has no problem imposing that belief on any citizen who doesn't share it. So something doesn't seem to quite add up in this supposed disarticulation. However, at a minimum, the refusal to impose categorical morality *seems* to indicate that, in the case of organ procurement, one is not dealing with the same degree or seriousness of moral code as murder; suffice to acknowledge the substantive tensions between public policy/governing relativism and moral relativism.

69 The quote is from *Fear of Knowledge* (New York: Oxford University Press, 2007), 2. The "mutually incompatible" part is not from the book but is important in that differences are not necessarily and always incompatible. The addition is made in his "Précis of *Fear of Knowledge*," *Philosophical Studies* 141, no. 3 (2008): 377–8.

70 Boghossian, *Fear*, esp. 15–24, 112–15.

71 Ancient Greeks believed in a flat earth, and rather than basing that belief on mere intuition or some divinely revealed truth, they based it precisely on evidence (lack of curvature, etc.). But Aristotle and his evidence and reasoning (on lunar eclipses, shadows, etc.) revealed otherwise, and significantly more evidence (photos from space, etc.) confirms that the earth is indeed not flat. The point is that there is *not*

       a difference between flat-earth conclusion and round-earth conclusion in terms of
       reasoning; both are examples of *evidence-based* reasoning, and both (pre-Aristotelians
       and post-Aristotelians) were *justified* in holding their beliefs. Yet it would be perverse
       to say that they are both *true.*

72 Boghossian, *Fear*, 116.

73 There is good reason to reject the type of relativism I've discussed here. Again, the
       more subtle end-relational or standards-based relativism type, if the theories hold for
       the possibility of a moral act or code being wrong across all societies or standards,
       would not be dismissed in this same way. While this is a footnote, the matter is impor-
       tant insofar as indexical-type theories that treat moral terms like *good* as akin to *tall*
       show, correctly, that the salient ends (good for what; taller than what?) are pragmati-
       cally picked out by the context in a type of conversational implicature. I buy this story.
       There is an additional step that I hold: there might be things that are good, or tall,
       across any and all standards. I'll call this the *Yao Ming Argument.* The statement "Ryan
       Gillespie is tall" would be semantically incomplete in such views, needing something
       such as tall *for* an average US adult male, or for an average adult male across the
       globe, or whatever. This matters because I am *not* tall for a basketball player, nor for
       a host of other classes of things. But when we say, "Yao Ming is tall," we can generate
       any number of classes – for a Chinese person, for a basketball player, for a human,
       etc. – and he is tall compared to any and all of them. Now I grant that there is still
       conversational implicature here, for the sentence *is* semantically incomplete – he is
       tall *for a human but short for a mountain*, for example. And that such an example seems
       silly is precisely to underscore the power of implicature.

74 The idea here is that, as discussed in the Yao Ming example, some things hold across
       any number of contexts and situations, whereas others do not. That some societies
       are tolerant of gay relations and others are not seems to be, regardless of how one
       feels about the matter, of a different order than societies that are tolerant of non-con-
       sensual sex, period, and those that are not, for example.

75 The only alternative, as I see it, is that morality is a *useful* fiction or a *necessary* illusion
       in practical human life and society. I think this view is mistaken, of course, but cannot
       fully argue against it here.

76 As the chapter continues, it will be clear that I reject his distinction of *real* and *appar-
       ent* reasons. Desires and false beliefs both provide *reasons* to be weighed in moral
       deliberations. The idea is that deliberators are looking for the reasons with the most
       weight, a feature that many desires do not have and something that no false beliefs
       have. This is a sort of ecumenical view of reasons, in which, in practical deliberations,
       what does and doesn't count as a reason is almost irrelevant; what matters is what the
       good reasons are and how they stack up against each other. Normative force will be
       used often and it is (almost necessarily?) quasi-mysterious.

77 See Parfit, *Matters Vol. 1*, 35.

78 On a view like Parfit's, normative force is not reducible to natural facts and hence nor-
       mativity in general is non-natural. A compelling objection is that normative force comes
       from a combination of desires and natural facts under a naturalistic theory. As I'm using
       the term, naturalism is a form of cognitive moral realism in that it holds moral truths as
       part of reality, but that these moral truths are reducible to non-moral facts. The reduc-
       tion is really the key here, given that it is possible to say *natural* and by that mean *consist-
       ent with reality* or something like that, in which nonmaterialist/nonphysicalist ontologies
       are not empirical but still a part of reality and hence *natural* in some sense.

79 To naturalists, once one has reported the relevant descriptive facts, as Frank Jackson
       says, "There is nothing more 'there.'" In David Copp's words, "When a naturalist

hears us say that something is right or wrong, just or unjust, she takes the truth of what we say to depend on whether the relevant thing has the relevant property, and she takes this to depend in turn exclusively on the way things are in the natural world." So in the case of Q1, the issue is that selling human organs is wrong if indeed *selling human organs* has the property of moral wrongness (or is absent the property of moral rightness). This property, however, is a natural property, not some non-natural or existing in a Platonic realm and hence "metaphysically queer" property, to use Mackie's language. On this, then, the moral inquirer's job is reductive: that is, it is not simply to redescribe moral facts into natural, empirical ones but that moral facts are reducible to natural facts. Non-naturalists hold that moral facts cannot be reducible to natural facts, with one significant motivation being Moore's Open Question Argument, in which a report of all the relevant natural facts can still intelligibly yield a response from an interlocutor that runs, "Yes, I see that. But still, is the act *wrong?*" A recent take on the latter is found in Matthew S. Bedke, "Against Normative Naturalism," *Australasian Journal of Philosophy* 90, no. 1 (2011): 111–29. For the above quotes, see Frank Jackson, *From Metaphysics to Ethics* (New York: Oxford University Press, 1998), 124; Mackie, *Ethics*, esp. 38–42.

80 Monir Moniruzamman, "'Living Cadavers' in Bangladesh: Bioviolence in the Human Organ Bazaar," *Medical Anthropology Quarterly* 26, no. 1 (2012): 69–91. Cf. Scheper-Hughes, "Bodies,"; "Commodity,"; "Mr. Tati."

81 The parallel here is Lewis Carroll's case for principles or rules being unable to count as further premises in arguments, ending in infinite regress: when the Tortoise wonders whether he must indeed accept a conclusion given certain premises, Achilles responds by saying, Yes, of course you must. As the famous exchange goes, "'Suppose I still refused to accept ... ' offers the Tortoise. 'Then Logic would take you by the throat, and *force* you to do it!' Achilles triumphantly replied." Lewis Carroll, "What the Tortoise Said to Achilles," *Mind* 104, no. 416 (1995): 692–3.

82 Mark Schroeder, *Slaves*, 34.

83 This is fundamental, answering the question of where reasons come from, and it is seen most clearly in other views of moral cognitivism. For example, the most promising conceptual analysis of normative terms is that offered by Stephen Finlay's end-relational theory. In his view, normative terms are relativized to ends, pragmatically picked out by the context of the conversation. Moral disagreement then is often a matter of conflicting ends. This strikes me as wholly plausible, if not actually correct; where his view and mine part company is on whether there are *right* ends or not, and subsequently, then, on how to weigh them. That is, both views share the end-relational theory, but in a broad stroke, mine is Socratic to his Humean. I discuss and implement his theory in my "The Art." His end-relational theory is seen in several papers: "What Ought Probably Means, and Why You Can't Detach It," *Synthese*, 177, no. 1 (2010): 67–89; "Oughts,"; "Reasons That Matter." The fuller statement is his *Confusion of Tongues: A Theory of Normative Language* (New York: Oxford University Press, 2014).

84 Finlay, "Reasons," 16.

85 Finlay, "Reasons," 17.

86 Boghossian, *Fear*, 110.

87 The quote is from Parfit, *Matters, Vol. 2*, 363. The metaphor is how he concludes Vol. 1, saying, "It has been widely believed that there are such deep disagreements between Kantians, Contractualists, and Consequentialists. That, I have argued, is not true. These people are climbing the same mountain on different sides." *Matters, Vol. 1*, 419. Putting all three of them together is his Triple Theory, all under the

banner of non-natural, non-reductive, value-based objective normative realism. The metaphor forms Peter Singer's front-page *Times Literary Supplement* review of the book when it was released as well. See Peter Singer, "One Mountain," *Times Literary Supplement*, 20 May 2011, 3–4.

88　Ethical disagreement as explained by differences in conductive reasoning, the conclusion I've just offered, was suggested by Carl Wellman in 1975. His conclusion is worth quoting at some length:

> Our disagreement on ethical principles, fundamental as it is, does not prove that we lack the premises required to rationally justify our ethical conclusions because the ultimate reasons for our ethical conclusions are not ethical principles but factual statements and the experiences on which our factual knowledge is grounded. Our disagreement on ethical reasoning, especially on the validity of conductive inferences from factual descriptions of individual objects and acts to judgments of value or obligation of them, does not show that our ethical conclusions cannot be justified by objective reasoning because it remains possible that the critical community can come to agree on the validity of ethical arguments by continuing the process of rational criticism indefinitely in time.

The contractualist element rings out in the "critical community" line, sounding very much like what Habermas discusses as intersubjective norm-constitution processes. See his "Ethical Disagreement and Objective Truth," *American Philosophical Quarterly* 12, no. 3 (1975): 220.

7. Weighing Reasons: Telic Orientation, Rhetorical Force, and Normative Force

1　This doesn't seem inconsistent with a view such as Mark Schroeder's that also endorses distinctions of acting for good reasons. For example, in responding to Jonathan Dancy's objection, and using Bernard Williams's famous gin-and-tonic case, he distinguishes between *beliefs about* and the actual *content* of *belief*. The initial worry was that Bernie takes a sip from his glass because he *believed* it contained gin and tonic rather than the content of that belief (that it *does* or *doesn't*). As he says, "Like Dancy, in the book and in other work I have consistently identified motivating reasons with the contents of beliefs which play a role in motivation, and for the same reasons as he does – in order to make sense of how agents can act for good reasons." Mark Schroeder, "Reply to Shafer-Landau, Mcpherson, and Dancy," *Philosophical Studies* 157, no. 3 (2012): 464.

2　My argument so far is meant to be consistent with rational and desire-based views of normativity. For example, in desire-based views, what counts in favour of some act is that it fulfils my desire, and opponents worry that this leads to strange conclusions and mistaken applications of the concept of *reason*, like a person with a weird desire to eat their car then having a *reason* to eat their car. For Parfit, the desire-based view, stemming from Hume, is not only silly, but is "much of what went wrong in the moral philosophy of the mid twentieth century." One might have *a* reason to eat one's car in a Humean picture, but under such a picture few believe that to be a *good* or *overriding* reason, and so the picture isn't exactly as silly as Parfit makes it out to be. Parfit, *Matters Vol. 2*, 373.

3　There is a distinction between weighing reasons, which is a psychological process, and the weight of reasons, in which some reasons are *heavier* than others on the Big Objective Scale. That is, further discussion is required on whether reasons have a weight *outside* of the people weighing them or whether reasoners assign weights as they see fit. I can't go into this here, but I believe that context matters in the weighing of reasons. For example, that a car is expensive is a reason for a poor person not to get it; but is that a reason for a rich person not to get it, given that expensive is a relative term? Details like that matter, in which reasons end up being *close* to diet – at one level, it is very subjective, because people are different sizes and have different capabilities. But in another sense there are reasons that transcend these sort of local details, that have a (relatively fixed) weight regardless of context and situation. The objection that disagreement can and does still exist on such matters (i.e., non-consensual sex) is explained by the fact that some people's scales, so to speak, are broken.

4 Cf. Samuel Fleischacker on *telic arena* in his *Divine Teaching and the Way of the World* (New York: Oxford University Press, 2011).

5 Allan Gibbard, *Wise Choices, Apt Feelings: A Theory of Normative Judgment* (Cambridge, MA: Harvard University Press, 1990), 100.

6 Gibbard, *Wise*, 72–3.

7 Gibbard, *Wise*, 102.

8 Kant, *Ethical Philosophy*, trans. James W. Ellington (Indianapolis: Hackett Publishing Company, 1994), 16.

9 There is a distinction to be made here between inclinations and desires. Kant wants to take the step of reason commanding inclinations and desires. I side with him on inclinations and am agnostic about desires. I think it is conceivable that desire is that which structures human agency, and that reasoning must spring forth from a desire to be rational, or something along those lines.

10 My target here is views that think it is wrong to assert one's will over and above rationality, for I deny that there is such a kind of rationality. The target view is expressed, for example, by Nagel, when he writes that philosophy "must produce or destroy belief, rather than merely provide us with a consistent set of things to say. And belief, unlike utterance, should not be under the control of the will, however motivated. It should be involuntary." Thomas Nagel, *Mortal Questions* (Cambridge: Cambridge University Press, 1979), xi.

11 Following the quote on rational necessity, his words are, "There is, I believe, no normativity here." Derek Parfit, *On What Matters, Vol. 2* (New York: Oxford University Press, 2011), 291. The idea that such might be normative for something such as angels, in the sense that they are perfect agents who respond to logical and normative necessity in a way that imperfect agents such as humans do not, is beyond my ability to say. For speculation sake, though, I think that angels respond to normativity and necessity the way that humans do given that they are also endowed with free will. But I'm not prepared to defend that.

12 If it is not clear, *faith* and *conviction* are used interchangeably, and thereby nothing necessarily religious is meant by invocation of the former. The idea is to translate *pistis* – which is traditionally translated in Aristotle with *proof*, but has the connotation of faith in the sense of *trust in*. The point is that this is something more than mere opinion (doxa) but not certainty or knowledge (episteme). A brief explication of this *naturalizing faith*, so to speak, as juxtaposed with religious faith, is found in my "Uses" and "Reason" articles. Similar usage exists in Stanley Fish's chapter "Faith Before Reason," in his *The Trouble with Principle* (Cambridge, MA: Harvard University Press, 1999), 263–75; and in Annette Baier, "Secular Faith," *Canadian Journal of Philosophy* 10, no. 1 (1980): 131–48.

13 The clearest discussion to support this is found in (144a6–35). Most particularly,

> In order to be good one must be in a certain state when one does the several acts, i.e. one must do them as a result of choice and for the sake of the acts

themselves. Now excellence makes the choice right, but the question of the things which should naturally be done to carry out our choice belongs not to excellence but to another faculty … called cleverness … Now if the mark be noble, the cleverness is laudable, but if the mark be bad, the cleverness is mere villainy; hence we call clever both men of practical wisdom and villains. Aristotle, *Nicomachean Ethics*, 1807.

14 *Rhetorical force* here means the degree to which it will secure interlocutor adherence. Richard Weaver's use of rhetorical force as attached to ultimate terms is similar to what I have in mind. For example, ultimate terms (which in his era of the 1950s were things like *progress* or *science*) – God-terms that forced other terms and concepts into subservience and were significantly likely to secure adherence if they could be attached to the argument being presented – are the source from which power flows. In his words, "Rhetorical force … is power transmitted through the links of a chain that extends upwards to some ultimate source." He seems to mean *concepts* as opposed to terms, but otherwise his analysis is highly relevant to the present effort. See Weaver, *The Ethics of Rhetoric* (Davis, CA: Hermogoras Press/Routledge, 1953/1985), 211.

15 Frank Jackson, *From Metaphysics to Ethics* (New York: Oxford University Press, 1998), 127.

16 At one level, pointing out that an act has a property of wrongness *just is* the act of point out that it is wrong. In such a picture, this is precisely the kind of thing that does, or ought to, change someone's mind about the act. But my point here is about the rhetorical force of pointing out abstract properties in ethical debates. That is, some disagreements can be settled quite simply by one party saying, "But you shouldn't do that because it is ethically wrong." But in debates about whether or not the act in question *is* wrong, a simple claim of or appeal to properties will lack rhetorical force – amounting instead to a form of foot stamping.

17 Stephen Finlay, "The Reasons That Matter," *Australasian Journal of Philosophy* 84, no. 1 (2006): 17.

18 David Copp, *Morality, Normativity, and Society* (New York: Oxford University Press, 1995), 222–3, emphasis added.

19 This is on par with the emphasis on moral judgment and moral complexity in the tradition of virtue ethics. An excellent characterization of this point is offered by Russ Shafer-Landau:

> Virtue ethicists sometimes invite us to appreciate the complexity of morality by having us imagine a moral rule book. The book would contain all the true rules of ethics, and all of the precise methods for applying them. It would state when exceptions were called for and when they were forbidden. It could be applied in a mechanical way, without any need of judgment.

No such book, virtue ethicists claim, could ever exist. See Russ Shafer-Landau, *The Fundamentals of Ethics*, 2nd ed. (New York: Oxford University Press, 2012), 255.

20 Ralph Wedgwood, "The Moral Evil Demons," in *Disagreement*, ed. Richard Feldman and Ted A. Warfield (New York: Oxford University Press, 2010) 244.

21 I take this to be, in one sense, *the* important conclusion to my argument. But in another sense, it is largely the goal of moral matters in the Aristotelian tradition, in which we feel our moral emotions "at the right times, with reference to the right objects, towards the right people, with the right aim, and in the right way." See Aristotle, *Nicomachean* (II.6.1106b.20), 1747.

What's offered is a way of making sense of that claim and the interrelationship between discursive rationality and desire-based normativity as affect backed, as well as to accommodate for *changes* to communal norms based on *reason* and not just preference or desire. This is to accommodate a critique made by Bernard Williams: Aristotelian approaches give "an account of moral development in terms of habituation and internalization that leaves little room for practical reason to alter radically the objectives that a grown-up person has acquired." See his *Ethics and the Limits of Philosophy* (Cambridge, MA: Harvard University Press, 1985), 38.

22 But it might be some evidence against it. Dworkin makes a point similar: "It would tell against my view that I could not convince you of it, but I would not count this as a refutation." Ronald Dworkin, "Objectivity and Truth: You'd Better Believe It," *Philosophy & Public Affairs* 25, no. 2 (1996): 133.

23 Gibbard, *Wise*, 235–50.

24 Intersubjective here means collectively determined and collectively binding rules, laws, and norms.

25 This is loosely based on Parfit, *Matters, Vol. 2*, 266–8.

26 The quote is from Jürgen Habermas, *Between Naturalism and Religion*, trans. Ciaran Cronin (Malden: Polity, 2008), 143; the contractualist picture is one shared by nearly all deliberative democratic scholars.

8. The Scope of the Market: Exploitation, Coercion, Paternalism, and Legal Consistency

1 Nancy Scheper-Hughes, "Commodity Fetishism in Organ Trafficking," *Body & Society* 7, nos. 2–3 (2001): 31.

2 Steve Farber and Harlan Abrahams, *On the List: Fixing America's Failing Organ Transplant System* (New York: Rodale, 2009), 51.

3 This is why a Marxian framework (property is theft) is at least internally coherent in a way that many armchair liberal theories are not.

4 Jeffrey Goldberg, "Involuntary Servitude: A Property-Based Notion of Abortion-Choice," *UCLA Law Review* 38, no. 6 (1991): 1657.

5 For example, Roy Hardiman, "Toward the Right of Commerciality: Recognizing Property Rights in the Value of Human Tissue," *UCLA Law Review* 34, no. 1 (1986): 207–64; Danielle M. Wagner, "Property Rights in the Human Body: The Commercialization of Organ Transplantation and Biotechnology," *Duquesne Law Review* 33, no. 4 (1995): 931–58.

6 Judith Jarvis Thomson, "A Defense of Abortion," *Philosophy & Public Affairs*, 1, no. 1 (1971): 48–9.

7 Following Ronald Dworkin's claim that there is good reason to draw a line around the body as inviolate for social resources, Satz says that "there is something to this line of thought, and indeed that a horror at the thought of the conscription of our bodies by others may lie behind the repugnance people feel toward kidney markets." Debra Satz, *Why Some Things Should Not Be for Sale: The Moral Limits of Markets* (New York: Oxford University Press, 2010), 201.

8 Furthermore, it is necessary to note that there is a significant distinction in terms of moral gravity in the abortion–organ sales cases, and the weight pulls much more heavily in the case of abortion over organ sales. In one instance, we are weighing a person's right to property and bodily self against the possible exploitation and coercion of vulnerable social members, and in the other, we are weighing bodily property rights against the possible elimination of a human life. To make the cases symmetrical in terms of gravity, the organ procurement issue would not involve selling organs but asking whether or not taking an organ was akin to killing a person. But that latter part is not entirely pertinent to the case of organ sales, showing more the gravity of the abortion debate – even if that is the one that is legally settled.

9 Margaret Jane Radin, "Market Inalienability," *Harvard Law Review* 100, no. 8 (1987): 1849–937.

10 Radin, "Market Inalienability," 1855, esp. fn 23.

11 Radin, "Market Inalienability," 1904.

12 The main arguments are found Satz, *Why Some Things*, 91–112.

13 Satz, *Why*, 98.

14 Satz, *Why*, 98.

15 Some noxious markets might be rejected by otherwise universal commodificationists on a Millian harm principle. The harm element is discussed explicitly by Epstein in several places (e.g., *Principles for a Free Society: Reconciling Individual Liberty with the Common Good* [Cambridge, MA: Basic Books, 1998], 71–104), while sometimes Posner discusses everything as commodifiable weighed against simply the cost of implementing the system. There is always the problem under these types of views of voluntary slavery as well. For baby selling, see Richard Epstein, *Mortal Peril* (New York: Addison-Wesley Publishing, 1997); Elisabeth Landes and Richard Posner, "The Economics of the Baby Shortage," *Journal of Legal Studies* 7 (1978): 323–48.

16 For some of Aristotle's discussions on different kinds of justice (natural, political, distributive, commutative), see *Nicomachean Ethics*, Book V.

17 Gerald Dworkin, *Morality, Harm, and the Law* (Boulder, CO: Westview Press, 1994), 156.

18 Recall that this was done by explicitly saying that NOTA does not extend to bone marrow (by defining marrow as not an "organ"). See "Bone Marrow Donors Can Be Compensated, Appeals Court Rules," *Los Angeles Times*, 1 December 2011. http://latimesblogs.latimes.com/lanow/2011/12/bone-marrow-donors-can-be-compensated-appeals-court-rules.html.

19 *Assessing Initiatives to Increase Organ Donations: Hearing before the House Committee on Energy and Commerce, Subcommittee on Oversight and Investigation*, 108th Cong. (2003), 69.

20 Michele Goodwin, "Altruism's Limits: Law, Capacity, and Organ Commodification," *Rutgers Law Review* 56, no. 2 (2004): 389.

21 Goodwin, "Altruism," 386–7.

22 Wagner, 958.

23 Satz, *Why*, 167.

24 Satz, *Why*, 169.

25 Satz, *Why*, 153; on degradation in this context, see 142–3.

26 Satz, *Why*, 93.

27 John Lawrence Hill, "Exploitation," *Cornell Law Review* 79, no. 3 (1993–4): 699.

28 *Assessing*, 64.

29 Benjamin Hippen, "Pro: Saving Lives Is More Important Than Abstract Moral Concerns: Financial Incentives Should Be Used to Increase Organ Donation," *Annals of Thoracic Surgery* 88, no. 4 (2009): 1055.

30 L.D. de Castro, "Commodification and Exploitation: Arguments in Favour of Compensated Organ Donation," *Journal of Medical Ethics* 29, no. 3 (2003): 146.

31 As I write this amid the COVID-19 pandemic, price gouging on everything from hand santizer to face masks to Costco pizza runs rampant.

32 There are a number of complicated issues at work here that would take me too far afield from organ procurement. A good discussion of exploitation and law can be found Hill, "Exploitation," 631–99.

33 *Assessing*, 4.

34 de Castro, "Commodification," 145.

35   Mark J. Cherry, *Kidney for Sale by Owner: Human Organs, Transplantation, and the Market* (Washington, DC: Georgetown University Press, 2005), 89.

36   Goodwin, "Altruism," 329.

37   While he does not make claims regarding labour and exploitation, Paul Hughes thinks that a Marxian-derived notion of exploitation is precisely the way to defend against what he perceives are moral derelictions stemming from market encroachment. See Paul Hughes, "Exploitation, Autonomy, and Organ Sales," *International Journal of Applied Philosophy*, 12, no. 1 (1998): 89–95.

38   Cherry, *Kidney*, 91.

39   Sally Satel, "Death's Waiting List," *New York Times*, 15 May 2006, http://www.nytimes .com/2006/05/15/opinion/15satel.html.

40   Monir Moniruzamman, "'Living Cadavers' in Bangladesh: Bioviolence in the Human Organ Bazaar," *Medical Anthropology Quarterly* 26, no. 1 (2012): 69; Sallie Yea, "Trafficking in Part(s): The Commercial Kidney Market in a Manila Slum, Philippines," *Global Social Policy* 10, no. 3 (2010): 358.

41   Cherry, *Kidney*, 158.

42   Cherry, *Kidney*, 151.

43   This is meant to be a straightforward case given only this information. Exploitation has much to do with background conditions, of course, and revelation along those lines could make a claim of exploitation here intelligible. For example, if the son couldn't read and had no understanding of the value of money, he might claim that the father exploited this to his advantage (by having to shell out only $15 instead of $20). Even then, the gift/giving was still voluntary and so exploitation doesn't seem to apply, really. Maybe if it had been a contract the father had gotten the two kids to sign or something to that effect.

44   Oft-used in conversations about morality under conditions of ethical pluralism, the story of the Tower of Babel is found in Genesis 11. It tells of a time when the whole earth spoke one language, and through the coordination that this provided, people decided to build a tower that reached to Heaven. God disapproved of the act, and says, "Let us go down, and there confound their language, that they may not understand one another's speech." (Gen. 11:6, KJV). Toulmin uses the image when discussing the proposal for bioethical standards for human-subjects research: "Before the Commission began work, many onlookers assumed that its discussions would degenerate into a Babel of rival opinions." Stephen Toulmin, "The Tyranny of Principle," *Hastings Center Report* 11(1981): 31. Cf. Stephen Finlay's *Confusion of Tongues: A Theory of Normative Language* (New York: Oxford University Press, 2014); Cf. Jeffery Stout, *Ethics after Babel* (Boston: Beacon Press, 1988).

45   Cherry, *Kidney*, 159.

9. What Money Cannot Buy and What Money Ought Not Buy: Dignity, Motives, and Markets

1   Portions of this chapter were published as Ryan Gillespie, "What Money Cannot Buy and What Money Ought Not Buy: Dignity, Motives, and Markets in Human Organ Procurement Debates," *Journal of Medical Humanities*: DOI: 10.1007/ s10912-016-9427-z.

2   For example: Arthur L. Caplan, *If I Were a Rich Man, Could I Buy a Pancreas? And Other Essays on the Ethics of Health Care* (Bloomington: Indiana University Press, 1992); Alexander Capron and Gabriel Danovitch, "We Shouldn't Treat Kidneys as Commodities," *Los Angeles Times*, 30 June 2014; Delmonico, Arnold, Scheper-Hughes,

et al., "Ethical Incentives – Not Payment – for Organ Donation," *New England Journal of Medicine* 346, no. 25 (2002): 2002–5; Jeffrey Prottas, *The Most Useful Gift: Altruism and the Public Policy of Organ Transplants* (San Francisco: Jossey-Bass Publishers, 1994); Margaret Jane Radin, "Market Inalienability," *Harvard Law Review* 100 (1987): 1849–1937; Debra Satz, *Why Some Things Should Not Be for Sale: The Moral Limits of Markets* (New York: Oxford University Press, 2010).

3   A sampling: Mark J. Cherry, *Kidney for Sale by Owner: Human Organs, Transplantation, and the Market* (Washington, DC: Georgetown University Press, 2005); L.D. de Castro, "Commodification and Exploitation: Arguments in Favour of Compensated Organ Donation," *Journal of Medical Ethics* 29, no. 3 (2003): 142–6; Satel, *When Altruism Isn't Enough* (Washington, DC: The American Enterprise Institute Press, 2008). Congressional hearings on the subject of compensation for organs have occurred as well, including NOTA 1983; NOTA 1984; *Assessing Initiatives to Increase Organ Donations: Hearing before the House Committee on Energy and Commerce, Subcommittee on Oversight and Investigation,* 108th Cong. 1 (2003). See also Michele Goodwin, ed., *The Global Body Market: Altruism's Limits* (Cambridge: Cambridge University Press, 2015).

4   The National Organ Transplant Act (NOTA) in 1984, in addition to creating the Organ Procurement and Transplant Network (OPTN), explicitly created a prohibition of organ sales under Section 301(a): "It shall be unlawful for any person to knowingly acquire, receive, or otherwise transfer any human organ for valuable consideration for use in human transplantation if the transfer affects interstate commerce" (NOTA 1984). On the growing demand, see Barbara Mantel "Organ Donations: Can the Growing Demand Be Met?" *CQ Researcher,* 21, no. 15 (2011): 346–50.

5   For example, Pinker writes, "Of course, institutional affiliation does not entail partiality, but, with three-quarters of the invited contributors having religious entanglements, one gets a sense that the fix is in. A deeper look confirms it." The fix, it seems, is religiously motivated and/or grounded views of public policy and human social relations. Steve Pinker, "The Stupidity of Dignity," *The New Republic,* 28 May 2008. Cf. Ruth Macklin, "Human Dignity Is a Useless Concept," *British Medical Journal* 327 (2003): 1419–20.

6   Cf. an overview at James F. Childress, *Practical Reasoning in Bioethics* (Bloomington: Indiana University Press, 1997), 282–300.

7   This is meant to be applicable to those who hold the essentiality for religious or non-religious reasons alike, and as a (potential) ground for the extension of rights (e.g., the Basic Law of Germany) and/or the essential *thing* that rights defend (e.g., the Geneva Convention). For discussion of this seeming duality of dignity and rights – that human dignity is both the grounds for and the subject of human rights – see Jeremy Waldron, *Dignity, Rank, and Rights* (New York: Oxford University Press, 2015), esp. 16–19.

8   Arthur Schopenhauer, *On the Basis of Morality,* trans. by E.F.J. Payne (Indianapolis, IN: Hackett Publishing Company, 1995), 100.

9   The statement of this is found in several places in Genesis (e.g., 1:27–8; 5:1–3; 9:6). The notion of *imago Dei* as part of what makes humans beyond animals is made by Thomas Aquinas (in *ST,* 1.Q3), who argues particularly that it is in reason and the intellect that we are *imago Dei*: "Man is said to be after the image of God, not as regards his body, but as regards that whereby he excels other animals ... Now man excels all animals by his reasoning and intelligence; hence it is according to his intelligence and reason, that are incorporeal, that man is said to be according to the image of God."

10   A passage from *Grounding* (§434) is often quoted: "In the kingdom of ends everything
     has either a price or a dignity. Whatever has a price can be replaced by something
     else as its equivalent; on the other hand, whatever is above all price, and therefore
     admits of no equivalent, has a dignity." See Immanuel Kant, *Ethical Philosophy*, trans.
     James W. Ellington (Indianapolis: Hackett Publishing Company, 1994), 40.

11   Michael Rosen, *Dignity: Its History and Meaning* (Cambridge, MA: Harvard University
     Press, 2012).

12   Leon Kass, "Death with Dignity and the Sanctity of Life," in *A Time to Be Born and a
     Time to Die*, ed. B.S. Kogan (New York: Aldine de Gruyter, 1991), 127.

13   Rosen, *Dignity*, 159, 156.

14   Daniel Dennett, "How to Protect Human Dignity from Science," in *Human Dignity
     Human Dignity: The President's Council on Bioethics, 2008*, 39–59: https://bioethicsarchive
     .georgetown.edu/pcbe/reports/human_dignity/index.html.

15   In addition to Waldron, *Dignity*, see Stéphanie Hennette-Vauchez, "Human Dignitas?
     Remnants of the Ancient Legal Concept in Contemporary Dignity Jurisprudence,"
     International Journal of Constitutional Law 9, no. 1 (2011):32–57. These arguments of
     dignity as rank, as inherent status, are derived from the class-based hierarchies of
     either (or both) Rome or Victorian England, and democracy grants us all from birth
     the inherent status of kings, so to speak, or the inherent status of humanity in general
     as more than animal, as explicated, perhaps most famously, in Cicero's *De Officiis* (e.g.
     I, 30).

16   Jürgen Habermas, "The Concept of Human Dignity and the Realistic Utopia of
     Human Rights," *Metaphilosophy* 41, no. 4 (2010): 469.

17   The opening of Germany's Constitution (*Basic Law*, 1.1.) runs, "Human dignity shall
     be inviolable. To respect and protect it shall be the duty of all state authority."

18   NOTA 1984, 26.

19   *Assessing*, 66.

20   Cynthia B. Cohen, "Selling Bits and Pieces of Humans to Make Babies," *Journal of
     Medicine & Philosophy*, 24 (1999): 292–3.

21   *Assessing*, 82.

22   For example, Sally Satel, "Death's Waiting List," *New York Times*, 15 May 2006, http://
     www.nytimes.com/2006/05/15/opinion/15satel.html; "Altruism + Incentive = More
     Organ Donation," *The Times* [online], 11 June 2010, https://www.aei.org/publication
     /altruism-incentive-more-organ-donations/. Cherry makes some interesting moves in
     regard to dignity in *Kidney for Sale*, esp. 36–40, 91–102, 113–46.

23   Satel, "Concerns about Human Dignity and Commodification," in *When Altruism Isn't
     Enough*, ed. Sally Satel (Washington, DC: The American Enterprise Institute Press,
     2008), 64.

24   Viviana Zelizer, *Morals and Markets: The Development of Life Insurance in the United States*
     (New York: Columbia University Press, 1978).

25   Alvin E. Roth, "Repugnance as a Constraint on Markets," *Journal Economic Perspectives*,
     21, no. 3 (2007): 38.

26   Adam Smith, *The Essential Adam Smith* (New York: Norton, 1986), 214.

27   Martha Nussbaum, "'Whether from Reason or Prejudice': Taking Money for Bodily
     Service," *Journal of Legal Studies* 27, no. 2 (1998): 693. This type of discussion still per-
     sists in certain artistic circles that think the concept of *selling out* means receiving pay-
     ment for one's work. These tend to be Marxist-flavoured or those who seem to either
     misunderstand the nature of art or forget that some of the greatest art in the history
     of the world (e.g., Michelangelo's Sistine Chapel Frescos, Da Vinci's *Mona Lisa*, or
     Beethoven's *Ninth*) were commissioned.

28 Satel, "Concerns about Human Dignity," 68.
29 Peter Singer, "Altruism and Commerce: A Defense of Titmuss against Arrow."
     Philosophy & Public Affairs 2, no. 3 (1973): 316.
30 Satel, "Concerns about Human Dignity," 69.
31 Michael Sandel, "What Money Can't Buy: The Moral Limits of Markets," *The Tanner Lectures on Human Values* (Oxford: Brasenose College, 11–12 May 1998): https://tannerlectures.utah.edu/_documents/a-to-z/s/sandel00.pdf, 89. Cf. his *What Money Can't Buy: The Moral Limits of Markets* (New York: Farrar, Straus, Giroux, 2012).
32 Satel, "Concerns about Human Dignity," 68.
33 Uri Gneezy and Aldo Rustichini, "A Fine Is a Price," *Journal of Legal Studies* 29, no. 1 (2000): 1–17; Bruno S. Frey and Felix Oberholzer-Gee, "The Cost of Price Incentives: An Empirical Analysis of Motivation Crowding Out," *The American Economic Review* 87, no. 4 (1997): 746–55.
34 Satel, "Concerns about Human Dignity," 75.
35 Childress, *Practical*, 295, 300.
36 Satel, "Concerns about Human Dignity," 72.
37 Satel, "Concerns about Human Dignity," 75, 77.
38 Satel, "Concerns about Human Dignity," 76.
39 This mentality, this attitude of "you should be willing to do it for free," is one that is ripe for exploitation, as Goodwin and Cherry in particular argue. It is an exploitation seen readily in the contemporary music business, in which the claim that "you should want to do this for free because that's what real artists do, so therefore give away your music," is used to exploit and/or guilt-trip artists away from charging or receiving payment. Meanwhile companies profit, sometimes significantly, from the playing or hosting of the music.
40 Satel, "Concerns about Human Dignity," 70.
41 The connection between moral responsibility and political economy under global capitalism is becoming much more prevalent in general, with strident critiques of *homo economicus* abounding. For a recent discussion, particularly adding the potentialities of religion, see Christina McRorie, "Rethinking Moral Agency in Markets: A Book Discussion on Behavioral Economics," *Journal of Religious Ethics* 44, no. 1 (2016): 195–226.
42 This example is extrapolated and expanded from Cherry, *Kidneys for Sale*, 125.
43 Cherry, *Kidneys for Sale*, 125.
44 Though dignity is not removed, it might be diminished by the presence of money, insofar as "diminished" means not acting in a way as to accurately reflect and promote human dignity, a point that will be made subsequently in the main text.
45 Satel, "Concerns about Human Dignity," 71.
46 Hennette-Vauchez, "Human Dignitas," 51–2.
47 Most notably Richard Epstein, and famous discussions of baby selling. Sometimes universal commodificationists talk of rejecting violations of liberal harm principles, while other times everything is seen as potentially commodifiable, weighed against the cost of implementing the system. See Richard Epstein, *Principles for a Free Society* (Cambridge, MA: Basic Books, 1998). On baby selling, see Elisabeth Landes and Richard Posner, "The Economics of the Baby Shortage," *Journal of Legal Studies* 7, no. 2 (1978): 323–48.
48 From the 1961 preface to his *Screwtape Letters*: "We must picture hell as a state where everyone is perpetually concerned about his own dignity and advancement and where everyone has a grievance." C.S. Lewis, *The Screwtape Letters: Annotated Edition* (New York: Harper Collins, 2013), xxxv.

49 The key turn is that autonomous agents (meant in a wide-scope, non-Kantian view of autonomy) have a right to legislate for themselves anything and everything, resulting in a sort of moral subjectivism. The universal commodificationist view, in one sense, is a flat rejection of dignity as inherent value or status or special rank, instead viewing dignity as reducible, simply, to autonomy. While this might be a valid view, to reiterate, I am most concerned with the role of nonreductive uses of dignity in organ procurement rhetoric, those arguers on the market and altruistic sides who both hold a view of dignity as more than autonomy.

50 Even Cole Porter invokes "truly" rhetoric to distinguish love-as-sex from true love in his song "Love for Sale," written/sung from the perspective of a prostitute: "If you want the thrill of love / I've been through the mill of love / old love / new love / every love but true love / love for sale."

51 Satel, "Concerns about Human Dignity," 71.

52 Satz, *Why Some Things*, 112.

53 Toulmin, "The Tyranny of Principle," *Hastings Center Report* 11, no. 6 (1981): 31.

54 Radin, "Market Inalienability," 1936.

55 Radin, "Market Inalienability," 1909–17; cf. Margret Jane Radin, "Justice and the Market Domain," in *Markets and Justice*, ed. John W. Chapman and J. Roland Pennock, 165–97 (New York: New York University Press, 1989).

56 The centrality of autonomy is often a significant motivation for universal commodificationists. But the pragmatic philosophical question about the coercive use of power in a democracy is about legitimate vs. illegitimate uses of coercive power, not that coercive power *per se* in a democracy is illegal or immoral, even if coercive power *per se* seems to violate the standard of liberal democracy itself, thus resulting in a paradox of liberal democracy (with many works in democratic political philosophy aiming to clarify and/or answer that paradox).

57 Joel Feinberg, "The Mistreatment of Dead Bodies," *The Hastings Center Report* 15, no. 1 (1985): 36, 37.

58 Sarah Banet-Weiser, *Authentic TM: The Politics of Ambivalence in Brand Culture* (New York: New York University Press, 2012), esp. 51–90.

59 Rupal Parekh, "The New Buzzword in Marketing? Human," in *Advertising Age*, 20 September 2013: http://adage.com/article/cmo-strategy/brands-behave-humans/244261/.

Conclusion: What Kind of Policy for What Kind of Society?

1 Debra Satz, *Why Some Things Should Not Be For Sale: The Moral Limits of Markets* (New York: Oxford University Press, 2010), 112.

2 Emanuel, *Ends of Human Life: Medical Ethics in a Liberal Polity* (Cambridge, MA: Harvard University Press, 1991), 246.

3 I am sympathetic to this description of *market-tested betterment*, meaning that the relative ease and reach of everyday life (compared to feudalism) are better explained by innovation and testing than by the accumulation of capital (as suggested by the word capitalism). There is still, however, this persistently puzzling issue of widening inequality in the past two decades in which growth has seemingly concentrated into just the narrowest sliver of the pie. For a lively discussion of what she calls The Great Enrichment, see Deirdre McCloskey, *Bourgeois Equality: How Ideas, Not Capital or Institutions, Enriched the World* (Chicago: University of Chicago Press, 2016), esp. 5–84.

4 Global anti-capitalist movements looked large and influential in the 2000s and so did Sanders in 2016 or McGovern in 1972, so the size and political purchase of present

political movements is an open question. Writing the first version of this footnote in 2019 amid fired-up strikes, protests, and campaigns, frequent trumpeting of "Medicare for All" policy proposals (single-payer system such as Canada and many other Western nations), to say nothing of Yellow Vests in Paris and calls for antitrust enforcement of major tech companies and the like, politically the pendulum seemed poised to swing back towards the collective, and in a big way, for better or worse. Now writing amid the COVID-19 pandemic, sheltering-in-place in Los Angeles as almost half the world sits under lockdown orders, with virus contractions and deaths seemingly doubling every few days and fears of not just a global recession but depression looming, I'm struck by duelling thoughts: the potential for major political and social upheaval in the direst of expressions, and the potential for relational renewal across the globe. The confluence of political, economic, moral, and health uncertainty is more profound than any I've ever experienced.

5 Wayne Booth, *Modern Dogma and the Rhetoric of Assent* (Chicago: University Press of Chicago Press, 1974), 15.

6 From the conclusion to his *General Theory*:

> The ideas of economists and political philosophers, both when they are right and when they are wrong, are more powerful than is commonly understood. Indeed the world is ruled by little else. Practical men, who believe themselves to be quite exempt from any intellectual influences, are usually the slaves of some defunct economist. Madmen in authority, who hear voices in the air, are distilling their frenzy from some academic scribbler of a few years back.

John Maynard Keynes, *The General Theory of Employment, Interest, and Money* (New York: Harcourt, 1964), 383.

7 Derek Parfit, *On What Matters, Vol. 2* (New York: Oxford University Press, 2011), 462, 463.

8 Parfit, *Matters, Vol. 2*, 463.

9 Market language itself as symbolically degrading of human dignity is presented in Scheper-Hughes, "Fetish." Hippen provides a clean rebuttal in "In Defense of a Regulated Market in Kidneys from Living Vendors," *Journal of Medicine and Philosophy* 30, no. 6 (2005): 603–4.

10 Diedre McCloskey, *The Bourgeois Virtues: Ethics for an Age of Commerce* (Chicago: University of Chicago Press, 2006), 507. The following description is culled from 507–8.

11 McCloskey, *Bourgeois Virtues*, 507. For more on (re)connecting virtue and capitalism, see Russ Roberts, *How Adam Smith Can Change Your Life: An Unexpected Guide to Human Nature and Happiness* (New York: Penguin, 2014).

12 In medical and health care ethics, some prominent advocates of such approaches are Ezekiel Emanuel, who argues for a liberal communitarian theory, and Donna Dickenson, who captures the recovery of *we* medicine against *me* medicine. Paul Farmer, with his emphasis on reduction of social and medical inequality, frequent quoting of Rousseau, and foregrounding of medicine needing a preferential option for the poor combined with rich anthropological data, is a clear articulator of the position. Catholic social theory also offers a vision resonant with these themes and thinkers as well, as does a rejection of contractual social relations in favour of a covenantal approach. Renewed interest in rethinking spirituality and religion within the context of (bio)medicine, such as Daniel Sulmasy's project, represents a powerful rearticulation of what healing and health care practice is. I am sympathetic, in particular, to the covenantal approach, and William May's presentation of covenant as something deeper than the self-interest of both parties

and the minimalism of stranger medicine resonates for the practice and sustainment of medicine and health care writ large. While covenanted institutions for society writ large sounds ideal, I am sceptical of such a broad agenda taking root under the conditions of ethical pluralism in liberal democracies. The emphasis on specific institutions – such as medicine and health care – adopting and sustaining a covenantal identity and practice sounds more plausible, albeit still a significant challenge. And just to be clear that the vision on offer is hardly synonymous with collectivism or socialism, a serious kind of "humane libertarianism" vision works here, too (and that is not just because I'd prefer McCloskey's company at the barstool to Picketty's). See, for example, Emanuel, *Ends of Human Life: Medical Ethics in a Liberal Polity* (Cambridge, MA: Harvard University Press, 1991), esp. 155–244; Dickenson, *Me Medicine v. We Medicine* (New York: Columbia University Press, 2013); Paul Farmer, *Infections and Inequalities* (Berkeley, CA: University of California Press, 1999); Lisa Sowle Cahill, "Bioethics, Relationships, and Participation in the Common Good," in *Health and Human Flourishing*, ed. Carol Taylor and Robert Dell'Oro (Washington, DC: Georgetown University Press, 2006), 207–24; Daniel Sulmasy, *The Rebirth of the Clinic* (Washington, DC: Georgetown University Press, 2006); William May, *The Physician's Covenant* (Louisville, KY: Westminster John Knox Press, 2000).

13 *Assessing Initiatives to Increase Organ Donations: Hearing before the House Committee on Energy and Commerce, Subcommittee on Oversight and Investigation,* 108th Cong. (2003), 82.

14 *Assessing,* 82.

15 The assumption is that sellers would be limited to a country's citizens. But the question of global capitalism and global trade is necessarily posed here, however: why would we limit the pool in such a way? Janet Radcliffe Richards makes this point; asking the final question, she notes, non-rhetorically:

> Of course there is something undesirable about a one-way international traffic from poor to rich; but that is not enough to settle the all-things-considered question of whether it should be allowed. Much international trade is currently objectionable on the same grounds, but simply stopping it would be worse for the poor countries. It is much better, for them, to improve the conditions of trade than to prevent it altogether. Is the case different with organs?

Janet Radcliffe Richards, "An Ethical Market in Human Organs," *Journal of Medical Ethics* 29, no. 3 (2003): 140.

16 Andrew Michael Flescher, *The Organ Shortage Crisis in America* (Washington, DC: Georgetown University Press, 2018), 138–59.

17 I borrow the quote from Flescher, *Organ,* 1.

18 *Assessing,* 82.

19 I borrow the phrase *moral flickering* from Roland Benabou and Jean Tirole, who offer a theory of moral behaviour in which the "demand side" is the satisfaction of some desire (pleasure, social standing) and the "supply side" is an agent's past actions, which thereby suggests that when "contemplating choices, they then take into account what kind of a person each alternative would "make them" and the desirability of those self-views – a form of rational cognitive dissonance reduction." In general I am sympathetic to their account (which is basically neo-Aristotle), but of course find their formal analytical equations challenging (and not just as a bit of methodological difference) – to say nothing of the notion that moral behaviour can involve "self-signaling." While Benabou and Tirole are clearly more careful and subtle than many, the behavioural-economist penchant for explaining so much in terms of signalling, so much so to include *self*-signalling, starts to sound like the monotonically grand talk of Freudian

projection and illusions. Benabou and Tirole, "Identity, Morals, and Taboos: Beliefs as Assets," *The Quarterly Journal of Economics* 126, no. 2 (2011): 805–55.

20   Adam Smith in part III, chapter II of *Theory of Moral Sentiments*:

> Man naturally desires, not only to be loved, but to be lovely ... He desires, not only praise, but praise-worthiness ... we must believe ourselves to be admirable for what they are admirable. But, in order to attain this satisfaction, we must become the impartial spectators of our own character and conduct. We must endeavor to view them with the eyes of other people.

Socrates, Plato, and Aristotle (and most ancient ethical theorists) are concerned, significantly, with honour, reputation, and influence – not as ends in themselves but as the result of moral excellence and character. Consider, for example, the Socrates of Plato's *Apology* (36e) consistently imploring the pursuit of not just the appearance of worthiness but actual worthiness, for most in Athens "give the semblance of success, but I give you the reality," or the opening book of *Nicomachean Ethics*, in which Aristotle suggests that, while indeed pleasure and honour are choice-worthy pursuits, they are chosen in relation to the end of *eudaimonia* (happiness), and that *eudaimonia* is the highest end because it is not chosen in relation to anything else. Eudaimonia, though, is not merely the state of feeling good about oneself; it requires actual excellence of the soul (1098a15). See Adam Smith, *The Essential Adam Smith* (New York: Norton, 1986), 103; Plato, *The Collected Dialogues of Plato*, ed. Edith Hamilton and Huntington Cairns (Princeton: Princeton University Press, 1989), 22; Aristotle, *The Complete Works of Aristotle*, ed. Jonathan Barnes (Princeton: Princeton/Bollinger Series, 1995), 1729–42.

21   Nina Mazer, On Amir and Dan Ariley, "The Dishonesty of Honest People: A Theory of Self-Conception Maintenance," *Journal of Marketing Research* 45, no. 6 (2008): 635.

22   I should be clear that the key discussions from this study had more to do with the degree to which participants could act dishonestly while still maintaining a self-conception as an honest person than it did notions of behavioural nudging. See Mazer, Amir, and Ariley, "Dishonesty," 633–44.

23   Immanuel Kant, *Ethical Philosophy*, trans. James W. Ellington (Indianapolis: Hackett Publishing Company, 1994), 40.

24   Kant, *Ethical*, 40–1.

25   Kant, *Lectures on Ethics*, ed. Peter Heath and J.B. Schneewind, trans. Peter Heath (Cambridge: Cambridge University Press, 2001), 150.

26   Bernard Williams, *Ethics and the Limits of Philosophy* (Cambridge, MA: Harvard University Press, 1985), 67. He is particularly attacking Kant in this passage.

27   Søren Kierkegaard, *Sickness unto Death*, ed. and trans. Howard V. Hong and Edna H. Hong (Princeton: Princeton University Press, 1980), 29.

28   Kierkegaard, *Sickness*, 21.

29   Recall that this feeling was part of Satel's desire to pay for the organ, discussed in chapter 4, and thereby making the relationship tidier, more manageable, and, bluntly, transactional. Her honesty in the appeal of such should be praised, not condemned; it *is* easier to mediate monetarily, and I imagine nearly everyone reading this to have preferred transactional encounters at times to the messiness of relationality and social expectations. The phrase *tyranny of the gift* is invoked most influentially in Nancy Scheper-Hughes, "The Tyranny of the Gift: Sacrificial Violence in Living Donor Transplants," *American Journal of Transplantation* 7, no. 3 (2007): 507–11.

30   Daniel Sulmasy argues for understanding the dialectic of healing as a finite-transcendent relation in his *The Rebirth of the Clinic* (Washington, DC: Georgetown University Press, 2006), esp. 6–88.

31 I discuss the relationship and differences between a naturalized faith and a religious faith in my "Reason, Religion, and Postsecular Liberal Democratic Epistemology," *Philosophy & Rhetoric* 47, no. 1 (2014): 1–24.

32 Theodor W. Adorno, *Negative Dialectics*, trans. E.B. Ashton (New York: Continuum, 1973), 385.

33 Arthur Kleinman, *The Illness Narratives: Suffering, Healing, and the Human Condition* (New York: Basic Books, 1988), 244.

34 See, for example, Edmund Pellegrino and David C. Thomasma, *The Virtues in Medical Practice* (New York: Oxford University Press, 19913); Tom Koch, *Thieves of Virtue: When Bioethics Stole Medicine* (Cambridge, MA: MIT Press, 2012). I'm also working on a project linking Socratic flourishing and rhetorics of health.

35 Aristotle, *Politics*, in *The Complete Works*, 2028.

36 David Keyt, "The Good Man and the Upright Citizen in Aristotle's *Ethics* and *Politics*," *Social Philosophy and Policy* 24, no. 2 (2007): 220–40.

37 Keyt, "The Good Man," 240.

38 For an excellent account of the relationship between reason, faith, religion, politics, and morality, see Samuel Fleischacker, *Divine Teaching and the Way of the World* (New York: Oxford University Press, 2013), esp. 279–410.

Bibliography

30 Rock. "Kidney Now!" Television show. National Broadcasting Company. 14 May 2009.

Adams, John. "John Adams, Defense of the Constitutions of Government of the United States." University of Chicago website. http://press-pubs.uchicago.edu/founders/documents/v1ch16s15.html.

Adorno, Theodor W. *Negative Dialectics.* Translated by E.B. Ashton. New York: Continuum, 1973.

Alexander, Jeffrey. *Cultural Trauma and Collective Identity.* Los Angeles: University of California Press, 2004.

Allen, Jonathan. "'Israeli Man Gets 2 ½ Years in U.S. Kidneys-for-Cash Case." Reuters.com, 13 July 2012: https://www.reuters.com/article/us-usa-kidneys-idUSBRE86B00020120712.

Andrews, Lori B. "My Body, My Property." *The Hastings Center Report* 16, no. 5 (1986): 28–38.

Arendt, Hannah. *The Human Condition.* Chicago: University of Chicago Press, 1958.

Aristotle. *The Complete Works of Aristotle,* edited by Jonathan Barnes. Princeton: Princeton/Bollinger Series, 1995.

Asen, Robert. "A Discourse Theory of Citizenship." *Quarterly Journal of Speech* 90, no. 2 (2004): 189–211.

Asen, Robert, and Daniel C. Brouwer. *Argumentation and Advocacy* 39, no. 3 (2003).

Assessing Initiatives to Increase Organ Donations: Hearing before the House Committee on Energy and Commerce, Subcommittee on Oversight and Investigation. 108th Cong. 2003.

Aquinas, Thomas. *Summa Theologica, Vol. 1, Part 1.* New York: Cosimo, 2007.

Audi, Robert. *Religious Commitment and Secular Reason.* New York: Cambridge University Press, 2000.

Bacon, John. "Tropes." *Stanford Encyclopedia of Philosophy* online. Accessed 1 December 2011: https://plato.stanford.edu/archives/win2011/entries/tropes/.

Baier, Annette. "Secular Faith." *Canadian Journal of Philosophy* 10, no. 1 (1980): 131–48.

Bailey, Ronald. "The Case for Selling Human Organs." *Reason Magazine,* 18 April 2001: http://reason.com/archives/2001/04/18/the-case-for-selling-human-org.

Banet-Weiser, Sarah. *Authentic TM: The Politics of Ambivalence in Brand Culture.* New York: New York University Press, 2012.

Bator, Paul. "The 'Good Reasons Movement': A 'Confounding' of Rhetoric and Dialectic?" *Philosophy & Rhetoric* 21, no. 1 (1988): 38–47.

Bedke, Matthew S. "Against Normative Naturalism." *Australasian Journal of Philosophy* 90, no. 1 (2011): 111–29.

Benabou, Roland, and Jean Tirole. "Identity, Morals, and Taboos: Beliefs as Assets." *The Quarterly Journal of Economics* 126, no. 2 (2011): 805–55.

Benhabib, Seyla. *Democracy and Difference.* Princeton: Princeton University Press, 1996.
– *Situating the Self: Gender, Community and Postmodernism in Contemporary Ethics.* New York: Routledge, 1992.
Bilefsky, Dan. "Black Market for Body Parts Spreads among the Poor in Europe." *The New York Times,* 29 June 2012: https://www.nytimes.com/2012/06/29/world/europe/black -market-for-body-parts-spreads-in-europe.html.
"Bill Summary & Status, S.1435." *The Library of Congress.* 7 July 2009: http://thomas.loc.gov.
Black, Edwin. *Rhetorical Criticism: A Study in Method.* Madison: University of Wisconsin Press, 1965.
Boettcher, James. W. "The Moral Status of Public Reason." *Journal of Political Philosophy* 20, no. 2 (2012): 156–77.
– "Respect, Recognition, and Public Reason." *Social Theory and Practice* 33, no. 2 (2007): 223–49.
Boghossian, Paul. *Fear of Knowledge.* New York: Oxford University Press, 2007.
– "Précis of *Fear of Knowledge.*" *Philosophical Studies* 141, no. 3 (2008): 377–8.
Bohman, James, and William Rehg. *Deliberative Democracy: Essays in Reason and Politics.* Cambridge, MA: MIT Press, 1997.
Boltanski, Luc, and Laurent Thévenot. *On Justification: Economies of Worth.* Translated by Catherine Porter. Princeton: Princeton University Press, 2006.
– "The Sociology of Critical Capacity." *European Journal of Social Theory* 2, no. 3 (1999): 359–77.
"Bone Marrow Donors Can Be Compensated, Appeals Court Rules." *Los Angeles Times* online, 1 December 2011: http://latimesblogs.latimes.com/lanow/2011/12/bone -marrow-donors-can-be-compensated-appeals-court-rules.html.
Booth, Wayne. *Modern Dogma and the Rhetoric of Assent.* Chicago: Chicago University Press, 1974.
– *Now Don't Try to Reason with Me: Essays and Ironies for a Credulous Age.* Chicago: University of Chicago Press, 1970.
Braeckman, Antoon. "Neo-liberalism and the Symbolic Institution of Society: Pitting Foucault against Lefort on the State and the 'Political.'" *Philosophy and Social Criticism* 41, no. 9 (2015): 945–62.
Broome, John. "Reason Versus Ought." *Philosophical Issues* 25, no. 1 (2015): 80–97.
Brown, Wendy. *Undoing the Demos.* New York: Zone Books, 2015.
Burke, Kenneth. *Attitudes toward History.* Los Angeles: University of California Press, 1937.
– *A Grammar of Motives.* Los Angeles: University of California Press, 1969.
Bynum, W.F., Anne Hardy, Stephen Jacyna, Christopher Lawrence, and E.M. Tansey. *The Western Medical Tradition: 1800–2000.* New York: Cambridge University Press, 2006.
Cahill, Lisa Sowle. "Bioethics, Relationships, and Participation in the Common Good." In *Health and Human Flourishing,* edited by Carol Taylor and Robert Dell'Oro, 207–24. Washington, DC: Georgetown University Press, 2006.
Calhoun, Craig. *Habermas and the Public Sphere.* Cambridge, MA: MIT Press, 1993.
– "Imagining Solidarity: Cosmopolitanism, Constitutional Patriotism, and the Public Sphere." *Public Culture,* 14, no. 1 (2002): 147–71.
Campbell, Denis, and Nicola Davison. "Illegal Kidney Trade Booms as New Organ is 'Sold Every Hour.'" *Guardian,* 27 May 2012: http://www.guardian.co.uk/world/2012/may/27 /kidney-trade-illegal-operations-who.
Campion-Vincent, Veronique. "Organ Theft Narratives as Medical and Social Critique." *Journal of Folklore Research* 39, no. 1 (2002): 33–50.
Caplan, Arthur L. *If I Were a Rich Man, Could I Buy a Pancreas? And Other Essays on the Ethics of Health Care.* Bloomington: Indiana University Press, 1992.

Caplan, Arthur L., and Paul Welvang. "Are Required Request Laws Working? Altruism and the Procurement of Organs and Tissues." *Clinical Transplantation* 3, no. 3 (1989): 170–6.

Capron, Alexander, and Gabriel Danovitch. "We Shouldn't Treat Kidneys as Commodities." *Los Angeles Times*, 30 June 2014.

Carney, Scott. *The Red Market: On the Trail of the World's Organ Brokers, Bone Thieves, Blood Farmers, and Child Traffickers*. New York: William Morrow, 2011.

Carroll, Lewis. "What the Tortoise Said to Achilles." *Mind* 104, no. 416 (1995): 692–3.

de Castro, L.D. "Commodification and Exploitation: Arguments in Favour of Compensated Organ Donation." *Journal of Medical Ethics* 29, no. 3 (2003): 142–6.

Chambers, Marcia. "Tough Questions about Transplants Raised by New Heart for 'Baby Jesse.'" *The New York Times*, 15 June 1986: http://www.nytimes.com/1986/06/15/us /tough-questions-about-transplants-raised-by-new-heart-for-baby-jesse.html.

Chen, Karen. "Inspired by Hélène Campbell, Ottawa Sees Increase in Organ Donor Registrations." *The Ottawa Citizen* online, 26 July 2012: http://www.ottawacitizen.com /health/Inspired+Hélène+Campbell+Ottawa+sees+increase+organ+donor+registrations /6990127/story.html.

Cherry, Mark J. *Kidney for Sale by Owner: Human Organs, Transplantation, and the Market*. Washington, DC: Georgetown University Press, 2005.

– "Why Should We Compensate Organ Donors When We Can Continue to Take Organs for Free? A Response to Some of My Critics." *Journal of Medicine and Philosophy* 34, no. 6 (2009): 649–73.

Childress, James F. "The Body as Property: Some Philosophical Reflections." *Transplantation Proceedings* 24, no. 5 (1992): 2143–8.

– *Practical Reasoning in Bioethics*. Bloomington: Indiana University Press, 1997.

"China 'Kidney for iPad' Trial Begins in Hunan." BBC.com, 9 August 2012: http://www.bbc .co.uk/news/world-asia-china-19197542.

Chisholm, Roderick M. "The Ethics of Requirement." *American Philosophical Quarterly* 1, no. 2 (1964): 147–53.

Cicero. *Cicero III*. Translated by H. Rackham. Cambridge, MA: Harvard University Press /Loeb, 1942.

– *Cicero IV*. Translated by H. Rackham. Cambridge, MA: Harvard University Press/Loeb, 1942.

Clanton, J. Caleb. *The Ethics of Citizenship: Liberal Democracy and Religious Convictions*. Waco, TX: Baylor University Press, 2009.

Clay, Megan, and Walter Block. "A Free Market for Human Organs." *The Journal of Social, Political, and Economic Studies* 27, no. 2 (2002): 227–36.

Cleveland, Sidney E. "Personality Characteristics, Body Image, and Social Attitudes of Organ Transplant Donors versus Non-Donors." *Psychosomatic Medicine* 37, no. 4 (1975): 313–19.

Cohen, Cynthia B. "Selling Bits and Pieces of Humans to Make Babies." *Journal of Medicine & Philosophy*, 24, no. 3 (1999): 288–306.

Cohen, G.A. *Rescuing Justice and Equality*. Cambridge, MA: Harvard University Press, 2008.

Cohen, Lloyd R. "Increasing the Supply of Transplant Organs: The Virtues of a Futures Market." *George Washington Law Review* 58, no. 1 (1989): 1–51.

Comaroff, Jean, and John Comaroff. *Millennial Capitalism and the Culture of Neoliberalism*. Durham, NC: Duke University Press, 2001.

Condit, Celeste M. "Crafting Virtue: The Rhetorical Construction of Public Morality." *Quarterly Journal of Speech* 73, no. 1 (1987): 79–87.

Conrad, Lawrence I., Michael Neve, Vivian Nutton, Roy Porter, and Andrew Wear. *The Western Medical Tradition: 800 BC to AD 1800*. New York: Cambridge University Press, 1995.

Copp, David. *Morality, Normativity, and Society*. New York: Oxford University Press, 1995.

Culross, Melissa. "Organ Donation Becomes Part of California's Curriculum." *CBS News*, 28 September 2012: http://sanfrancisco.cbslocal.com/2012/09/28/organ-donation -becomes-part-of-californias-curriculum/.

Curb Your Enthusiasm. "Lewis Needs a Kidney." Television show. Home Box Office, 30 October 2005.

Dagger, Richard. "The Sandelian Republic and the Encumbered Self." *The Review of Politics* 61, no. 2 (1999): 181–208.

Daniels, Norman. "Health Care Needs and Distributive Justice." In *Bioethics*, edited by John Harris, 319–46. Oxford: Oxford University Press, 2001.

Delmonico, Francis L., Robert Arnold, Nancy Scheper-Hughes, Laura Siminoff, Jeffrey Kahn, and Stewart Youngner. "Ethical Incentives – Not Payment – for Organ Donation." *New England Journal of Medicine* 346, no. 25 (2002): 2002–6.

Dennett, Daniel. "How to Protect Human Dignity from Science." In *Human Dignity: The President's Council on Bioethics*, 2008: https://bioethicsarchive.georgetown.edu/pcbe /reports/human_dignity/index.html.

DeRoos, Luke J., Wesley J. Marrero, and Elliot B. Tapper. "Estimated Association Between Organ Availability and Presumed Consent in Solid Organ Transplant." *JAMA Network Open* 2, no. 10 (2019): doi:10.1001/jamanetworkopen.2019.12431.

Devitt, Michael. "Against Incommensurability." *Australasian Journal of Philosophy* 57, no. 1 (1979): 29–50.

Dickenson, Donna. *Me Medicine vs. We Medicine.* New York: Columbia University Press, 2013.

Dirty Pretty Things. Film. Directed by Stephen Frears. New York: Miramax, 2002. DVD.

Donate Life website. Accessed 11 January 2013: http://donatelife.net/understanding -donation/statistics/.

Dostoevsky, Fyodor. *The Brothers Karamazov.* Translated by Richard Peaver and Larissa Volokhonsky. New York: Farrar, Straus, Giroux, 2002.

Duerr, Benjamin. "Should Patients Be Able to Find Organ Donors on Facebook?" *The Atlantic* online, 15 April 2015: https://www.theatlantic.com/health/archive/2015/04 /should-patients-be-able-to-find-organ-donors-on-facebook/390144/.

Dworkin, Gerald. *Morality, Harm, and the Law.* Boulder, CO: Westview Press, 1994.

Dworkin, Ronald. "Objectivity and Truth: You'd Better Believe It." *Philosophy & Public Affairs* 25, no. 2 (1996): 87–139.

Edelstein, Ludwig. *Ancient Medicine.* Baltimore: Johns Hopkins University Press, 1967.

Elias, Julio J., Nicole Lacetera, and Mario Macis. "Sacred Values? The Effect of Information on Attitudes Toward Payments for Human Organs." *American Economic Review* 105, no. 5 (2015): 361–5.

Emanuel, Ezekiel J. *The Ends of Human Life: Medical Ethics in a Liberal Polity.* Cambridge, MA: Harvard University Press, 1991.

Engelhardt Jr., H. Tristram, and Kevin Wm. Wildes. "Postmodernity and Limits on the Human Body: Libertarianism by Default." In *Medicine Unbound: The Human Body and the Limits of Medical Intervention*, edited by Robert H. Blank and Andrea L. Bonnicksen, 61–71. New York: Columbia University Press, 1994.

Epstein, Richard A. *Mortal Peril.* New York: Addison-Wesley Publishing, 1997.

– *Principles for a Free Society: Reconciling Individual Liberty with the Common Good.* Cambridge, MA: Basic Books, 1998.

Ericcson, Anders K., Neil Charness, Paul Feltovich, and Robert R. Hoffman. *Cambridge Handbook of Expertise and Expert Performance.* Cambridge: Cambridge University Press, 2006.

Evans, John H. *The History and Future of Bioethics.* New York: Oxford University Press, 2012.

Facebook. Accessed September 2018: https://newsroom.fb.com/company-info/.

Farber, Steve, and Harlan Abrahams. *On the List: Fixing America's Failing Organ Transplant System*. New York: Rodale, 2009.

Farmer, Paul. *Infections and Inequalities*. Berkeley, CA: University of California Press, 1999.

Farrell, Thomas. "Knowledge, Consensus, and Rhetorical Theory." *Quarterly Journal of Speech* 62, no. 1 (1976): 1–14.

Feinberg, Joel. "The Mistreatment of Dead Bodies." *The Hastings Center Report* 15, no. 1 (1985): 31–7.

Ferngren, Gary. *Medicine and Health Care in Early Christianity*. Baltimore: Johns Hopkins University Press, 2009.

– *Medicine and Religion: A Historical Introduction*. Baltimore: Johns Hopkins University Press, 2014.

Finlay, Stephen. *Confusion of Tongues: A Theory of Normative Language*. New York: Oxford University Press, 2014.

– "Four Faces of Moral Realism." *Philosophy Compass* 2, no .6 (2007): 829–49.

– "Oughts and Ends." *Philosophical Studies* 143, no. 3 (2009): 315–40.

– "The Reasons That Matter." *Australasian Journal of Philosophy* 84, no. 1 (2006): 1–20.

– "What Ought Probably Means, and Why You Can't Detach It." *Synthese* 177, no. 1 (2010): 67–89.

Fish, Stanley. *The Trouble with Principle*. Cambridge, MA: Harvard University Press, 1999.

Fisher, Walter. "Narration as a Human Communication Paradigm: The Case of Public Moral Argument." *Communication Monographs* 51, no. 1 (1984): 1–22.

– "Toward a Logic of Good Reasons." *Quarterly Journal of Speech* 64, no. 4 (1978): 376–84.

Fleischacker, Samuel. *Divine Teaching and the Way of the World*. New York: Oxford University Press, 2011.

Flescher, Andrew Michael. *Heroes, Saints, and Ordinary Morality*. Washington, DC: Georgetown University Press, 2003.

– *The Organ Shortage Crisis in America*. Washington, DC: Georgetown University Press, 2018.

Flescher, Michael, and Daniel L. Worthen. *The Altruistic Species*. Philadelphia, PA: Templeton Foundation Press, 2007.

Foucault, Michel. *The Birth of the Clinic*. New York: Vintage, 1994.

Fox, Renee, and Judith P. Swazey. *Spare Parts: Organ Replacement in American Society*. New York: Oxford University Press, 1992.

Frankena, William. *Ethics*. Englewood-Cliffs, NJ: Prentice-Hall, 1973.

Frey, Bruno S., and Felix Oberholzer-Gee. "The Cost of Price Incentives: An Empirical Analysis of Motivation Crowding Out." *The American Economic Review* 87, no. 4 (1997): 746–55.

Friedman, Milton. "The Social Responsibility of Business Is to Increase Its Profits." *The New York Times*, 13 September 1970.

Garsten, Bryan. *Saving Persuasion: A Defense of Rhetoric and Judgment*. Cambridge, MA: Harvard University Press, 2006.

Garver, Eugene. "Aristotle on the Kinds of Rhetoric." *Rhetorica* 27, no. 1 (2009): 1–18.

– *For the Sake of Argument: Practical Reasoning, Character, and the Ethics of Belief*. Chicago: University of Chicago Press, 2004.

Gawande, Atul. "The Heroism of Incremental Care." *New Yorker*, 23 January 2017.

Gerbner, George, Larry Gross, Michael Morgan, Nancy Signorielli, and James Shanahan. "Growing Up with Television: Cultivation Processes." In *Media Effects*, 2nd ed., edited by Jennings Bryant and Dolf Zillmann, 43–67. Mahwah, NJ: Lawrence Erlbaum, 2002.

Gibbard, Allan. *Reconciling Our Aims: In Search of Bases for Ethics*. New York: Oxford University Press, 2008.

– *Thinking How to Live*. Cambridge, MA: Harvard University Press, 2003.

– *Wise Choices, Apt Feelings: A Theory of Normative Judgment.* Cambridge, MA: Harvard University Press, 1990.

Gillespie, Ryan. "The Art of Criticism in the Age of Interactive Technology: Critics, Participatory Culture, and the Avant Garde." *International Journal of Communication* 6 (2012): 56–75.

– "Normative Reasoning and Moral Argumentation in Theory and Practice," *Philosophy & Rhetoric* 49, no. 1 (2016): 49–73.

– "The Normative Relationship between Rhetoric and Judgment: On Pistis, Krisis, and Moral Inquiry." In *Rhetoric in the Twenty-First Century*, edited by Nicholas Crowe and David Frank, 39–52. Newcastle Upon Tyne: Cambridge Scholars, 2016.

– "Reason, Religion, and Postsecular Liberal Democratic Epistemology." *Philosophy & Rhetoric* 47, no. 1 (2014): 1–24.

– "Religion and the Postsecular Public Sphere," *Quarterly Journal of Speech* 102, no. 2 (2016): 194–207.

– "The Role of Intuition, Emotion, and Reason in the Act of Judgment: Implications from Moral Psychology and Metaethics for Argumentation Studies." In *Reasoned Argument: Selected Papers from the 16th Biennial AFA/NCA Conference on Argumentation*, edited by Robert Rowland, 95–103. Washington, DC: National Communication Association, 2011.

– "Uses of Religion." *International Journal of Communication* 5 (2011): 1669–86.

– "What Money Cannot Buy and What Money Ought Not Buy: Dignity, Motives, and Markets in Human Organ Procurement Debates." *Journal of Medical Humanities* 40, no. 1 (2019): 101–16.

Giner, Salvador, and Sebastian Sarasa. "Civic Altruism and Social Policy." *International Sociology* 11, no. 2 (1996): 139–59.

Gneezy, Uri, and Aldo Rustichini. "A Fine Is a Price." *Journal of Legal Studies* 29, no. 1 (2000): 1–17.

Goldberg, Jeffrey. "Involuntary Servitude: A Property-Based Notion of Abortion-Choice." *UCLA Law Review* 38, no. 6 (1991): 1597–658.

Goodnight, G. Thomas. "Controversy." In *Argument in Controversy: Proceedings of the NCA/AFA Conference on Argumentation*, edited by Donn Parsons, 1–11. Annandale, VA: Speech Communication Association, 1991.

– "The Engagements of Communication: Jürgen Habermas on Discourse, Critical Reason, and Controversy." In *Perspectives on Philosophy of Communication*, edited by Pat Arneson, 91–106. West Lafayette, IN: Purdue University Press, 2007.

Goodnight, G. Thomas, and David B. Hingstman. "Studies in the Public Sphere." *Quarterly Journal of Speech* 83, no. 3 (1997): 351–99.

Goodwin, Michele. "Altruism's Limits: Law, Capacity, and Organ Commodification." *Rutgers Law Review* 56, no. 2 (2004): 305–407.

– *The Global Body Market: Altruism's Limits.* Cambridge: Cambridge University Press, 2015.

Greenblatt, Alan. "Have You Friended Your Favorite Cause Lately?" NPR.org, 4 May 2012: http://www.npr.org/2012/05/04/152018256/have-you-friended-your-favorite-cause.

Griffiths, James. "Report: China Still Harvesting Organs from Prisoners at a Massive Scale." CNN.com, 25 June 2016: https://edition.cnn.com/2016/06/23/asia/china-organ-harvesting/index.html.

Grimaldi, William M.A. "Rhetoric and Truth: A Note on Aristotle 'Rhetoric' 1355a.21–24." *Philosophy & Rhetoric* 11, no. 3 (1978): 173–7.

– "Rhetoric and the Philosophy of Aristotle." *The Classical Journal* 53, no. 8 (1958): 371–5.

Gross, Alan G., and Marcelo Dascal. "The Conceptual Unity of Aristotle's Rhetoric." *Philosophy & Rhetoric* 34, no. 4 (2001): 275–91.

Gutmann, Amy, and Jonathan D. Moreno. *Everybody Wants to Go to Heaven but Nobody Wants to Die: Bioethics and the Transformation of Health Care in America.* New York: Liveright, 2019.

Gutmann, Amy, and Dennis Thompson. *Democracy and Disagreement*. Cambridge, MA: Belknap/Harvard University Press, 1996.
- *Why Deliberative Democracy?* Princeton: Princeton University Press, 2004.
Guyer, Paul. "Review of Kant's Moral Metaphysics." *Notre Dame Philosophical Reviews*, 24 April 2012: http://ndpr.nd.edu/news/30472-kant-s-moral-metaphysics-god-freedom -and-immortality/.
Habermas, Jürgen. *Between Facts and Norms: Contributions to a Discourse Theory of Law and Democracy*. Translated by William Rehg. Cambridge, MA: MIT Press, 1998.
- *Between Naturalism and Religion*. Translated Ciaran Cronin. Malden: Polity, 2008.
- "The Concept of Human Dignity and the Realistic Utopia of Human Rights." *Metaphilosophy* 41, no. 4 (2010): 464–80.
- *The Inclusion of the Other: Studies in Political Theory*. Edited by Ciaran Cronin and Pablo De Grieff. Cambridge, MA: MIT Press, 1998.
- *Religion and Rationality: Essays on Reason, God, and Modernity*. Edited by Eduardo Mendieta. Cambridge, MA: MIT Press, 2002.
- *The Structural Transformation of the Public Sphere*. Translated by Thomas Berger. Cambridge, MA: MIT Press, 1989.
- *Theory of Communicative Action, Vol. 1: Reason and the Rationalization of Society*. Translated by Thomas McCarthy. Boston: Beacon Press, 1984.
Haidt, Jonathan. "The Emotional Dog and Its Rational Tail: A Social Intuitionist Approach to Moral Judgment." *Psychology Review* 108, no. 4 (2001): 814–34.
- *The Righteous Mind: Why Good People Are Divided by Politics and Religion*. New York: Pantheon, 2012.
Haidt, Jonathan, and Fredik Bjorklund. "Social Intuitionists Reason, in Conversation." In *Moral Psychology, Vol. 2: The Cognitive Science of Morality: Intuition and Diversity*, edited by Walter Sinnott-Armstrong, 241–54. Cambridge, MA: MIT Press, 2008.
Hansmann, Henry. "The Economics and Ethics of Markets for Human Organs." *Journal of Health Politics, Policy and Law* 14, no. 1 (1989): 57–85.
Hardiman, Roy. "Toward the Right of Commerciality: Recognizing Property Rights in the Value of Human Tissue." *UCLA Law Review* 34, no. 1 (1986): 207–64.
Hariman, Robert. "Norms of Rhetorical Theory." *Quarterly Journal of Speech* 80 (1994): 329–32.
Hart, Roderick P., and Courtney L. Dillard. "Deliberative Genre." In *Encyclopedia of Rhetoric*, edited by Thomas Sloane, 210–11. New York: Oxford University Press, 2001.
Harvey, David. *A Brief History of Neoliberalism*. Oxford: Oxford University Press, 2007.
Hauerwas, Stanley. "Whose Conscience? Whose Emotion?" *The Hastings Center Report* 22, no. 1 (1992): 48–9.
Hauser, Gerard, and Amy Grim. *Rhetorical Democracy: Discursive Practices of Civic Engagement*. Mahwah, NJ: Lawrence Erlbaum Associates, 2004.
Healy, Kieran. "Altruism as an Organizational Problem: The Case of Organ Procurement." *American Sociological Review* 69, no. 3 (2004): 387–404.
Hennette-Vauchez, Stéphanie. "Human Dignitas? Remnants of the Ancient Legal Concept in Contemporary Dignity Jurisprudence." *International Journal of Constitutional Law* 9, no. 1 (2011): 32–57.
Henry, Samantha, and David Porter. "Levy Izak Rosenbaum Pleads Guilty to Selling Black Market Kidneys." *Huffington Post*, 27 October 2011: Reposted on http://donatelife -organdonation.blogspot.com/2011/10/levy-izhak-rosenbaum-pleads-guilty-to.html.
Hensley, Scott. "Poll: Americans Show Support for Compensation of Organ Donation." NPR.org, 16 May 2012: http://www.npr.org/blogs/health/2012/05/16/152498553 /poll-americans-show-support-for-compensation-of-organ-donors.
- "What's on Facebook's Mind? Organ Donation." NPR.org, 1 May 2012: http://www.npr .org/blogs/health/2012/05/01/151768743/whats-on-facebooks-mind-organ-donation.

Hill, John Lawrence. "Exploitation." *Cornell Law Review* 79, no. 3 (1994): 631–99.

Hippen, Benjamin. "In Defense of a Regulated Market in Kidneys from Living Vendors." *Journal of Medicine and Philosophy* 30, no. 6 (2005): 593–626.

– "Pro: Saving Lives Is More Important Than Abstract Moral Concerns: Financial Incentives Should Be Used to Increase Organ Donation." *Annals of Thoracic Surgery* 88, no. 4 (2009): 1053–61.

Hippen, Benjamin, and J.S. Taylor. "In Defense of Transplantation: A Reply to Nancy Scheper-Hughes." *American Journal of Transplantation* 7, no. 7 (2007): 1695–7.

Hollihan, Thomas A., and Kevin T. Baaske. *Arguments and Arguing: The Products and Process of Human Decision Making.* Prospect Heights, IL: Waveland Press, 1994.

Horton, R.L., and P.J. Horton. "A Model of Willingness to Become a Potential Organ Donor." *Social Science and Medicine* 33, no. 9 (1991): 1037–51.

Horkheimer, Max, and Theodor W. Adorno. *Dialectic of Enlightenment.* Translated by John Cumming. New York: Continuum, 2002.

Huang, Elbert S., Nidhi Thakur, and David O. Meltzer. "The Cost-Effectiveness of Renal Transplantation." In *When Altruism Isn't Enough,* edited by Sally Satel, 19–33. Washington, DC: The American Enterprise Institute Press, 2008.

Hubbard, Amy. "Now Live-Tweeting: Play-by-Play of a Kidney Transplant." *Los Angeles Times,* 13 June 2012: https://www.latimes.com/nation/la-xpm-2012-jun-13-la-na-nn-live-tweeting -kidney-transplant-20120613-story.html.

Hughes, Paul. "Exploitation, Autonomy, and Organ Sales." *International Journal of Applied Philosophy* 12, no. 1 (1998): 89–95.

Human Dignity and Bioethics: Essays Commissioned by the President's Council on Bioethics. Washington, DC: available from https://bioethicsarchive.georgetown.edu/pcbe/reports /human_dignity/.

Humphrey, Hubert H. "Remarks at the Dedication of the Hubert H. Humphrey Building, November 1, 1977," *Congressional Record,* 4 November 1977, vol. 123, p. 37287; taken from *Bartleby's Respectfully Quoted: A Dictionary of Quotations:* https://www.bartleby.com /73/724.html.

Ikels, Charlotte. "Kidney Failure and Transplantation in China." *Social Science & Medicine* 44, no. 9 (1997): 1271–83.

– "The Anthropology of Organ Transplantation." *Annual Review of Anthropology* 42 (2013): 89–102.

Interlandi, Jeneen. "Not Just Urban Legend." *Newsweek,* 19 January 2009: https://www.ncbi .nlm.nih.gov/pubmed/19496356.

Isocrates. *Isocrates, Vol. II.* Translated by George Norlin. Cambridge, MA: Harvard University Press/Loeb, 1929.

Jackson, Frank. *From Metaphysics to Ethics.* New York: Oxford University Press, 1998.

Jasper, J.D., Carol A.E. Nickerson, Peter A. Ubel, and David A. Asc. "Altruism, Incentives, and Organ Donation." *Medical Care* 42, no. 4 (2004): 378–86.

Jonsen, Albert R. *The New Medicine and the Old Ethics.* Cambridge, MA: Harvard University Press, 1990.

Joralmon, Donald. "Shifting Ethics: Debating the Incentive Question in Organ Transplantation." *Journal of Medical Ethics,* 27, no. 1 (2001): 30–5.

Kant, Immanuel. "An Answer to the Question: What is Enlightenment?" In *What Is Enlightenment?* edited by James Schmidt, 58–64. Berkeley: University of California Press, 1996.

– *Critique of Judgment.* Translated by James Creed Meredith. Edited by Nicholas Walker. New York: Oxford University Press, 2007.

– *Ethical Philosophy.* Translated by James W. Ellington. Indianapolis: Hackett Publishing Company, 1994.

– *Lectures on Ethics.* Edited by Peter Heath and J.B. Schneewind. Translated by Peter Heath. Cambridge: Cambridge University Press, 2001.

Kass, Leon. "Death with Dignity and the Sanctity of Life." In *A Time to Be Born and a Time to Die,* edited by B.S. Kogan, 117–45. New York: Aldine de Gruyter, 1991.

Kenny, Martin. *Biotechnology: The University Industrial Complex.* New Haven: Yale University Press, 1988.

Keshavjee, Salmaan. *Blind Spot: How Neoliberalism Infiltrated Public Health.* Berkeley, CA: University of California Press, 2014.

Keynes, John Maynard. *The General Theory of Employment, Interest, and Money.* New York: Harcourt, 1964.

Keyt, David. "The Good Man and the Upright Citizen in Aristotle's *Ethics* and *Politics.*" *Social Philosophy and Policy* 24, no. 2 (2007): 220–40.

"The Kidney Project: Statistics." UCSF Schools of Pharmacy and Medicine: Department of Bioengineering and Therapeutic Sciences website: https://pharm.ucsf.edu/kidney/need/statistics.

Kierkegaard, Søren. *Sickness Unto Death.* Edited and translated by Howard V. Hong and Edna H. Hong. Princeton: Princeton University Press, 1980.

Kleinman, Arthur. *The Illness Narratives: Suffering, Healing, and the Human Condition.* New York: Basic Books, 1988.

Knox, Richard. "Tax Breaks for Organ Donors Aren't Boosting Transplant Supply." NPR. org, 31 August 2012: http://www.npr.org/blogs/health/2012/08/30/160338259/tax-breaks-for-organ-donors-arent-boosting-transplant-supply.

Koch, Tom. *Thieves of Virtue: How Bioethics Stole Medicine.* Cambridge, MA: MIT Press, 2012.

Kopfman, Jenifer E., and Sandi W. Smith. "Understanding the Audiences of a Health Communication Campaign: A Discriminant Analysis of Potential Organ Donors Based on Intent to Donate." *Journal of Applied Communication Research* 24, no. 1 (1996): 33–49.

Korsgaard, Christine. *Sources of Normativity.* Cambridge: Cambridge University Press, 1996.

Landes, Elisabeth, and Richard Posner. "The Economics of the Baby Shortage." *Journal of Legal Studies* 7, no. 2 (1978): 323–48.

Lanham, Richard A. *A Handlist of Rhetorical Terms,* 2nd ed. Berkeley, CA: University of California Press, 1991.

Levine, Marianne. "Stanford Hospital Awarded National Gold Medal of Honor." *The Stanford Daily* online, 5 October 2012: http://www.stanforddaily.com/2012/10/05/stanford-hospital-awarded-national-gold-medal-of-honor/.

Lewis, C.S. *The Screwtape Letters: Annotated Edition.* New York: Harper Collins, 2013.

"Life Stories: Having the Heart to Survive Years of Waiting." OrganDonor.gov. Accessed 8 December 2011: http://organdonor.gov/lifestories/lifewong.html.

"Life Stories: New Heart Turns Sick Child into Active Girl." OrganDonor.gov. Accessed 8 December 2011: http://www.organdonor.gov/lifestories/lifebaladez.html.

"Life Stories: The Real Heroes Are the Donor Families." OrganDonor.gov. Accessed 8 December 2011: http://organdonor.gov/lifestories/lifeabrown.html.

Lipscomb, Benjamin J. Bruxvoort, and James Krueger. *Kant's Moral Metaphysics: God, Freedom, and Immortality.* Berlin: De Gruyter, 2010.

"Longest Kidney Chain Ever Wraps at UW Hospital and Clinics." *UW Health News and Events,* 14 April 2015: https://www.uwhealth.org/news/longest-kidney-chain-ever-completed-wraps-up-at-uw-hospital-and-clinics/45549.

Lord, Errol, and Barry Maguire. *Weighing Reasons.* New York: Oxford University Press, 2016.

Lott, Micah. "Restraint on Reasons and Reason for Restraint: A Problem for Rawls' Ideal of Public Reason." *Pacific Philosophical Quarterly* 87, no. 1 (2006): 75–95.

Lundin, Susanne. "Organ Economy: Organ Trafficking in Moldova and Israel." *Public Understandings of Science* 21, no. 2 (2012): 226–41.

MacFarquhar, Larissa. "The Kindest Cut: What Sort of Person Gives a Kidney to a Stranger?" *The New Yorker*, 27 July 2009, 38–51.

MacIntyre, Alasdair. *After Virtue*. 2nd ed. Notre Dame, IN: University of Notre Dame Press, 1984.

Mackie, J.L. *Ethics: Inventing Right and Wrong*. New York: Penguin, 1977.

Macklin, Ruth. "Human Dignity Is a Useless Concept." *British Medical Journal* 327 (2003): 1419–20.

Mahoney, Julia D. "Altruism, Markets, and Organ Procurement." *Law and Contemporary Problems* 72, no. 3 (2009): 17–35.

Mantel, Barbara. "Organ Donations: Can the Growing Demand Be Met?" *CQ Researcher* 21, no. 15 (2011): 346–50.

"The Market for Human Organs?" *Think Tank*/PBS.org, 16 July 2006: http://www.pbs.org /thinktank/transcript1248.html.

Martin, Dominique, and Gabriel M. Danovitch. "Banking on Living Kidney Donors – A New Way to Facilitate Donation Without Compromising on Ethical Values." *Journal of Medicine and Philosophy* 42, no. 5 (2017): 537–58.

Matas, Arthur. "A Gift of Life Deserves Compensation: How to Increase Living Kidney Donation with Realistic Incentives." *Cato Policy Analysis*, 7 November 2007: https://www .cato.org/publications/policy-analysis/gift-life-deserves-compensation-how-increase -living-kidney-donation-realistic-incentives.

–   "Organ Transplant Expert Answers Our Viewer Questions about Kidney Sales." *ABC News* online, 22 November 2007: http://abcnews.go.com/print?id=3902508.

Mauss, Marcel. *The Gift*. New York: Norton, 2000.

May, William. *The Physician's Covenant*. Louisville, KY: Westminster John Knox Press, 2000.

Mazer, Nina, On Amir, and Dan Ariley. "The Dishonesty of Honest People: A Theory of Self-Conception Maintenance." *Journal of Marketing Research* 45, no. 6 (2008): 633–44.

McClain, Linda C. "Inviolability and Privacy: The Castle, the Sanctuary, the Body." *Yale Journal of Law and Humanities* 7, no. 1 (1995): 195–242.

McCloskey, Deirdre. *Bourgeois Equality: How Ideas, Not Capital or Institutions, Enriched the World*. Chicago: University of Chicago Press, 2016.

–   *The Bourgeois Virtues: Ethics for an Age of Commerce*. Chicago: University of Chicago Press, 2006.

McKeon, Richard. "Communication, Truth, and Society." *Ethics* 67, no. 2 (1957): 89–99.

McRorie, Christina. "Rethinking Moral Agency in Markets: A Book Discussion on Behavioral Economics." *Journal of Religious Ethics* 44, no. 1 (2016): 195–226.

"Millennials in Adulthood: Detached from Institutions, Networked with Friends." Pew Research Center, March 2014: http://www.pewsocialtrends.org/2014/03/07/millennials -in-adulthood/.

Moniruzamman, Monir. "'Living Cadavers' in Bangladesh: Bioviolence in the Human Organ Bazaar." *Medical Anthropology Quarterly* 26, no. 1 (2012): 69–91.

Morais, Richard C. "Desperate Arrangements." Forbes.com, 29 January 2007: http://www. forbes.com/forbes/2007/0129/072.

Moreno, Jonathan D. *Deciding Together: Bioethics and Moral Consensus*. New York: Oxford University Press, 1995.

–   "The Triumph of Autonomy in Bioethics and Commercialism in Health Care." *Cambridge Quarterly of Healthcare Ethics* 16, no. 4 (2007): 415–19.

Morgan, Susan. "The Intersection of Conversation, Cognition, and Campaigns: The Social Representation of Organ Donation." *Communication Theory* 19, no. 1 (2009): 29–48.

Morgan, Susan, and Jenny Miller. "Beyond the Organ Donor Card: The Effect of Knowledge, Attitudes and Values on Willingness to Communicate about Organ Donation to Family Members." *Health Communication* 14, no. 1 (2001): 121–34.

– "Communicating about Gifts of Life: The Effect of Knowledge, Attitudes, and Altruism on Behavior and Behavioral Intentions Regarding Organ Donation." *Journal of Applied Communication Research* 30, no. 2 (2002): 163–78.

Munson, Ronald. *Raising the Dead: Organ Transplants, Ethics, and Society.* New York: Oxford University Press, 2002.

Murphy, James. J. *Rhetoric in the Middle Ages.* Los Angeles: University of California Press, 1974.

Murphy, John. "Civic Republicanism in the Modern Age: Adlai Stevenson in the 1952 Presidential Campaign." *Quarterly Journal of Speech* 80, no. 3 (1994): 313–28.

My Sister's Keeper. Film. Directed by Nick Cassavettes. Burbank, CA: Warner Home Video, 2009. DVD.

"My Sister's Keeper (2009)." IMDB.Pro. Accessed 10 December 2011. http://pro.imdb.com /title/tt1078588/boxoffice.

Nagel, Thomas. *Mortal Questions.* Cambridge: Cambridge University Press, 1979.

"National Events." U.S. Department of Health and Human Services website. Accessed 6 December 2011: http://www.organdonor.gov/materialsresources/materialsntlevents.html.

National Organ Transplant Act. Pub.L. No. 98–507. 98 Stat 2339 (1984): http://history.nih .gov/research/downloads/PL98-507.pdf.

National Organ Transplant Act: Hearings on H.R. 4080 Before the Subcommittee on Health and the Environment of the House Committee on Energy and Commerce. 98th Cong. 1983.

National Speech and Debate Association. "Past Topics: Public Forum Debate." https://www .speechanddebate.org/topics/.

"NBA's Alonzo Mourning Touts 'Resilience' in Memoir." NPR.org, 5 October 2008: https:// www.npr.org/templates/story/story.php?storyId=95387250.

Nussbaum, Martha. "'Whether from Reason or Prejudice': Taking Money for Bodily Services." *Journal of Legal Studies* 27, no. 2 (1998): 693–723.

Nutton, Vivian. *Ancient Medicine.* New York: Routledge, 2004.

Ong, Walter J. *Ramus, Method, and the Decay of Dialogue: From the Art of Discourse to the Art of Reason.* Cambridge, MA: Harvard University Press, 1983.

"OPTN/UNOS Ethics Committee Report to the Board of Directors." 2–3 March 2009, Houston, TX.

Organ Procurement and Transplant Network: https://optn.transplant.hrsa.gov.

Organs for Sale: China's Growing Trade and Ultimate Violation of Prisoner's Rights: Hearing of the Committee on International Relations, Subcommittee on International Operations and Human Rights. 107th Cong. 2001.

Parekh, Rupal. "The New Buzzword in Marketing? Human." *Advertising Age* online, 20 September 2013: http://adage.com/article/cmo-strategy/brands-behave-humans /244261/.

Parfit, Derek. *On What Matters, Vol. 1.* New York: Oxford University Press, 2011.

– *On What Matters, Vol. 2.* New York: Oxford University Press, 2011.

Parker, Ian. "The Gift." *The New Yorker,* 2 August 2004, 54–63.

Perelman, Chaim. *The Realm of Rhetoric.* Translated by William Kluback. Notre Dame, IN: Notre Dame University Press, 1982.

Perelman, Chaim, and Lucie Olbrechts-Tyteca. *The New Rhetoric: A Treatise on Argumentation.* Translated by John Wilkinson and Purcell Weaver. Notre Dame, IN: University of Notre Dame Press, 1969.

Pellegrino, Edmund. "Families' Self-Interest and the Cadaver's Organs: What Price Consent?" In *The Ethics of Organ Transplants: The Current Debate,* edited by Arthur Caplan and Daniel Coelho, 205–7. New York: Prometheus Books, 1998.

Pellegrino, Edmund, and David C. Thomasma. *The Virtues in Medical Practice.* New York: Oxford University Press, 1993.

Picoult, Jodi. *My Sister's Keeper.* New York: Atria, 2003.

Pinker, Steve. "The Stupidity of Dignity." *The New Republic,* 28 May 2008: http://pinker.wjh
.harvard.edu/articles/media/The%20Stupidity%20of%20Dignity.htm.

Plato. *The Collected Dialogues of Plato.* Edited by Edith Hamilton and Huntington Cairns.
Princeton: Princeton University Press, 1989.

Pollack, Wendy. "Organ Brokers Flourish Online." Wall Street Journal.com, 11 January 2007:
http://blogs.wsj.com/informedreader/2007/01/11/organ-brokers-flourish-online/.

Porter, Cole. "Love for Sale." From *The New Yorkers,* 1930: https://www.ibdb.com/broadway
-production/the-new-yorkers-11281/#songs

Poulakos, Takis. *Speaking for the Polis: Isocrates on Civic Education.* Columbia: University of
South Carolina Press, 1997.

Poulakos, Takis, and David Depew. *Isocrates and Civic Education.* Austin: University of Texas
Press, 2004.

Prottas, Jeffrey. "Encouraging Altruism: Public Attitudes and the Marketing of Organ
Donation." *Milbank Memorial Fund Quarterly/Health & Society* 61, no. 2 (1983): 278–306.

– *The Most Useful Gift: Altruism and the Public Policy of Organ Transplants.* San Francisco:
Jossey-Bass Publishers, 1994.

*Putting Patients First: Increasing Organ Supply for Transplantation: Hearing Before the House
Committee on Commerce, Subcommittee on Health and Environment.* 106th Cong. 1999.

Quintilian. *IV: Institutio Oratoria, Books 9–10.* Translated by Donald A. Russell. Cambridge,
MA: Harvard University Press/Loeb, 2001.

Radin, Margaret Jane. "Justice and the Market Domain." In *Markets and Justice,* edited
by John W. Chapman and J. Roland Pennock, 165–97. New York: New York University
Press, 1989.

– "Market Inalienability." *Harvard Law Review* 100, no. 8 (1987): 1849–937.

Rawls, John. *Political Liberalism: Expanded Edition.* New York: Columbia University Press, 2005.

– *Theory of Justice.* Cambridge, MA: Harvard University Press, 1971.

Raz, Joseph. *Engaging Reason: On the Theory of Value and Action.* New York: Oxford
University Press, 1999.

– "Value Incommensurability." *Proceedings of the Aristotelian Society* 86, no. 1 (1985–6):
117–34.

Repo! The Genetic Opera. Film. Directed by Darren Lynn Bousmann. Los Angeles: Lionsgate,
2009. DVD.

Repo Men. Film. Directed by Miguel Sapochnik. 2010. Universal City, CA: Universal Studios,
2011. DVD.

Reynolds, Dean. "Strangers Kidney Donation Sets Off a Chain Reaction of Good Deeds."
CBS News, 28 February 2018: https://www.cbsnews.com/news/strangers-kidney
-donation-sets-off-chain-reaction-of-good-deeds/.

Richards, Janet Radcliffe. "An Ethical Market in Human Organs." *Journal of Medical Ethics*
29, no. 3 (2003): 139–40.

Roberts, Russ. *How Adam Smith Can Change Your Life: An Unexpected Guide to Human Nature
and Happiness.* New York: Penguin, 2014.

Rosen, Michael. *Dignity: Its History and Meaning.* Cambridge, MA: Harvard University Press,
2012.

Ross, W.D. *The Right and the Good.* New York: Oxford University Press, 1930.

Roth, Alvin E. "Repugnance as a Constraint on Markets," *Journal Economic Perspectives* 21,
no. 3 (2007): 37–8.

Saletan, William. "Shopped Liver: The Worldwide Market in Human Organs." Slate,
14 April 2007: http://www.slate.com/articles/health_and_science/human_nature/2007
/04/shopped_liver.html.

Sandel, Michael J. *Democracy's Discontent*. Cambridge, MA: Belknap/Harvard University Press, 1998.
– *Justice: What's the Right Thing to Do?* New York: Farrar, Straus, & Giroux, 2009.
– "Political Liberalism." *Harvard Law Review* 107, no. 7 (1994): 1765–94.
– "The Procedural Republic and the Unencumbered Self." *Political Theory* 12, no. 1 (1984): 81–96.
– "What Money Can't Buy: The Moral Limits of Markets." *The Tanner Lectures on Human Values*. Oxford: Brasenose College, 11–12 May 1998: http://tannerlectures.utah.edu /_documents/a-to-z/s/sandel00.pdf.
– *What Money Can't Buy: The Moral Limits of Markets*. New York: Farrar, Straus, & Giroux, 2012.
Sandel, Michael J., and Thomas Nagel. "The Case for Liberalism: An Exchange." *The New York Review of Books*. 5 October 2006.
Sanner, Margareta. "Attitudes toward Organ Donation and Transplantation: A Model for Understanding Reactions to Medical Procedures after Death." *Social Science and Medicine* 38, no. 8 (1994): 1141–52.
Satel, Sally. "Altruism + Incentive = More Organ Donation." *The Times* online, 13 June 2010: https://www.thetimes.co.uk/article/altruism-incentive-more-organ-donations-qw0qhdtbbbg.
– "Death's Waiting List." *The New York Times* online, 15 May 2006: http://www.nytimes.com /2006/05/15/opinion/15satel.html.
– "Concerns about Human Dignity and Commodification." In *When Altruism Isn't Enough*, edited by Sally Satel. Washington, DC: The American Enterprise Institute Press, 2008.
– *When Altruism Isn't Enough*. Washington, DC: The American Enterprise Institute Press, 2008.
Satel, Sally, and Alan D. Viard. "The Kindest (Tax) Cut: A Federal Tax Credit for Organ Donations." *AEI's Tax Notes* 155, 12 June 2017: https://www.aei.org/wp-content/uploads /2017/07/Tax-Credit-for-Organ-Donation.pdf.
Satz, Debra. *Why Some Things Should Not Be for Sale: The Moral Limits of Markets*. New York: Oxford University Press, 2010.
Scanlon, T.M. *Being Realistic about Reasons*. New York: Oxford University Press, 2014.
– *What We Owe Each Other*. Cambridge, MA: Harvard University Press, 1998.
Scheper-Hughes, Nancy. "Bodies for Sale – Whole or in Parts." *Body & Society* 7, nos. 2–3 (2001): 1–8.
– "Commodity Fetishism in Organ Trafficking." *Body & Society* 7, nos. 2–3 (2001): 31–62.
– "Mr Tati's Holiday and João's Safari: Seeing the World through Transplant Tourism." *Body & Society* 17, nos. 2–3 (2011): 55–92.
– "The Rosenbaum Kidney Trafficking Gang." *Counterpunch*, 30 November 2011.
– "The Tyranny of the Gift: Sacrificial Violence in Living Donor Transplants." *American Journal of Transplantation* 7, no. 3 (2007): 507–11.
Schopenhauer, Arthur. *On the Basis of Morality*. Translated by E.F.J. Payne. Indianapolis, IN: Hackett Publishing Company, 1995.
Schroeder, Mark. "Reply to Shafer-Landau, Mcpherson, and Dancy." *Philosophical Studies* 157, no. 3 (2012): 463–74.
– *Slaves of the Passions*. New York: Oxford University Press, 2007.
Schultz, David. "The 'Facebook Effect' on Organ Donation." NPR.org, 20 September 2012: http://www.npr.org/blogs/health/2012/09/18/161358304/the-facebook-effect-on -organ-donation.
Scott, A.O. "An I.R.S. Do-Gooder and Other Strangeness." *The New York Times* online, 19 December 2008: http://movies.nytimes.com/2008/12/19/movies/19seve.html.
Scott, Russell. *The Body as Property*. New York: Viking, 1981.

"Seven Pounds (2008)." IMDB.Pro. Accessed 10 December, 2011: http://pro.imdb.com /title/tt0814314/boxoffice.

Shafer-Landau, Russ. *The Fundamentals of Ethics*. 2nd ed. New York: Oxford University Press, 2012.

"Should We Legalize the Market in Human Organs?" NPR.org, 21 May 2008: http://www .npr.org/templates/story/story.php?storyId=90632108.

Signorielli, Nancy, and Michael Morgan. *Cultivation Analysis: New Directions in Media Effects Research*. Newberry Park, CA: Sage, 1990.

Simmel, Georg. *The Philosophy of Money*. Edited by David Frisby. Translated by Tom Bottomore and David Frisby. New York: Routledge, 1978.

Simmons, Roberta. "Presidential Address on Altruism and Sociology." *The Sociological Quarterly* 32, no. 1 (1991): 1–22.

Singer, Peter. "Altruism and Commerce: A Defense of Titmuss Against Arrow." *Philosophy & Public Affairs* 2, no. 3 (1973): 312–20.

– "One Mountain." *Times Literary Supplement*, 20 May 2011, 3–4.

Skorupski, John. *The Domain of Reasons*. New York: Oxford University Press, 2010.

Smith, Adam. *The Essential Adam Smith*. New York: Norton, 1986.

Smith, Steven. *The Disenchantment of Secular Discourse*. Cambridge, MA: Harvard University Press, 2010.

Starr, Paul. *The Social Transformation of American Medicine*. New York: Basic Books, 1984.

Stevens, Margaret. "Factors Influencing Decisions about Donations of the Brain for Research Purposes." *Age and Aging* 27, no. 5 (1998): 623–9.

Stevenson, Charles. "The Emotive Meaning of Ethical Terms." In *Moral Discourse and Practice: Some Philosophical Approaches*, edited by Stephen Darwall, Allan Gibbard, and Peter Railton, 71–82. New York: Oxford University Press, 1997.

Stiglitz, Joseph. *Globalization and Its Discontents*. New York: Norton, 2003.

Stolberg, Sheryl Gay. "Pennsylvania Set to Break Taboo on Reward for Organ Donation." *The New York Times* online, 6 May 1999: http://www.nytimes.com/1999/05/06/us /pennsylvania-set-to-break-taboo-on-reward-for-organ-donations.html.

Stout, Jeffery. *Ethics after Babel*. Boston: Beacon Press, 1988.

Sulmasy, Daniel. *The Rebirth of the Clinic*. Washington, DC: Georgetown University Press, 2006.

Sunstein, Cass R. *Republic.com*. Princeton: Princeton University Press, 2001.

Sweet, Victoria. *God's Hotel*. New York: Riverhead Books, 2012.

Tao, Dominick. "Worldwide Market Fuels Illegal Traffic in Organs." *The New York Times* online, 30 July 2009: http://www.nytimes.com/2009/07/30/nyregion/30organs.html.

Taylor, Charles. *A Secular Age*. Cambridge, MA: Belknap/Harvard University Press, 2007.

– *Sources of the Self*. Cambridge, MA: Harvard University Press, 1989.

Taylor, James Stacey, and Marcy C. Simmerling. "Donor Compensation without Exploitation." In *When Altruism Isn't Enough*, edited by Sally Satel, 50–62. Washington, DC: The American Enterprise Institute Press, 2008.

Tilney, Nicholas. *Transplant: From Myth to Reality*. New Haven: Yale University Press, 2003.

Titmuss, Richard. *The Gift Relationship*. New York: Vintage, 1971.

Tober, Diane. "Kidneys and Controversies in the Islamic Republic of Iran: The Case of Organ Sales." *Body & Society* 13, no. 3 (2007): 151–70.

Thompson, Dennis. "Public Reasons and Precluded Reasons." *Fordham Law Review* 72, no. 5 (2003–4): 2073–88.

Thomson, Judith Jarvis. "A Defense of Abortion." *Philosophy & Public Affairs* 1, no. 1 (1971): 47–66.

Toulmin, Stephen. *Return to Reason*. Cambridge, MA: Harvard University Press, 2003.

– "The Tyranny of Principle." *Hastings Center Report* 11, no. 6 (1981): 31–9.

– *The Uses of Argument*. Cambridge: Cambridge University Press, 1958.

"Tracy Morgan Interview 04/05/11." TeamCoco website. Accessed 1 April 2020: https://teamcoco.com/content/tracy-morgans-new-kidney-making-him-crazy.

Transplant Games of America website. Accessed 11 January 2013: http://www.transplantgamesofamerica.org.

"Transplants: New Italy-Spain-France Organ Network." Ansamed.info, 1 October 2012: http://www.ansamed.info/ansamed/en/news/nations/france/2012/10/01/Transplants-new-Italy-Spain-France-organ-network_7560025.html.

"UCLA Kidney Chain." UCLA website: https://www.uclahealth.org/transplants/kidney-exchange/kidneychain.

UNOS Ethics Committee Report and White Paper. "Are Financial Incentives for Obtaining Organs Ethically Justifiable?" Subcommittee of Incentives for Donation. UNOS Ethics Committee. May 1991.

Urmson, J.O. "Saints and Heroes." In *Essays in Moral Philosophy*. Edited by A.L. Melden, 198–216. Seattle: University of Washington Press, 1958.

Utilizing Public Policy and Technology to Strengthen Organ Donor Programs: Hearing before the House Committee on Oversight and Government Reform, Subcommittee on Information Policy, Census, and National Archives. 110th Cong. 2007.

Veatch, Robert. "Why Liberals Should Accept Financial Incentives for Organ Procurement." *Kennedy Institute of Ethics Journal*, 13, no. 1 (2003): 19–36.

Venkataramani, A.S., E.G. Martin, A. Vijayan, and J.R. Wellen. "The Impact of Tax Policies on Organ Donations in the United States." *American Journal of Transplantation* 12, no. 8 (2012): 2133–40.

Vickers, Brian. *In Defense of Rhetoric*. Oxford: Oxford University Press, 1989.

Wagner, Danielle M. "Property Rights in the Human Body: The Commercialization of Organ Transplantation and Biotechnology." *Duquesne Law Review* 33, no. 4 (1995): 931–58.

Waldron, Jeremy. *Dignity, Rank, and Rights*. New York: Oxford University Press, 2015.

Wallace, Karl. "The Substance of Good Reasons." *Quarterly Journal of Speech* 49, no. 3 (1963): 239–49.

Weaver, Richard M. *The Ethics of Rhetoric*. Davis, CA: Hermogoras Press/Routledge, 1985.

Wedgwood, Ralph. "The Moral Evil Demons." In *Disagreement*, edited by Richard Feldman and Ted A. Warfield, 216–46. New York: Oxford University Press, 2010.

Weithman, Paul J. *Religion and the Obligations of Citizenship*. New York: Cambridge University Press, 2002.

Wellington, Allison J., and Edward Sayre. "An Evaluation of Financial Incentive Policies for Organ Donations in the United States." *Contemporary Economic Policy* 29, no. 1 (2011): 1–13.

Wellman, Carl. "Ethical Disagreement and Objective Truth." *American Philosophical Quarterly* 12, no. 3 (1975): 211–21.

Williams, Bernard. *Ethics and the Limits of Philosophy*. Cambridge, MA: Harvard University Press, 1985.

Wittgenstein, Ludwig. "Lecture on Ethics." In *Moral Discourse and Practice*, edited by Stephen Darwall, Allan Gibbard, and Peter Railton, 65–70. New York: Oxford University Press, 1997.

Wood, Gordon S. *The Radicalism of the American Revolution*. New York: Knopf, 1991.

The World Transplant Games Federation. Accessed 11 January 2013: http://www.wtgf.org.

Yea, Sallie. "Trafficking in Part(s): The Commercial Kidney Market in a Manila Slum, Philippines." *Global Social Policy* 10, no. 3 (2010): 358–76.

"Your Decision to Donate." Donate Life California.org. Accessed 8 December 2011; https://www.donatelifecalifornia.org/.

Zelizer, Viviana. *Morals and Markets: The Development of Life Insurance in the United States*. New York: Columbia University Press, 1978.

Ziff, Paul. *Semantic Analysis*. Ithaca, NY: Cornell University Press, 1960.

Index

civic republicanism; *communitas*;
constitutional patriotism
communitas, 35, 58, 101, 192, 246n76
community: as altruistic argument, 53–5,
232n71; Aristotle and, 18, 120; calculus
of needs vs. wants, 54; vs.
categoricity,
15, 19, 224n47; desires, and relativism,
131, 255n48; vs. incentives, 31,
185, 226n38, 227n39; of judgment
(Gibbard), 99–100, 152; and morality,
32–5, 216, 227n41, 257n64; and public
reason, 93–4. *See also* civic community
compensation, 68, 184, 186, 187. *See also*
art and economics; financial incentives
competition, 29, 88, 189, 200
compromise,75, 151, 183, 204–5, 214
Comte, Auguste, 33
Condit, Celeste, 32
congressional hearings, 42, 43, 55, 63,
182, 232n84. See also *Assessing Initiatives
to Increase Organ Donation*; *Putting
Patients First*
conscience: and autonomy, 177, 248n91;
and markets, 69, 81, 111; and morality,
91, 105, 109, 248nn89–91, 210;
neoliberalism and, 89; stories of, 44, 47
consistency: legal, 71, 163, 166–70; and
orders of worth, 93; rational, 111, 117,
238n110; in rhetoric, 22, 78, 81–2, 196,
238n110
constitution, ideal, 213–14
constitutional patriotism, 99, 100, 192
contractualism, 17, 153, 233n90, 257n64.
See also Scanlon, T.M.
Copp, David, 149, 255n49, 258–9n79
costs, 70, 71, 152. *See also* economics;
value(s)
court cases, 64, 65, 72, 167, 234n14,
264n18
Cubin, Barbara, 54–5
cultivation theory, 47, 57

debate about organ supply: approach,
8, 10, 12, 14–16, 18; common ground,
13–14, 79, 113, 170, 221n22;
compromise, 204–5; context, 13, 203–4
(*see also* neoliberalism); as debate about
society, 23, 194, 198–9, 217; disputed
norms, 104–5; epistemic reasoning,
97–8, 242–3n42; existential overlay,

211–14; key questions, 15–16, 103,
116–17, 140, 216, 259n79; metaethics
of, 125–30, 253n27; of morality *and*
markets, 20–3, 199–204, 270–1n12.
See also rhetoric of altruistic supply;
rhetoric of market-based supply;
weighing reasons in the organ debate
debt, emotional, 73–4, 212, 215
de Castro, L.D., 71, 171
DeGette, Diana, 137, 172
De Leon, Eric, 65
Delmonico, Francis, 55, 75, 171, 182, 183
democracy: deliberative, 9, 219n2, 219n6,
221–2n26; grants humanity, 267n15;
and individual preferences, 116;
justification in, 244n63; neoliberalism
and, 15, 18–19, 87–9, 114–15, 250n106.
See also coercion
Dennett, Daniel, 181
desire(s): and categorical morality, 18,
136; to excel, 33–4, 227–8n53; vs.
inclinations, 261n9; and morality,
271–2n19, 272n20; and normative
force, 257n78; and normativity, 260n2,
262–3n21; reason and, 123–4, 141–2,
145–6, 202, 250n5, 252n15, 254n34,
258n76; and relativism, 131, 255n48
DeVos, Richard, 76, 77, 167
Dickens, Charles, 229n23
Dickenson, Donna, 9, 270n12
dignitas, 58, 119, 181, 189, 250n4
dignity. *See* human dignity
dilemma, 71, 129; of commodification,
193; liberal-democratic, 110–14; moral,
104, 115, 117, 187–9
distanced self, 110, 177, 247n84; and
unencumbered/encumbered self,
107–9
Donate Life California, 41, 49
donation networks, 25, 28, 39, 40, 48, 75,
76, 220n15, 266n4
Donnett, Sarah, 41
donor registration, 12, 49, 78, 220n16
Dostoevsky, Fyodor, 108, 109, 246n78,
248n89
doubt, 79, 106–7, 246n78, 247n79–80. *See
also* uncertainty
Dworkin, Gerald, 71–2, 167
Dworkin, Ronald, 131, 132–4, 255–6n57,
256n60, 263n7, 263n22

Printed and bound by CPI Group (UK) Ltd, Croydon, CR0 4YY

16/04/2025

14658336-0002